June 2, 2013

Dear S.S. Essie,
may this book be
as big a blessing
to you as it has been
to me. Please Read
Isa. 55: 8-11

With Love
Joan Cummings

The Gospel
From Patmos

The Gospel
From Patmos

Everyday Insights for Living
From the
Last Book of the Bible

Jon Paulien

REVIEW AND HERALD® PUBLISHING ASSOCIATION
HAGERSTOWN, MD 21740

This book was
Edited by Gerald Wheeler
Copyedited by James Cavil
Cover design by Trent Truman
Typeset: Bembo 10.5/12.5

PRINTED IN U.S.A.

10 09 08 07   5 4 3 2 1

R&H Cataloging Service
Paulien, Jonathan Karl, 1949-   .
    The gospel from Patmos.

    1. Devotional calendars—Seventh-day Adventists.   2. Devotional literature.
3. Bible. N.T. Revelation—Study and teaching.   I. Title.

                    242.2

ISBN 10: 0-8280-2092-3
ISBN 13: 978-0-8280-2092-3

Dedication

PAMELLA

The joy of my life,

my wife,

my best friend.

Preface

The Philosophy of This Devotional Book

"Prophecy is given not to satisfy our curiosity about the future, but to teach us how to live today."

The devotional volume you are about to read is unlike any previously written on the book of Revelation. I could be wrong on this, but I have looked at more than 1,000 different titles on Revelation, and I am not aware that anyone has ever tried consistently to draw from the Apocalypse practical, everyday insight for living.

Why start now? Because the Bible clearly declares that God's purpose for prophecy is not to satisfy our curiosity about the future, but to teach us how to live today. The big issues of the end-time arise from the little decisions we make each day. Prophecy has a practical purpose. Studying the book of Revelation should make us better people, not just dispensers of "heavenly intelligence."

Nowhere in the Bible do we find this taught more clearly than in the twenty-fourth chapter of Matthew. There the disciples come to Jesus full of curiosity about the future (Matt. 24:1-3). "When will the Temple be destroyed? When will the end come? When will You return? What signs can You give us so that we will know these things are about to take place?" But instead of indulging their curiosity about the future, Jesus tells them that wars, rumors of wars, earthquakes, and famines are not signs of the end (verses 6-8). He recites many other kinds of events that the Jews of the time believed were signs of the Messiah or indications of the end-time (verses 9-31). But the only usable sign He offers them is His coming itself (verse 30)!

So what was His point? A series of parables make it clear (Matt. 24:32-25:46). Jesus is not giving them information about the timing of the end or the exact nature of the events leading up to it. He wants them to live each day with the end in mind—He wants them to treat other people with kindness and caring concern, knowing that they will one day have to give account of all that they have done (Matt. 25:31-46; 24:45-51). Christ wants them to pay careful attention to His words and to strive by their actions each day to be more and more like Him (Matt. 25:1-13; 7:24-27). And He wants them to make the most of their talents, to be all they can be each and every day (Matt. 24:14-30). In other words, the purpose of prophecy is not to satisfy our curiosity about the future, but to teach us how to live today.

This obviously does not deny the prophetic dimension of the text and our need to pay close attention to it. I have done that in other places. My main emphasis will be on the devotional aspect or the practical elements of the message of the book.

So in this daily devotional we will not be looking for signs of the end or a deeper understanding of the order of events in the last days of earth's history. Nor will we be dissecting beasts in detail as representatives of sweeping events in history. Instead, we will be looking for the "revelation of Jesus Christ" in the kind of insight for daily living that can get saints ready for what is to come. It is a "view from the heart."

Each devotional will be based on a fresh translation of the text. Some devotionals are closely tied to scholarly exegesis. But in parts of Revelation, such as the seven trumpets, scholarly exegesis tends to produce little devotional payoff. In such cases the text may be used more as a springboard for a particular topic than as the primary source for the devotional thought. In either case, points of emphasis are highlighted in bold (the translations are the author's own). I invite the reader to make the prayer at the bottom of each devotional his or her own. It is the author's desire that this devotional will make the "revelation of Jesus" personal for each reader. (Those interested in a more scholarly and apologetic study of the nature and themes of Revelation should consult my series of volumes on the book, beginning with *The Deep Things of God* [Hagerstown, Md.: Review and Herald Publishing Association, 2004]).

—Jon Paulien
Andrews University

THE REVELATION OF JESUS CHRIST, *which God gave Him, to show to His servants what must soon take place. And He signified it, sending it through His angel to His servant John, who testified concerning the word of God and the testimony of Jesus, which he saw.* REV. 1:1, 2.

Y ou are vacationing on a lovely island. One day you walk along the edge of a cliff, occasionally stopping to peer over the edge at the waves crashing against the rocks below. The combination of wind, waves, and noise is exhilarating. Suddenly you stumble upon a very old man sitting on a flat spot near the top of the cliff that overlooks the sea. His gaze fixed far out to sea, he doesn't seem to notice you.

"What are you looking at, sir?" you ask. "Are you waiting for a ship to come in?"

He doesn't answer.

You start toward him, yet he still doesn't seem aware of your presence. Although his eyes are open, you get the impression that he is not really there with you, that his eyes are not focused on anything you can see.

"What are you looking at, sir?" you repeat.

Again, no response.

Approaching still closer, you wave your hand in front of the man's eyes.

Still he remains oblivious to you.

Torn between shaking the man, calling the police, or sitting down nearby to see what will happen next, you decide to sit and wait a while.

After a few minutes the old man takes a deep breath and his eyes focus. Then he looks around and sees you. You position yourself in case you need to get up and flee, but he smiles in a friendly way and says, "I suppose you are wondering what is going on."

Tentatively you nod.

Smiling again, he says, "You probably won't believe this, but I just had an encounter with Jesus Himself! And you wouldn't believe how awesome and great He has become since He ascended to heaven. Not only that, but He told me all about the future and the end of the world. Would you like me to describe it to you?"

Would you be interested? Or would you put him off as just another crank? I don't know how I would respond if I ran into someone like John. But I do know this: the book of Revelation has survived many detractors. Today it is a guaranteed classic. It can bring you into a closer walk with Jesus. I invite you to journey through this book with me.

Lord, I'm starting a new year with a book that has raised more questions than answers in the past. Help me to find the key to a deeper relationship with You this year.

January 2

THE REVELATION OF JESUS CHRIST, *which God gave Him, to show to His servants what must soon take place. And He signified it, sending it through His angel to His servant John.* REV. 1:1.

We are living in a time of massive change. It seems almost impossible now, particularly for the younger generation, but 25 years ago we had no personal computers, no cell phones, no VCRs or DVD players, no PDAs, and no Internet. These few items alone have changed our lives as much as all the inventions from the dawn of time until 1980.

The era when the biblical author wrote the book of Revelation also witnessed a significant change in technology. The turn of the first Christian century witnessed a transition from scrolls to the codex style of making books. A scroll consisted of a single long sheet of paper (made from animal skins or papyrus reeds) that would be rolled up on a stick, while a codex involved gluing or stitching many pieces together at one end, much like the book you have in your hand at this moment.

Before John's time no one even dreamed of carrying a "Bible" around. Scrolls were so heavy and awkward that nothing larger than one of the New Testament Gospels could fit onto a single one. The codex style allowed books to be smaller in size and more manageable. It also made it possible for them to be much larger in content, somewhat like increasing your hard drive space tenfold. While scrolls the size of Isaiah and the Psalms were unthinkable, it was possible to include many Bible books in a single codex. So the codex style rapidly replaced the scroll as the format of choice. The major exception was the Jewish synagogue, which still continues to use the scroll format for Scripture.

Writers often put book titles on the outside of scrolls, so that the reader could identify the contents without opening them. But with the arrival of the codex, scribes frequently placed the title of a work in the opening line. So "The Revelation of Jesus Christ" is more than just the first line of the book—it is also the title.

Right from the start we learn that the Apocalypse is not the revelation of the Middle East, the Christian church, or the Islamic world. The title of the book is not even "The Revelation of the End-time"—*it is the revelation of Jesus Christ.* As difficult as the book may be to understand, its primary purpose is to teach us about Jesus. If my interpretation of Revelation doesn't lead to a clearer picture of Christ, you can be pretty sure I haven't really understood the book.

Lord, thank You so much for the advances in technology that have made Your Word more accessible than ever before. But in all my use of technology or Scripture, help me never to lose sight of Jesus. May this new year bring me a clearer picture of Him than I have ever had, a clearer view of just how He would have lived the life I face.

THE REVELATION OF JESUS CHRIST . . . Rev. 1:1.

Our household and many others share a certain custom. When young people get hungry, they tend to shout, "Mom, what's there to eat?" But if Mom is too busy to answer or has stepped outside, the next step is to head into the kitchen and see if something is cooking. If there is, they lift the cover off the pots on the stove (or open the oven door if something is baking) to see what is inside. Cooking smells can be a wonderful thing, but often they raise a good deal of curiosity. What is it that smells so good? What can we look forward to eating in a few minutes?

The word for "revelation" in the original is *apokalupsis,* the Greek word from which the English word "apocalypse" comes. The word *apokalupsis* consists of two Greek words, *apo,* "from," and *kalupto,* "to cover." So the word *apokalupsis* means "to take the cover off" something. If that something were a pot, removing the lid allows you to see what's cooking. You are "unveiling" the pot's contents. In the book of Revelation you are "taking the cover off" Jesus—learning something about Him that would be hidden if you didn't have access to this book of the Bible.

In what sense does Jesus need uncovering in the book of Revelation? Think for a minute what we would be missing if it hadn't made it into our Bibles. When Jesus was on the earth, He was a human being, in the flesh. He walked as any other person, talked in human language, and dressed like the people around Him. Jesus lived in a particular culture, time, and place. As did others, He got tired, dirty, and sweaty. It would be easy to look at that Him and say, "Well, He is a great teacher, a great man, and a great prophet. But surely He's not the king of the universe, is He? Would the king of the universe get sweaty and tired?"

If all we knew about Jesus were what we have in the Gospels, we would be missing a great deal. The book of Revelation "takes the cover off" Jesus of Nazareth. It shows us that He is no longer just a human being who came from Nazareth but the one who sits on the throne in heaven and who has rulership over the entire universe.

If we did not have the book of Revelation, we would not have a full picture of who Jesus is. It was the King of the universe who was willing to become a human being, willing to serve and bless, willing to subject Himself to shame and abuse, willing to suffer and die for us. The greatness of Jesus makes His sacrifice all the more remarkable. The book of Revelation takes the cover off that greatness so everyone can see it.

Lord, give me a "hunger" to know Jesus as I have never known Him before. May the images of His greatness in Revelation open my eyes to the privilege of relationship with Him.

January 4

The revelation of Jesus Christ, **WHICH GOD GAVE HIM,** *to show to His servants what must soon take place. And He signified it, sending it through His angel* **TO HIS SERVANT JOHN,** *who testified concerning the word of God and the testimony of Jesus, which he saw.* REV. 1:1, 2.

When our oldest daughter was 5 years old, our lives got out of control. My wife became pregnant with our third child. Why were our lives out of control? Just do the math. From the birth of Kimberly on, our family would have two parents and three children. The children outnumbered my wife and I!

I don't know if you think this was a good idea or not, but shortly before the birth we pulled Tammy (our oldest) aside and said, "You know, Tammy, two adults and three children is just not going to work! From now on, we need you to help us with the little ones and be like half a parent. Do you think you could be our little helper?"

Did she agree? Did she ever! Does the word "bossy" come to mind? Though we came to regret the conversation at times, Tammy has proved to be a most efficient cook, housekeeper, and family counselor! Recently we took a family vacation. Tammy (21 at the time) cleaned the living room and the kitchen, helped her brother pack, prepared all food items, and loaded the car. While Dad kept a watchful eye, everything was done in superior fashion!

But while the roles occasionally get a little fuzzy in our family, no one questions who has the final word when it comes to the younger children. The parents do. Whenever we left Tammy in charge of the younger ones, she was to do exactly as her parents said.

The lines of authority in Revelation are similar. The author is John, but the content of the book is from Jesus, rather than the human prophet. While the symbols reflect the apostle's world, Jesus chose them ("signified"—Rev. 1:1). The book of Revelation is not John's own idea. He received these things in a vision from Jesus Christ. His authority, therefore, is like that of the Old Testament prophets and also the apostles of the New Testament. The "words of this prophecy" are to be obeyed (verse 3, NIV). Their authority is so unquestionable that not a word is to be added or subtracted (Rev. 22:18, 19).

God's wisdom and knowledge are certainly bigger than anything written in the book of Revelation. The great God has bent down and used John to speak to us, the way a parent talks to a 2-year-old, getting down to their level and using their language. The Scriptures are our clearest witness to God, one that is within our capacity to understand.

Lord, thank You for reaching out to me in the book of Revelation. I will follow You with all my heart today.

The revelation of Jesus Christ, which God gave Him, to show to His servants what must **SOON** *take place . . .* Rev. 1:1.

The text says that the events described in Revelation will "soon" take place. Where did the revelator come up with that? Would anyone in their right mind say 1,900 years is soon? What could he possibly mean?

Some interpreters suggest that we must understand this "soon" from God's perspective rather than ours. After all, a day with the Lord is like 1,000 years (2 Peter 3:8)! In that sense the coming of Jesus has always been soon. To God the passage of 1,000 years is only a single grain in the infinite sands of time.

That answer may be useful, but it is not enough for most of us. After all, John did not write the book of Revelation for God's benefit, but rather "to show his servants what must soon take place." When the angel came to Peter in prison (Acts 12:7, NIV) and said, "Quick, get up!" (the same Greek word as "soon" in Revelation 1:1), the angel certainly wasn't suggesting that Peter should snooze for another 1,900 years! What would the first readers of Revelation have made of this comment? Was Jesus (or John) mistaken here? How are we to make sense of this?

For one thing, such declarations seem to be a pattern with God. Even in Old Testament times you often receive the impression that God's great final act is just around the corner. When you get to the Gospels, the sayings of Jesus don't seem to suggest more than a few years or decades either. Scripture throughout presents the time until the end as short.

It is as if God knows that something in the human psyche goes wrong every time the future seems to lengthen. We may know in our heads that every moment could be our last, yet we live as though our personal history will continue for decades at the least. Portraying time as short meets a human need. It helps us to focus on the things that matter the most. It enables us to set the right priorities for whatever remains of our lives.

A student approached a rabbi and asked, "When should I get right with God?"

The rabbi replied, "The day before you die."

"But when am I going to die?" the student retorted.

The rabbi replied, "No one knows; therefore, the Scriptures say, 'Today, if you will hear His voice, harden not your hearts.'" One way or the other, things will take place soon. What counts is how we respond to that reality.

Lord, help me to live this day with the perspective of eternity. May I experience each moment and treat each person as if I am about to give a final accounting of my life.

January 6

The revelation of Jesus Christ, which God gave Him, to show to His servants what must soon take place. And **HE SIGNIFIED IT,** *sending it through His angel to His servant John.* REV. 1:1.

Stefanie's mother was born on a small island called Krk, off the coast of Croatia in the former Yugoslavia. As a child she swam daily in the transparent waters of the Adriatic and picked wild asparagus along the rock-laced coast. Somewhere in the middle of her adolescent years her father's name finally surfaced from an immigration list into which it had been dropped years before, and she found herself transplanted with her parents and sister into the whirling, horn-honking, exhaust-filled cacophony that is New York City.

Perhaps the most disorienting element of her new environment was the language. While many Americans may not realize it, American English is loaded with idiomatic sayings that are extremely difficult for new immigrants to fully understand. Imagine the wonder when a newcomer to America hears that someone is "head over heels in love." Even more puzzling to an immigrant's sense of normalcy is the expression "it's a dog-eat-dog world." And consider the puzzlement when a trusted friend instructs a new immigrant to "break a leg."

None of these expressions make a lot of sense the instant a new American hears them. But to those who grew up in the States, they communicate significant information, especially when combined with just the right tone of voice. The best way to learn such idioms is to spend a lot of time listening to those who have been around for a while.

Jesus often used similar expressions. When he warned His disciples against "the leaven of the Pharisees," He was certainly not suggesting that the religious leaders were undercover bakers, churning out poisonous loaves to sell in the marketplace! And think of how we use the word "heart." Even though we live in a medically advanced society, we still consider the emotional center of the human body to be the "heart." [1]

When our text says that the revelation of Jesus Christ has been "signified" it warns us to be careful how we move from the words of Revelation to its meaning. Things will often turn out vastly different than our first impressions might suggest.

So like immigrants, students of Revelation should not try to make too much sense of the book on their own. They need to compare their impressions with those who have carefully studied the book before them. When it comes to Revelation, we will find great safety in a "multitude of counselors."

Lord, give me a learning spirit as I work my way through this book. Help me carefully consider the ideas of others before I become too confident in my own opinions about it.

WHO TESTIFIED CONCERNING THE WORD OF GOD AND THE TESTIMONY OF JESUS, WHICH HE SAW.

Blessed is the one who reads and those who hear **THE WORDS OF THIS PROPHECY** *and keep* **THE THINGS WHICH ARE WRITTEN IN IT,** *for the time is near.* REV. 1:2, 3.

The book begins with the phrase "the revelation of Jesus Christ." Verse 1 goes on to report that the revelation is signified, and in verse 2 it becomes the testimony of Jesus, something that John can see. So John speaks of two things: the "word of God" and the "testimony of Jesus." The word of God is likely a reference to what was John's Scriptures, the collection of writings that we know today as the Old Testament.

The book of Revelation alludes to the Old Testament hundreds of times, employing a word here, a phrase there, a name somewhere else. It recalls the places of the Old Testament—Babylon, Egypt, and Jerusalem—as well as the people of the Old Testament: David, Jezebel, and Balaam. The Old Testament is like a current flowing under the surface of the book, yet affecting everything it touches.

A few years ago I visited Russia with my oldest daughter to teach a couple classes. At the time it wasn't certain if Communism was gone or would make a comeback. So one of the "must sees" on my to-do list was Red Square, Lenin's tomb, and the Kremlin in the capital city of Moscow. Tammy, on the other hand, was more interested in shopping for a nesting doll. So after we did the tourist stuff we headed for Moscow's street market, where you could bargain for local handicrafts.

Nesting dolls are a Russian specialty. Usually made of wood, they are a series of hollow dolls beautifully decorated on the outside and that can be opened to reveal successively smaller versions of the outer doll. After some searching we found a black doll in seven layers with a beautiful multicolored scene on each one, all emphasizing the color red. Tammy was pleased with the doll and negotiated with enthusiasm, bringing the price down to $7 (a good deal at the time).

In its use of the Old Testament the book of Revelation is like a nesting doll. You could read the book without reference to the Old Testament and think you have grasped the whole picture. But when you discover the text beneath the surface, it begins revealing the deeper truths placed in the book. The book of Revelation is like the finale of the biblical symphony, drawing all of the Bible's themes together in a thrilling conclusion.

Lord, thank You for the deep things of Your Word. It keeps me coming back to the Bible again and again, helping me grow spiritually as I continue to study. May I never be satisfied with a surface understanding.

January 8

BLESSED IS THE ONE WHO READS AND THOSE WHO HEAR *the words of this prophecy and keep the things which are written in it, for the time is near.* REV. 1:3.

The text says, "Blessed is the one who reads . . . and those who hear . . ." What does that mean? Why does one person read and many persons hear? Because books in New Testament times were scarce and expensive to produce, most people would encounter one only when someone read it out loud to them. The book of Revelation was meant to be read in church. It was intended, not as a written work for study by individuals, but rather to be heard orally by groups of people. A special blessing rests on the public reading of the book of Revelation.

In 1995 I had the privilege of leading a tour of the seven churches of Revelation in Turkey. The trip was an adventure in many ways. Thirty-nine people, including my family, crowded into a single bus with a Turkish driver and a Muslim tour guide. Our driver took more chances on the road than any driver I have ever experienced, yet he did so with a calmness that made it seem like the right thing to do!

Another memorable aspect of the trip was that everyone but the two Turks got sick with some sort of stomach flu by the second day. That made for many desperate stops at remote pharmacies or even more isolated places as the passengers scattered in all directions looking for trees and bushes to hide behind. What was even more embarrassing was that most of the sick ones were vegetarians who professed healthy living. The two Turks who didn't get sick were chain smokers who also transgressed Muslim strictures against alcohol!

A highlight of this trip was the chance to visit the ruins of the seven ancient cities that once contained the churches of Revelation. A young woman in our group prepared a dramatic reading of Jesus' message for each of those churches. As prescribed in the text, one or more read out loud as the rest of us listened. After each reading we sang a song that she had written based on the messages to the seven churches. The impact was unforgettable. We heard the letter to each church right on the spot where those congregations originally listened.

I doubt that most churches today would have the patience to hear the entire book of Revelation read out loud (it takes about an hour and a half)! But in small pieces we were able to re-create some of the original setting on our trip. In Pergamum we heard the letter while standing on the site of the "seat of Satan," the great altar of Zeus. Then in Thyatira we listened while surrounded by a friendly group of Turkish schoolchildren whose teachers then treated us to apple tea. John encourages every Christian to experiment with dramatic readings of Revelation in church and in family worship.

Lord, give me attentive ears to listen to You and Your Word as never before. I also pray for a heart that is willing to obey.

John to the seven churches which are in Asia: Grace to you and peace . . . **FROM JESUS CHRIST.** REV. 1:4, 5.

In the opening lines of most books the author tries to bring the reader up to speed on his or her purpose for that book. The book of Revelation is no exception. The first eight verses of the book form a prologue that presents the major themes and intentions for the book. The style of the prologue (Rev. 1:1-8), however, is different from the rest of the book. It is fairly normal and straightforward, the typical language of the New Testament. As a result it is quite unlike the apocalyptic language of the rest of the book, which is filled with complex symbolic images that have vexed interpreters for nearly 2,000 years.

What do you do with a book that describes an animal with seven heads and 10 horns and that has the body of a leopard and feet of a bear (Rev. 13:1, 2)? What do you do with a book in which eagles speak (Rev. 8:13), but gigantic cities are silent (Rev. 18:22, 23)? And what do you do with a book in which blood flows as high as a horse's bridle (Rev. 14:20)? With images like that, it is no wonder that 12 people trying to interpret Revelation will often come up with 13 different opinions about what the book means!

The good news is that before you get into the bizarre stuff, John takes a moment to let you know why he wrote the book. And he does this in plain language—straightforward prose. Yes, the book of Revelation *does* have a strong focus on end-time events (Rev. 1:1, 7). But above all else the theme of the book is Jesus. It comes from Him (verse 1), it is His testimony (verse 2), and it is grounded in His death, His resurrection, and His work for us (verses 5, 6). The reader must not forget this beginning, no matter how confusing the journey gets.

You see, the book of Revelation is like a riddle. And everybody loves riddles. Riddles present you with a puzzle that needs to be solved. Let me share one with you: "The majority of people on earth live within 50 miles of what place?" When most people hear this riddle, they start thinking about the world's most populated places. They quickly realize that no place on earth has even a tenth of the world's population located within a 50-mile radius, much less the majority. So the solution to the riddle will not be found in a certain spot on the globe. What is the answer? Most people live within 50 miles of the place in which they were born! Once you have the key to the riddle, the response is obvious.

In Revelation the key to the riddle is Jesus Christ! The key that John has placed at the door of Revelation transforms its meaning. No matter how weird the images get, the correct interpretation of any passage will always open up a clearer picture of Jesus.

Lord, give me a clearer picture of Jesus today. I want to be more like Him.

January 10

John, to the seven churches which are in Asia: Grace to you and peace from the One who is, and who was, and who is to come, and from the seven spirits which are before his throne, and from **JESUS CHRIST, THE FAITHFUL WITNESS, THE FIRSTBORN FROM THE DEAD, AND THE RULER OF THE KINGS OF THE EARTH.** REV. 1:4, 5.

It is probably only superstition, but the North Dakota farm culture my wife grew up in believed that things happen in threes. If two people you knew died, you began to wonder whom the third one would be. Or if two of your friends and relatives decided to get married, you speculated whom would be next. People believed that both good and bad things tended to happen in groups of three.

In the book of Revelation a lot of things also occur in patterns of three. We find three angels (Rev. 14:6-12) and three frogs (Rev. 16:13). John talks about three beasts (Rev. 12 and 13, cf. Rev. 16:13) and three woes (Rev. 8:13). The passage above describes the Godhead as a complete "trinity" of persons: the Father, the Son, and the Holy Spirit. Revelation 1:4-6 has, in fact, three "trinities." Today's devotional will focus on the second of the three.

John the revelator describes Jesus as "the faithful witness, the firstborn from the dead, and the ruler of the kings of the earth" (verse 5, NIV). These phrases describe the main characteristics—or qualities—of Jesus. You won't read about such qualities in *USA Today* or hear about them on CNN. The teens at the local disco are not talking about Jesus as they dance. Our world is largely oblivious to the marvelous qualities of Jesus. That's why the book of Revelation is so important. It openly and publicly reveals the secret things about Jesus.

Jesus is "the faithful witness." In the original language the word for "witness" is the one from which we get the English word "martyr." In the self-sacrificing love of Jesus on the cross, we see a clear demonstration of the character of God.

Christ is also "the firstborn from the dead," a reference to His resurrection. When God raised Jesus from the tomb, He pronounced a blessing on the whole human race (Acts 13:32, 33). From then on a human being was seated at the right hand of God (Heb. 8:1, 2)!

That means He is the "ruler of the kings of the earth." While most people do not acknowledge Him as such, we can become citizens of His kingdom and receive all the benefits of citizenship in it. Because He rules the kings of the earth we don't have to be afraid of oppressive governments anymore. They govern only by permission (John 18:36, 37). In the book of Revelation Jesus is everything we need.

Lord, I see the greatness of Jesus more clearly than ever. I will worship Him today with all my heart.

To the One who loves us and **HAS FREED US FROM OUR SINS BY HIS BLOOD,** *and has made us a kingdom, priests before God, even His Father—to Him be glory and power for ever and ever, Amen.* REV. 1:5, 6.

I didn't show much interest in golf until I turned 40. That year I spoke at a conference at which two pastors invited me to join them for a round at a nearby course. Borrowing a set of clubs, I went with them on a blisteringly hot summer day. It wasn't long before I learned about a special rule that most pastors seem to have if and when they golf. One of them, Ben, was on the tee of a narrow hole that had thick forest on both sides of the fairway. He shanked the ball off the heel of his club, and it bounced harmlessly into the woods less than 50 yards away. With a look of disgust on his face he said, "I think I'll take a mulligan."

My puzzlement over this term did not last long. He reached into his pocket, pulled out another ball, and set up to drive all over again, as if the first shot had never happened. I found out that mulligans are something like a second chance, an opportunity to do things over, to get them right. Somewhat to my amusement, as the game went on Ben's performance got worse and worse. Instead of an occasional mulligan he began to take one after another. One time he even did a mulligan, a "secondary" mulligan, and a "tertiary" mulligan (I made the adjectives up on the spot) before he was satisfied with his shot.

While the golf purist will be horrified with me, I find it a relief to be able to play golf without my life hanging on every swing. The occasional chance to start over takes the pressure off and makes the whole game more enjoyable. Computers have a similar feature—the "undo" key. Whenever your finger slips and hits a key that totally skews everything, and you have no clue what went wrong or how to fix it, you just hit the undo key, and everything gets restored the way it was before your mistake.

The analogies are not perfect, of course. But something like a mulligan happens in your life when you give yourself to Jesus. You have a chance to start over, to undo the guilt and burden of the past. The blood of Jesus frees us from sin. His death makes it possible for us to break the chains of the past, to have a fresh start, to be forgiven. The blood of Jesus frees us not only from sin but from fear—the fear that something we do will make us unacceptable to Him. The fear that our best will never be good enough. I don't know about you, but I could use a mulligan now and then.

Lord, thank You that I am no longer a prisoner of the past, that my sins can be forgiven, that I can start over again today. Help me to bring all my sins and shortcomings to the blood of Jesus. Give me the sense of freedom that comes from being right with God.

January 12

To the One who loves us and has freed us from our sins by His blood, **AND HAS MADE US A KINGDOM, PRIESTS BEFORE GOD,** *even His Father—to Him be glory and power for ever and ever, Amen.* REV. 1:5, 6.

Nothing can get you down like being fired. But being expelled from a job is not the worst thing that could happen to you. In his book *We Got Fired! . . . And It's the Best Thing That Ever Happened to Us,* Harvey Mackay shares inspirational stories of rejects turned celebrities.

A music studio fired Elvis Presley in 1954. "You ain't goin' nowhere, son," its representative declared. "Go back and drive a truck." Tell that to the thousands of Elvis impersonators who sing his tunes decades after his death.

A newspaper terminated Walt Disney because he had run out of ideas. The Disney Company, with its movies, theme parks, television stations, and more, is now a multibillion-dollar empire.

A French cycling team dropped Lance Armstrong after he began treatment for testicular cancer in 1997 (with just a 50 percent chance of survival). They even refused to pay his remaining salary or his medical bills. Big mistake. Armstrong not only beat the cancer, but he won seven consecutive Tour de France races after recovery.

Before he ruled CNN, Larry King wrote a column for the Miami *Herald.* The *Herald's* editor let him go for being too chummy with his subjects. His way with people paid off, though. Few politicians or celebrities ever bypass *Larry King Live* today.

Steve Jobs cofounded Apple Computer in his garage, then got thrown out by his own company. Jobs picked up the pieces and bought a majority share in Pixar in 1986. Nine years later he won an Oscar for *Toy Story.* By 1997 he was back at Apple![2]

I can relate to how it feels when life dishes out rejection. But the above examples make it clear that no matter how bad things get (Armstrong could have been dead by 1998), God can use it as a stepping-stone to greatness.

I certainly don't always feel like a king, do you? When you feel as if nothing will ever go right for you—that everybody's against you—it is easy to wonder whether life is worth living. Yet Revelation insists that we are elevated to the status of kings and priests in Jesus Christ. Should you ever you think that you are nobody—that no one cares—grab the book of Revelation and scatter those thoughts with the clear assertions of God's Word! Instead of being nobodies, through Jesus Christ we have been elevated to the highest places. The book of Revelation not only tells us who Jesus Christ is but also who we can become in Him.

Lord, all the glory and all the praise belong to You. Burn into my heart today a strong sense of the value I have in Your eyes.

Behold, **HE IS COMING WITH THE CLOUDS, AND EVERY EYE WILL SEE HIM, INCLUDING THOSE WHO PIERCED HIM, AND ALL THE TRIBES OF THE EARTH WILL MOURN OVER HIM.** *Yes, Amen.* REV. 1:7.

In verse 7 we find a combination of two texts from the Old Testament. The "coming with the clouds" reminds us of the Son of man in Daniel 7:13. That those who pierced him will mourn over him, echoes Zechariah 12:10. Matthew 24:30 also combines the same two texts, so Revelation 1:7 may reflect Jesus' earlier teaching.

In Zechariah the ones who pierce and mourn are "the house of David" and the "inhabitants of Jerusalem." But Revelation changes it to "all the tribes of the earth," a common shift in the book. It applies the literal and local things of the Old Testament in a spiritual and worldwide manner. The concept of "Israel" expands to include people of any race and place who are in relationship with Jesus.

So the key to inclusion among the people of God is a connection with His Son. But how can you have a relationship with Jesus when you can't see, hear, or touch Him? That possibility was abundantly illustrated by the most-watched movie of all time, *Titanic*. *Titanic* earned twice as much money from theater admissions as any other movie until then. The popularity of the film had a rather trivial reason. Millions of teenage girls in North America became smitten with the handsome young male lead, Leonardo DiCaprio. Many went back to see the movie several times. Some claimed to have seen it more than 40 times! They were developing a relationship with someone they couldn't see, hear, or touch in person! Few of them had ever encountered DiCaprio in real life.

How could this be? The movie was not Leonardo himself. But it was a *witness* to the reality that was the actor. And millions of teenage girls found that witness sufficient for a serious relationship. Whereas millions will testify to the existence of Leonardo DiCaprio and the influence he may have had in their lives, *billions* through the centuries have testified to the reality of Jesus, most basing it on the testimonies found in the sacred and inspired pages of Scripture.

It is clear that you *can* have a living relationship with someone you cannot see, hear, or touch. When it comes to Jesus, you develop that relationship by *spending time* with the witness about Him in His Word. You need to invest in serious Bible study as well as talk to other people who know Him and hear their testimonies about His impact in their lives. And you need to get involved in the mission that He left for His disciples (Matt. 28:20) to accomplish. Those in relationship with Jesus will one day participate in the glorious victory portrayed in Revelation.

Lord, I need the presence of Jesus to be real in my life today. May His Word become flesh in everything I do or say.

January 14

"I AM THE ALPHA AND THE OMEGA," SAYS THE LORD GOD, "THE ONE WHO IS AND WHO WAS AND WHO IS TO COME, THE ALMIGHTY." Rev. 1:8.

One Friday in October news reached a community that locusts were on the way and would devastate any crops still in the field. The community's farmers immediately went into "around the clock" mode. Beginning Friday afternoon they harvested all night Friday and all day Saturday to get the crop in before the locusts arrived. That is, everyone except one individual.

A Seventh-day Adventist farmer followed his normal Friday afternoon routine, putting away equipment and setting aside all chores that he could do another day. Anticipating his response, a few of his neighbors came over to plead with him. The labor of an entire year was at stake. Surely God wouldn't mind if the Adventist farmer "took care of business" just this one time?

"I will keep the Sabbath as usual," the man told his neighbors. "I trust God to deal with the locusts."

The neighbors tried once more to dissuade him, but his mind was made up, so they returned to their farms and their desperate effort to get the crops in before the locusts arrived. All night Friday and all day Saturday they labored, managing to save most of what they had grown.

Sunday morning dawned, and the Adventist farmer looked out the window at the remnants of what had once been a thriving crop. The locusts had come through during the night and eaten up everything. The neighbors returned, to comfort the farmer as much as to chide him. But they did ask him to explain God's failure to compensate him for his faithfulness.

"God does not always make a final settlement in October," the farmer replied.

In our text God is the Alpha and Omega (beginning and ending of the Greek alphabet). He is the one who is, was, and is to come (the one in control of the past, the present, and the future), and the Almighty. God is the Lord of history. No situation that we encounter could possibly take Him by surprise. Everything that happens to us is part of a larger plan. But how do we explain the farmer's misfortune?

God's judgments on wicked nations and systems fill the book of Revelation. But His true people can be found in those same nations and systems. They experience the "side effects" of divine judgment. Because of the mixed nature of human systems, God's faithful people should never expect perfect security in this life. Faithfulness does not always receive an immediate reward. The Lord does not always make a final settlement in October.

Lord, give me the confidence today to know that You are in control, even when things seems totally out of control. Give me patience to wait for Your justice.

I, John, **YOUR BROTHER AND COMPANION IN THE AFFLICTION AND KINGDOM AND PATIENT ENDURANCE WHICH IS IN JESUS,** *came to be on the island which is called Patmos, on account of the word of God and the testimony of Jesus.* Rev. 1:9.

It is all too easy to pontificate about the sufferings of others when you haven't experienced what they have gone through. I remember a beloved teacher whose wife was dying of cancer. His graciousness to each student in spite of the horrible burden that he carried to school every day awed me. The power of his life and of his impassioned expositions on love, marriage, and suffering in the Christian life constantly stirred me. I wanted nothing more than to be like him when I finished my education.

Things went from bad to worse. Day after day we saw less of our teacher as he was more and more needed to care for his wife's deteriorating condition. Occasionally he let us peek briefly through the curtain of his stoic fortitude and sense the pain that he and his wife were experiencing. The funeral was an awesome moment of melancholy in which we all embraced our beloved professor in his spiritual and emotional pain. The one who had so often carried us in our troubles now needed our support.

Loving and admiring this man, I wanted so badly to do or to say something that would be helpful. In my mind I ranged through my seven years of ministry, thinking of all the brilliant things I might have said at funerals. Yet I had never, up to that point, lost anyone who was truly close to me. Aunts, uncles, and parents were still alive, and my grandparents had been somewhat distant.

Taking my teacher aside one day, I shared some theological thoughts that I hoped would be helpful to him in his loss. His response stunned me. It was the only time I ever saw him angry. "Don't you ever do that to anyone again!" he said. "None of that theology is worth a piece of manure right now. You don't know what it means to lose your wife, and your words only make it worse." If the ground had opened up just then, I would gladly have jumped in!

Only those who have truly suffered know how to comfort the suffering. John knows what they are going through from experience. Those who share in suffering or persecution often find themselves unified in ways that transcend all barriers. Race, culture, and denominational differences matter little when experiencing the consequences of opposition to the gospel. Knowing that others have felt what we do has healing power for our own pain. And through what we have endured we learn how to minister to others who suffer.

Lord, steer me away from theologies of success and prosperity. Help me embrace the hard things of this life. May my wounds have healing power in the lives of others.

January 16

I, John, your brother and companion in the **AFFLICTION** *and kingdom and patient endurance which is in Jesus,* **CAME TO BE ON THE ISLAND WHICH IS CALLED PATMOS,** *on account of the word of God and the testimony of Jesus.* REV. 1:9.

I was born on the upper east side of Manhattan when the area was poor. I grew up in a nearby suburb and attended church in Manhattan. If you can drive in New York City, I always thought, you can do it anywhere. I found it rather amusing to have people visit from other parts of the country and have them frozen in horror as I drove at breakneck pace, weaving in and out of traffic. I was sure that my driving abilities were superior to anyone who had learned how to drive in less interesting parts of the world.

But as I grew older God provided me with opportunities to travel and find out that my confidence as a driver rested on fairly limited experience. While the drivers in New York City are fast and often reckless, they don't hold a candle to those of Paris or Rome. And for sheer audacity, no one can compare with the cab drivers of Caracas, Venezuela!

But for me the most challenging places to operate a car in are the former British countries of the Southern Hemisphere, such as Australia, New Zealand, and South Africa. Not only do people drive on the left there, but the driver sits in the right-hand seat and shifts gears with the left hand! And imagine figuring out how to drive on the left and then discovering the marvelous British legacy known as the roundabout. Instead of having everyone stop at an intersection, in such countries the cars participate in a free-for-all merry-go-round that sucks you in and then spits you out somewhere else, sometimes in the right direction! While I thought driving in these places was great fun, I made plenty of foolish moves along the way, humbling my New York confidence.

When John received the vision on Patmos, he was not in his usual environment. He was far away from the comfortable routines of his past. And the changes in his life included experiences he called "affliction." But as difficult as life on Patmos was for him, he knew that God had brought him there.

When life is routine it is easy to feel as if we are in control, as if we can handle whatever may come. Quickly we may lose our sense of need for God. So sometimes God moves us away from our usual round of activities and puts us in places where we have to depend more fully on Him. Approaching the end of time, followers of God will find themselves placed in new and challenging circumstances. As a result they will come to rely on Him more consistently and completely than ever before.

Lord, help me to remember You in the prosperous and easy times. Bring me experiences that will prepare me for whatever may come, yet keep me humble in my need for You.

I was in the Spirit during **THE LORD'S DAY,** *and I heard a loud voice like a trumpet behind me.* REV. 1:10.

What did John mean by the "Lord's Day"? When did the prophet receive his vision? As scholars look at this text, they don't find the question easy to answer. They offer at least five plausible options. First is the day we call Saturday. Saturday is the seventh day of the week on the Hebrew calendar, known to the Jews as the Sabbath. Scripture frequently refers to the Sabbath as "the Lord's Day." In Isaiah 58 the Lord Himself speaks of the Sabbath as "my holy day." And in Mark 2:27, 28 Jesus declares that He is the "Lord of the Sabbath." So a strong biblical option for understanding John is that he was alluding to these earlier texts to identify the Sabbath as the day on which the vision came. Since he shows a great deal of interest in the Sabbath command in chapter 14, I believe this is the best option.

The second option is the day now named Sunday. Christian writings from the second century (as close as 35-40 years after the book of Revelation) clearly use the phrase "the Lord's Day" as a figure of speech for Sunday. The idea developed in relation to the fact that Jesus rose from the dead on the first day of the week (our Sunday), so "the Lord's Day" could allude to that. But we have no evidence that Christians in the first century kept Sunday.

A third possibility is that John was referring to what we regard as Easter. Jesus rose on Sunday, the first day of the week. But it was also at the time of the Jewish Passover. Christians celebrate Easter every year around the time of Passover. If that is what the prophet had in mind, he is telling us he received the vision in the spring, around Passover season.

Fourth, perhaps John had in mind the Old Testament Day of the Lord, a phrase used in the Bible for God's great intervention at the end of earth's history. In this case the revelator would be saying something like "I saw this vision with the end of the world in mind."

Fifth, some ancient documents suggest a special "Emperor's Day" once a year, when people would gather for worship. John might be "thumbing his nose" a bit at the Roman emperor by asserting that God intervened on the very day when the enemy seemed in full control. Revelation shows that Jesus is Lord, not a human emperor.

At at moral spiritual level, it doesn't hurt to remind ourselves that every day is a gift from God. Every day is a day "that the Lord has made" (Ps. 118:24), a time to be used to glorify Him and to bless others. Every day is to be enjoyed with thanksgiving. Have a good one today!

Lord, You have given this day to me. I return it to You with my thanks. I dedicate all my thoughts and actions to Your service.

January 18

"Write what you see in a book and send it to the seven churches, **TO EPHESUS, SMYRNA, PERGAMOS, THYATIRA, SARDIS, PHILADELPHIA, AND LAODICEA."** Rev. 1:11.

The seven churches are the first of a series of sevenfold visions in the book of Revelation. John describes seven churches, seven seals, seven trumpets, and seven bowl-plagues. An introductory scene precedes each of these sevenfold visions. For example, the vision of Christ among the seven lampstands (Rev. 1:12-20) comes before the vision of the seven letters (Rev. 2; 3). The introductory scenes are like stage backdrops in front of which the actions of each vision take place. As a result, John Bowman (in *The Interpreter's Dictionary of the Bible*) persuasively sets out the thesis that Revelation is modeled on the form of an ancient Greek play, with seven acts and seven scenes played out against the backdrop of each vision's introduction.[3]

In the book of Revelation, then, God has used the familiar form of the drama to communicate a message about what is real in the universe. While actors often speak of things that are not as if they were true, drama can be a powerful vehicle to express truth. A former student of mine, Dan, always wanted to become a famous actor. Perhaps that was why his sister Cindy said what she did at their father's funeral. She observed to him that being a minister seemed a lot like theater.[4]

Somewhat to his surprise, Dan later entered ministry and found out that his sister was right in a way. He discovered that ministers play a role of great power and influence. They represent God to people. Ministers may have inappropriate thoughts at times, but they dare not act on them or they will bring the name of Christ into disrepute among the weak, the young, or the unbelieving.

Ministers, therefore, play a role. They must set an example, because they represent Christ to the world. They must keep true to the script and not goof around, flirt, or tease. At the same time they need to be accessible enough that people will share their pain with them. It's a rather challenging task. So when Dan told Cindy that he had decided to become a minister, she said to him, "Good, Danny, that's theater."

The role of the Christian in a secular world is equally challenging. We must always act with the mission in mind, yet be accessible to those in need. Who is skillful enough to meet the challenge? No one, but with God all things are possible. He chose a murderer with a speech impediment to lead His people out of Egypt (Moses). He selected the runt of the litter to slay the giant (David). He was born in a manger, yet changed the world! He summons the unlikely to do what seems impossible. And He doesn't call the equipped, but equips the ones He calls.

Lord, help me keep the mission in mind in all I do and say today.

January 19

And I turned to see the voice that was speaking to me. And when I turned I saw
SEVEN GOLDEN LAMPSTANDS. REV. 1:12.

O
n Easter in 1969 I had the privilege of being in Rome. After attending the pope's Easter remarks in St. Peter's Square, my three friends and I went to see the ruins of the ancient Roman Forum. It was quite a thrill to stroll on ground that Peter and Paul must have walked, looking at the remains of buildings that had been once grand, but still made of the same stones that the apostles would have seen and touched.

Most tourists visiting the Forum start opposite the Mamertine Prison (where Paul may have been confined). You then move past the temple of the Vestal Virgins, up and down Palatine Hill, and past the Basilica of Constantine to the other end of the Forum. There we came across the Arch of Titus, the Roman general who conquered the city of Jerusalem in the year A.D. 70. Imagine our excitement when we saw in sharp relief an illustration of soldiers parading around Rome with the seven-branched lampstand removed from the Temple in Jerusalem! We felt truly close to the world of the Bible.

Throughout the ancient Roman world the seven-branched menorah (lampstand) was the most common symbol for Judaism,[5] just as the fish and the cross later became emblems for Christian faith. In a striking way, the book of Revelation adopts this image of Judaism to represent the churches of Asia Minor. By this means John clearly understood that true Christian faith was heir to Israel's heritage, even if at times the synagogue did exclude Christians (Rev. 2:9; 3:9). It was those who did the expelling that had lost touch with their Jewish heritage, not the faithful followers of Yeshua the Messiah.

Were the Nazis right, then? Has the church replaced Israel? Was the Holocaust a judgment from God rather than human wickedness? It is hard to imagine first-century Christians taking such a position. They proclaimed a Jewish Messiah, who fulfilled the ancient promises made to Israel. They converted pagans to Israel's one true God. While not requiring Gentiles to be circumcised, Jewish Christians such as Paul embraced them as new participants in their Jewish faith in Jesus. Gentile believers were the spiritual children of Abraham (Gal. 3:28), inwardly circumcised (Rom. 2:28, 29) and grafted into Israel's tree while unbelieving branches were broken off (Rom. 11:17).[6]

In the book of Revelation the lampstand image stresses the Jewishness of Christian faith and the intimate connection between that faith and the ancient heritage of Israel.

Lord, help me to learn more about my Jewish roots and appreciate them the way Paul and John did.

January 20

And I turned to see the voice that was speaking to me. And when I turned I saw
**SEVEN GOLDEN LAMPSTANDS, AND IN THE MIDST OF
THE LAMPSTANDS WAS ONE LIKE A SON OF MAN,** *dressed
in a foot-length robe wrapped around the chest with a golden sash.* REV. 1:12, 13.

One day a highway patrolman in South Dakota was heading north on Interstate 29 just as I was heading south past him. Since my speed control was set at the speed limit (65 miles per hour), I was not concerned about His presence. I was obeying the law. So when the lights on his car began flashing and he slowed to make a U-turn, I remained calm with a clear conscience. I figured he must be after someone else (although the road was fairly deserted at the time).

As he came up and moved behind me it was clear that I was the one he was after. With a clear conscience I pulled over, curious as to what the problem was. "Did you know that you were traveling kind of fast?"

"No, sir," I replied courteously, "I had my speed control set at 65 miles per hour."

His next assertion startled me. "You registered 77 miles per hour on my radar."

"That's impossible," I responded as courteously as outrage would allow. "I've been traveling at this setting for 3,000 miles now and no one has stopped me. Are you sure there isn't something wrong with your radar?"

That comment was probably a negotiating mistake, correct as it may have been. It required me to make a substantial contribution to the well-being of the community I was passing through. Although I felt angry about it for weeks, I could do nothing about it.

John sees Jesus among seven golden lampstands, which represent the seven churches of Asia Minor (Rev. 1:20). The vision portrays Jesus as walking among the lampstands, ministering to the churches. The background to this idea is the Old Testament covenant: "I will walk among you and be your God, and you will be my people" (Lev. 26:12, NIV).

One of the best things about the covenant concept is that God is not arbitrary. He subjects Himself to the covenant. "Know therefore that the Lord your God is God; he is *the faithful God, keeping his covenant* of love to a thousand generations of those who love him and keep his commands" (Deut. 7:9, NIV). God is not like the ancient pagan gods who couldn't be trusted. The Hebrew God approaches His people in a consistent fashion, obeying His own rules. This is a tremendous source of security and stability for our spiritual life. We know what to expect from Him. I'm thankful God is not like that highway patrolman in South Dakota.

Lord, I commit myself anew to You today. I desire the spiritual stability that You have promised in Your covenant with us.

And I turned to see the voice that was speaking to me. And when I turned I saw
**SEVEN GOLDEN LAMPSTANDS, AND IN THE MIDST OF
THE LAMPSTANDS WAS ONE LIKE A SON OF MAN,** *dressed
in a foot-length robe wrapped around the chest with a golden sash.* Rev. 1:12, 13.

W̲e noticed yesterday that the concept of a "son of man" in the midst
of the golden lampstands echoes images of the Old Testament
covenant. A major aspect of the Old Testament covenant resembles what we could call a contract today. In a "covenant" two parties enter into a relationship of some kind—to build a house, to get married, to go to school. All these things involve a connection between people or between a person and an institution.

An interesting aspect of the Old Testament covenant is the part about "blessings" and "curses" (see Deuteronomy 28, for example). While such language sounds strange in today's world, the idea behind it is not. Let me illustrate.

A few years back the bridge collapsed in my hometown. It was a terrible thing for the community because it turned the downtown business section into a dead-end street. And that pretty much destroyed the place economically. The merchants no longer had customers. Not only that, but it became necessary to travel anywhere from seven to 15 miles out of our way in order to cross a river only a few dozen feet wide.

The situation was so desperate that when the Department of Transportation made a contract for a new bridge, the community leaders said, "You must put a date in that contract." The authorities set the bridge's completion for May 26, about nine months later. The community leaders put "blessings and curses" in the contract. For every day that they finished the bridge ahead of schedule, the builders would receive $10,000 extra. And for every day that completion was late, $10,000 would be deducted from their final payment. The contractors finished the bridge on May 1, 26 days early!

The good news of the gospel is that God in Christ has already met the obligations of the covenant at the cross and the resurrection (Acts 13:32, 33; 2 Cor. 1:20). For those in relationship with Jesus, the covenant contains nothing we need to fear. The promises of God are all freely available in Christ. We can have security in our relationship with Him.

Many Christians are insecure. They don't know if they have done enough or if they are right with God. To them, Jesus says, "I am here among you." Are these churches perfect? Have they done all the right things? No. It's very clear that they are fallible, make mistakes, and, in some ways, are even turning away from Jesus. Yet He continues to walk among those lampstands as the faithful God of the covenant who is always there for His people.

I believe that your sacrifice is sufficient to save me. Make this concept real to me today.

January 22

And in the midst of the lampstands was One like a Son of man, dressed in a foot-length robe wrapped around the chest with a golden sash. **HIS HEAD AND HIS HAIRS WERE WHITE LIKE WOOL, WHITE AS SNOW;** *and His eyes were like a flame of fire. His feet were* **LIKE POLISHED BRASS** *which had been purified in a furnace, and His voice was like the sound of many waters. He had seven stars in His right hand, a sharp, two-edged sword was coming out of His mouth, and His face was like the sun shining in its strength.* REV. 1:13-16.

When I was in college, I naturally assumed that Jesus looked roughly like the pictures of Him that I had seen growing up in church. While I was not aware of any need for Jesus to resemble a German-American, the difference between the usual pictures of Jesus and the kind of people you see in the Middle East was lost on me.

It was in the late-1960s, and I was at the ground zero of college protests, the first Earth Day, the arrival of Black History Week, and lots of marches for racial equality and against the war in Vietnam. An African-American student pulled me aside one day to catch me up on neglected aspects of my education.

He explained that Jesus was definitely not "White," that in fact He had African features. Pulling out our text for today, he explained to me that Jesus had hair like wool. Pointing to his Afro, he said, "Just like me, not like you." He also noted that the color of polished brass was a lot closer to the color of his feet than of mine. This encounter provided quite a jolt to my comfortable mental pictures of Jesus, and I am grateful for it.

What is especially interesting is that White supremacists in the American South used the same text to prove that Jesus was White. After all, His *head* as well as His hair were white like wool. According to them, the reference to wool had to do with the color of the hair rather than its texture. It goes to show that we can easily use the book of Revelation to support opinions not actually addressed in the book.

It was not Jesus' purpose in this vision to give us an exact portrait of what He looks like. After all, it would be a horrible picture of anyone to have a sword sticking out of their mouth. And the whiteness of Jesus' head and hair is not to show that He is blond—rather, it recalls the "Ancient of Days" in Daniel 7. Jesus comes to John directly from the throne of God to give him divine encouragement for the difficulties that would lie ahead for him and for his churches. It would be a shame to miss the greatness of Jesus in order to focus on the color of His skin.

Lord, help me not to be distracted by the many interesting sidetracks that Revelation seems to offer. Keep my eyes focused on the message about who You really are.

And in the midst of the lampstands was One like a Son of man. . . . **HIS FACE WAS LIKE THE SUN SHINING IN ITS STRENGTH.**
REV. 1:13-16.

The appearance of Jesus on Patmos was dazzling. At the sight of Him John essentially collapsed from astonishment (Rev. 1:17). Jesus wasn't anything like the ordinary-seeming human being the prophet had known back in Galilee. What was the significance of this stunning description? The passage presents Jesus as dazzling and impressive as the angel of Daniel 10. But He is even more than that. He also bears the characteristics of God. The hair like wool, the comparison with snow, and the flaming fire are characteristics of the Ancient of Days Himself in Daniel 7:9. When He calls Himself the first and the last (Rev. 1:17, 18), without question Jesus comes to John as the God of the Old Testament (Isa. 44:6; 48:12). Jesus is truly a "star" in every sense of the word.

I am reminded of Ben Stein's last column. He got tired of reporting on Hollywood stars when it seemed there were more important things to be excited about. Here are his own words:

"I no longer think Hollywood stars are terribly important. They are uniformly pleasant, friendly people, and they treat me better than I deserve to be treated . . . [But] how can a man or woman who makes an eight-figure wage and lives in insane luxury really be a star in today's world, if by a 'star' we mean someone bright and powerful and attractive as a role model? Real stars are not riding around in the backs of limousines . . . while they have Vietnamese girls do their nails. They can be interesting, nice people, but they are not heroes to me any longer. . . .

"A real star . . . is the U.S. soldier in Baghdad who saw a little girl playing with a piece of unexploded ordnance on a street near where he was guarding a station. He pushed her aside and threw himself on it just as it exploded. . . . There are plenty of other stars in the American firmament . . . the policemen and women who go off on patrol in South Central [Los Angeles] and have no idea if they will return alive. The orderlies and paramedics who bring in people who have been in terrible accidents and prepare them for surgery, the teachers and nurses who throw their whole spirits into caring for autistic children, the kind men and women who work in hospices and in cancer wards. Think of each and every fireman who was running up the stairs at the World Trade Center as the towers began to collapse.

"Now you have my idea of a real hero. . . . God is real, not a fiction. . . . We make ourselves sane when we fire ourselves as the directors of the movie of our lives and turn the power over to Him. I came to realize that life lived to help others is the only one that matters. . . . This is my highest and best use as a human."[7]

Lord, I appoint Jesus as the director of my life. He is my ultimate action hero.

January 24

And **WHEN I SAW HIM, I FELL AT HIS FEET LIKE A DEAD MAN.** *And He placed His right hand on me, saying, "Do not be afraid. I am the First and the Last, and the One who lives. I became dead, and behold I am alive for ever and ever, and I have the keys of death and of Hades."* REV. 1:17, 18.

One day a very strange thing happened to me and to my family. My wife and I had spent the afternoon shopping with our children. As we were about to turn into our house we noticed with alarm that all the lights in our house were turned on and that a large and unfamiliar pickup truck sat parked in our driveway. We sat frozen in place for at least a minute, uncertain what to do. With fear and trembling I decided to leave the wife and kids in the car and walk right in to confront whoever it was.

I was no less shocked, but considerably relieved, to discover that the "invader" was none other than my wife's father. Grandpa had decided on the spur of the moment to surprise us by driving 800 miles to Michigan from his farm in North Dakota. And surprise us he did! When he didn't find us at home, a neighbor woman helped him break in and get settled.

Now, Grandpa's visit wouldn't have been so unforgettable if he had lived across town. At that time my father (who did live on the other side of town) often dropped in without warning to check on things or fix something while we were out. But we thought our other grandpa was 800 miles away! We never expected him to show up unannounced. The incident has helped me understand a little of John's reaction when he met Jesus on the island of Patmos.

You see, John had known Jesus pretty well in the flesh (see 1 John). But that had been 60 years ago. And Jesus wasn't in North Dakota—He had ascended to some other part of the universe. The prophet certainly wasn't expecting Christ to show up in his back yard at any moment.

Not only that, this Jesus had the kind of dazzling qualities that John would have associated with God Himself. He is the "first and the last," terms that describe the great Lord of the Old Testament (Isa. 44:6; 48:12). Jesus comes to John as the deity of the Old Testament, the one who made the world, gave the law on Mount Sinai, and filled the Temple with glory in Solomon's day. It must have been a staggering shock for John to take in. As a result he goes down like a dead person would if someone had stood them up on their feet. *Thud!* It was more than he could handle.

This is the revelation of Jesus Christ. He is more than a man—He is the God-man. When, like John, we recover from this realization, we can be comforted to know that He is well able to provide everything we need, including eternal life.

Lord, give me a glimpse of Your greatness today. I want to walk in true humility, a humility that comes from a sense of Your surpassing greatness.

AND WHEN I SAW HIM, I FELL AT HIS FEET LIKE A DEAD MAN. Rev. 1:17.

As we saw yesterday, encountering Jesus in vision greatly shocked John. You could say that the book of Revelation arose out of some "shock therapy" that Jesus administered to the prophet. Jesus comes to him in a totally unexpected form. He breaks the mold into which the apostle had placed Him. He stretches the boundaries of the revelator's experience, challenging him to a bigger picture of Jesus. And the reality is that we all struggle to move past our own limitations when it comes to our understanding of God.

If I were a Muslim I'd probably have a hard time grasping that God could be pleased with someone who doesn't fast one month out of the year and pray five times a day. I would have no problem eating snakes or rabbits, but I would have a hard time imagining a God who could overlook the consumption of pork. I'd look down on Christians who drink, while smoking like a chimney!

If I were a Jehovah's Witness I would probably have a hard time accepting that God could use a blood transfusion to save the life of a child. And if I were a Mormon I might have a difficult time acknowledging a God who could do mighty acts through such people as Moses and Peter who didn't know enough to wear special underwear.

Many Catholics have a hard time believing that a minister or priest can truly please God without being celibate. In Jesus' day some Jews had a hard time watching the disciples pick a little grain and munch on it while walking through a field on the Sabbath. Who could do that and still be in the service of God? Hindus can't eat beef, but pork is OK. Many Christians thought that the Crusades were a just and holy war. Protestants on both sides of the American Civil War prayed that God would bring victory to their cause.

All of this reminds me of one of the best book titles I have ever heard: *Your God Is Too Small!* The Jesus of Revelation is the antidote to "small God syndrome." We call Him meek and mild, yet many who knew Him best thought He was a dangerous revolutionary. After all, He called upstanding clergy, labeling them hypocrites. He referred to the local governor as "that fox." Earnest religious people He labeled "sons of the devil." And He kept company with prostitutes and tax swindlers.

Twice He crashed a temple yard sale, knocking over the merchandise, mixing up money they had neatly separated into various accounts, and driving the members off the property. He went out of His way to heal a homeless person, but seemed to have little respect for important people. Jesus sure would be nice to have around if He would just do things our way.

Lord, help me to accept You as You really are, not just the way I wish You were.

January 26

Do not be afraid. I am **THE FIRST AND THE LAST,** *and the One who lives. I became dead, and behold I am alive for ever and ever, and I have* **THE KEYS OF DEATH AND OF HADES.** REV. 1:18.

Scholars have noticed a surprising thing in this text. We find similarities between the description of Jesus here and the greatest, most popular goddess of Asia Minor, Hekate. Hekate was renowned as the one who possessed the keys to Hades, the mythological realm of the dead. The ancients called her *trimorphos,* that is, having three different forms or shapes related to the three great parts of the universe: heaven, earth, and the underworld (Hades). In her heavenly form she went by the name Selene or Luna (the moon). On earth she was called Artemis or Diana (see Acts 19). And in the underworld the Greeks referred to her as Persephone. She was also known as "the beginning and the end" (Rev. 22:13).[8]

As the one who freely moves between heaven, earth, and the underworld, Hekate would be the goddess of revelation. She would be able to reveal on earth the things that went on in heaven and in Hades. As the holder of the keys to Hades she would also be the one who could provide salvation.

Why would Jesus refer to Himself in ways that so strikingly resemble a pagan goddess? Because God always meets people where they are (see 1 Cor. 9:19-23). Do you remember the day you met Jesus? Do you remember the words or actions on His part that reached your heart? Each conversion story is unique, because God is creative in His approach.

A young man in Arizona was searching for Jesus, though he didn't really know it at the time. He lay on his couch one day, high on drugs, listening to the Rolling Stones rock music group (in his words, he was "stoned on the Stones"). As he stared up at the ceiling in his altered state of mind, not particularly looking for God, he suddenly saw a face that he recognized as that of Jesus. Jesus said to him, "When this song is over, you need to get your life in order and follow Me!" The music died and, stunned, the young man raised himself to a sitting position. He looked around and saw no one.

Responding to God's call, he quit the drugs and the wild life and went back to school. A few years later he finished seminary and entered the ministry! It's an incredible testimony to Jesus' ability to reach anyone, even in a drug- and rock music-infested room. I am in no way suggesting that drugs and the Rolling Stones are a useful path to faith—I simply want to underline the infinite grace of Jesus Christ, who pulls branches out of the fire and puts them to good use! That means there's hope for you and me, too.

Lord, thank You for doing whatever it took to draw me into a relationship with You.

WRITE, THEREFORE, WHAT YOU HAVE SEEN, NAMELY, THE THINGS WHICH ARE AND THE THINGS WHICH MUST HAPPEN AFTER THESE THINGS. REV. 1:19.

In verse 11 the angel told John to "write what you see in a book and send it to the seven churches." The word for "see" in that verse is a present tense, indicating that John was already in vision and that the vision would continue for a time. Verse 19, on the other hand, has the prophet instructed to "write what you *have* seen." The word for seeing is no longer in the present tense. This suggests that John received the whole vision between verse 10, when he went into the spirit, and verse 18, when he finished the narrative of his encounter with Jesus. By verse 19 the vision was over—it was time for the writing to begin.

According to verse 19, the content of Revelation fits into two categories: the things that are and the things that must happen *after these things*. Revelation 4:1 repeats the language of 1:19: "Come up here and I will show you *what must take place after these things.*" Verse 19, then, seems to be a structuring device for the rest of the book. The first part of the vision involves the "things which are"— that is, the messages to the seven churches (Revelation 2 and 3). The rest of the vision focuses primarily on events that are future from John's perspective. But what good is it to the churches to learn about events beyond their day?

My wife and I recently flew from South Bend, Indiana, to New Zealand. It was an extremely complicated itinerary, involving three separate flights and a lay-over in Los Angeles. We left on Tuesday and arrived on Friday. Snowstorms in Chicago complicated matters greatly by causing the cancellation of a number of flights into and out of the city. As a result my wife and I ended up having to take different flights to Los Angeles. How did we manage to meet again there?

We were able to get together in Los Angeles because we knew something about the future. Because we were aware of our ultimate goal we were able to make the right decisions along the way. We knew that whatever our separate routes, United Airlines would hold our luggage at Los Angeles International Airport. As it turned out, I landed at a gate far from the terminal normally served by United Airlines. For a time I could find neither my wife nor my baggage. But she wisely waited at the United Baggage Office in Terminal 7. Eventually I found my way to her and our things. We might never have reunited if we had not both known where we were going.

Likewise, God tells us about the future so that we can get where we are going today. Each day is a piece of our itinerary toward God's purpose. With an eye on His Word we can find our way through the maze of life.

Thank You, Lord, for making Your ultimate purpose clear through Your Word. May my steps today keep me heading in the direction of Your ultimate purpose for me.

January 28

The mystery of the seven stars, which you saw in My right hand, and the seven golden lampstands; **THE SEVEN STARS ARE THE ANGELS OF THE SEVEN CHURCHES,** *and the seven lampstands are the seven churches.* REV. 1:20.

I drowned about 10 years ago. Funny, though, I'm still here. Snorkeling in the Great Barrier Reef off Australia, I was about 400 yards from shore in five-foot-deep water, so when my strength began to give out I wasn't worried. That was when I discovered the water wasn't five feet deep—it was seven feet deep! And I was in big trouble.

Fortunately I spotted a rock about 18 inches high and 18 inches wide in the sand below the water. Standing on the rock, I managed to get my nose above water. Unfortunately, waves kept washing me off the rock, so I couldn't get my strength back. I called to my wife, who is a better swimmer than I am. To make a long story short, she came over and helped me stay balanced on the rock until help arrived.

A few months later we told the story to a friend who had done a lot of diving. "How were you able to keep your nose above water and hold your husband up when you're so much smaller than he is?" he asked my wife.

"I balanced myself on the tips of my fins," she said.

His eyes grew wide. "That's impossible! Fins won't support your weight."

"Well, that's what I did! They felt as solid as my own legs!"

He thought for a minute. "There's no way that could work. An angel must have held you up!"

I'm inclined to agree. In my desperate situation I didn't know how she did it—I was just grateful that my wife was as solid as a pillar next to me. As I think about her explanation, I'm also convinced an angel held us up.

What are the angels of the seven churches? Some interpreters think they are the messengers that carried John's apocalypse and read it to the churches. Others consider them the pastors or leaders of the churches. Still others conclude that they are God's secret guardians that step in to help when needed, such as what I experienced in Australia.

The book of Revelation is full of angels. Most of them are clearly not human beings. In Jewish tradition, angels guide the activities of earthly rulers (Daniel 10:13, 20, 21, for example) and are sometimes held responsible for the earthly ruler's behavior.[9] Perhaps these seven angels watched over the leaders of the churches. It is nice to know that the church, feeble and defective though it may be, has the same kind of watchcare from God's angels that every one of us has.

Thank You, Lord, for the messengers that watch over all of Your people.

The mystery of the seven stars, which you saw in My right hand, and the seven golden lampstands. The seven stars are the angels of the seven churches, and **THE SEVEN LAMPSTANDS ARE THE SEVEN CHURCHES.** REV. 1:20.

Revelation 1:12-20 presents a fantastic description of "one like a son of man" (Jesus) standing in the middle of seven golden lampstands. In verse 20 we learn that the seven lampstands represent seven churches in Asia Minor. So the key idea in this part of chapter 1 is that Jesus is in close relationship with His churches.

What adds spice to this observation is the fact that the second part of each letter (the description of Jesus) in the two chapters that follow includes characteristics of Him already mentioned in chapter 1. For example, the letter to Ephesus (Rev. 2:1) describes Jesus as the one who holds the seven stars in His hand (Rev. 1:20) and walks among the seven golden lampstands (verses 12, 13). In the letter to Smyrna (Rev. 2:8) He is the first and the last, the one who died and came to life (Rev. 1:17, 18). Then in the letter to Pergamum (Rev. 2:12) He approaches with a sharp, two-edged sword (Rev. 1:16). So it goes throughout.

In other words, Jesus presents Himself differently to each of the seven churches. No individual church has the full picture of Jesus. Respecting the unique needs and characteristics of each church, He is able to adapt to their particular needs and circumstances. Or to put it another way, He offers different strokes for different folks!

These descriptions of Jesus have some incredible implications for everyday Christian life. For one thing, He knows all about each church (Rev. 2:2, 9, 13, etc.), even before they are aware of His presence. And He knows everything there is to know about me, even before I tell Him! That means we have no need to hide anything from Jesus. He already knows! The truth about me is safe with Him.

Since He already knows, He can approach each one of us in just the way we need Him most. Jesus respects our uniqueness, He is aware of our different personalities and needs, and He graciously deals with each of us in the way that will do us the most good.

Consider still another implication. If no church and no Christian has the complete picture of Jesus, then we all have every reason to be humble. We are all learners. And we can all teach each other. While I may know a lot more about Jesus than someone I meet, that person may have just the perspective on Jesus that I need that day. The smartest position for a Christian to take is to be a learner in every situation.

Lord, help me to learn from everyone I meet today. Help me also to share with them the unique picture of You that You have given to me.

January 30

To the angel of the church of . . . write. REV. 2:1, 8, 12, 18; 3:1, 7, 14.

While Revelation has many similarities with other ancient apocalyptic books, the letters of Revelation 2 and 3 are somewhat out of character in such a work. Some scholars suggest that they are "prophetic letters," a type of writing that appears in the Old Testament (2 Chron. 21:12-15; Jer. 29) and early Jewish literature (2 Baruch 77:17-19; Epistle of Jeremiah 1). Such letters carried a great deal of authority, and people treated them as if they were royal or imperial edicts.[10]

The Roman world had no official postal system, except for governmental business. Friends who happened to be traveling in the right direction, or designated messengers, carried most letters. But the empire's superb road system, combined with efficient shipping on the Mediterranean Sea, made travel easier and faster than it had ever been before. Archaeologists have found evidence of people in Egypt sending letters to Asia Minor and receiving replies in as short a time as 25 days. That isn't all that much different than today!

Letters almost always introduce an element of suspense. The envelope gives some idea as to sender and purpose, but the content may still be a surprise. I have often received letters that look like official business, including a see-through panel. Opening them, I expect a bank statement or official correspondence, only to find another credit card offer or an enticement to enroll in a book club. I have learned to look at the postage stamp or mark on such correspondence. If the sender paid full rate, the contents will probably be important to me. But if the letter went by bulk mail, the contents will most likely be a waste of my time.

Once I received a brown envelope from the Internal Revenue Service, the tax collection office of the United States. Such letters might as well have black borders, as they usually portend great financial loss to the receiver! Since I was in school at the time and funds were limited, I opened the letter with a heavy heart. But to my joyous surprise I found a check inside! Someone had decided to audit my last tax return and discovered a mistake that I had made to my disadvantage. Obviously, one has to open a letter to be certain of its contents.

I can imagine the suspense in the cities of Asia Minor as the readers of the Apocalypse came to the part that said, "To the angel of the church of *Ephesus,* write," or "To the angel of the church of *Smyrna,* write." The members of these respective churches must have held their breath as they awaited a message directly from Jesus. And the collection of letters contained a lot of surprises!

Lord, I eagerly await instructions through Your Spirit today. Be straight with me. I am willing to accept and carry out Your message to me.

To the angel of the church of . . . write. REV. 2:1, 8, 12, 18; 3:1, 7, 14.

When I was a teenager, television had an extremely popular show called *Star Trek.* It was about the starship *Enterprise,* an outer space battleship that roamed the galaxy defending the United Federation of Planets against Klingons and other evil species. The ship's captain was a normal human being named Kirk who expressed the typical range of emotions from elation at victory in battle to panic when everything was going wrong. His subordinate was Mr. Spock, a humanoid with pointed ears who came from the planet Vulcan and was totally devoid of emotion.

A running subplot in nearly every show was Captain Kirk losing his cool in a crisis and Mr. Spock interjecting in a dry tone of voice, "Captain, that is not very logical." You see, unlike beings from "Vulcan," human beings have two major ways to assess any situation: one is reason and logic, and the other feeling. Emotions, of course, can be a major protective device for human beings, but they can also lead people to do silly and unproductive actions, as the show often illustrated.

We can illustrate Western logic by the equation: $A + B = C$. Everything drives toward the conclusion. But the Hebrew logic of the Bible is different: $A + B = A$! Hebrew logic returns back on itself. It is like the notes on a piano. As you go up the musical scale (do, re, mi, etc.) you keep coming back to the same notes, but they are at a higher, more advanced level than before. Western logic emphasizes the conclusion, while Hebrew logic stresses the center.

The seven churches seem to be structured along the lines of Hebrew logic: A-B-A. Jesus does not criticize Smyrna and Philadelphia (the second and the sixth) at all; Pergamum and Sardis (the third and the fifth) seem to be in serious decline; Ephesus and Laodicea (the first and the last) have similar problems. The church in the middle—Thyatira—appears to have two phases, and the message to it is the longest.

The resulting structure is like a seven-branch lampstand with three branches on each side, one in the middle and pairs of branches meeting at the same point on the stem of the lampstand: Ephesus and Laodicea are at opposite ends of the candlestick; Smyrna and Philadelphia are the next level; Pergamum and Sardis above them; and Thyatira, the top.

God did not apply Western logic to the churches of Asia Minor. He cared so much for them that He met them where they were.

Lord, I'm so grateful to know that You can reach me at my level of understanding.

February 1

To the angel of the church of Ephesus write, "These things are spoken by the One who holds the seven stars in His right hand, **THE ONE WHO WALKS IN THE MIDDLE OF THE SEVEN GOLDEN LAMPSTANDS."**
REV. 2:1.

To many people, golf is the dumbest sport ever invented. People wander all over the face of the earth, chasing a ball, only to drive it away from themselves again as soon as they find it. Yet something about the strange game seems to draw many people back again and again. One big reason, I suspect, is the fact that no matter how many times a golfer plays the same course, it is never truly the same.

Every time you play a hole, the tee is in a different place, and you approach the green from a different direction. When the ground is dry, the ball will bounce farther than when it is wet. In dry air the ball will fly farther than when it is humid. Because the grass is a quarter-inch longer than it was the day before, the ball will behave in new ways. And if the wind is in your face, a particular hole will play very differently than it would if the wind were at your back.

But that is far from the sum total of complications one can face in golf. Every golfer knows that the ball seems to have a mind of its own and goes where it wants to. The place where it lands is called the "lie." A lot of the skill involved in the game is learning how to handle the different lies, which can include soft, hard, up-hill, downhill, sidehill, rough, smooth, wet, dry, or any combination of the above. Success requires adjusting one's swing to the requirements of the specific lie.

What does all this have to do with the book of Revelation? Not much, I suppose, but it does illustrate a point that we noticed in one of the earlier devotionals. Jesus "adjusts His swing" to deal with the realities of each of the seven churches. He meets each of them where they are and shares with each a unique picture of Himself fitted to the exact circumstances in which they live.

If we want to make a difference in our world, we will want to become more like Jesus in the way we treat people. In the words of Paul: "I have become all things to all men so that by all possible means I might save some" (1 Cor. 9:22, NIV). Just like the variety of conditions in golf, no two human beings are alike. Even more than that, no person we meet is exactly like he or she was the day before! To be a blessing to everyone we meet, we need to meet them where they are. We need to "adjust our swing" to the unique context of each encounter with others. This makes life not only a lot more complicated, but also a lot more interesting!

Lord, help me to see each person I meet today through Your eyes. Enable me to adjust my approach to each person to reflect their unique needs.

I KNOW your works. REV. 2:2. I KNOW your affliction and your poverty.
VERSE 9. *I KNOW where you live. VERSE 13. I KNOW your works. VERSE 19.*
I KNOW your works. REV. 3:1. I KNOW your works. VERSE 8. I KNOW
your works. VERSE 15.

A common message to each of the seven churches is the clear assertion that Jesus knows everything about each of them. Early in each letter is a statement along the lines of "I know your works." Jesus knows not only everything we do but also what we can become. He wants each church to become all that it can be and desires that each church live according to His design.

Christ knew all about John as well. He had a plan and a purpose for his life. Jesus recognized that the prophet could handle the powerful visions that form the core of the message of Revelation (Rev. 1:1). In writing out the book, John was acting out Jesus' purpose for his life (verses 11, 19).

God has a design and a purpose for every person's life. He told Jeremiah, "Before I formed you in the womb I knew you, before you were born I set you apart" (Jer. 1:5, NIV). If God had a unique plan for Jeremiah and for John as well as each of the seven churches, we can have little doubt that He has a specific one for each of us. But God's design for our temperament and spiritual purpose is not always immediately obvious.

My wife, Pamella, once believed that God's design for her was to be a pastor's wife, to simply be and do whatever that required. But over time she came to realize that it was a secondary purpose. Although supportive of mine and important in itself, it was not by itself her own unique mission for God.

She then plunged for more than a decade into the full-time role of mother and home school teacher. Such responsibilities were and are extremely important, and many, such as Mary, the mother of Jesus, have found fullness of purpose in them. But my wife often felt frustrated and empty, sensing that somehow that was not all there was to God's design for her.

More recently she has plunged into a college education, preparing to assist God in the beautification of our planet through the skills of horticulture and landscape design. These activities have been intensely satisfying at times, and yet the question for her has lingered: *Is that all God wants me to do?*

Her uncertainty has actually been a great blessing. It has plunged my wife into an intense study of the process by which people can come to know God's design and purpose for them (see tomorrow's devotional). How is it with you? Do you understand God's plan for you? If so, are you living by it, or have you let the cares of this life distract you from it?

Lord, I submit myself entirely to Your design and purpose for me. I am willing to be and do according to Your will.

February 3

I KNOW your works. Rev. 2:2. *I KNOW your affliction and your poverty.* Verse 9. *I KNOW where you live.* Verse 13. *I KNOW your works.* Verse 19. *I KNOW your works.* Rev. 3:1. *I KNOW your works.* Verse 8. *I KNOW your works.* Verse 15.

We saw yesterday how God had a unique intent for John's life and for each of the seven churches. The Lord clearly spelled out that design for them in everyday Greek. But most of us do not get that kind of direct word from Him. While some have a strong sense of "calling" in their lives, most do not. So how do the rest of us discover God's purpose for us? My wife, Pamella, offers the following practical suggestions.

1. *Submit to God's purpose for your life.* Why should He reveal His plan to you if you have no intention of following it? To paraphrase something Jesus said, "If you are willing to do His will, you will know" (John 7:17). Seek His purpose through prayer and study, and as it becomes clearer to you, put it immediately into practice. Rick Warren's book *The Purpose-Driven Life* blessed Pamella in this process.

2. *Learn all you can about your childhood.* Children are often more faithful to God's design than grown-ups are (Mark 10:14, 15). So talk to older relatives and friends about your interests and personality as a child. Read things your parents may have written down about your sayings and actions. One of my wife's sweetest memories as a child was making little dresses for her dolls, working late into the night, so happy and focused that she had lost all track of time.

3. *Take advantage of tests and inventories.* Today we have many resources that can help us better understand our temperament, spiritual gifts, brain tendencies, and personality. A brain tendency inventory recently revealed that my wife and I are almost identical in all areas of innate personality. It greatly surprised us, as we had always thought we were opposites. This has made her more open to teaching and writing as part of God's design for her.

4. *Invite honest feedback about your life today.* Others often see us more clearly than we do ourselves. Several women have recently told my wife that her life story had profoundly blessed them. She is now sharing it with a variety of audiences.

5. *Experiment.* Try out the ideas that emerge from the above processes. Ask yourself three questions as you experiment: (a) do I enjoy this (would God design you to do something you hate)? (b) am I good at it? and (c) do other people (particularly fellow Christians) think I'm good at it? If the answer to all three is a resounding yes, you have probably grasped another piece of God's purpose for your life.

Lord, I want my life to be centered on Your design and purpose for me. Teach me all I need to know as soon as I can handle it (John 16:12).

To the angel of the **CHURCH OF EPHESUS** *write, "These things are spoken by the One who holds the seven stars in His right hand, the One who walks in the middle of the seven golden lampstands." REV. 2:1.*

That Ephesus is the first church the angel addresses makes sense. If one were traveling from Patmos to Asia Minor, Ephesus would be the first of the seven cities that one would encounter. Also the most prominent of them, it was politically more powerful than Pergamos and more favored than Smyrna with regard to the cult of emperor worship.

Symbols of the civil religion filled the city. Augustus (27 B.C.-A.D 14.) had allowed Ephesus to build temples in his honor, although he himself did not care for emperor worship. Domitian (A.D. 81-96) proclaimed the city the foremost center of the imperial cult in Roman Asia. Also it became renowned for the worship of Artemis (Acts 19:23-40), the practice of magic (verses 13-19), and its large Jewish community (verses 8, 9). All of these elements would have made the book of Revelation relevant to the church in Ephesus.[11]

Shortly after the time of Revelation the church received another letter, this time from Ignatius, the bishop of Antioch in Syria. Ten Roman soldiers had taken him into custody and were transporting him through Asia Minor to Rome, where he would die in the arena. Along the way the soldiers allowed him to meet with other Christians. One memorable encounter was the warm welcome in Smyrna from Polycarp, the leader of the local church there (we will meet him again in a later devotional).

While Ignatius was in Smyrna, four representatives also came from Ephesus to encourage him. They included the bishop of Ephesus, Onesimus, possibly the former runaway slave mentioned in Paul's letter to Philemon. Ignatius responded to their visit by sending a letter to the church at Ephesus. Later on he also dispatched letters to Philadelphia and Smyrna.

In his letter to the Ephesians Ignatius thanks the church for its kindness, praises its unity, and warns them to be subject to their bishop and not allow divisions in the church. As did John in the three New Testament Epistles, Ignatius considered Docetism, a theory that rejected the full humanity of Jesus, as the greatest threat facing the church at that time.

Ignatius also sent a letter to the Christians in Rome, asking them not to intercede with the emperor in his behalf. He seems to have been almost eager for martyrdom, in order that he might sooner be with Christ. In fact, he declared that if the wild beasts were not hungry he would urge them on! While his eagerness for martyrdom may strike us as odd, his love for Jesus would have been a great model for a church that was lacking in love.

Lord, I too want to be faithful to You, no matter what the cost.

February 5

I KNOW YOUR WORKS, *even your labor and your patience, and that you are not able to endure evil people. You have also tested those who call themselves apostles and are not, and found them to be liars. You also have patience and endure hardship because of My name and have not grown weary.* **BUT I HAVE THIS AGAINST YOU, THAT YOU HAVE LEFT YOUR FIRST LOVE.** REV. 2:2-4.

In this passage we see Jesus' analysis of the church at Ephesus. He has a number of positive things to say about it. An energetic church that knows how to work (verse 2), it is also a patient one that endures without getting weary (verses 2, 3). It has discernment and is doctrinally sound (verses 2 and 6). Interested in truth, it does not want to see falsehood gain entry among the believers. At first glance it would be easy to get excited about this very effective church, but it has one small problem: the church is backsliding in love (verse 4).

Christian life contains many paradoxes, and they can be hard to maintain. On one hand, we have the call to be faithful, energetic, discerning, and doctrinally sound. On the other hand, God summons us to be masterful in love. Keeping them in balance can be a difficult tension. Checking someone out to see if they are doctrinally sound at the same time we are trying to love them can be hard to do. The desire for sound doctrine and decisive action often leads to the loss of mutual love, which is the badge of discipleship. "By this all men will know that you are my disciples, if you love one another" (John 13:35, NIV).

It reminds me of a story that Martin Luther told about drunken peasants. He would ask people, "Do you know what happens when you put a drunken peasant on a horse? The one thing you know for sure is that he is going to fall off the horse! What you don't know is whether he will fall off the horse to the right or the left!" Luther felt that Christians often resembled drunken peasants on a horse. We have a hard time maintaining our balance between the gospel of free acceptance, on the one hand, and keeping the commandments, on the other. Luther felt that every time he proclaimed the gospel, the people forgot to obey. And every time he preached obedience, they forgot the gospel.

I find that true in my own experience. When I emphasize love and the gospel, obedience seems a little less important. But I find encouragement in the experience of Ephesus. While the early Christians had the memory of walking with Jesus and even had living apostles among them, they still had to deal with some of the same issues we struggle with today. If the early Christians had this same problem, we should not expect to have an easy time of it today. We need the Holy Spirit's presence at all times if we want to keep our balance.

Lord, I need Your Spirit to keep my balance today.

I know your works, even your labor and **YOUR PATIENCE,** *and that you are not able to endure evil people. You have also tested those who call themselves apostles and are not, and found them to be liars.* **YOU ALSO HAVE PATIENCE AND HAVE ENDURED HARDSHIP** *because of My name and have not grown weary.* REV. 2:2, 3.

Here Jesus uses two different Greek words to express the idea of "patient endurance" and "enduring hardship or difficulty." In a sense the words express two different ways of saying the same thing. But put the two concepts together, and we have the combined sense of moving on when you cannot advance anymore, or of continuing to carry a burden when the weight is pressing you down. It is a combination of the English word "patience" with the English word "endurance."

I remember a time when my family was visiting relatives in the Denver area. We decided to drive up the road to the top of Mount Evans, a 14,000-foot peak in plain sight outside the Mile-High City, Denver. The drive was beautiful, even though the weather at the top was blustery and cold. On the way down people expressed an interest in hiking a bit to get in closer touch with the scenery. Looking at a map I noticed a trail that left the road at the 12,500-foot mark, wandered for a mile or so, and returned to the road at the 11,500-foot mark.

I had a "brilliant" idea. We could park the car by the trailhead and hike down together to the next turnout in the road. Then I'd walk back up to the car and pick everyone up! I was in good physical shape, and it sounded like fun to me.

The hike down was great, the weather had warmed up a bit, and the wildflowers were spectacular. As we got in sight of the road I bade my family farewell and headed back up toward the place where I had parked the car. It was *only* 1,000 feet farther up, and I hurried so as not to keep the family waiting below. But the air was so thin and the trail was so steep that it was difficult to take 10 or 20 steps without stopping to gasp for air. My heart was pumping at 180 beats per minute even though I was walking at a snail's pace! Every step was a struggle, every inch gained by slow and arduous effort.

The easiest thing would have been a short siesta. But I patiently endured, knowing that my family was waiting below. The Christian life is sometimes like that. In the valleys we skip along and seem to make wonderful progress. But if we choose to come up to God's vision for us we must eventually ascend to the upper mists of the high mountains. We must go into the thin air of high places. And in the process, we learn what patient endurance is all about.

Lord, when things get tough today, help me keep my mind on You. Strengthen me to keep on keeping on. And help me endure the feelings of the moment and continue to do the right thing.

February 7

But I have this against you, that **YOU HAVE LEFT YOUR FIRST LOVE.** Rev. 2:4.

The Ephesus church seems to have been replaying the experience of Israel before the exile to Babylon. In the words of Jeremiah to the people of Jerusalem: "I remember the devotion of your youth, how as a bride you loved me and followed me through the desert" (Jer. 2:2, NIV). The early years of Israel's experience in the wilderness were a time of relative devotion and faithfulness. But now things have changed: "I had planted you like a choice vine of sound and reliable stock. How then did you turn against me into a corrupt, wild vine?" (verse 21, NIV).

If you had to emphasize either strong doctrinal soundness or love in a situation, which would you choose? When we don't know what to do, the safest course of action is to love. First Corinthians 13 tells us that we could have doctrinal soundness and all kinds of helpful works but if we don't have love, those works are of no value. Ellen White concludes, "In reforms we would better come one step short of the mark than to go one step beyond it. And if there is error at all, let it be on the side next to the people." [12]

I remember a time I went to visit a man who was committing adultery. My mind swirled the whole way over, wrestling with just how to approach the issue. I determined to confront him boldly, because I knew that if he didn't make a change in his life, Satan would use the situation to draw him completely away from Christ.

When I arrived at the home, somehow it just didn't seem appropriate to start with that situation. We talked about other things instead. Repeatedly I considered bringing up my purpose for the visit, but it never seemed quite right. Instead I was kind and supportive. Finally I left, kicking myself mentally. *What a wimp,* I told myself. *He was right there, and you didn't have the guts to tell the truth.* For the next two days I berated my own cowardice.

Then I received a phone call from him. "Pastor, ever since you left the other day the Holy Spirit has been hammering me about my situation. You knew exactly what I was doing yet you didn't try to humiliate me and make me feel bad. Instead you treated me with love and respect. I was ready for a fight, but your kindness was harder on me than anything you could have said. I have to get my life in order. Will you come back and teach me how?"

By nature we tend to be severe with others and merciful toward ourselves. Any church that loses touch with the centrality of the gospel will begin to wound people even in its faithfulness and sound doctrine. So whenever we are not sure how to handle a specific situation, it is the safest course to err on the side of love and mercy.

Lord, help me never to criticize another until I see them through Your eyes and love them as You love them.

But I have this against you, that **YOU HAVE LEFT YOUR FIRST LOVE.** Rev. 2:4.

Nothing could be colder than a church that doesn't love. And the love that truly matters must go beyond formalities—beyond the meeting of basic needs—to compassionate connection with others.

In 1992 Jack Harris received, along with a group of hospital administrators, an invitation to visit the People's Republic of China. The sponsoring organization asked him to present a paper entitled "Healing Through Kindness." Prior to the weeklong seminar in which he was participating, the group visited hospitals across the nation to observe their methods and procedures. It found a number of potentially useful differences, such as acupuncture. At the same time it also encountered some strange and questionable practices.

In one hospital they witnessed people being examined for various ailments. Lined up on crude benches, the patients waited for their turn. One by one someone called out their names over the loud public address system. The patients entered a very large room in which medical personnel stood beside beds waiting for the next individual to examine.

Harris watched a man treat three different people, two women and a man. When the examiner finished with a patient he simply thumped them on the head. That was his signal that he was through with them. They got up and walked away. Neither doctor nor patient made any comment. It was like a medical assembly line, cold and indifferent.

On another occasion Harris visited a nursery with two nurses and 47 babies. It seemed that all the babies were crying at once. Harris approached the closest baby. She lay there screaming and kicking like babies anywhere else in the world. Her little black-haired head rolled back and forth in the crib, and her little feet stroked the air with fervor. The grandfather in him made him reach down and touch her cheek. Instantly the little girl stopped kicking and crying and looked up into his face. In moments her face broke into a smile. It was as if she spoke perfect English. Or is a touch and a smile the same in any language?

Many in this world endure lives of loneliness and emptiness. They are worth more than a thump on the head. Your touch and your smile have tremendous power to express the kind of love that changes people. The adults around you may not be kicking and screaming, but they are longing for the practical touch of love. Ephesus was a church that used to love like that, but had forsaken this course in the name of doctrinal purity. In our zeal to make sure that the "Nicolaitans" around us do not infiltrate the church, we often freeze out the lonely and neglected along with them.[13]

Lord, I know how easy it is for my love to fade. Help me to be more aware of the crying needs of others today.

February 9

But I have this against you, that **YOU HAVE LEFT YOUR FIRST LOVE.** Rev. 2:4.

The church at Ephesus is largely faithful to Jesus, but it does have a problem. It has "left [its] first love" and has taken that first fateful step down a slope to disaster. No one but Jesus may have been aware of it. Ephesus itself may not have realized what it was doing, at least until the book of Revelation arrived. The first steps in spiritual decline are usually quiet ones.

One time I was in Kruger National Park, South Africa. People there can drive along roads occupied by lions, giraffes, elephants, and much more. You could say that the animals roam free in Kruger, while the people find themselves restricted to four-wheeled cages (their cars)! Visitors are expected to spend the night in fenced-in "rest camps" for their safety.

Late one day we were about 15 miles from the next rest camp. We needed to be safely inside by 6:00 in the evening. At the moment we had just stopped at a spot where someone had seen a leopard in the past half hour. When the leopard failed to return, we decided we had better get to camp. As I pulled out of the parking spot I drove over some small bushes. A loud thumping sound came from under the car, louder than small bushes should make, but nothing seemed wrong, so I drove on.

A few moments later I noticed that the battery gauge had slipped from 16 to 14 (don't ask me what the numbers meant). The car's owner thought that that meant the alternator was no longer charging the battery. Having only a limited stretch of time before the engine would die, we decided to stop at no more water holes but head straight toward the rest camp. The thought of being stranded in the African wilderness at night was not a welcome one.

Can you remember a time when your gas gauge read empty with no gas station in sight? Then you will understand a fraction of the concern that gripped our stomachs as the needle on the battery gauge moved from 14 to 12 to 10. When the gauge reached 8, the fence of the rest camp appeared on the horizon. As we approached the entrance the engine began to stutter. I worked down through the gears, trying to keep the vehicle moving. The engine kept hesitating and finally died 100 feet from the gate. We rolled in with a silent engine and came to a stop at the fuel station just inside the entrance! Our gratitude to God knew no bounds!

It is easy enough to know when our cars break down, but how is it with our spiritual lives? In the easy comfort of a consumer society, it is easy to think that all is spiritually well, when in reality our spiritual batteries have been running down for quite some time. To us the words of Jesus come home with considerable force: "You have left your first love."

Lord, don't hold back. I need to know the truth about myself and receive the remedy only You can give.

REMEMBER, *therefore, the place from which you have fallen.* **REPENT AND DO THE FIRST WORKS,** *but if not, I will come to you and remove your lamp from its place, if you do not repent. But you do have this: you hate the works of the Nicolaitans, which I also hate.* REV. 2:5, 6.

iven Jesus' analysis of the Ephesus church, what counsel would He offer to them? The first thing He says is "remember." In the original Greek the word is a present imperative. This means that they have not forgotten their former level of relationship with God. But the church needs to internalize a sense of growing loss, to be motivated by the fact that they are in decline.

The next thing He tells them to do is to repent. The form of this word is different, reflecting a one-time action. Here He is commanding them to get started. Their repentance is to be a one-time decisive turnaround. While the church is used to remembering, it has forgotten how to repent. It needs a fresh start and to bring its actions in line with its intentions.

Third, He counsels them to do the things that they did at first. This is also something that they must start doing. Revive the earlier circumstances that caused your love to blossom in the first place. Go back in your mind to a time you were truly close to the Lord and renew those thoughts and actions. "Repent and do the first works."

Marriage counselors will tell you that a couple who has fallen out of love needs to go back through the steps that bonded them together in the first place. Nearly every married couple was in love at one time. No matter what is going on between them today, they were once attracted to each other. If that happened before, it can occur again.

A couple that is fighting and angry needs to start over. It can be good to back off sexually and go back to square one in the relationship. Go out on dates—if possible, to the places where your relationship got its start. Rekindle the joy in holding hands, kind words, and gentle attentions. Take time off from work, reduce the pressure, and act young again. Restore the bonds that have weakened or broken.

The same principle can apply to spiritual life. If you have fallen out of love with God, go back to the things that bonded you to Him in the first place. Where were you when you first felt His presence? What kinds of things did you do to respond? We don't have to take the initiative in restoring our relationship with God. The gospel tells us that He has already done that. We love God because He first loved us. He is the initiator. Our task is to respond to what He has already done. We love Him because He first loved us.

Lord, I remember the fires of our first love, and I choose to respond to You in the way I have done before.

February 11

Remember, therefore, the place from which you have fallen. Repent and do the first works, but if not, **I WILL** *come to you and* **REMOVE YOUR LAMP FROM ITS PLACE,** *if you do not repent.* REV. 2:5.

In 1995 I led a group of students from Andrews University on a tour of Turkey, the modern-day nation that includes the locations of Revelation's seven churches. Our local tour guide, Murat, was a secular Turk of Muslim background who had taken an interest in the Christian heritage of his country.

One day road signs reported that we were nearing the city of Konya, in a section of central Turkey where Paul had worked during his first and second missionary journeys. Murat told us that Konya was a city of more than 500,000, but only three or four of them were Christians, and Murat knew them all personally. When he also told us that Konya was the Turkish name for the ancient city of Iconium, I realized that this city had been the site of a flourishing Christian community founded by Paul (Acts 13:51-14:6). We then learned that the whole area of the seven churches of Revelation shared a common condition. Ephesus is now Kusadasi, Philadelphia is Alashehir, and Christians are nowhere to be found.

When John wrote his book, Christianity was strongly established in central and western Asia Minor. In fact, many scholars believe Christians were more numerous in first-century Asia Minor than anywhere else in the world. But through the centuries these churches gradually declined, until Islam virtually eradicated them. The regions where the early church was once strongest (including Syria and North Africa) are now overwhelmingly Islamic. As Jesus warns in our text above, lampstands can be removed from their place.

Yet it was not Islam that destroyed the church. In North Africa doctrinal and ethnic controversies weakened Christianity. Christians in the Middle East failed to engage the local culture, leaving the way open for Muhammad's more contextualized faith. During the Middle Ages the European church leadership sought to revitalize Christianity in the Middle East. But they misunderstood the gospel and chose a method (the Crusades) that made things even worse. It was the church that destroyed Christianity in the eastern Mediterranean.[14]

Such history should be a warning to us. Where the gospel once flourished (including Europe, North America, and Australia), it is now in decline. Yet regions that hardly knew the gospel two centuries ago (Africa and Asia) are rapidly becoming the center of the faith. You and I dare not take our role in God's plan for granted. If we abandon our mission, the Lord will raise up others to fulfill it. Lampstands can be removed from their place.

Lord, rekindle the clarity of my mission today. Keep my lamp trimmed and burning.

He that has an ear, let him hear what the Spirit says to the churches. To the one who overcomes I will give to eat of **THE TREE OF LIFE,** *which is in the paradise of God.* REV. 2:7.

God offers the overcomers in Ephesus a special reward. They will eat from the tree of life, now located in the paradise of God. If it takes deep repentance to eat from that tree, it will be worth it. The reward is far greater than the sacrifice along the way (cf. Rev. 22:2).

Nearly everyone knows the story of Gideon, how he defeated the Midianites with 300 men bearing torches and trumpets. Most have never heard the rest of the story. After the battle the people asked him to become king. But he said, "I will not rule over you, nor will my son rule over you. The Lord will rule over you" (Judges 8:23, NIV).

Gideon had 70 sons from various marriages. He had at least one other, Abimelech, as a result of an extramarital affair. After Gideon's death, Abimelech plotted with his mother's relatives to murder all the other sons of Gideon and proclaim himself king (you can read the story in Judges 9). The only son of Gideon to escape, Jotham, disrupted Abimelech's coronation ceremony by taunting him from a distance with the following parable:

"One day the trees went out to anoint a king for themselves. They said to the olive tree, 'Be our king.' But the olive tree answered, 'Should I give up my oil, by which both gods and men are honored, to hold sway over the trees?' Next, the trees said to the fig tree, 'Come and be our king.' But the fig tree replied, 'Should I give up my fruit, so good and sweet, to hold sway over the trees?' . . . Finally all the trees said to the thornbush, 'Come and be our king.' The thornbush said to the trees, 'If you really want to anoint me king over you, come and take refuge in my shade'" (Judges 9:8-15, NIV).

The sting in this parable is in the nature of the "thornbush" (Hebrew: *atad*). Most trees are an asset to the environment. Animals feed off the fruit and rest in the shade. Birds nest in the branches of the tree. The organic matter that drops from the tree nourishes other plants. So in the ancient world a healthy tree represented the caretaking role of properly constituted authority. But when I saw one of these *"atad"* trees in the area where Jotham made his speech, nothing—absolutely nothing—grew under that tree, not even a weed! Jotham was satirizing the cruel and abusive nature of the kingship Abimelech would exercise.

The reign of God will not be like that of Abimelech. Instead of a "thorn tree," Revelation depicts it by a "tree of life," which enhances every life that encounters it. There the overcomer will find an abundant life that never ends. And we will never regret yielding our lives to the rule of God.

Lord, I surrender my life to You again today. Help me to trust Your directions.

February 13

And to the angel of the church in Smyrna write: These things says the First and the Last, who died and came to life. **I KNOW YOUR AFFLICTION AND YOUR POVERTY; NEVERTHELESS YOU ARE RICH.** Rev. 2:8, 9.

Commentators widely agree that the poverty in this passage is literal, while the riches are spiritual. The Smyrnians were poor in this world's goods, but they were rich in the goods of the gospel, wealthy in the things of the Spirit.

In practical terms, a big difference exists between poverty and riches.[15] People born rich have an entirely different mentality than the average person. For most of us, financial limitations affect nearly every decision we make. We choose inexpensive restaurants for lunch and buy our clothes at Wal-Mart or Penney's instead of Nieman-Marcus or Gucci. In our free time we go to a public beach instead of a tropical vacation at Club Med. Our lack of unlimited money shapes every choice we make.

Compare this lifestyle with that of the megawealthy. If you want to go skiing, or even shopping, in the Alps at a moment's notice, drive to the airport and grab the next available first-class seat. If the weather is too cold, head for the tropics or the other hemisphere. Should you not feel like washing clothes, just hire someone to buy a new designer wardrobe for each day. Want a new speedboat or sports car? Then hire someone to purchase it and deliver it to the place of your choice. While most of us are limited in our daily decisions, the superrich have the world at their fingertips. They can do anything and be anything they want whenever they desire. And the rest of us tend to watch enviously from a distance, thinking of everything we are missing out on.

But the church at Smyrna discovered a different kind of riches, one that the rich rarely attain (Matt. 19:24). Those who know Jesus are liberated from enslavement to money. They realize that we find the true riches of life in loving relationships. To have a clean conscience, to be able to forgive and to be forgiven, is to be truly rich. It is far better to know the Word of God than to be able to rush from one empty round of entertainment to another.

The truth is that the wealthy have a hard time with relationships. They never know whom they can trust. Everyone wants to "be their friend," not because of personal qualities, but because being a friend of the rich is a path to wealth and power of one's own. The rich avoid a relationship with Christ, sometimes because they are too distracted and busy and sometimes because they fear the call to "sell all you have" more than poor people do. The truest of all riches are found in Christ, not in material wealth.

Lord, turn my affections to the true riches You offer in Christ.

I know **YOUR AFFLICTION** *and your poverty;* **NEVERTHELESS YOU ARE RICH.** *I also know the blasphemy of those who call themselves Jews. They are not real Jews; they are the synagogue of Satan.* Rev. 2:9.

I have a friend named Ted who used to fly combat missions in a fighter jet for the United States Marine Corps. Shortly after a practice landing at an Air Force base, he overheard a pilot radio the tower that he was descending through 70,000 feet. *Seventy thousand feet? Descending? How high can this guy's plane fly?* my friend thought. After making inquiries, he discovered that it was the top-secret (at the time) SR-71 reconnaissance plane, able to travel at unheard-of heights and at extremely fast speeds.

His appetite whetted, Ted pushed his way through a bunch of "red tape" to get permission to look the SR-71 over for himself. Finally his superiors allowed him to walk past the security detail and observe this awesome technological achievement inside a hangar. Its great size and sleekness impressed him. But as he got up close he was stunned and disappointed. The thing was leaking all over the floor. A number of drip pans dotted the floor under it. It looked as if this "bucket of bolts" was ready to fall apart! Then he found out it was being readied for takeoff. He asked what was the matter with it.

"Nothing," the ground crew told him. It was in great shape. It was just right for flying at high altitudes and airspeeds. What Ted didn't realize was the incredible stresses the plane's makers had designed it to withstand. Once the plane got up to speed and reached its cruising altitude, its skin would expand, and the resulting heat would cause the dripping to stop. Not only that, but much of the plane consisted of titanium, a metal that actually gets stronger as it heats up.

This story helps me understand the text. How can Christians be poor and rich at the same time? How is it that we should welcome suffering and affliction as riches (James 1:2)? I think Christians are a lot like the SR-71. In ordinary life they don't stand out at all—they may even look like a bigger mess than the average secular person. It is when the trials and stresses of life show up that the real Christian begins to shine.

God doesn't permit His people to go through trials in order to find out what they are made of. He already knows. But one reason He allows trials is so that we can discover what He has been remaking us to be. As we learn to stay close to God in trial He redesigns us so we can fly higher and faster than we could possibly have imagined. If our lives were easier we might never discover the rich fulfillment that comes from soaring at God's altitude.[16]

Lord, You know how to fit us for the kind of life You had in mind when You designed us. Help me to resent the "training" but to see eternal riches in life's setbacks.

February 15

I know your affliction and your poverty; nevertheless you are rich. **I ALSO KNOW THE BLASPHEMY OF THOSE WHO CALL THEMSELVES JEWS. THEY ARE NOT REAL JEWS; THEY ARE THE SYNAGOGUE OF SATAN.** REV. 2:9.

It appears from today's text that the church's relationship with the Jews of Smyrna was at risk.[17] The church faced a perilous situation. By the second century the Roman Empire expected everyone except the Jews to venerate the emperor. The authorities exempted Jews out of respect for the antiquity of their religion. Since the Romans usually identified early Christians as Jewish, they often escaped unnecessary persecution.

The Jews themselves, on the other hand, had reason to be cautious about any association with Christians. Twenty-five years earlier Jewish apocalyptic excitement had provoked the Romans to destroy Jerusalem and its Temple, leaving behind thousands of dead. It was loud and clear that Jewish status in the empire could get revoked at a moment's notice if Christian talk of the Messiah created Roman suspicion against the Jews.

At the time John wrote Revelation the Jewish community was finding itself in some difficulty with the local leaders of Smyrna. When Christian Jews talked about Jesus the Messiah and the end of the world, it only made things even more difficult. So we should understand the word "blasphemy" in our text in terms of "slander." Historical records suggest that the following scenario may have occurred a number of times in first-century Smyrna.

Let's say Jason was a Christian member of the synagogue. Theudas, a non-Christian Jewish neighbor, never liked him. His "crazy ideas" embarrassed the Jews among their pagan neighbors. One day Theudas discovers that Jason's goats have escaped their enclosure again and munched and trampled his prized rhododendrons. In a fit of anger he "informs" the local authorities that Jason was an enemy of the emperor and the state but stayed "under the radar" by masquerading as a Jew. Then he gives evidence of Jason's "un-Jewish" ideas.

Roman authorities at that time would rarely seek out Christians, but when faced with a specific charge, they would have to investigate. It would not do to have potential revolutionaries multiplying undetected. When they interviewed Jason's neighbors they soon discovered that he was a no-show at civic events. If the Jewish community did not like him and supported Theudas' contention that Jason was not a real Jew, execution was the likely fate.

After such incidents, it is understandable that Christians would begin to think that Jews such as Theudas were not real Jews, but tools of Satan.

Lord, reveal Your presence to all Christians who face slander and persecution in Today's world. Show me ways that I can encourage and support them.

DO NOT BE AFRAID OF WHAT YOU ARE ABOUT TO
SUFFER. *Behold, the devil is about to throw some of you into prison, to test you, and you will suffer affliction for ten days. Be faithful until death, and I will give you the crown of life.* Rev. 2:10.

J esus says, "Do not be afraid of what you are about to suffer." Why? Because "there is no fear in love. . . . Perfect love drives out fear." And "we love because he first loved us" (1 John 4:18, 19, NIV).

Those who fear God have placed themselves in His control and do not let anybody else worry them. They have learned to trust Him in all situations, because He knows all circumstances. He permits nothing that wouldn't be for our good in the long run. And He allows nothing that we can't handle if we are in a relationship with Him.

Sometimes we get into situations that overwhelm us. But we still don't need to be afraid. Do you remember the story about the time I was snorkeling near Heron Island in the Great Barrier Reef? I had injured my leg the week before and was getting a little tired. I decided to rest from my snorkeling by standing up occasionally and keeping my nose above the water while I rested. But as I carried out my plan I discovered that the water was not five-feet but seven-feet deep and that the shore was 400 yards away.

Realizing that I did not have the strength to make it back, I began to panic. Convinced that my life was over, I began to swallow ocean water. A rock suddenly appeared in the sand below, barely large enough to balance on. Then my wife swam over and was able to help me stay upright. Professional help arrived, and I was on my way safely toward shore.

The overwhelming thought in my mind as I reached the beach was that I must be alive for a purpose. God had a reason for me to go on living and had intervened to accomplish that. What is most pertinent to our text today is that the incident has taken away my fear. I know that God is in control of my existence. You could say that I am already on borrowed time, so I really don't need to be afraid anymore.

A year or so later I was strolling where tourists don't often go—through a deserted Muslim section of the old city of Jerusalem. Some of my students saw me walking alone and hid around a corner. When I passed by they came roaring out and hollering as if they were going to kill me. I didn't know who they were, but I did not react. To my surprise and theirs, I was not afraid.

Now, I don't intend to be stupid and go places where I don't belong, but if God is in control of my life, I don't have to be afraid. If He is with me and it's time, then so be it. I don't have to worry about when. Fear is no longer in control.

Lord, thank You for those times that I instinctively live by faith. Increase my faith.

February 17

Do not be afraid of what you are about to suffer. Behold, the devil is about to throw some of you into prison, to test you, and **YOU WILL SUFFER AFFLICTION FOR TEN DAYS.** *Be faithful until death and* **I WILL GIVE YOU THE CROWN OF LIFE.** Rev. 2:10.

Daniel and his friends experienced 10 days of trial in Daniel 1. The church at Smyrna would also experience 10 days of testing. But faithfulness in it would prepare them for future glory. Like Daniel and his three friends, we prepare best for future challenges by passing the tests we encounter in the present.

The game was on the line. As the ball was snapped, Mike, the defensive end, charged into the opposing left tackle with his right shoulder, freed himself for a spin move with his left forearm, and dropped the scrambling quarterback with an ankle tackle. The quarterback fumbled the ball and Mike's teammate recovered, ensuring victory.

While all this happened in three and a half seconds, the play itself was years in the making. Lifting 80 tons of weights four or five times a week gave Mike the arm and leg strength to free himself from a clutching offensive tackle. Hundreds of tennis matches and agility drills created the ability to change directions quickly.

Thousands of 40-yard dashes and wind sprints meant he could keep going in the fourth quarter when his opponents were gasping for air. Hundreds of hours in the film room taught him that a particular tackle always leaned back a bit on pass plays, or that a certain quarterback would always pump-fake with the ball or scramble to his left whenever an opponent was about to tackle him.

In the span of about three and a half seconds Mike made a great play that turned the game around. A great deal of suffering went into the strength, the agility, the speed, and the strategy he employed to defeat his opponents. None of this was fun, except perhaps for the tennis. But each exercise would enable him to be a bit faster, a bit quicker, a bit stronger, and a bit more agile than he had been before. It all added up to small advantages on the football field.

The sum total of Mike's success was determined less by what happened on the playing field than by what happened in the training room.[18] The "victory crown" of life (Olympic gold medal) that Jesus promised the Smyrnians was not a casual result of their behavior. God used the grievous things they had suffered to prepare them for the ultimate victory of human existence—eternal life.

Lord, help me to remember that the difficult issues in my life today are not obstacles— they are opportunities to prepare for the ultimate battle of human history.

BE FAITHFUL UNTIL DEATH, *and I will give you the crown of life. He that has an ear, let him hear what the Spirit says to the churches.* **THE ONE WHO OVERCOMES WILL NOT BE HURT BY THE SECOND DEATH.** REV. 2:10, 11.

Polycarp was the elderly bishop of Smyrna around A.D. 155. A crowd in the stadium clamored for his arrest. But when mounted police arrived at his cottage to arrest him, he served them a banquet, requesting an hour of prayer before they took him away. The officers marveled at his graciousness and lamented that they had to arrest him. As he marched into the stadium to the roar of the crowd a voice from heaven said, "Be strong, Polycarp, and play the man."

The proconsul (governor), out of respect for his age, tried to persuade Polycarp to avoid death by offering a simple way out. "All you have to do is say, 'Away with the atheists.'" The crowd had earlier used the phrase to refer to the Christians, calling them atheists because they wouldn't worship the community's idols and had no shrines of their own. Polycarp waved his hand toward the pagan crowd in the stadium and said, "Away with the atheists." Not satisfied, of course, the proconsul said, "Just curse Christ, and I will let you go."

"Eighty and six years have I served him and he has done me no wrong," the bishop replied. "How then can I blaspheme my king who saved me?"

When the proconsul then threatened him with fire, Polycarp responded, "You threaten me with a fire that burns for just an hour, because you don't know about the fire of judgment that will come upon all the ungodly. But why do we delay? Bring what you will!"

When they had placed Polycarp on the wood they wanted to nail him to the stake, but he said, "Let me be as I am. The one who will help me endure the fire will also help me stay here, even without nails." When they lit the fire it formed a vault around him, looking like an oven. The bishop stood in its center, unconsumed. The crowd, not able to bear their defeat, prevailed upon the executioner to reach in and kill him with a dagger. And so Polycarp died for his faith.[19]

The threat of death for Christians is not an issue in much of today's world. It may be easy to consider texts and stories like this irrelevant to our daily lives, especially if we live comfortably in the suburbs. But we have still much to learn here. The martyrdom of our brothers and sisters in the past and even in the present challenges us to count the cost of our faith. How would we fare if placed in similar circumstances? Can our faith grow and mature without such challenges? How much is Jesus truly worth to us?

Lord, help me to count the cost of faith. I want to embrace the little challenges now so I can face whatever may be in store for me.

February 19

And to the angel of **THE CHURCH IN PERGAMUM** *write: These things says the One who has the sharp, two-edged sword.* **I KNOW WHERE YOU LIVE,** *where the throne of Satan is. You are holding fast to My name and have not denied My faith even in the days of Antipas, My faithful martyr who was put to death among you,* **WHERE SATAN LIVES.** REV. 2:12, 13.

Some students of this passage have suggested that the church at Pergamum was a compromising one. This could explain the reason that Jesus approaches it with a sharp, double-edged sword. It needs the cutting discernment that comes by the Word of God. "For the word of God is living and active. Sharper than any double-edged sword, it penetrates even to dividing soul and spirit, joints and marrow; it judges the thoughts and attitudes of the heart" (Heb. 4:12, NIV).

The church at Pergamum seems to be the opposite of Ephesus, which had sound doctrine and lacked love. The Pergamum church is weak in the very area that Ephesus is strong—sound doctrine.

According to Jesus, Pergamum was a dangerous place for Christians to live. In some sense He considered it the dwelling place of Satan. Pergamum was probably the most impressive of the seven cities listed in this part of Revelation. Its primary ruins lie on top of a steep hill hundreds of feet above the plain. The largest remaining structure is that of the amphitheater, capable of seating some 15,000 people. Built into a steep hillside, it overlooked the valley to the west.

Archaeologists took a part of the most spectacular of its many temples, the Pergamon Altar, and rebuilt it inside a museum in the eastern part of Berlin. The temple included a huge marble staircase (nearly 20 feet high and 100 wide) surrounded and topped in a horseshoe shape by colonnaded statuary carved into the marble itself. It was an incredible piece of work, exuding confidence in human genius and the overwhelming power of the religion it represented. Such magnificence would have attracted onlookers to the pagan religions of Rome. Compromise would have easily crept in without Christian believers even being aware of it.

The power of human achievement is even more impressive today. Giant skyscrapers, awesome technological advances, dazzling sports events and shows, all subtly suggest that real life is to be found in human achievement and pride. The Word of God is a sharp, two-edged sword revealing this false reality to be the illusion that it is. Events such as September 11 underline the accuracy of Jesus' diagnosis. After all, mighty Pergamum is largely in ruins today.

Lord, apply Your discerning Word to my life today. Expose my tendency to compromise.

You are holding fast to My name and **HAVE NOT DENIED MY FAITH** *even in the days of Antipas, My faithful martyr who was put to death among you, where Satan lives.* Rev. 2:13.

The statement "have not denied my faith" is the natural reverse of "hold on to your confession of faith" (Heb. 4:14; 10:23, author's translation). The believers in Pergamum have not only retained their trust and confidence in God in the good times, but also refused to deny that faith when placed under the pressure of persecution. We develop our faith in God and His teachings by applying His Word to everyday life. As we see God's hand at work in everyday experience, our faith grows. As our faith passes smaller tests, it strengthens until it can survive the more serious challenges that may come our way.

An example of how faith develops in small steps occurred in the fall of 2003. During a school board meeting the Eau Claire, Michigan, Seventh-day Adventist Church learned that its school faced an $8,000 deficit. When the church board could not come up with any solution, the church made an appeal to the entire congregation. An anonymous donor came forward and offered to match all funds raised, thinking that he could spare $4,000 from a savings account.

Prayers ascended, and letters went out to the members. On December 7 the school's Christmas program took up an offering. At the end of the program someone called the principal up to the front of the church and announced that the total amount raised that night was $12,160! And it did not include the pledged funds.

Approached with the results, the anonymous donor was stunned at the generosity of the members. Even if he cleaned out all his savings, he would be thousands of dollars short of what he had pledged. At first he considered just donating the $4,000 he had intended to give. Then he decided to stand by his promise and trust God to make up the difference. He emptied his bank account and prayed for a miracle.

Before the end of the week, unexpected funds arrived at his home, not only finishing off his pledge, but also replenishing his bank account! The man's act of faith not only received its reward, but the entire church was amazed to see the hand of God work so powerfully and with such miraculous timing. One small act of faith snowballed to the point at which an entire congregation of several hundred people could perceive the hand of God.[20]

It is in the small things that our faith learns to grow. And it is in the large challenges that our faith gets tested.

Lord, increase my faith. Send me the kinds of experiences today that will expand my trust in You. Prepare me and those I love for the big challenges to come.

February 21

You are holding fast to My name and have not denied My faith even in the days of
ANTIPAS, MY FAITHFUL MARTYR *who was put to death among you, where Satan lives.* REV. 2:13.

The book of Revelation reports the execution of a Christian named Antipas. His name has an interesting meaning: "against everyone." It fits in well with the typical Gentile accusation against Christians that they were "haters of the human race." The people of the Roman Empire applied it to Christians because they refused to participate in various aspects of the civil religion expected of all good Roman citizens. At the very least, many considered Christians as antisocial and regarded their presence as bad luck for any community.

While Scripture does not give any details, it is clear that Antipas died a martyr to his faith. "You did not renounce your faith in me, even in the days of Antipas, my faithful witness, who was put to death in your city—where Satan lives" (Rev. 2:13, NIV). Pergamum was one of the sites where the Roman governor held court and made judicial decisions. It is possible that early Christians would see in the "sharp, two-edged sword" of Christ (verses 12, 16) a contrast to the governor's power over the "sword," the death sentence. If so, the Roman governor probably executed Antipas for being a Christian.

The procedure in Antipas' case may have been that described by the governor Pliny some 15 years later in a letter to the emperor Trajan:

"I have asked the accused whether they were Christians. If they confessed, I asked a second and a third time, threatening penalty. Those who persisted I ordered to be executed, for I did not doubt that, whatever it was they professed, they deserved to be punished for their inflexible obstinacy. . . . I dismissed those who said they were not or never had been Christians, and who in my presence supplicated the gods and placed wine and incense before your [Trajan's] image, and especially cursed Christ, which I hear no true Christian will do." [21]

Trajan responded that the authorities should not seek Christians out or try them on the basis of anonymous accusations. If openly brought to the governor's attention, however, officials should handle them as Pliny had described. Probably a hostile neighbor, either Jew or Gentile, accused Antipas to the governor. Imagine living in a place where you never knew which neighbor might suddenly report your faith to the authorities! If it could happen to Antipas, it could happen to any Christian.

Lord, I am grateful for the relative safety in which I live today. Give me the wisdom and strength to serve You well when times are good.

But I have a few things against you, namely that you have some there who hold to **THE TEACHING OF BALAAM,** *who taught Balak to place an occasion for sin before the sons of Israel, to eat food offered to idols and to commit fornication. Similarly, you have those who hold to* **THE TEACHING OF THE NICOLAITANS.** Rev. 2:14, 15.

Apparently, some in the church at Pergamum held teachings similar to those of Balaam. They, like him, attempted to entice others astray with their ideas. The text also mentions the teaching of the Nicolaitans. The Greek root for the word Nicolaitans (nikolaos) means "the one who conquers the people" while the Hebrew name Balaam means "one who swallows up the people." These two terms, though from different languages, mean essentially the same thing.

When the king of Moab saw the Israelites coming, he realized that the God of Israel was far too powerful for his armies to overcome. So the monarch, Balak, had a brilliant idea. He would find a true prophet of their God who was willing to curse them. Then perhaps their deity would forsake them and Balak could conquer them in battle.

Having heard about Balaam, Balak sent a representative to him: "The king of Moab is offering you a large sum of money if you will come and curse Israel." A greedy sort, the prophet decided to accept the offer in spite of Yahweh's displeasure.

On his way to Moab Balaam had his famous conversation with a donkey. In spite of the divine hint that he was on the wrong track, he continued on his journey and tried to curse Israel. But instead of curses, blessings spilled from his mouth. The king who hired him was furious (see Num. 22-24 for the larger story).

Balaam's consistent message, however, was "I'm a prophet of Yahweh and can say only what Yahweh puts in my mouth." No matter what Balaam did, he could not curse Israel and, therefore, could not earn his money. Then he had a brilliant idea.

"If we could figure out a way to lead Israel astray," he suggested, "God would forsake them, and they would be defeated in battle." As part of his fiendish scheme, Balaam used the fascination of pagan feasts and the lure of sexual immorality to attract a number of Israelites to sin through food sacrificed to idols and sexual immorality. As a result, God withdrew His protection from Israel, and a great plague destroyed many of them (see Num. 25 and 31:16).

The story of Balaam illustrates our dependence on God's protection. The sins that seem so innocuous to us have disastrous implications if they succeed in separating us from the Lord. The church at Pergamum felt justified in its compromises, yet placed itself in grave danger.

Lord, help me discern the unintended consequences of my daily actions and respond accordingly.

February 23

But I have a few things against you, namely that you have some there who hold to the teaching of Balaam, who taught Balak **TO PLACE AN OCCASION FOR SIN BEFORE THE SONS OF ISRAEL, TO EAT FOOD OFFERED TO IDOLS AND TO COMMIT FORNICATION.**
REV. 2:14.

Eating food offered to an idol may seem like a rather small issue to complain about. And young people often ask, "What could possibly be wrong with 'a little harmless sex'?" The actions that Balaam and Balak led Israel into must not have seemed so wrong to many Israelites. But when temptation leads to sin, we often discover that its consequences vastly outweigh any pleasure that may have occurred. The end result of Baal-Peor, the event in the Old Testament that our text refers to, was the death of 24,000 Israelites.

Recent discoveries give us a new understanding of the complexities of outer space. Long supposed by theory but never confirmed, scientists now know that so-called black holes are massive fields of gravity that can literally rip a star apart. Invisible to the naked eye, X-ray telescopes such as those at the Chandra X-ray Observatory Center, in Cambridge, Massachusetts, can detect them.

Photographs made at Chandra are the first strong evidence for this phenomenon. They show a star disintegrating from the pull of a black hole. "Stars can survive being stretched a small amount, as they are in binary star systems, but this star was stretched beyond its breaking point," said Stefanie Komossa of the Max Planck Institute for Extraterrestrial Physics in Germany. "This unlucky star just wandered into the wrong neighborhood."

The interesting part is that the black hole did not swallow the star. It consumed only 1 percent of the star's total mass. But the momentum and energy it triggered actually flung most of the star's gas away from the black hole. All the black hole did was initiate the process by eroding the star's critical mass. Once the black hole disrupted the star in this way, the star's destruction took on a life of its own, and it disintegrated from there.

Sin is like this black hole. Its attraction on our lives is as powerful as gravity. Seductive temptations draw us constantly and steadily into the hold of its gravitational pull. And like the black hole that destroys the star by just breaking apart its vital structure, yielding to sin can damage us just enough to set a process of ultimate annihilation into motion. The Word of God is clear that even small sins can lead to destruction and eventually death![22]

Lord, help me to take sin very seriously. I know that salvation is by grace, yet sin attracts me away from You and Your grace, leading in dangerous and destructive directions. I therefore choose to yield my body and mind to Your complete control today.

But I have a few things against you, namely that you have some there who hold to the teaching of Balaam, who taught Balak to place an occasion for sin before the sons of Israel, to eat food offered to idols and to **COMMIT FORNICATION.** *Similarly, you have those who hold to the teaching of the Nicolaitans.* REV. 2:14, 15.

The word for fornication in Greek is closely related to the word for prostitution. Christians are often horrified that people would value themselves so lowly as to offer their bodies sexually in exchange for a relatively small amount of money. Yet those same Christians sometimes think that a little sex between "consenting adults" should not be a major issue. But if it is wrong to sell our sexuality to another, is it any better to give it away for free? The Bible teaches us to save our sexuality for the one who will value us so highly that he or she will be willing to commit their entire life to us. Promiscuous sexuality tends to occur when people have a low sense of worth. What they do not value they freely throw away.

"But isn't sexual purity until marriage an old-fashioned idea?" a parishioner asked his pastor. "Sure, it's dumb to play around with all the disease that's out there, but we love each other and plan to get married some day. Give me one reason we should wait."

"I'll do better than that," the pastor replied. "I'll give you three. First, if you are preparing for marriage, you need to build a relationship that will last a lifetime. To achieve that, you will need a strong relational 'infrastructure,' and that means spending a lot of time getting to know each other mentally, emotionally, and spiritually. Once a couple gets physical they start neglecting the other aspects of their relationship, and those are the ones that really count if you're going to spend the rest of your lives together.

"Second, sex before marriage weakens your resistance to affairs within marriage. The brain tends to take the path of least resistance. Once you have worn down a certain path for a while, it is much easier to go that way again in the future. A 'trial marriage' is one of the best ways to ensure that the marriage itself will not last.

"Third, even if you never have an affair later on, having sexual relations with your spouse before marriage leads to issues of trust. No matter how faithful you are, she will think, *Well, he did it with me when we weren't married, so what's to stop him doing it with someone else he isn't married to?* Marriage is tough enough without throwing that kind of distrust into the mix."

"Wow," the parishioner said. "I didn't know the Bible was that practical."

Lord, help me to stop listening to the Balaams of Hollywood and Madison Avenue. I choose to put my trust in the whats of Your Word, even when I don't understand the whys.

February 25

REPENT, *therefore, but if not, I will soon come to you and make war with them by means of the sword of My mouth. He that has an ear, let him hear what the Spirit says to the churches. To the one who overcomes I will give some of* **THE HIDDEN MANNA.** *And I will give him* **A WHITE STONE, AND UPON THAT STONE A NEW NAME WILL BE WRITTEN,** *which no one can know except the one who receives it.* REV. 2:16, 17.

The church at Pergamum is *drifting* into compromise, not rushing in intentionally. People don't just get up one morning and decide to give up their relationship with God or become totally secular. When Christians become secular, it is because they allow themselves to wander gradually into it. Perhaps they are not praying, or wrestling in private prayer, as much as they used to. Maybe they are just not reading the Bible and other spiritual books the way they did before. The slide into secularism is gradual.

The problem with compromise is that people slip into it without even realizing what is happening. Compromise tends to be popular—it makes everybody happy and offends no one. But it disturbs God. I should probably qualify that last statement. Conciliation and compromise are not the same thing. The former is good. The results of compromise, on the other hand, are not spiritually healthy.

With compromise comes lower personal standards. People don't naturally drift upstream. The normal tendency in any church is downstream toward a lower standard and less clarity in doctrine. Unless people are willing to swim against the tide through vigorous application of Scripture, a church will inevitably move to lower standards—as Pergamum did.

What is Jesus' solution to compromise? He leaves us in no doubt. *Repent!* The Greek form of the word implies that repentance is something they must start. The Pergamenes evidently don't think they need to repent, but Jesus insists that the wrong kind of tolerance requires repentance. If the church's leadership won't confront the people who are destroying the church, He will come and "make war with them by means of the sword of His mouth."

The remedy for a compromising spirit is, first of all, a firm decision. To repent is to make a total turn in your life, to renew spiritual disciplines. It means to stop drifting along and doing what feels good or what comes naturally. Repentance requires that you become intentional in what you do spiritually by scheduling time for prayer and study. And to provide time in your life for the things that God would have you to do, such as sharing your faith.

No matter what you've done or where you've been, it's not too late to turn things around.

Lord, open my eyes to the hidden compromises in my own life. I invite the spirit of repentance into my heart.

And to the angel of **THE CHURCH IN THYATIRA,** *write: "These things says the son of God, the one whose eyes are like flaming fire and whose feet are like polished brass. I know your works, even your love, your faith, your service, and your patience, and* **YOUR LATTER WORKS ARE GREATER THAN THE FORMER.** REV. 2:18, 19.

When one thinks of vacation spots or places to see in North America, several immediately come to mind. Among the major destinations are such places as Orlando, Florida; New York City; Washington, D.C.; the Grand Canyon; and Yellowstone Park. Most of them have a worldwide reputation, and people will go out of their way in order to visit them.[23]

Still other destinations are almost as well known. Most of these involve bodies of water or mountains, places such as Colorado and the California coast. It may surprise people to find out that my home state of Michigan has more boat registrations than any other state. Bordering on the three largest of the Great Lakes makes a great deal of water recreation possible. Water and mountains provide weary people from the city with a reason to make that long drive with the family in order to have a few moments of quiet recreation.

One place that doesn't seem to be on anyone's vacation list is the state of Oklahoma. It was nearly 10 years after I had visited my forty-ninth state (Alaska) before I made Oklahoma the fiftieth. Most people probably know Oklahoma best for the "dust bowl," Will Rogers, and a Broadway musical of the same name. Possessing neither large bodies of water, nor mountains, nor a major theme park, the state is a vast plain that most travelers pass through hurriedly on their way to somewhere else.

But if you chose to visit Oklahoma after all, you would find that the place has a quiet beauty all its own. Breeze-filled plains rise up to meet an endless sky. And the people who live there exhibit a rugged work ethic that fills life in this unpretentious place with meaning and satisfaction. While the life there is simple and straightforward, the people are well worth getting to know.

Like Oklahoma, Thyatira was like a neglected sister among the seven churches. The other six cities had major economic and political importance. In ancient lists of the great cities of Asia Minor the other six appear near the head of the list, while Thyatira is usually missing. But Jesus does not look at things the way we do. He recognizes value where others see dross. The simplest of Christians often have the most profound walk with God. If you sometimes feel like an "odd person out" in your local church community, God says to you, "Welcome to Thyatira (Oklahoma)!"

Lord, thank You for Thyatira and Oklahoma, which remind me to respect those that are marginalized in today's world, and may I take courage in You when I feel left out myself.

February 27

To the angel of the church in Thyatira, write, "These things says **THE SON OF GOD,** *the One whose eyes are like flaming fire and whose feet are like polished brass. . . . And I will give [the overcomer]* **THE MORNING STAR."** Rev. 2:18-28.

I started playing golf about 12 years ago. It is a very challenging game. You would think that it shouldn't be too hard to hit a ball lying stationary on the ground. And I almost always hit it. But how you hit it is another matter. One time you may shank the ball off to the right or the left, while another time you fail to hit it square and the ball doesn't go as far as you planned. Other times it arcs to the right (slice) or to the left (hook).

When I took up golf, my biggest problem was the slice, in which the ball starts out in the direction I want it to go, but then begins to arc or curve to the right. A small slice of 10 yards or so is not a problem—you can control that. But when the slice gets really big—30, 40, or 50 yards to the right—your results will not be very successful.

A friend of mine, Jim Park, had a slice even worse than mine, so he decided to go to the "swing doctor," a golf teacher who teaches people for a living (they're often called "golf pros").[24] In the midst of his first lesson the "pro" told him that the reason he was hitting the ball to the right was that he was not "following through." In other words, the ball would go not where Jim intended but rather where his body was facing after he swung the club.

Park immediately questioned the pro's logic. What difference would it make where the swing ended up if he had already hit the ball? His teacher assured him again that he was slicing the ball because he was not following through on the swing and that his body was facing to the right of the target after he had hit the ball. When everything is going wrong, you become willing to try almost anything! So Park began to follow through more with his swing. The difference it made absolutely amazed him. He now hit the ball straighter and farther than ever before.

The church at Thyatira received a head-to-toe vision of Jesus. Their success depended on maintaining that vision of Jesus. Like them, our success in any aspect of the spiritual life results from "following through"—from making sure that all of our efforts focus on Jesus. When we take our eyes off Him and concentrate on the problem or the mission, our "swing" (strategy, organization, talent, etc.) may seem perfect, but our results will wander far from the goal. Everything we do in the spiritual life must happen in relation to Jesus. Or to use the language of Hebrews 12:2 (the golfer's translation): We need "to fix our eyes on Jesus, the beginning and follow-through of our faith."

Lord, my life is filled with distractions, many of them very good things. Help me to "follow through" by keeping my eyes and whole body directed toward You in all I do today.

And I have against you that you permit **THE WOMAN JEZEBEL,** *who calls herself a prophet, to teach and* **DECEIVE MY SERVANTS TO COMMIT FORNICATION AND EAT FOOD OFFERED TO IDOLS. I HAVE GIVEN HER TIME IN ORDER THAT SHE MIGHT REPENT,** *but she was not willing to repent* **OF HER SEXUAL IMMORALITY.** REV. 2:20, 21.

Jesus here calls John's Christian opponents followers of Jezebel. Whoever she was, she appears to represent the Thyatira branch of the group labeled "Nicolaitans" and "those who hold to the teaching of Balaam" (Rev. 2:14, 15). Apparently all three names represent the same group, because all three names involve the same two problems: eating food offered to idols and committing fornication. Interestingly enough, when you go to the Christian writings of the following century, the same two issues appear front row center.

The Roman Empire required all non-Jews to participate in the civil religion. The Romans tolerated all kinds of religious practices, but no matter what your religion was or where you came from, they also expected you to take part in the ceremonies and public events of Roman society. Such events were somewhat like the Fourth of July parade in the United States. It did not matter what religion you were—it was part of your duty as a citizen to be involved in them.

Serious consequences awaited those who did not participate in the civil religion, even when the death penalty was not in view. For example, they would be ostracized from the trade guilds, in which people networked to build their businesses. They would lose their influence on the development of society or the improvement of their position within it. Lack of involvement in the civil religion also deprived them of social opportunities. As a result those who avoided Roman civil religion became poor, powerless, social outcasts.

For the Western world today wealth and security seem to represent the highest goals of secular society. But the Greco-Roman world had an even higher goal: status. It was a world that reveled in the honor and esteem of others and poured shame on those who did not conform. In such a world the restrictions of Christian life and practice virtually guaranteed exclusion from honor and status in one's own neighborhood.

So first-century Christians who refused to participate in Roman civil religion suffered serious consequences in business, civil affairs, and social contact. The gospel is free, but it can cost us our reputations, our families, our jobs, and even our lives. Jesus calls His followers to total commitment, no matter what the consequence. But He rewards that total commitment with meaning and purpose in this life and exalted status in the life to come.

Lord, too often I have compromised my commitment to You because of the attractions of this life. I renew my commitment to You from this day forward.

February 29

And I have against you that you permit **THE WOMAN JEZEBEL,** *who calls herself a prophet, to teach and* **DECEIVE MY SERVANTS TO COMMIT FORNICATION AND EAT FOOD OFFERED TO IDOLS.** Rev. 2:20.

We catch a glimpse in this text of a "conservative/liberal" conflict in the late-first-century church. Conservatives no doubt pointed out the seventh commandment: "Thou shalt not commit adultery." Given its pointed nature, could a serious Christian even think about participating in cultic prostitution? Some Christians may have found a theological justification for this kind of activity in the writings of Paul, who argued that the state had authority to require certain things.

"Everyone must *submit himself to the governing authorities,* for there is no authority except that which God has established. *The authorities that exist have been established by God.* Consequently, he who rebels against the authority is rebelling against what God has instituted, and those who do so will bring judgment on themselves. . . . Therefore, it is necessary to *submit to the authorities,* not only because of possible punishment but also *because of conscience.* This is also why you pay taxes, for the authorities are God's servants, who give their full time to governing" (Rom. 13:1-6, NIV).

The Nicolaitans could have used this remarkable passage as a justification for participating in the requirements of civil religion (see also 1 Tim. 2:2, 3, NIV). We are to pray for, obey, respect, and honor the authorities. But I'm sure Paul would not have approved of cultic prostitution. In 1 Corinthians 8-10, however, Paul is fairly clear that eating food offered to idols is not a major issue in itself. One suspects that sincere Christians who differed with the perspective of Revelation might have found encouragement in Paul's letters, whether or not they were reading him correctly.

The reality is that Paul's situation was quite different from John's. *Circumstances may alter cases.* The book of Revelation recommends social, political, and economic withdrawal from society, if necessary, in order to be faithful to the instructions of Jesus. John takes a hard line with fellow believers that Paul did not feel was necessary in his day. Evidently circumstances had changed in the 40 years between Paul's letters and Revelation. Actions that would have been acceptable in the past were no longer so, because of changing circumstances.

Lord, help me to be discerning of the times. May I never use a plausible interpretation of Scripture as an excuse for sin. Help me to handle Your Word with careful attention to the original context.

And I have against you that you permit **THE WOMAN JEZEBEL,** *who calls herself a prophet, to teach and* **DECEIVE MY SERVANTS TO COMMIT FORNICATION AND EAT FOOD OFFERED TO IDOLS.** REV. 2:20.

As we have seen, Roman civil religion had two major elements in it that would involve a compromise with Christian faith: the issue of food offered to idols and the matter of "fornication." Why was food offered to idols a problem for John's churches? Doesn't Paul say that an idol is nothing and that offering food to it does not really matter, because idols cannot speak, hear, or feel (1 Cor 8:4, 7-9)? If something is offered to an idol, nothing has really happened, so in principle we have no big problem here. But by the time Revelation was written, the situation seems to have changed. When people regarded the idol feast as a way of putting the state before God, it would create a serious conflict of conscience for the Christian.

That was not all. A part of the ancient religious scene was ritualized prostitution. People believed that if sexual intercourse took place in the temple between the men of the city and cultic priestesses, rain would fall in abundance, the crops would grow, and the community would be prosperous. As strange as this sounds to us, it made sense to the ancients. People who held aloof from these "civic traditions" might be thought of as hostile to the welfare of the community.

In the Western world today wealth and security represent the highest goals of life. But the world of Revelation had an even higher goal: status. People reveled in the honor and esteem of others, and poured shame on those who did not conform. In such a world, to be a Christian virtually guaranteed exclusion from honor and status in one's own neighborhood.

Many Christians, however, were loath to give up the quest for a high place in the esteem of others. They wanted political and social opportunities and longed to accumulate some wealth and have some influence. But that was not going to happen unless they, occasionally at least, participated in the cultic feasts and in temple prostitution. The letters to the churches indicate that there were some Christians who weighed the options and asked, "Why not? After all, how can we reach the upper classes for Christ if we do not meet them where they are?"

So early Christians seem to have felt a tension between outreach to society, on the one hand, and faithfulness to the full counsel of God, on the other. God wants us to meet people where they are. But Revelation exposes the dangers of compromise even in the pursuit of souls. We must be prepared to leave our comfort zone for the sake of the gospel. But we must never betray our conscience. An empty vessel cannot fill others.

Lord, help Your church today to strike the balance between outreach and faithfulness. Help us to be faithful as we call others to faithfulness.

March 2

Behold, **I AM THROWING HER INTO A BED,** *and those who have committed adultery with her into extremely hard circumstances, unless they repent of their works. And* **I WILL KILL HER CHILDREN WITH DEATH,** *and all the churches will know that I am the one who searches minds and hearts. And I will give to each of you according to your works.* REV. 2:22, 23.

The punishment here fits the crime. Since Jezebel has led others to commit fornication, she herself gets thrown into a bed, the place where sexual relations usually take place (cf. Heb. 13:4). But it is not clear if the passage has sexual relations in mind. The bed is also the place where people have to go when struck down by severe illness. The word "death" here probably means "pestilence" or contagious disease.

The phrase "I will kill her children with death" does not sit too well with people in today's world. It has an abusive ring to it. While He was on earth, Jesus always loved children and would never wish them harm. Children often suffer, however, from the consequences of adult action, including those of their parents. In this case the "children" are probably adult disciples of Jezebel, those who believe and act on her teachings.[25]

The passage reminds us that even gifted people can be wrong. Jezebel was a highly gifted person, one recognized as a prophet and teacher with great authority and a following. Though she may not have realized it at first, she was leading her people into darkness. How does this text apply to church leaders today? If you and I find ourselves placed in leading positions in the church, how can we know when we are wrong? How can we recognize when we are using the gifts that God has given us to lead people in the wrong direction?

More than once I have run into individuals who seem to be sincerely following God to the best of their ability and yet their followers are constantly getting into one difficulty or another. It has led me to ponder very carefully what the behavior of a disciple says about someone's actions or teachings.

If you are the leader of a church, watch your "disciples" very carefully. What is their behavior like? What kinds of things are they presenting to others? Followers often "catch" nuances in a teaching that the teacher may not even be aware of. The flaws in such instruction may only become clear in the later behavior of those who love the teacher. It is those who adore the teacher the most whose behavior will most clearly demonstrate the flaws in his or her teaching.

Lord, I need greater discernment to fully understand the implications of everything I believe and teach. Help me be willing to submit to Your correction, even when it comes through individuals I may not particularly like.

But **TO THE REMNANT** *of you in Thyatira, as many as do not hold her teaching,* **THOSE WHO HAVE NOT LEARNED THE "DEEP THINGS OF SATAN,"** *as they call them (I place no other burden upon you), I say nevertheless,* **"HOLD ON TO WHAT YOU HAVE UNTIL I COME."** Rev. 2:24, 25.

Jesus offers counsel to the faithful ones in the church. He calls them a "remnant." Here is the first time the word appears in the book of Revelation. The remnant in this text are those who, while they may tolerate Jezebel's role in the church, do not accept or practice her teachings. In this they anticipate God's final remnant at the end of time (Rev. 12:17).

Scholars are not certain as to the meaning of "Satan's deep secrets." Sometimes people become so confident in Christ that they think they can toy with the devil. It may well be that "Jezebel" was claiming that from her deep experience of the things of Satan she could teach people how to control him and thus triumph over him. While the text is not clear, she may have been exercising some type of exorcist ministry (casting out demons).

It is true that Christians will have victory over Satan in Christ. When oppressed by Satan, we can call on God in the name, the power, and the blood of Jesus Christ. And when we encounter others similarly afflicted we can do the same. The power of Jesus Christ is real and at such times manifests itself in remarkable ways. I am speaking from experience.

But we face danger here as well. Encounters with Satan are more scary and thrilling than bungee jumping or sky diving! If we let the power of Christ in such situations "go to our heads" we may find ourselves tempted to seek out more such encounters to show off "our power" to others. But in the subtle selfishness of our mixed motives we open ourselves up to the very oppression we are claiming to free people from. While Satan is subject to the power of Christ, he is certainly smarter and more powerful than we are in our own strength. Delivering Satan's captives for Christ should never be an excuse for us to boast. Pride in our effectiveness for Christ, as was the case with "Jezebel," puts us on the pathway to unexpected destruction.

The remnant in Thyatira face enormous challenges. Jesus doesn't heap His criticisms on them. He places no other burden on them than to "hang on" until He comes. It would be easy for the remnant to fall into a cycle of guilt and shame over their past failures to confront Jezebel and her disciples. But Jesus asks no more of them than to hold the course that they are capable of if they will trust completely in Him. They are not perfect, but Jesus says, "I will not put any further burdens on you. Hang on to what you already have."

Lord, I am tired of one mistake after another. Help me to "hang on" one day at a time. Help me to grow on Your schedule into the person You want me to be.

March 4

The one who overcomes and keeps My works until the end, **I WILL GIVE HIM AUTHORITY OVER THE NATIONS.** *He will rule them with a rod of iron the way a ceramic vessel is shattered, just as I have received [authority] from My Father. And* **I WILL GIVE HIM THE MORNING STAR.** *He that has an ear, let him hear what the Spirit says to the churches.* Rev. 2:26-29.

What is it that motivates people to accomplish difficult tasks? How is it that some people can endure all kinds of hardship and difficulty for a relatively minor reward? Some individuals, for example, and I'm one of them, will tolerate all kinds of sweat, pain, and exhaustion for a mountaintop view. Others will travel as much as a half day for a meal at their favorite restaurant. Students will work five times as hard at their studies to get a good grade at the end of the course.

I have a daughter who loves winter camping. She is truly amazing. Once she spent a whole week outdoors in the Upper Peninsula of Michigan *in February!* She and about 17 others dragged 100-pound packs on sleds behind them in the snow, slept in teepees, and cooked their food over tiny camp stoves that they had to carry along with their clothing, bedding, flashlights, and other supplies. Special clothing and supplies for the trip cost almost $1,000!

One of the most interesting features of dragging a sled through the snow is how hot it gets! While the temperature at the beginning of the day might be as low as −18°F, the warmth of the winter sun, combined with the high-end camp clothing, led to waves and waves of sweat. My daughter's number one desire at the end of the week was to find a shower.

Although she cannot wait to go winter camping again, one day she complained about how hard it was—the aching muscles, the sweat, the shortness of breath. I asked her what kept her going at those times. "I didn't want to fall behind everybody else!" she said. For her that was powerful motivation!

Jesus knows that everyone needs motivation to change their ways or to accomplish something great. In the letter to the church at Thyatira He tells them to keep their eye on the reward. The day is coming when Jesus will endow them with dominion over the nations. Kings and priests in heavenly places, they will have authority like His. He will also give them the morning star. Revelation 22:16 tells us that Jesus is the morning star—that He is giving them Himself. So the ultimate motivation is a close relationship with Jesus.

Lord, help me to keep my eye on the reward today. I can accomplish amazing things when I know that You are with me.

March 5

And to the angel of the church in Sardis, write: These things says the one who has the seven spirits of God and the seven stars. I know your works. **YOU HAVE A NAME THAT YOU ARE ALIVE, YET YOU ARE DEAD.** *Be continually watchful and begin to strengthen the things which remain, which are* **ABOUT TO DIE.** *For I have not found your works complete before my God.*
Rev. 3:1, 2.

From this testimony of Jesus it is clear that a church can have a great name and yet die. Just because it was faithful in times past doesn't mean it will always remain that way. God can approve of a religious movement at one point in time, and yet it can lose its way.

Scripture offers an interesting example from biblical times. John the Baptist was the greatest of the prophets and a faithful man. He baptized Jesus when He came and introduced his own disciples to Him. Without question God approved of his ministry. Jesus even considered him to be a fulfillment of prophecy. He was the Elijah to come predicted by Malachi (Matt. 11:11-14; Luke 1:13-17; cf. Mal. 4:5, 6).

But scholars have noticed that the Gospel of John treats the Baptist a bit differently than those of Matthew, Mark, and Luke do. Matthew, Mark, and Luke present John as the exalted prophet who plays the role of Elijah in preparing the way for the Messiah. But the later Gospel of John has John the Baptist constantly lowering himself in comparison with Jesus. Speaking of Jesus, John says such things as "He must increase, but I must decrease" (John 3:30, KJV), and "A man who comes after me has surpassed me because he was before me" (John 1:30, NIV).

Why does the Gospel of John highlight John's self-deprecating statements? Because we have evidence that many of the followers of the Baptist failed to follow Jesus. They considered John greater than Christ because in the Jewish theology of the time earlier was better. The one who comes first is the greatest. So at the end of the first century a number of people still clung to the Baptist. The author of the Fourth Gospel challenges them to move on and follow Jesus all the way. To continue to be just a disciple of the Baptist was really *not* to follow him. It was to be part of a religious movement that had served its purpose and was now outmoded from God's point of view.

Clinging to a religious tradition simply because we have always done so or because our parents did so is a dangerous thing. Sometimes movements fall back or God moves on. We are each responsible to search out God's ways for ourselves—we cannot trust just in the findings of our spiritual forebears.

Lord, help me to follow You wherever You may lead, even when You head in directions I didn't think You would go. Keep me close to Your Word and moved by Your Spirit.

March 6

YOU HAVE A NAME THAT YOU ARE ALIVE, YET YOU ARE DEAD. *Be continually watchful and begin to strengthen the things which remain, which are* **ABOUT TO DIE.** *For I have not found your works complete before my God.* REV. 3:1, 2.

Pastor Charles (not his real name) could not put his finger on it, but something was wrong. Although he spent his usual hour in devotions each morning, nothing he read seemed to connect. When he prayed, his prayers seemed to get no higher than the ceiling. People received his sermons well, and they were often powerful. They seemed to change lives. Yet the joy of ministry was gone. He knew how to be an effective pastor, and everyone around him thought he was one, yet he knew deep inside that he was just going through the motions.

We call it "ministerial burnout." Burnout can also occur in lay Christians. Jesus described it as "having a name that you are alive yet you are dead." Sometimes burnout is a sign that we have overcommitted ourselves. Other times it indicates that we have allowed people to move us away from our divine purpose. We are busy, but the things that really matter aren't getting done.

Sardis had a great name—it had "star status"—and yet Jesus thought it was dead. What happened to it represents a threat that faces every church and every Christian. Many are the Christians whose hearts are in the right place but who have no delight in the faith and find it difficult to serve God. What do you do when you sense that the things of Christ are not as exciting to you as they once were? I have found the following to be helpful.

1. *Have a willingness to change.* If you don't feel willing to change, let God know that you are willing to be made willing (John 7:17). Many times I feel spiritually divided: 30 percent of me wants to serve God with all my heart, and 70 percent of me is tired and doesn't feel like it right now. If you put what you have on the altar, He can grow your commitment into a firm decision.

2. *Make a radical and firm decision.* Jesus used the strong word "Repent!" You may have to take decisive action, throw things out, change your job, do something radical. Say to yourself, "I am not going to let another day go by without taking action to be where God wants me to be."

3. *Go back to the place where you last saw the light.* Keep a journal and write down the high points of your spiritual life. When things are not going so well, you can read the journal and be encouraged. The best devotional book you'll ever find is the one you write yourself.

4. *Develop a sense of eschatological accountability.* Jesus is returning and will ask all of us to give an account of our lives. When we realize the value of every thought and action in the light of eternity, it will motivate us to move with decisive action.

Lord, rekindle the fire of the Spirit in my heart today.

BE CONTINUALLY WATCHFUL *and begin to strengthen the things which remain, which are about to die. . . .* IF YOU WILL NOT WATCH, THEREFORE, I WILL COME AS A THIEF, *and you will not know at what hour I will come to you.* REV. 3:2, 3.

For Christians, staying awake spiritually is the hardest when the world around you is asleep. Soon after Hitler's ascent to power in 1933, 7,000 of the 18,000 Lutheran pastors opposed the "Aryan clause" that forbade Christians of Jewish descent from working for the church. In protest these pastors broke away from the state church and formed the Confessing Church.

One of the pastors, Dietrich Bonhoeffer, left a prestigious teaching post at the University of Berlin and moved to London. But at the request of the Confessing Church he courageously returned to Germany in 1935 to lead a Confessing seminary for young ministers. He was only 29 years old at the time himself. By 1936 the authorities banned him from further lecturing at the University of Berlin, and the seminary went more and more underground.

Hitler turned his charm on the Confessing Church. Allowing them to keep some of their distinctives, he offered them legitimacy in exchange for overall support of his plans for the country (at least the ones he was willing to share at that time).

Bonhoeffer fought such compromise, believing that good and evil could not live together. His position became more and more isolated as the Confessing Church felt that its precarious situation required limited cooperation with the state. But Bonhoeffer claimed that "the failure of German Christians to resist the Nazi rise to power stemmed from their lack of moral clarity."

In 1939 he accepted a lecture tour in the United States. While there, American theologians pressed him to stay in America and continue his work of protest in safety. But his conscience did not allow him to choose a life of relative ease. When it became clear that war was about to break out, he took one of the last ships to leave for Germany. His resistance to the Nazi government became so direct that the German leadership had him arrested. On April 9, 1945, a few weeks before the end of the war, he was executed for his resistance at a concentration camp called Flossenbürg.

Whether we seek to convert the lost or to fight for social justice, it is easy to grow weary in well-doing and follow the crowd as Sardis did. This is particularly true when the church itself has become part of the crowd. The only people who can stand at such times are those whose moral compass does not rest on reason or conscience alone but on the clear teachings of God's Word.[26]

Lord, direct my conscience to the Word of God. May I never compromise with evil while showing mercy on those whose conscience is not yet clear. May Your thoughts become my thoughts and Your ways my ways.

March 8

Remember, therefore, the things you have received and heard. Pay attention to them and repent. **IF YOU WILL NOT WATCH, THEREFORE, I WILL COME AS A THIEF, AND YOU WILL NOT KNOW AT WHAT HOUR I WILL COME TO YOU.** REV. 3:3.

The history of Sardis in ancient times bears some resemblance to Jesus' description. It was once the supreme city of the region, the capital of the kingdom of Lydia, ruled by the famous king Croesus. His wealth was so great that even today people recognize the expression "rich as Croesus." But by the time John wrote Revelation Sardis had slipped to secondary status behind Ephesus, Pergamum, and even Laodicea. So in the first century the reputation of the city far exceeded its reality.

The parallels of history to text may be even closer. Ancient historians suggest that Croesus consulted the oracle at Delphi before heading into battle against Cyrus, the Persian ruler who would conquer Babylon eight years later. He asked the oracle if he should cross the Halys River to attack Cyrus or not. The oracle responded that if he crossed the Halys River, a mighty empire would fall.

Confident that he had a promise of victory, the king assembled an army and forded the Halys to meet Cyrus. The Persian leader overwhelmingly defeated him. But Croesus was not greatly concerned. Not only did he have the oracle's promise (he thought), but he knew that he could retreat to his impregnable fortress (Sardis) and raise an even larger army for the following year. But Cyrus pursued rapidly and surrounded Sardis before Croesus could gather the new army. The king was still unconcerned, thinking that Cyrus was vulnerable so far from his base and that the forces of Sardis would in time crush his army against the cliffs below the city.

The acropolis of Sardis sat on the top of Mount Tmolus. The sides of the mountain (which I have visited) are nearly sheer, almost like having walls hundreds of feet high. On such a height it must have seemed that a child could guard the city against an army. So Croesus retired one night in confidence that things would soon turn in his favor. He woke up to find the enemy in control of the acropolis and his kingdom now history.

What seems to have happened is that while the rock face below the city was almost perpendicular, a crevice had developed in the rock, allowing infiltrators to climb up one at a time to enter the city. Such an attack would work only if the defenders were unawares, so Cyrus' attack must have been at night. Along the lines of Jesus' message, destruction came upon Sardis like "a thief in the night." [27]

Lord, heighten my spiritual alertness so I can be constantly aware of the angles of attack that Satan would use against me. May Your coming find me on guard.

But you have a few names in Sardis who have not **DEFILED THEIR GAR-MENTS;** *they will walk with Me in white, because they are worthy. The one who overcomes will likewise be* **DRESSED IN WHITE GARMENTS.** Rev. 3:4, 5.

It is a humiliating thing to be underdressed in a large gathering. I remember one time receiving an invitation to address about 400 pastors and lay church leaders at a conference in northern California. Don Schneider, who later became president of the North American Division of Seventh-day Adventists, headed the conference at the time. Those who know him best report plenty of stories about his practical jokes, from short sheets to the use of a starter's pistol to shock people. But I didn't know him well enough then.

I had prepared for the trip and was putting in a final couple hours at the office when Schneider called my wife at home. He explained who he was and said, "I just wanted to let your husband know that the meetings will be held at our camp in Leoni Meadows. It is way up in the mountains, so he should plan to dress warm and casual."

My wife decided to help me out by removing the suits from the garment bag and replacing them with lumber jackets and jeans. When I came home I was delighted at the news, since I have never been a big fan of uncomfortable ties! Gathering up the baggage, I headed for the airport. Later that day I drove up to Leoni Meadows from the airport in Sacramento and got everything hung up. I put on a nice red-and-black-plaid flannel shirt and my best pair of jeans and headed downstairs for the first meeting. When I arrived at the meeting hall I discovered 400 people awaiting me in three-piece suits and elegant dresses. It was at that moment that it dawned on me that I had been tricked! I was about to be the tramp at the ball.

Not knowing what else I could do, I went straight to the microphone and said, "Most of you don't know him well yet [Schneider had just arrived in the area two months before], but Don Schneider is widely known as a practical joker of menacing proportions." I then explained what he had done to me and used the rest of the weekend to even the score!

It's no fun to be badly dressed for an occasion. Neither is it pleasant to behave in a way out of touch with our surroundings. The garment language in this text is spiritual. Jesus is looking around Sardis to find candidates for heaven. No one will be out of place there. God's judgment will not rest on outward appearance but will take into account the true character of each person as they respond to the saving sacrifice of Jesus. Those who follow Christ now will not be out of place then!

Lord, cleanse my heart from all that spiritually stains. May the life of heaven be a reality in my life even now.

March 10

But you have a few names in Sardis who have not defiled their garments;
THEY WILL WALK *with Me in white, because they are worthy.* Rev. 3:4.

In the Hebrew language "walking" was a metaphor for the total experience of everyday life. Our character is the sum total of the way that we "walk" from day to day. The church at Sardis had some serious deficiencies on the whole, but there still remained a few believers there whose character suggested that they would one day walk with Jesus in eternity.

In the old city of Jerusalem you can tell the age of a pavement or a staircase by the amount of wear in the stones. Considering the hardness of most rocks, it is an amazing thing to realize that over a few hundred years the constant shuffling of sandaled feet can actually cut grooves and depressions into granite, slate, marble, and other types of paving stones. Each time a foot slides over a stone, it wears away a microscopic puff of dust from a stone. Tens of thousands of steps leave a permanent impression.

My favorite spot to observe this is the newly excavated staircase below the south wall of the Temple mount. It was the main entrance into the Temple courts from the south. Pilgrims coming up from Bethlehem, Beersheba, or Hebron would ascend these stairs to gates that passed under the royal portico and into the Court of the Gentiles, where Jesus drove out the moneychangers. While the gates into the Temple area have long ago been bricked over, archaeologists have newly exposed the steps leading up to them. Sitting on those stairs one can view the City of David (the original city) angling down toward the Pool of Siloam and covered in part by the Arab village of Silwan. One can also see the hills that continue to separate Jerusalem from Bethlehem.

Since the staircase was unearthed in severely damaged form, experts have restored a portion with fresh stones so that visitors can gain a sense of what it must have looked like in Jesus' day. Interspersed among the fresh stones, however, are the rounded remnants of paving stones that withstood the grinding of countless feet for more than 1,000 years. It is thrilling to walk or sit on these stones, realizing that Jesus and His disciples had certainly passed over them.

In today's world, where constant change is the norm, it is helpful to remember that others have gone before us. Never alone in our spiritual pilgrimage, we can seek out mentors and guides to help us overcome our most difficult moments. And above all, the well-worn steps that lead to God are before us every day in the Bible. When we open the ancient Word and listen to its voice, we can find solid ground for our feet.

Lord, open my mind today to learn something of value from everyone I meet.

The one who overcomes will likewise be dressed in white garments, and **I WILL NOT REMOVE HIS NAME FROM THE BOOK OF LIFE,** *and I will confess his name before My Father and before His angels. He that has an ear, let him hear what the Spirit says to the churches. Rev. 3:5, 6.*

I n some parts of the ancient Greek world, when the authorities were about to execute a person for a crime they would first erase his name from the roll of the citizens. This seems to have been a necessary step before the state could condemn a citizen to death.[28]

It seems clear from this text that Jesus didn't believe in the popular version of "once saved always saved." Remaining in the book of life is the result of an ongoing process of "overcoming" (a Greek participle in the present tense). Thus remaining in the book of life rests on continuing relationship with Jesus, not some arbitrary decree on God's part. While our works are never the basis for our salvation, good works are the ongoing evidence that people are saved (Rev. 19:7, 8). Righteous deeds are the garments of the righteous.

The promise that God gives to those who continue to overcome—that He will not blot their names out of the book of life—is a warning to all Christians who think that mere profession or church attendance will be sufficient to ensure their salvation. When Mickey Cohen, a famous Los Angeles gangster of the 1940s, made a public profession of Christian faith, Christians everywhere were elated. They considered it a marvelous example of God's saving grace. But as time passed they began to wonder why he did not renounce his gangster lifestyle.

Sometime later when Christian friends confronted him about it, he responded, "You never told me I had to give up my career. You never told me that I had to give up my friends. There are Christian movie stars, Christian athletes, Christian businessmen. So what's the matter with being a Christian gangster? If I have to give up all that—if that's Christianity—count me out." Cohen gradually drifted away from his Christian friends and ultimately died alone and forgotten.[29]

Christians need to realize that when we take the name of Jesus, we immediately become witnesses for Him. But when we merely go through the motions, when we don't allow Him to change us, we give others the excuse not to allow Jesus to change their lives either. We may not be gangsters, but if we take on Christian faith as a thin veneer over our selfishness, we bear witness to a faith that will not change the world. It is a faith that may seem alive to others, but is nevertheless either about to die or is already truly dead.

The victory of faith comes to those who persevere in overcoming.

Lord, I pray that I will never be satisfied with merely a veneer of faith. Take over the core of my being and transform me into a true witness for You.

March 12

And to the angel of the church in **PHILADELPHIA,** *write . . .* REV. 3:7.

As most Americans know, the name *Philadelphia* means "brotherly love." Philadelphia, Pennsylvania, has become called, therefore, the City of Brotherly Love. I'm not sure how the ancient city of Philadelphia received its name, but the Turkish people who live there now still exhibit this characteristic.

I have visited the ancient site of Philadelphia twice. It is located in the modern city of Alashehir. I have never been in a place that more warmly receives strangers. The first time we visited I was not feeling well. So I was walking down the street on market day, noticing my surroundings, but not wanting to talk or be involved with people.

Suddenly a man rushed toward me from behind a vegetable stand. Unable to speak English, he pointed to my camera and then himself and his vegetable stand. He wanted me to take a picture. I was used to this Middle Eastern drill—or so I thought. "You take picture—I take baksheesh." In other words, the privilege of taking his picture would relieve me of some of my dollars. In a bad mood to begin with, I was not interested in a picture of his vegetable stand. But for some reason I went along, expecting to get fleeced.

When I finished taking the picture, an amazing thing happened. He motioned for me to wait, pulled out a paper bag and filled it with vegetables from his stand, then handed them to me and said, "Welcome!" With a smile and a wave he sent me on my way. I was truly humbled and somewhat ashamed of my attitude. It dawned on me at that moment that here was a great example of the brotherly love that lay behind the ancient name of the place.

A little later my family and three students found a place to eat. It was a little restaurant a few hundred meters from the market square. Their specialty was Turkish cheese bread and salad. As we were vegetarians, that sounded like the perfect meal for a traveler. We watched, fascinated, as the baker laid out long strips of bread, filled a tiny trench with local cheese, and then put the results in a brick oven with an open fire. The food was delicious and cost the eight of us only US$5! I was so moved by the experience that I left a 25 percent tip in gratitude. Since the children were sometimes slow, we left ahead of the students to head for the bus.

The students arrived 15 minutes later with another whole meal of cheese bread. The man had been so moved by my tip that he refused to let the students go until he had prepared a second meal for all of us as a gift! It deeply touched me. Brotherly love is a wonderful thing that brings profound joy to both the giver and the receiver. I will never forget my Turkish friends!

Lord, I want to show Your love today by giving of myself to others. May You exhibit the meaning of Your love through me.

And to the angel of the church in Philadelphia, write: These things says the Holy and True One, **THE ONE WHO HAS THE KEY OF DAVID, WHO OPENS AND NO ONE WILL SHUT, WHO SHUTS AND NO ONE OPENS.** Rev. 3:7.

J esus declares Himself to be the one who holds the key of David. He has the authority to open and to shut, making Him the one who controls entrance to the royal palace, the place where the authority of the kingdom concentrates.

The language of this text is based on Isaiah 22:22. Sennacherib of Assyria was attacking Jerusalem. The leaders of the nation had gathered weapons, shored up the city walls, and secured the water supply of the city. But God criticized their work because in all their preparations they never asked Him for help. Instead, when they realized that their situation was hopeless, they decided to party and enjoy what few resources they had left before death overtook them (verses 1-13).

Shebna, who was in charge of the royal palace, proved to be as materialistic as the people, commissioning a spectacular grave to be carved out for himself in a prominent place (verses 15, 16). The Lord deposed him from his position and gave the key of David to Eliakim, the son of Hilkiah, instead (verses 17-21). From then on Eliakim would be the one with the authority to open and shut the doors of the kingdom (verse 22).

In the American government we would call the position described here as chief of staff. This position came to the attention of the American people during the Watergate crisis of 1973-1974. H. R. Haldeman, President Nixon's chief of staff, had full control of the president's schedule. He decided who could get in to see the president and who could not. If he didn't like someone, that person would never have access to the president unless the president intervened personally!

Many people have the idea that the top leaders of American government meet with the president on a daily basis. Actually very few have that privilege. Above all others the chief of staff is in constant contact with the president. If he wishes and the president allows, the chief of staff can become the most powerful and influential position in the U.S. government, even though the individual is neither elected by the people nor ratified by Congress.

As in Smyrna, the members of the church at Philadelphia experienced conflict in relation to the local synagogue. It is likely that the Christians of Philadelphia found themselves disfellowshipped from the synagogue, and they may have questioned whether they had lost their place in heaven as well. Jesus assures them that He, and He alone, decides who enters the temple of God. As long as they remain in relationship with Him, their position with God is secure.

Lord, I treasure the access I have with You in Christ. Help me to serve You today with joy and confidence, knowing that Jesus has set before me an open door.

March 14

And to the angel of the church in Philadelphia, write: These things says the Holy and True One, the One who has the key of David, who opens and no one will shut, who shuts and no one opens. I know your works. **I HAVE PLACED BEFORE YOU A DOOR ALREADY OPENED, AND NO ONE IS ABLE TO SHUT IT.** *Although you have little strength, you have kept My word and have not denied My name.* Rev. 3:7, 8.

In the heart of Beijing, China, lies the old imperial palace called the Forbidden City. Within the walled boundaries of this network of buildings the ancient emperors of the Chinese dynasties once lived and ruled. Common people could never set foot on grounds considered sacred, hence the name Forbidden City.

In order to enter the well-fortified "city" one must go through the very large and imposing Meridian Gate, which consists of five entrances. The central and grandest of them was reserved only for the emperor himself. All the other officials and royal family members had to pass through one of the other four gates. The only exception was that a princess on her wedding could enter the city through this special gate. Also, once a year, the three top scholars in China had the rare honor of using the emperor's gate.[30]

The letter to Philadelphia has a unique feature. Jesus does not just analyze the church's past and offer a remedy—He describes what He is doing for them in the present, having placed before them an open door that no one can shut. The ultimate Emperor does not reserve that door for Himself but throws it open to His followers from Philadelphia.

What is this door, and why does Jesus offer it and hold it open? Commentators have three main suggestions.

1. Jesus as the door. As in John 10, He is the one who guards the entrance to the church. Nothing can deny access to His faithful Philadelphians.

2. A door of missionary opportunity. Jesus promises them that their efforts to evangelize the lost would be successful (cf. 1 Cor. 16:9; 2 Cor. 2:12; Col. 4:3).

3. The door of heavenly knowledge. If this is Jesus' intention, it would be in anticipation of Revelation 4:1, which depicts a door standing open in heavenly places. The people of the church of Philadelphia have the knowledge about heavenly things that they are receiving from John in the book of Revelation.

While all three suggestions have scriptural support, I particularly like the first. Although others (the synagogue in Philadelphia) have excluded them from salvation, Someone far greater than their opponents welcomes them!

Thank You, Lord, for providing a full and free salvation in Christ. As I continue in my walk with You, help me never to doubt my access to You.

Behold, I will cause those of the synagogue of Satan—who say that they are Jews, but are not, they are actually liars—I will cause them to come and **BOW DOWN BEFORE YOUR FEET** *and acknowledge that I have loved you.* Rev. 3:9.

ecause the place where I teach has long had a strong contingent of Korean students, I have become intrigued by aspects of Korean culture. One of the most interesting involves bowing. As with many Asian cultures, ritualized bowing is part of the Korean greeting process, as well as in the expression of thanks and apologies.

I have observed that "bows" come in a variety of forms. When two individuals of equal status meet, the bows are roughly equal in proportion, low but not too low. As a person of higher status meets a person of lower status, he or she acknowledges that person with a bow, but the bow is not as low as the one directed toward the higher status person. And when someone has made a nice gesture toward another or has given a gift, the depth of the bow is proportionate to the appreciation for the gift or gesture.

Something similar holds true for the apology bow. It is an aphorism in the Korean culture that when one has truly messed up, the situation can be redeemed only if one "remembers to bow very low." The deeper the bow the greater the contrition. This can be helpful even in the Western context. My wife can be ever so upset with me, but something about a male bowing in contrition to a woman melts her heart (or triggers amusement) and defuses what could otherwise turn into an ugly situation.

It is affirming for teachers to bow to a Korean student in greeting, but it is usually a shallow bow, almost a nod. But for Koreans this system of bowing is not a carefully calculated action. Rather, it is instinctive, a spontaneous cultural reaction to events and people. Similar rituals must have been common in the Greco-Roman world of antiquity.

The Greek word behind "bow down" in our text is the typical one for "worship" in the book of Revelation. As such it implies a willing acknowledgment that someone else is superior, worthy of adoration and praise. The background to this text appears in the Old Testament. The sons of those who oppressed the Jews in Babylon would bow down to them, showing that the exiles were no longer despised, but now were honored (Isa. 45:14; 49:23; 60:14). The Jews would not need to avenge their own humiliations. God Himself would reverse their fortunes. Likewise, Christians, oppressed by both Jew and Gentile, would be exonerated one day by God (Rev. 3:9).

Lord, when I get put down or others get the opportunities I feel I deserve, help me to trust in You to right wrongs in Your good time. Help me not to take things into my own hands, but to wait patiently for Your timing.

March 16

Behold, I will cause those of the synagogue of Satan—who say that they are Jews, but are not, they are actually liars—I will cause them to come and bow down before your feet and acknowledge that **I HAVE LOVED YOU.** REV. 3:9.

Bob is a Presbyterian minister from the Philippines. Some call him a "natural-born" pastor. To speak with him is to know that you have been with a believer.

One day, on his way to the pulpit to preach, he stopped near his wife and picked up his 10-month-old daughter. Carrying her in his arms, he stepped up to the podium and began his sermon. At first the little girl stared wide-eyed at the people before her, but soon she reached out and grabbed her dad's tie, and put it in her mouth. Everyone laughed. Pastor Bob freed his tie and put it back in his suit, and continued his sermon.

His tiny daughter then grabbed his glasses and pulled them off. People chuckled. Retrieving his glasses, Pastor Bob put them back in place and kissed his daughter. Then he continued to preach. After a minute or so, the little girl reached out and grabbed him by the nose! Everyone, including Pastor Bob, broke out in laughter.

When it finally became still, Pastor Bob said to the congregation, "Is there anything that she could do that you could not forgive her for?" People began to nod, thinking of their own children and grandchildren.

"And when does that end?" Pastor Bob continued. "At 3? At 15? At 30? How old does someone have to be before you forget that everyone is a child of God?"

The audience fell totally silent. You could hear a pin drop.

Very softly the pastor asked, "And when did you forget that you too are a child of God?"[31]

Does God love us less than we love our children? Is a 3-year-old's continuation as part of the family conditional upon never making a mess? Conditional on earning his or her keep? Do we think God is a poorer parent than most of us? Do we feel inside that we could never be good enough to merit His acceptance and favor? Consciously, or unconsciously, we often operate from a fear-driven covenant with God, many of our behaviors and relationships motivated by an effort to avoid His judgment.

Many of us strive fearfully to deserve God's love. We are reluctant to believe that we belong. Perhaps that is the cause of most of our stress. Maybe we need to become like children again to know just how much God loves us.

Lord, thank You for accepting me as part of Your family in Christ. Thank You for the many tokens of love You have placed in the world around me. I will rest in Your love today.

Because **YOU HAVE KEPT THE WORD OF MY PATIENCE**
I will keep you from the hour of trial which is about to come upon the whole inhabited world to test those who live on the earth. REV. 3:10.

The game wasn't a sellout, by any stretch of the imagination. It lured 25,623 fans, more than half of them Black Americans, to the 32,000 seats in Ebbets Field, Brooklyn, New York. What they saw was a slice of history in the making: a Black man playing in a major league game for the very first time.

Of course, Jackie Robinson didn't break the color line in baseball all by himself. He needed Branch Rickey, the president and general manager of the Brooklyn Dodgers, to help him do it. Rickey was the one with the will and the power to ignore the idiotic myopia of the sport's other leaders. Were the rulers of baseball afraid that Blacks couldn't play baseball? Or were they afraid that they would play it too well?

For some time Rickey had been searching for a special Black athlete, someone whose poise matched his skills. Robinson needed to be able to swallow the racist insults he would surely face from both players and fans. Rickey told Robinson at their first meeting that he had to have "guts enough not to fight back."

And Robinson proved to be that man. The first four-sport star at UCLA, an Army veteran, and a budding Negro League phenom, Robinson neither smoked nor drank and possessed a heroic reserve off the field to complement his fiery resolve on it. As he stepped to the plate in a Dodgers uniform, he was a mature 28 years old (by contrast, Derek Jeter was playing in his eighth major league season when he turned 28).

But in a magnificent 10-year Hall of Fame career Robinson made up for lost time, his and that of the great Negro League ballplayers who never got the chance to shine in the big leagues. When Robinson conducted himself with dignity in the face of insult, the game of baseball truly became the "national" pastime.[32]

In our world today people prize athletes who brag and posture, doing their deeds "in your face." But real greatness is found in patient endurance, the kind that embodies the service and self-sacrifice of the Lamb. Jesus praises Philadelphians not for their skills, their wealth, or their worldly success, but for their patience in the face of poverty, weakness, and persecution. The message of Revelation turns the philosophy of this world on its head. Anyone can fight back when rage takes over. It takes strength of character not to respond to provocation.

Lord, You set the tone for Jackie Robinson and me when You endured insult and suffering with patience at Your trial and on the cross. I choose to follow Your example today.

March 18

I am coming quickly. **HOLD FAST TO WHAT YOU HAVE** *in order that no one might take your crown.* REV. 3:11.

I have three children who are just about grown up now. But while they were all born to my wife and me, they are all different. For example, when I used to read them stories in the evening, the oldest would tend to repeat everything I said, trying to tell the story better than I had just done. The middle child would try to get into my lap so he could see the pictures. The youngest would bounce around the room acting out the different parts of the story. While all of these behaviors were at times annoying, each child exhibited a unique learning style.

Now the differences show up in the way they handle money. One likes to hoard everything for a "rainy day." She usually has each semester of college paid up in advance before the application of subsidies or scholarships. Another child tends to spend every dollar as soon as it comes in, or even beforehand (a persuasive borrower), but almost always spends that money wisely on things that will make a difference in the long run. The third child is just as quick to spend money, but tends to use it for short-term indulgences such as candy, computer games, and cheese breadsticks. As parents we advise, but we also allow them to make some mistakes so they can learn.

When the oldest was about 3 years old we visited another couple who had a child her age. Early on the mother distributed some raisins to both children. Later in the day I noticed that my daughter was doing everything one-handed. In playing games she would move the pieces with the same hand each time, the other hand held out of sight. Even while eating she didn't dive into the food with her usual two-handed vigor. It finally became evident that she had balled the other hand into a fist and that she wouldn't loosen it for anything. When I asked her to show us what was in her hand, she shyly opened it for inspection to reveal about eight raisins. Liking raisins, she had decided to save them for a "rainy day." She hung on to those raisins as if her life depended on it.

Jesus encourages the Philadelphians to "hold fast" what they have. They must cling to certain values as determinedly as my daughter did to her raisins. Jesus wanted them to hang on tightly to their salvation (John 10:29). He wanted them to hang on to their patience and not move ahead of God's plans for their lives. And He wanted them to hang on to their consistency in obeying Him and in doing good.

So never give up! Hang on tight to all that truly matters. Jesus is coming soon.

Lord, help me identify the things in my life that truly matter to You. I want to hang on to them with all the strength You can give me.

The one who overcomes **I WILL MAKE A PILLAR IN THE TEMPLE OF MY GOD AND THAT ONE WILL NOT GO OUT OF THE TEMPLE ANYMORE.** *I will write upon him or her the name of My God and the name of the city of My God, the New Jerusalem, which comes down out of heaven from My God, and I will write upon that one My new name. He that has an ear, let him hear what the Spirit says to the churches.* Rev. 3:12, 13.

B ecause of difficulties with the local synagogue, the members of the Philadelphian church seem to have questioned their access to God. The divine letter assures them of their continued channel to God in Jesus Christ. Jesus is the one who holds the key of David. He opens the door into heaven for them, and He will make them like a pillar in the temple. That means they will always be a part of God's inner circle.

Access can make all the difference in this world as well as the next. I remember when I was a student at the seminary, more than 30 years ago. The Greater New York Conference sponsored us, and my wife's income added enough so that we were able to live comfortably, eat well enough, and take care of tuition expenses.

But then came the recession of 1974. People all over the area were losing their jobs. One day my wife learned that the farmer's market where she had been working could no longer afford to keep her. In one day we lost nearly half our income. Although I managed to increase my hours at the library where I had been working part-time, it would make only a small dent in our financial setback.

This placed me in a position that many other students had faced, but to which I had been a stranger. I needed to go to the officer for student finance to see about (beg for) any available loans or grants. For a long time I sat in the waiting room, cooling my heels. The door to the finance officer's office remained closed. Whatever was going on inside was more important than I was.

Just then a teenage girl walked into the waiting room and pointed toward the closed door. When the secretary nodded her head, the girl went right over to the door and opened it! How brazen! How unfair! Then she said in a plaintive voice, "Daddy?" Receiving a positive response, I suppose, she walked right in.

What was the difference between her and me? She had access to her father, something I couldn't claim. The door that was closed for me was open for her. That's the way it is when you know Jesus. In Him we have access with the Father.

Lord, thank You for full access to You in Christ. May I live and act today as one who knows that from experience.

March 20

The one who overcomes **I WILL MAKE A PILLAR IN THE TEMPLE OF MY GOD AND THAT ONE WILL NOT GO OUT OF THE TEMPLE ANYMORE.** *I will write upon him or her the name of My God and the name of the city of My God, the New Jerusalem, which comes down out of heaven from My God, and I will write upon that one My new name. He that has an ear, let him hear what the Spirit says to the churches.* REV. 3:12, 13.

Just outside Aswan, Egypt, in the middle of Lake Nasser, sits an island temple called Philae. It is reachable by *felucca* (Egyptian sailboat) or small motorized boats. On my visit a small, barefooted boy from Sudan, who didn't look a day over 10 years old, drove my boat. The Greek monarchy of the Ptolemies had built the Temple of Philae about two centuries before the time of Jesus. While the Greek rulers didn't worship Egyptian gods, they respected the venerable culture of Egypt and sought to provide temples that carefully copied the ancient Egyptian art and architecture of Thebes.

Because of its relative youth and the fact that sand had covered it for hundreds of years, Philae today remains in remarkable condition, compared to the ruins of Karnak and the area around the Valley of the Kings. Its roof is intact, and so is the artwork inside, including colorful paintings amazingly preserved even after 2,200 years.

Like other ancient Egyptian temples (and like the Temple to Yahweh in Bible times), one passes through a gigantic gate into an outer courtyard. Another gate opens into the temple structure itself, with successive chambers leading to the tiny inner shrine that is the holiest part of the whole complex. At each level of holiness, access became increasingly limited, until only the highest order of priests could enter the inner shrine.

The book of Revelation is full of allusions to the heavenly temple. Revelation 4 and 5 mention the lamps, the incense, the Lamb, the worship, and the presence of God Himself. Revelation 6:9 speaks of the altar of sacrifice, and Revelation 8:3-5 and 9:13 the altar of incense. Revelation 11:19 explicitly connects the ark of the covenant with the inner shrine of the heavenly tabernacle. That heavenly temple appears again in chapter 15, this time only to be emptied because of the glory of God manifested within (Rev. 15:5-8). The book declares that the people of God perform priestly service before Him day and night in His temple (Rev. 7:15-17; 22:2-5).

The promise to Philadelphia includes permanent dwelling in the innermost part of the heavenly temple. Christians will always be in the divine presence. This means that they will have a major role in the governance of the universe (see also Rev. 3:21). Though often weak and despised on this earth, God's servants will be elevated to the highest place in eternity.

Lord, prepare me now for the glorious role You have in store for all of your people.

And to the angel of **THE CHURCH IN LAODICEA,** *write . . .* Rev. 3:14.

The message to the church at Laodicea connects strongly with the history and the environment of the city. The city was infamous for its wretched water supply. Lukewarm in temperature, it was filled with sediment and lime. The water was too cold for bathing and too warm to be refreshing on a hot summer day. Jeremiah used rotten food to illustrate the disgust God felt for the behavior of the people (Jer. 24). In this text Jesus offers an image appropriate to the situation of Laodicea.

The city also had a reputation for its self-sufficiency. It was a prominent banking center during the time of the Roman emperor Domitian. Laodicea was so proud of its wealth that it refused aid from the emperor after a major earthquake. The city was also famous for its textiles, particularly cloth and carpets woven from black wool, a startling contrast to Jesus' offer of white garments. The city was also home to a first-century medical school that specialized in ear and eye ointments.

So Laodicea the city, like the church it housed, was a self-sufficient place that did not feel its need of outside support, even though its water system came from outside and was not palatable. Jesus used the history and environment of Laodicea as an illustration of the shortcomings of the local church.[33]

"[Why does God], contemplating the condition of the church of Laodicea, see one thing, while Laodicea, considering her own status, beholds an entirely different condition? The reason lies in the fact that God and Laodicea are really looking at two different things. Laodicea gazes upon material things.

"She tends to observe her achievements, which are not inconsiderable. She thinks of her missionaries at the end of the earth. She recalls the hospitals and dispensaries which her wealth has erected and which her generosity maintains. She surveys the schools and colleges in which she purposes to lead her young people in the way that is right. She counts her printing presses and publishing houses, established to enlighten the world. She remembers her stately houses of worship, erected in many cities of many lands. She counts her membership, and analyzes her offerings.

"Her mind goes back to her humble beginnings, and traverses with a subtle and unconscious pride the years of growth, of progress, of attainment. It is a splendid showing. Laodicea is happy, is complacent. She has a flawless doctrine, a competent organization, a triumphant message. Who can deny these things?"[34]

Lord, we cannot always control where we live. Help me to resist the things around me that draw me away from Your purpose for me.

March 22

And to the angel of the church in Laodicea, write: These things says the Amen, the Faithful and True Witness, **THE RULER OF GOD'S CREATION.** Rev. 3:14.

Instead of "the Ruler of God's creation," some translations read "the Beginning of God's creation." Why the big difference? Because the underlying Greek word (*arche*—pronounced roughly as *ar-kay*) is ambiguous. Jesus is the *arche* of God's creation. *Arche* can indicate "old" or "beginning," as in "*archaeology*," the study of old things. But it can also indicate rulership—the first in the kingdom. Our English word "patri*arch*" means "rule by the father," and "mon*archy*" means "rule of one." So the word *arche* has a double significance.

In the Greek Old Testament *arche* is the first major word in the Bible—"in the beginning *[en arche]* God created." So Revelation 3:14 points us to Genesis 1:1. Jesus comes to Laodicea as the "Ruler of God's creation." The counterpart of the original ruler of God's creation, Adam (Gen. 1:26-28), He is the "new" Adam or the "second" Adam (Rom. 5; 1 Cor. 15).

The biblical creation story describes Adam in terms of three basic relationships: 1. First of all, Adam was in relationship with God. As the "image of God" (Gen. 1:26, 27) he had great dignity, but his relationship with God was that of a subordinate to a superior. 2. The image of God included both male and female (verse 27). God created the human race for relationship with others, regardless of gender or ethnic background. 3. The image of God also included dominion over the earth (verses 26, 28). Adam ruled over the fish of the sea, the birds of the air, and the creatures that move along the ground.

When Jesus came to this earth, He was Adam as Adam was intended to be. 1. He had a perfect relationship with God, obeying everything that God told him to do (John 8:28; 14:28; 15:10). 2. He had a perfect relationship with others, living a life of humble service and self-sacrifice (Mark 10:45; John 13:1-17; Phil. 2:5-7). 3. And He had a perfect relationship with the earth and its creatures. Animals obeyed His commands (John 21:2-11; Matt. 17:24-27; Mark 11:1-7). The winds and the waves were subject to Him (Matt. 8:26, 27). In every sense Jesus was Adam as Adam was intended to be.

As the Second Adam, Jesus walked over the ground we all experience. Like the first Adam, we have a history of failure, dysfunction, and disgrace. But Jesus can replace my flawed personal history with His own perfect history. That leaves me the hope that I can be more like the Second Adam and less like the first.

Lord, thank You for the new history I have in Jesus Christ. Today I purpose to live as He lived, not to earn Your favor, but in gratitude for all He has done for me!

March 23

I know your works, that **YOU ARE NEITHER COLD NOR HOT.** *I wish you were either cold or hot. So* **BECAUSE YOU ARE LUKEWARM AND NEITHER HOT NOR COLD, I AM ABOUT TO VOMIT YOU OUT OF MY MOUTH.** Rev. 3:15, 16.

The letter to Laodicea describes the church in terms of lukewarm water. Hot drinks and cold drinks can both be refreshing. A cold drink on a hot day really hits the spot. A hot drink on a cold day warms your toes the way few things can. But lukewarm water on any kind of day is nauseating to most people.

About six miles from ancient Laodicea was the city of Heirapolis, the Yellowstone Park of the ancient biblical world. It had geysers, bubbling springs, and extensive terraces of mineral water. In fact, the terraces stand out visibly anywhere on the site of ancient Laodicea. The water in Hierapolis was and is hot. A few miles to the east of Laodicea was Colossae. There the groundwater was cold. But Laodicea had no natural source of water. The city was located where it was because it was the junction between two major roads. So Laodicea piped its water from the hot springs at Heirapolis, and by the time it reached the city the water was lukewarm.

The first time I visited Heirapolis, now the Turkish resort city of Pamukkale, my family discovered a wonderful illustration of this text at the Hotel Pam. Behind the hotel is a series of terraced pools that look like hot springs. A fountain at the top spills hot spring water into the pool. The water comes out at 56° C (roughly 135° F), and each pool spills over to the level below a little cooler than the previous one. At the bottom of the terraces is a waterfall that descends into a cool pool complete with stalactites and stalagmites (artificial). Next to the cool pool is an unheated pool the same temperature as the air.

You walk up and down the terrace, testing the temperature of the water. When you find the temperature you like, you get in. Then when you are tired of that level you go higher or lower, depending on your preference. I noticed that people flocked to the hot water at the top and the cold water pool at the bottom. Many would go back and forth between the hot and the cold. But nobody chose the middle, the lukewarm pools! It was just not comfortable or relaxing.

The point Jesus seems to have been making was that the church at Laodicea was unattractive and useless, like the lukewarm parts of the Pam Hotel pool. The church at Laodicea was satisfied with less than God's best—it was absorbed in mediocrity. Jesus' response to the church is arresting. "You make Me want to throw up!" Previous churches were in deterioration or decline, but this church is *really* in trouble.

Lord, save me from lukewarmness. May my witness be refreshing to all today.

March 24

Because you say, **"I AM RICH AND PROSPEROUS AND I HAVE NEED OF NOTHING,"** *and have not known that you are wretched and pitiable and poor and blind and naked.* Rev. 3:17.

What is wrong with Laodicea? In a human sense, nothing. It has achieved what all human beings desire: comfort, ease, the alleviation of all its needs. But Laodicea is a church, and Jesus Christ has called the church to a life of self-sacrificial service. The church must leave its comfort zone and take radical risks to share the gospel with those in need. Our comfort zone, however, can be deceptively hidden even from ourselves.

Bruce Olson tells of his efforts to take the gospel to the Motilón people in a remote part of South America. He learned to speak the language, and the people came to accept his presence. Eventually his closest Motilón friend became a Christian, but otherwise he had little response to his efforts.

One Motilón custom included marathon singing sessions in which, suspended in hammocks high above the ground, they sang out the news that each of them had heard and experienced during the previous days. During one of these festivals Olson listened as his friend, the first Motilón Christian, sang out the story of Jesus, and the story of his personal conversion. For 14 hours, while a formerly hostile neighboring chief repeated it word for word, note for note, the gospel rang out through the jungle night.

Although a positive development, the missionary himself was uncomfortable with what happened. "It seemed so heathen," he wrote. "The music, chanted in a strange minor key, sounded like witch music. It seemed to degrade the gospel. Yet when I looked at the people around me and up at the chief, swinging in his hammock, I could see they were listening as though their lives depended upon it. Bobby was giving them spiritual truth through the song."

To the missionary it sounded like witch music. Motilón music, as well as their language, had previously served false gods. Yet the missionary would not hesitate to translate the Bible into the Motilón language in spite of its pagan connotations. The gospel had to come to the Motilón people in a language they could understand.

The same was true of their music. How could God sing to the Motilón except in a musical language that communicated to them? Bach chorales and early-American folk hymns would not do the job. The missionary's Laodicean comfort zone had become an obstacle to the gospel. When it came to spiritual things he thought his way was the only right one, his favorite Christian music the only appropriate type for transmitting the gospel. Because he was unable to move past his comfort zone, God bypassed him and sang to the Motilón in their own way.[35]

Lord, disturb my comfort zone and use me to connect with some lost person today.

Because you say, "I am rich and prosperous and I have need of nothing," and have not known that **YOU ARE WRETCHED AND PITIABLE AND POOR AND BLIND AND NAKED.** Rev. 3:17.

Have you ever met a person who took better care of the dogs in their life than they did of their children? The dogs never receive a cross word, never go hungry, and receive every attention known to canines at any hour of day or night. No sacrifice seems too great. A friend of mine observed about one such situation: "I don't believe in reincarnation, but if I did, I would like to come back as one of Pat's dogs!" Dogs treated in such a way usually feel special and strut around assuming that they are entitled to such treatment.

At the opposite end of the dog spectrum are many animals I have seen in the course of my travels around the world. In places where the people are downtrodden and poor, dogs often get treated as the lowest of the low. Listless, underfed, and pitiful, they never wag their tails, and it seems that almost everyone kicks at them in order to add to their misery. The animals are dirty and shifty-eyed, cowering at the approach of humans.

The Laodiceans are like the pampered dogs. They assume that their prosperity and ease are rights that they are entitled to. As a result they have little sense that sin has relegated us all to a deep inner wretchedness that the outward marks of wealth and culture only mask. Yet the abused and mistreated in this world deeply feel the pitiful condition that the Laodiceans have hidden from themselves. They can hardly lift up their eyes to look in the face of another, much less pray for healing.

A middle-aged man worked in an office. Childhood molestation had left him vulnerable to the approach of sexual predators in academy and college. Although desiring to marry and have a family, he feared intimacy and emotionally ran for cover whenever a single woman tried to engage him in conversation. People thought he was a bit odd and were usually unwilling to go anywhere near the pain lodged in his heart. Finally a pastor saw through the guarded facade and invested many hours in a friendship that allowed the secrets to come out and be dealt with.

If we saw people as Jesus does, I think that we would be shocked by the miserable lives most live. Seldom nourished by the Word of God or the gentle touch of others, their spiritual lives are listless, and in the quiet moments of the night they indeed see themselves as miserable, poor, blind, and naked. If we have been touched and transformed by the grace of God, then we are called to go forth and be God's gentle healers of broken people. Would that life's Laodiceans were as aware of their own need.

Lord, open my eyes to those who are weak, whether or not they realize their weakness.

March 26

I COUNSEL YOU TO BUY FROM ME GOLD PURIFIED
IN THE FIRE, *in order that you might be rich, and white garments, in order
that you might be clothed, and that the shame of your nakedness might not be
revealed, and eyesalve to anoint your eyes, in order that you might see.* REV. 3:18.

The gold purified in the fire represents the kind of faith that lasts to the
end. I believe that faith is primarily a gift from God, but we can do
some things to increase it.

When I was working on my doctorate, I spent the majority of my
waking hours at a small desk in the library. While the general atmosphere of the
library was quiet, sometimes in our little corner vigorous discussions would take
place among two or three doctoral students. During one of those times a colleague
shocked me to the core. He had worked many years as a pastor outside of North
America. He told me that where he came from the number one topic of discussion among ministers was whether or not God exists! I don't share this to poke
fun or vent my horror, but simply to point out that maintaining a living walk with
God in the midst of a highly secular technological age is no easy matter. We live
in a time of spiritual crisis.

In the Western world this spiritual crisis particularly afflicts those that grew
up in the turmoil of the 1960s. Many things once handed down as certainties
have proved to be questionable as fact. Some things taught as "God's truth" seem
to have been more about keeping certain people in power. As a result, my generation has felt betrayed and has tended to lay everything open to question.

The advent of computer technology and the Internet has fundamentally
changed the way people think and reason. The speed and complexity of life have
accelerated rapidly. Nothing seems stable anymore. Jobs get downsized the minute
your salary becomes comfortable. Where you live seems subject to chance more
than intention. As a result, extended families find themselves ripped apart.

In these challenging times we need to consciously and intentionally cultivate
a relationship with God. One of the best ways to do so is to talk about it. Speak
about it often and in a wide variety of contexts. Faith strengthens when we share
it. In the words of Ellen White: "The more you talk faith, the more faith you will
have." [36] Spend time with people who are full of faith. Every day remind yourself
to accept the gold that Jesus offers and allow the circumstances of life to polish that
gold into an enduring luster.

Lord, in the busyness of the urgent it is so easy to live from hour to hour without reference to You. I want to keep You at the center of attention today. Increase my faith.

I counsel you to buy from Me gold purified in the fire, in order that you might be rich, and white **GARMENTS,** *in order that you might be clothed, and that the* **SHAME** *of your* **NAKEDNESS** *might not be revealed, and eyesalve to anoint your eyes, in order that you might* **SEE.** Rev. 3:18.

Although the messages to the seven churches have universal value, Jesus was certainly addressing a first-century church and its condition through His servant John. If the present condition of the ancient city of Laodicea is any indication, the church at Laodicea never accepted the counsel it received.

After passing by an ancient water channel, the bus lets you off at the base of Laodicea's tell (or mound), the top of which proves to be a farmer's field. As you walk through the field you look down and see chips of marble and clay piping scattered throughout the surface soil. With a sense of awe you realize that a great city lies just below the surface (archaeologists have never seriously excavated Laodicea). Further on one can see remnants of a public bath and other structures sticking up out of the ground. Laodicea has been deserted for more than 1,500 years! In a real sense the church at Laodicea did get spewed out of Jesus' mouth (Rev. 3:16), because it no longer exists.

But in another and deeper sense Laodicea still does survive. The author of Revelation seems to associate the church with the last-day people of God, who face the final battle of earth's history, Armageddon. You see, the counsel Jesus offers to Laodicea in our text for today echoes that given to those facing Armageddon (Rev. 16:15). The two passages have four Greek words in common: "garments," "shame," "nakedness" and the verb for seeing. No other text in the Bible has this exact same combination of words.

Notice Revelation 16:15: "Behold, I come like a thief! Blessed is he who stays awake and keeps his *clothes* with him, so that he may not go *naked* and be *shamefully exposed*" (NIV). The words for clothes and naked are fairly obvious, even in translation. The words translated "shamefully exposed" represent the two major Greek words for "see" and "shame." When God makes a call to the final generation of earth's history, He uses the language of Laodicea! While the city of Laodicea is dead, something of it lingers to the end of time.

So in some sense the message to Laodicea represents the followers of Jesus who experience the last crisis of earth's history. God summons the final remnant to accept the counsel to Laodicea and to take hold of the true wealth that God offers. The message to Laodicea is, in a special sense, to us as well.

Lord, I need Your garment of righteousness today. Give me clear vision to discern good from evil in everything that happens to me.

March 28

As many as **I LOVE** *I reprove and discipline; be earnest, therefore, and repent.*
Rev. 3:19.

Christmas is an exciting season for 6-year-olds. Nicholas was in kinder-garten, busily memorizing songs for his school's winter pageant. A dress rehearsal would take place the morning of the pageant, and parents who had scheduling conflicts that evening got a chance to view the presentations.[37]

Most American public schools have stopped referring to the holiday as "Christmas," so the Christian parents did not expect more than the typical holi-day entertainment, songs about reindeer and Santa Claus, snowflakes and good cheer. And to no one's surprise, the children were all dressed in fuzzy mittens and red sweaters, with bright knit caps on their heads. It was a bit surprising, there-fore, when Nicholas' class rose up to sing "Christmas Love."

The children in the front row of the class held up large letters, one by one, to spell out the title of the song. As the class would sing "C is for Christmas," a child would hold up the letter C. Then, "H is for Happy," and so on, until the whole group had spelled out the complete message, "Christmas Love."

The performance was going smoothly until everyone began to notice a small, quiet girl in the front row holding the letter M upside down, totally unaware that her letter looked like a W. The audience of first through sixth graders snickered at her mistake. But she had no idea that they were laughing at her, so she stood tall, proudly holding her W.

Although the teachers in the audience tried to quiet the children, the laugh-ter continued until the last letter was raised. A hush came over the audience and eyes began to widen. In that instant everyone realized the true reason they were there, the reason why anyone was celebrating the holiday in the first place, the real purpose for the festivities. For when one of the children held high the last letter, the message read loud and clear: Christ *was* love!

The word "love" is rare in the book of Revelation. Jesus loves us (Rev. 1:5); the Ephesians have left their first love (Rev. 2:4); and the church at Thyatira shows a lot of love, patience, and service (verse 19). Jesus loves the church at Philadelphia (Rev. 3:9); the people of God do not love their lives to the point of avoiding death (Rev. 12:11); and those outside the New Jerusalem love falsehood (Rev. 22:15). So Revelation seems to emphasize reproving and disciplining more than love. That makes this text very important, because it shows that while bad things sometimes happen to God's people, a loving hand still guides all things for our ultimate good.

Lord, You sprinkle tokens of Your love throughout my life, even though I tend to over-look them. Open my eyes to see them today.

As many as I love **I REPROVE AND DISCIPLINE;** *be earnest, therefore, and repent.* REV. 3:19.

We live in a world in which counseling and psychology have taught us all to be gentle with other people in recognition of our common suffering. As a result we see people's misbehavior more as sickness than as sin. And it is certainly true that all of us have been victimized to some degree. But the spiritual outcome of this approach can be an unwillingness to hear rebuke, even when it comes from the mouth of Jesus Himself. Few want to hear from a God who will speak harshly to us. But the fact is that Jesus confronts those He loves, and He often does so forcefully. Genuine confrontation can save a lot of heartache. Let me illustrate.

The lead elements of the German Army crest the hill. Below them lies the Rhine River, deep with runoff from melting snow. Even at this distance, the German presence violates the Versailles Treaty of 1918. Riding in the turret of the lead tank, the commander halts the column and scans into the distance. The French gun emplacements on the opposing shore remain silent.

The column moves forward slowly, listening for the first sounds of incoming artillery. The tanks make their way down to the waterfront and deploy without incident. Unwilling to start a war, the French do nothing. Only years later, after the end of the war, will the Allies discover Hitler's secret orders for the troops occupying the Rhine Valley on that March morning in 1936. He told them that at the first sign of French resistance they should beat a hasty retreat.

We'll never know for sure, but perhaps humanity could have averted World War II if the French had resisted that day. Had Hitler's reputation been damaged, the generals might not have been so cooperative with him. Millions of lives might have been saved had Hitler discovered in 1936 that other nations would hold him accountable for violating the peace.

Allied leaders feared armed conflict, but they failed to avoid it. And their inaction likely made it much worse. Neither the German people nor the leaders of their armed forces were prepared for war at the time. Resistance would have forced Hitler to back down. His army at that time was no match for the French alone, much less the combined weight of the Allies. The prestige he gained—the influence with both the German people and the general military staff—and the knowledge that the Allies were too fearful to confront him gave Hitler the opportunity to increase his armed forces and make several conquests through sheer intimidation. By the time war did come, Hitler's forces were much stronger, and he was able to initiate hostilities at the time of his choosing. Postponing confrontation only made the conflict more severe.[38]

Lord, thank You for the many times You have confronted me through Your Word and through other people. I choose to be more receptive in the future.

March 30

Behold, **I STAND AT THE DOOR AND KNOCK.** *If anyone should hear My voice and* **OPEN THE DOOR** *I will come in to him and dine with him, and he with Me.* REV. 3:20.

J esus presents Himself as standing outside the door into Laodicea, knocking and seeking an invitation to enter. Philadelphia's door is the door of salvation. Christ holds it open, and no one can shut it. But the door here is shut not by Jesus but by Laodicea itself. It is an allusion to the Song of Solomon. Note the story behind this imagery.

"I slept but my heart was awake. Listen! My lover is knocking:

" 'Open to me, my sister, my darling, my dove, my flawless one. My head is drenched with dew, my hair with the dampness of the night.'

" 'I have taken off my robe—must I put it on again? I have washed my feet— must I soil them again?'

"My lover thrust his hand through the latch-opening; my heart began to pound for him. I arose to open for my lover, and my hands dripped with myrrh, my fingers with flowing myrrh, on the handles of the lock. I opened for my lover, but my lover had left; he was gone. My heart sank at his departure. I looked for him but did not find him. I called him but he did not answer" (S. of Sol. 5:2-6, NIV).

Solomon's original wife was the daughter of Pharaoh, king of Egypt (1 Kings 3:1, 2). Though based on a political alliance, a loving marriage seems to have developed. While in later life Solomon assembled a massive harem, recent research suggests that he was monogomous for the first 20 years (1 Kings 9:9, 10; 11:1-4) (Richard Davidson, *Flame of Yahweh: A Theology of Sexuality in the Old Testament*). Affairs of state were such that direct contact between the king and queen may have been quite intermittent, since they lived in different but adjoining palaces (1 Kings 7:7, 8).

The story told in this song may reflect a night when the queen knew Solomon was in town and thinking of her.

The Song of Solomon is the story of a particular woman in Solomon's harem, who may have been his favorite. She had been hoping he would come for her that night. After waiting and waiting, she finally gave up and went to sleep. Then he arrives! But in her sleepiness she did not jump up and invite him in. "No, not now. I don't feel like getting up and putting my robe on again. My feet might get dirty on the floor." Finally she has a change of heart and runs to the door and opens it. The tragedy is that he is already gone.

This is a scary scenario when applied to a church. Jesus does not force His way in, but allows it to make the choice. The message here is that the church has no time to lose. If Laodicea does not act soon, it will be too late

Lord, am I ignoring You? Am I deaf to Your knocking at my heart? Draw me to the door of my heart today! I don't want to delay opening to You.

TO THE ONE WHO OVERCOMES I WILL GIVE TO SIT WITH ME ON MY THRONE, *just as I overcame and sat down with My Father on His throne. He that has an ear, let him hear what the Spirit says to the churches.* REV. 3:21, 22.

This promise contains something truly special that doesn't become obvious until you have looked at all seven overcomer promises in the seven letters to the churches. In stairstep progression each church receives more and more promises, perhaps to counter the increasing degeneration seen as one reads through the seven letters. The first church, Ephesus, has a single promise: the overcomer there will gain the right to eat from the tree of life.

The second church, Smyrna, gets two promises. Revelation 2:10, 11, offers the overcomer in Smyrna both the crown of life and the assurance that he or she will not be hurt by the second death.

Verse 17 offers the overcomer in Pergamum three things: the hidden manna, the white stone, and a new name, one that will be written on the white stone.

I think you can see where this is going. The fourth church, Thyatira, has a total of four promises in verses 26-28. The overcomer in Thyatira receives authority over the nations. He will rule them with an iron scepter, will dash them in pieces, and will also be given the morning star.

The overcomer in Sardis (Rev. 3:4, 5) walks with Jesus and dresses in white. Not only that—he or she has assurance that nothing will blot their names out of the book of life. Instead they will have their names acknowledged both before Jesus' Father and before His angels.

By now it should not surprise us that the sixth church, Philadelphia, receives no less than six promises from Jesus. According to Revelation 3:10-12 God will protect the overcomers from the hour of trial, they will be pillars in the temple of God, and they will never again leave it. That makes three. In addition, God will write His name on them as well as the name of the city of God and Jesus' own new name. Whatever that last item means, the promises are a total of six. And if you add up all the promises to the first six churches you get a total of 21 promises, seven times three!

Does that mean Laodicea is going to get seven promises? No. It actually has only one. But it is the promise to end all promises. In verse 21 the overcomer in Laodicea gets to sit with Jesus on His throne! That *one* promise incorporates all the 21 promises received by the other six churches. If you sit with Jesus on His throne, you have everything!

Just as Laodicea is the most hopeless of the seven churches, it is also the one that gets the best promise. The church who has nothing receives the promise of everything! "Where sin abounds grace does much more abound."

Lord, in my hour of greatest need, I claim Your greatest promise!

April 1

AFTER THESE THINGS I SAW, *and behold, a door was standing open in heaven, and the first voice which I heard, like a trumpet [cf. Rev. 1:10], said to me, "Come up here, and I will show you what must take place after these things."* REV. 4:1.

The scene of Revelation 4 and 5 is one of the most dramatic in the Bible. It is even more glorious in the original language than in translation. I have never read this passage in Greek without tears in my eyes and an unbelievable thrill as my mind envisions what worship in heaven must be like. The scene starts slowly but then crescendoes and crescendoes, until the entire universe becomes a single vast antiphonal choir ringing out the praises of the Lamb and the One sitting on the throne (Rev. 5:11-14). The scene then concludes as the four living creatures utter "Amen" followed by thunderous silence.

A danger that readers face when going through a passage such as Revelation 4 and 5 is the tendency to make too much of every detail and thereby miss its primary intent. That purpose is to set forth the greatness of the heavenly throne room, the greatness of God and, therefore, the surpassing greatness of the slain Lamb. The throne room of God lays all earthly claims to power and glory in the dust. When one has had a glimpse of the open gates of heaven, it makes no sense to continue to be afraid of earthly powers or even specific human beings. The passage invites us to shove all earthly intimidation into the shadows of God's transcending power and glory, and to acknowledge Him as the one true object of worship. When we really know Him, we will understand what true worship is all about.

It is a message I need to hear. I have often allowed other human beings to influence me away from the path God wants me to tread. I remember the 17-year-old in seventh grade who was twice my size and tried to intimidate me to shoplift some candy. I think of the conference president who questioned my commitment to ministry, causing me to excel in busywork that looked good at the office, but didn't accomplish God's best in real life.

A boss once used the time-honored technique of blackmail, with the result that I compromised my integrity in order to keep my job. Another time the influence of a teacher I admired led me to question teachings of the Bible that were perfectly clear. Can you understand why I buckled in these situations? Can you grasp the power of intimidation and human attraction that so often steer us away from God's purpose for our lives? In light of the heavenly throne room we can respond in only one way: repent, bow down, and acknowledge the only One who is truly worthy of my worship.

Lord, I feel convicted regarding the many times I have compromised my conscience to please some human being. I choose to repent and follow You alone today.

AFTER THESE THINGS I SAW, *and behold, a door was standing open in heaven, and the first voice which I heard, like a trumpet [cf. Rev. 1:10], said to me, "Come up here, and I will show you what must take place after these things."* REV. 4:1.

We have come to the portion of Revelation that offers interpreters more difficulty than any other part—the seals and the trumpets. Interpreters are seriously divided as to how to handle many of the texts in Revelation 4-11. It is important to bring to them a sound interpretation, not one based on feeling, or a gut sense of current events, but on what we actually find in the text. The only safe course in such passages as these is to determine, as far as possible, the author's actual intention in writing such passages. To the degree that we can determine the writer's intention in the original setting, we will be on much safer ground in drawing out applications for our own time.

From 1986 to 1992 I met with the Daniel and Revelation Committee of the General Conference. It was a rich and exciting experience, trading ideas with 20-25 outstanding Bible scholars from all over the world on issues related to the book of Revelation. In the course of three years we heard six different papers on Revelation 4 and 5. Each one, written by a respected scholar, made a case for a specific perspective on the text, yet the committee rejected all six papers. Such flat-out rejection puzzled me, but the committee was unanimous in suggesting that none of the perspectives grew naturally out of the text. They then turned to me and asked me to write a paper on the two chapters. Talk about intimidation!

I read through the Greek text of Revelation 4 and 5 many times. Suddenly it occurred to me: not a single one of the key words that would have backed up the six papers was present in the passage. Respected scholars had offered "gut impressions" of what they thought was going on, but the specific language to support their ideas was missing! In reading and rereading the passage, I came to very different conclusions about its message and purpose than the other authors had.

Our opinions about the Bible are not the thing that matters. What is vital is God's purpose through a human author and the method by which we discover that intent. We need to begin by committing ourselves to the Word of God, no matter what opinions we may have brought to our study. We must then give careful attention to the words of the text in context, and allow each word to have its place in revealing the message God would have us see. The only truth that matters is the one He intended.

Lord, I repent of all the times I have come to Your Word to confirm what I already think. Help me to be willing to accept Your wisdom on Your terms.

April 3

After these things I saw, and behold, a door was standing open in heaven, and the first voice which I heard, like a trumpet [cf. Rev. 1:10], said to me, "Come up here, and I will show you **WHAT MUST TAKE PLACE AFTER THESE THINGS."** Rev. 4:1.

After writing out the letters to the seven churches, John moves on to describe a scene in which a voice invites him to observe in heaven. From here on in the book the primary focus dwells on things that are future from John's point of view (perhaps A.D. 95). Why a book on future events? Because God wants us to know that we can trust Him to get us where we need to go.

In 1992 I had the opportunity to visit Disneyland in southern California with my extended family. My greatest fear on that occasion was that the group would somehow get split up. I was particularly concerned about my children, for they were 10, 6, and 4 years old at the time. I explained to the children that if any of them lost track of us, they should "freeze" at that spot and wait for us to come looking for them. If after an hour or so no one had shown up, their backup plan was to head for the park entrance and wait there.

Everything went fine until 9:30 that night. In the confusion right after the electrical parade, we lost our 10-year-old girl near the castle at the center of the park. I immediately told everyone else to stay where they were while I went back through the crowd to the place where we had stood during the parade. Back and forth I went, calling her name, but no response. Panic began to set in almost immediately. Where could she be? How could I find her in the crowd? When it was clear that she was no longer in that area, I took the group to the Tiki Birds, the next attraction on our agenda, and asked them to wait there while I checked the entrance of the park. In agony I prayed the whole way, my mind spinning. *What if she's not there? Then what? Whom do I talk to? How will we find her?* I walked down Main Street in fear and trembling.

When I got to the entrance, I did not see her. But I noticed a darkened area nearby and decided to see if she was hiding out there. I had just started in that direction when a feeble voice squeaked, "Daddy?" My head snapped around to see her on a bench. With inexplicable joy I hugged her. Not a word of rebuke came out of my mouth.

She had forgotten the "freeze" part of the instructions and had gone directly to Plan B, causing much anguish for her family. But we rejoiced that everything had worked out in the end. God gave us the book of Revelation in order to spare us similar anguish. Remembering its instructions will keep us from getting lost as the future unfolds.

Lord, thank You for providing us clear evidence that You know the future and can safely guide us home. Give us listening ears and understanding hearts.

Immediately I became in the Spirit, and behold, **A THRONE WAS THERE IN HEAVEN,** *and there was One sitting on the throne.* Rev. 4:2.

One of the highlights of any visit to Istanbul, Turkey, is a chance to tour Topkapi Palace, the famous palace of the sultan on a hill overlooking the Bosporus and the Golden Horn. I particularly enjoyed a visit to the palace museum that displayed the sultan's treasures. An especially memorable part of the museum is a view of the sultan's throne. I had never actually seen a throne before, and this one came as quite a surprise. It looked roughly like a highly decorated love seat, with comfortable cushions.

I had always thought that thrones were like armchairs, but this one was much too wide for that. And then I remembered the text: "To the one who overcomes I will give to sit with Me on my throne, just as I overcame and sat down with My Father on His throne" (Rev. 3:21). Obviously the throne of heaven is not an armchair! It is more like a couch, on which two or more people can sit. Suddenly the New Testament texts about Jesus sitting down at the right hand of God made sense (Acts 2:33; Heb. 1:3, 13; 8:1, etc.). Jesus here receives everything that the throne represents and offers a future place there to those who overcome.

A careful reading of Revelation 4 makes it clear that "throne" is the key word of the entire chapter. Appearing 12 times in the chapter, it is the center and focus of the scene. Everything that takes place in the heavenly throne room does so in relationship to the throne. A series of prepositions signals the various actions. Things happen "around" the throne, "upon" the throne, "out from" the throne, "before" the throne, "in the midst of" the throne, and "at the right side of" the throne. Clearly the central word of this passage, the throne represents the central theme of everything that takes place in it.

What is a throne and what does it symbolize? A throne represents the right to rule. The person who sits on it has the authority to govern a piece of territory, a nation, or a group of some kind. Since the throne is at the center, the key issue of this passage involves God's right to rule and how that functions in heavenly places. While the book of Revelation normally associates the word "throne" with God, it can apply to Satan and his cohorts as well (Rev. 2:13; 13:2). Thus the centrality of the throne here means this passage is a decisive development in the conflict between God and Satan over the dominion of the universe. Revelation 4 and 5 portrays the crucial event in that war—the death of the Lamb and His resulting exaltation to the throne of God.

Lord, I accept that You have the right to rule in my everyday life. May my decisions and actions today conform to Your gentle government of my life.

April 5

Immediately I became in the Spirit, and behold, **A THRONE WAS THERE IN HEAVEN,** *and there was One sitting on the throne. The One sitting there was like in appearance as a jasper and sardius stone. A rainbow, like an emerald in appearance, was all around the throne.* Rev. 4:2, 3.

What kind of scene are we looking at here? Is it a general description of the heavenly throne room or of a specific point in time? After careful study it seems clear to me that chapter 4 is describing not a specific event but rather a general view of the throne room in heaven and what goes on in it on a regular basis.

In our text, for example, it doesn't say that the throne was being set up—it simply states that "a throne *was there* in heaven." When John arrives on the scene, the throne is already there. Nothing new is taking place except that the prophet is now observing it. This scene looks a lot like the one in Daniel 7—but with a difference. Daniel 7 describes thrones "being set up" (Dan. 7:9). The passage depicts a specific event. But this is not the case in Revelation 4.

The general nature of this scene is even more obvious in Revelation 4:9. There it tells us that "whenever the living creatures give glory and honor and thanks to him who sits on the throne and who lives for ever and ever, the twenty-four elders fall down before him who sits on the throne, and worship Him who lives for ever and ever." The Greek grammar behind "whenever the living creatures . . . the twenty-four elders fall down . . ." indicates repetitive action, something that happens again and again and thus is not a specific time or event in either earth or heaven.

I think this is an interesting observation. We can, if we will, train ourselves to be much more observant of the Scriptures so that insights like this start popping up everywhere. It reminds me of a photography class I took. The first assignment was to photograph trees—single trees, multiple trees, a forest, branches, twigs, flowers on the trees. The teacher said, "Shoot a roll of film that features only trees in all types of places and circumstances."

At first it seemed like an impossible task. But after a while I started looking at my world in ways I had never done before. I found driftwood on the beach, stands of pines, trees losing their leaves, other trees in color, branches on the ground, etc. The point of the project was to teach me how to observe my environment and notice things I had failed to see before. Careful study of the Bible has the same effect. We become more and more aware of God's will and His ways, and as a result our lives are never the same.

Lord, give me new eyes, that I may view Your Word in ways I have never done before, ways that mirror what You see.

And all around the throne were **TWENTY-FOUR THRONES** *and on the thrones* **TWENTY-FOUR ELDERS WERE SITTING, DRESSED IN WHITE GARMENTS WITH GOLDEN VICTORY CROWNS ON THEIR HEADS.** Rev. 4:4.

Through the centuries one of the major issues in Revelation 4 has had to do with the 24 elders in this and other passages. Who are they? Where did they come from? What is their role in the heavenly throne room? The 24 elders surround the throne of God, and each sits on a separate throne. They seem to be heavenly beings of some kind, but the book of Revelation never tells us who they are. Let's take a quick look at some of the evidence.

The book of Revelation has several crucial numbers: 3, 4, 7, and 12. The root number for the elders is the number 12. 12 + 12 = 24. This raises the possibility that the elders are somehow related to the 144,000 of Revelation 7 and 14. The number 144 consists of 12 x 12, while the number 24 is made up of 12 + 12. This combination returns in the description of the New Jerusalem with its 12 foundations and 12 gates. The 12 foundations are connected with the 12 apostles of the Lamb, while the 12 gates are associated with the 12 tribes of Israel.

One popular opinion about the 24 elders is that they are a group of angels. While this may make a certain amount of sense, it is unlikely. Nowhere in the Bible or in early Judaism do we ever find angels called elders. Besides that, nowhere do ancient writings depict them as sitting on thrones, and nowhere do they wear victory crowns *(stephanos),* as the 24 elders do. Throughout the time and place of the composition of Revelation these terms are always associated with God Himself or with the people of God.

An excellent possibility is that these elders are the heads of the Old Testament and New Testament people of God. The description of the New Jerusalem might support this. If so, the 24 elders represent all God's believers throughout history, combining the roles of the 12 apostles and the 12 tribes. They represent humanity before God.

Does Revelation 4 imply that the elders are in the heavenly throne room before Jesus arrives there? But then, why not? As the preparations for the inaugural ceremony in heaven got under way, these representatives of humanity would be ushered in to the throne room before the ceremony began. This way, envoys from the whole universe—including the human race—would be able to express their approval at the time of Christ's enthronement.

The bottom line is this: Whoever these 24 elders are, they in some way exemplify humanity before God.

Lord, it is comforting to know that humanity is constantly represented before You. It helps me know that I can trust Your judgment in my case as well.

April 7

And **OUT FROM THE THRONE CAME LIGHTNINGS AND NOISES AND THUNDERS, AND SEVEN LAMPS OF FIRE,** *which are the seven spirits before the throne, were burning before the throne. And before the throne was, as it were, a sea of glass clear as crystal. In the midst of the throne and all around the throne were* **FOUR LIVING CREATURES** *full of eyes in front and in back.* REV. 4:5, 6.

The book of Revelation makes no distinction between God's throne room and the heavenly temple. It treats them as one and the same. The throne is the place of power and authority, and the lightnings, noises, and thunders that issue from the throne would certainly enhance that impression. The person who sits on the throne is the one in charge, the one who has the right to tell others what to do.

Today's text, however, mentions the throne together with seven lamps of fire and four living creatures. The lamps of fire recall the seven churches in chapters 1 through 3 (although the Greek words are different). They also recall the lampstand(s) in the Hebrew tabernacle and Solomon's Temple.

Most people are familiar with the covering cherubs on the ark of the covenant, guarding the spot where the glory of God would shine. But Solomon had an even grander idea for the Temple he built. He had some artists carve a pair of covering angels from olive wood. They towered over the ark 15-17 feet high (depending on how the ancients actually calculated a cubit). Also they had their wings spread out to a full span of 15-17 feet. They were stationed in the Most Holy Place in such a way that a wing tip of one cherub touched the wall, a wing tip of the other touched the opposite wall, and their other wings met in the center of the room.

This made a total of four cherubim or covering angels associated with the ark in the Most Holy Place. So the four living creatures probably allude to the four cherubim in Solomon's Temple. In that case our text describes both the heavenly throne room of God and the heavenly sanctuary. The two are one and the same.

Since the authority of God is based in the sanctuary, the government of the universe rests not on raw power but on the spiritual principles of the sanctuary. The God who exercises power and authority in the universe is also the deity who offers the kind of acceptance and forgiveness illustrated in the Old Testament sanctuary services. The safety of the universe is grounded in a combination of power and grace, authority and compassion. Our God can be trusted.

Lord, in my experience power almost always gets abused for selfish advantage. I am grateful for the assurance that Your ways are not like those of the world.

In the midst of the throne and all around the throne were **FOUR LIVING CREATURES** *full of eyes in front and in back. The first living creature was like a lion, the second was like a calf, the third had a human face, and the fourth living creature was like an eagle in flight. Each of the* **FOUR LIVING CREATURES** *had six wings, and the wings were full of eyes, all around and even underneath.* Rev. 4:6-8.

Here we run into a group of four "living things," the first of many strange and unusual creatures in the book of Revelation. The creatures are covered with eyes and have six wings each. Other strange beasts in Revelation include a slain lamb with seven horns and seven eyes, a talking vulture, locusts that have human faces and scorpion stingers, and a seven-headed, 10-horned dragon. While they are all interesting, you won't run into any of them in the forest or in a zoo—unless you've been drinking!

This reminds me of one of the most popular cartoon movies of all time—*The Lion King*. While *The Lion King* appears on the surface to be an animal story, it's not actually about animals. The creatures in the story represent people and how they relate to each other. *The Lion King* is, in fact, an African apocalypse. The cartoon begins with a perfect world, in which everything is in balance and harmony. The forces of evil then destroy that world, and eventually the heroic actions of a son restore it to harmony. The book of Revelation is a lot like that.

Writers of books and cartoons have often used animals to illustrate how people and groups of people behave. We find it easier to recognize ourselves and our behaviors if the insight comes through a story about animals. If a writer tries to make sensitive points more directly, we tend to resist or reject them because we feel under attack.

That's what makes the book of Revelation so powerful. Although it reads like an animal story, it's not really about animals. It is more like a cartoon drama about the interactions among groups of people, both good and evil. And it is about the relationship between God and the human race, and how the course of human history will eventually turn out.

Why then do people find the book of Revelation so tough to understand? It's because the author recorded the drama of Revelation not in the twenty-first century but rather in the 90s of the first century A.D., and it is directed to a group of seven churches in the Roman province of Asia. God spoke their language and encouraged them in their situation. But in His message to them He was creating a dramatic series of images that would continue to inspire His people for nearly 2,000 years.

Lord, thank You for reaching out to the human race in forms that we have learned to enjoy. Help us to see the deeper meaning behind Your words.

April 9

Each of the four living creatures had six wings, and the wings were full of eyes, all around and even underneath. And they have no rest day or night, saying, **"HOLY, HOLY, HOLY, LORD GOD ALMIGHTY,** *who was and is and is to come."* REV. 4:8.

The threefold phrase "holy, holy, holy" echoes the sixth chapter of Isaiah. In Isaiah's day Judah faced a serious crisis. King Uzziah had just died. To appreciate the significance of that event, it helps to know that he had reigned over Judah for 52 years. The vast majority of the people in Judah had never known any other sovereign. To make matters worse, Uzziah had been one of the most successful kings that had ever governed the people of God. So for the people, there seemed nowhere to go but down! With fear they faced an uncertain future.

At this time of crisis Isaiah has a vision of God's throne. He sees angelic creatures around the throne singing, "Holy, holy, holy is the Lord Almighty" (Isa. 6:3, NIV). Isaiah was a priest, a relatively holy man, in the holiest place (the Temple) among the holiest people on earth during one of most faithful periods of their history. Nevertheless, recoiling at his vision of the purity of God, He cries out, "Woe to me! . . . I am ruined! For I am a man of unclean lips, and I live among a people of unclean lips, and my eyes have seen the King, the Lord Almighty" (verse 5, NIV).

In the presence of God any sense of his own accomplishments or personal glory pales as he beholds absolute competence and total purity. Isaiah recognizes his own uncleanness, not because he has compared himself with anyone else, but because He has come face to face with God!

Here is a powerful spiritual principle. It is easy to be proud of one's spiritual growth and achievements when one compares them with the real and perceived foibles of others. The more you can put down what others do, the higher you can stand in your own observation. But this means that your eyes are no longer on God. You have built yourself up at the expense of a genuine relationship with Him!

One of the clearest signs that a person has lost touch with God, therefore, is a critical and faultfinding spirit. By way of contrast, the strongest indication that anyone has a living relationship with God is that he or she has a clear sense of personal depravity. Those who have looked in the face of God are painfully aware of their weaknesses, sins, and shortcomings. An authentic awareness of sin and guilt is the prerequisite for acceptance with God. When we have truly hit bottom, we have nowhere to go but up!

Lord, I must have a glimpse of Your face today. I need to remember that achievement is not the path to acceptance with You—instead that path is a humble and a contrite heart.

April 10

And whenever the living creatures express glory and honor and **THANKFULNESS** *to the One sitting on the throne, who lives for ever and ever . . .* Rev. 4:9.

According to this text, one of the marks of heavenly life is the constant expression of thankfulness. Those accustomed to having everything they need may find this difficult to understand. We are more likely to complain about our minimal lack of comforts than we are to give thanks for our abundance. What we need is a change of attitude. The difference between thanks and complaints has more to do with our point of view than it does with the actual facts. Let me illustrate.

As a husband I get a bit grumpy whenever my wife hogs the covers. But why don't I let the sudden breeze remind me to be thankful that she is not out somewhere with someone else? And as a parent I get more than grumpy when I've asked one of my children to clean their room and later find them in front of the TV instead. Why doesn't it occur to me to be thankful that my child is at home and not on the streets?

When tax time comes, I complain about all I have to pay. Shouldn't I be thankful instead that I am employed and that I make enough money to be worth taxing? When my children's friends leave a mess after a party, I find it easy to fuss, but wouldn't it be better to be thankful that my children have friends, and that they trust my wife and me enough to bring them over to our house?

The other day when I was complaining about clothes that fit a little too snug, why didn't it occur to me to be thankful that I have more than enough to eat? You see, the difference between complaining and thankfulness is primarily attitude!

When my lawn needs mowing, my windows could use some cleaning, and my gutters require fixing, it reminds me to be thankful that I have a home. When I hear lots of complaints about the government, I can be thankful that we have freedom of speech where I live. When the only parking spot is at the far end of the lot, I can be thankful that I am able to walk and that I have a car. Or when my heating bill is extra large, I can be thankful that I have been warm.

When the woman behind me in church sings off-key, I can be thankful that I can hear. When we have a pile of laundry to wash, dry, and fold, I can be thankful I have enough clothes. When my muscles ache at the end of the day, I can be thankful that I have the ability to work hard. And when the alarm goes off in the early-morning hours, I can be thankful that I am still alive.[39]

Lord, teach me anew an attitude of gratitude and praise. I want to use this day to practice for the heavenly chorus.

April 11

And whenever the living creatures express glory and honor and **THANKFULNESS** *to the One sitting on the throne, who lives for ever and ever . . .* REV. 4:9.

Bob and DeAnna Gulke, my wife's brother and sister, both kindly passed on a cute story a while ago that was food for some thought.[40] In the story someone was getting the proverbial tour of heaven from St. Peter. During part of the tour they walked side by side inside a large workroom filled with angels.

St. Peter stopped in the first part of the room and said, "This is the receiving section. Here we receive and handle all prayer requests."

The heavenly tourist looked around and saw countless angels sorting out petitions from people all over the world. The tour then moved on to the second section of the workroom.

"This is the packaging and delivery section," St. Peter explained. "Here the graces and blessings the people asked for are processed and delivered to those who asked for them."

Again it was an extremely busy place. Many angels were working hard, since so many blessings had been requested and were being packaged for delivery to earth.

Finally at the farthest corner of the room, the two of them stopped at a very small area. To the surprise of the heavenly tourist, it had only one angel, seated and idly doing nothing.

"This is the acknowledgment section," St. Peter announced.

"How is it that there's no work here?" the tourist asked.

"So sad," St. Peter sighed. "After people receive the blessings they ask for, very few send acknowledgments."

"How does one acknowledge God's blessings?"

"Simple," St. Peter answered. "Just say, 'Thank You, Lord.'"

But what if you can't think of any blessings from God? What if life for you has seemed an unending series of disasters and trials? Should heaven's acknowledgment section be unemployed on your account?

I'd suggest consulting a dictionary. Blessings we may never have acknowledged to God fill every page. Apes, apples, apricots—the Lord has given so many things to each of us. When was the last time you thanked Him for one of them? God is the author of life and every good thing. Let the acknowledgments begin!

Lord, I am ashamed of the many times You have reached out to me in blessing and I have taken You for granted. I thank You for this day and all that You have done for me.

The twenty-four elders fall down before the One sitting on the throne and
WORSHIP THE ONE WHO LIVES FOR EVER AND EVER,
and throw their crowns before the throne, saying, "You are worthy, our Lord and God."
REV. 4:10, 11.

When you open a Bible for the first time, you will find poetry and songs, prophecy and proverbs, but mainly narrative—a story of sorts. It tells the history of a people, but it is more than this. Scripture is the history of a nation in relationship with God. And it is not so much the history of a nation as it is the history of the acts of God.

We often think of worship as a time when some preacher reminds us of what we're supposed to do. But biblical worship is not about what we should do—it is about what God has done. "He has caused his wonders to be remembered" (Ps. 111:4, NIV). When Israel recounted what the Lord had done for them, it enhanced their relationship with Him. But more than this, the acts of God were powerful deeds, events that changed history in a mighty way. Rehearsing them rekindled the power of the original act. God would again break into history and change things for the better. When the Israelites recounted His deeds for them in the past, God became real to them in the present.

The lay leader of a large church felt his spiritual experience going dry. For whatever reason, he couldn't connect with the preaching in his church. His walk with God was slipping away, and he was about ready to give up. But he decided to give it one more chance. On Sunday morning he went down to the little Baptist church in town.

Bad luck. The preacher was away that week, and the deacon was up there reading something or other. As he mumbled along, the congregation seemed half asleep. *Here I've decided that this is to be the last chance I'm going to give this church, and this has to happen,* the lay leader thought. But a funny thing took place on the way to a nap. Every five or 10 minutes the deacon, who seemed totally clueless, lifted his eyes from the reading and said, "Well, I don't know about that, but I do know one thing: God is able," and then he mumbled on for another five or 10 minutes. Then he said again, "Well, I don't know about that point, but I do know this: God is able!"

About 20 minutes into that sermon the lay leader began to sense God's presence warming his heart. Later he reported, "I just suddenly realized God really *is* able. God is able to take me where I am. It doesn't matter who is preaching." And it doesn't matter how dead the congregation is or how out-of-date the worship service might be. If you rehearse the mighty acts of God, He is able to resurrect the dead!

Lord, turn my eyes away from the many distractions of life to the mighty things You have done for me. May Your character and Your actions become the substance and focus of my life.

April 13

"You are worthy, our Lord and God, to receive glory and honor and power, because **YOU CREATED ALL THINGS,** *and* **ON ACCOUNT OF YOUR WILL THEY CAME INTO EXISTENCE AND WERE CREATED."** Rev. 4:11.

The three great philosophical questions of life are: Why are we here? Where did we come from? Where are we going? We observe all three questions in play in Revelation 4 and 5, and nowhere more so than in this text.

Why are we here? To participate in continual, grateful, worshipful response to the God who made us.

Where did we come from? We all began in the mind and heart of God, who put shape on His thoughts when He created us.

Where are we going? To live with Him forever in a universe filled with love and peace.

What a wonderful framework to live by! How much better is Revelation's view of the world than one in which people answer the three great philosophical questions with a shrug!

Without the insights of God's revelations, we would be tempted to believe that we all ultimately descended from single-cell creatures in primordial mud. "Like father, like son" is a frightening concept when combined with that kind of past. Evolutionary science responds to the "Where did we come from?" and "Why are we here?" questions with something like "Whatever." I'd rather know that I originated with a thought in the mind of a loving God who wants me to live with a sense of purpose and meaning.

Without the insights of God's revelations, the future looks dark indeed. Science warns us that—given enough time—a collision between earth and a comet or asteroid is extremely likely. As recently as 1908 a meteorite only 50 meters across laid waste hundreds of square miles in Siberia. Had the meteorite been the size of the asteroid that recently passed closer to earth than the moon, it would have devastated much of the Eurasian land mass. Other perils also threaten us—such things as viral mutations and weapons of mass destruction. And even if we survive those threats, the sun will one day explode into a nova that will melt the planet and everything in it back to the core elements.

Many take the Christian worldview for granted. They aren't conscious of the degree to which it provides stability and meaning to life. Without that worldview, eating and drinking, waking and sleeping, tend to become empty routines, devoid of purpose.

Lord, help me not to take You for granted. Open my eyes to the ultimate purpose of my existence. May I make a difference in someone's life today.

April 14

You are worthy, our Lord and God, to receive glory and honor and power, because You created all things, and **ON ACCOUNT OF YOUR WILL THEY CAME INTO EXISTENCE AND WERE CREATED.** REV. 4:11.

In December of every year we receive a free calendar in the mail. The calendar contains pictures of local scenery and is nicely laid out. But its primary purpose is not to let us know what day it is. The calendar comes from the Cook Nuclear Plant, located about 10 miles to the west of our home. The free calendar seeks to make sure that every resident of the area knows the signals and the evacuation routes in case of a nuclear accident.

The plant nestles between sand dunes and the shore of Lake Michigan. Deep within its core is enough nuclear power to incinerate most of the county in which I live. To make matters worse, the prevailing wind blows directly from the location of the plant to the neighborhood where I live. I find it sobering, therefore, that the nearest evacuation bridge (to escape toward the east) is a mile closer to the plant than my house is. Potentially, that could be a most deadly mile.

The reason we have to live under such a shadow is our society's massive need for electricity. Life as we know it would not exist without it. Imagine having to preserve and cook food, bake and toast bread, or wash clothes without electricity. Without it the clocks, the water heater, the furnace, the lights, and the air-conditioner in my home would not function. Just about everything in today's world that enhances human comfort requires electricity. Anyone with electricity is infinitely richer than someone without it.

To put it another way, many of us have become totally dependent on the electricity monster. And perhaps such dependency isn't such a bad thing. God has designed a universe in which every part must rely on other parts. The trees absorb our exhaled breath and give us oxygen in return. Certain birds enjoy the food crawling on the backs of rhinos, giving the lumbering creatures relief from bugs and a comforting back scratch! The atomic and subatomic particles of the universe exist in intricate relationships with each other. Humans depend on plants and animals for their food, and we are all dependent on our Creator.

Jesus was the greatest human being who ever lived. Yet even Jesus depended on His Father for guidance and direction (John 5:19; 8:28). In His humanity He would rise each morning before sunrise, go off by Himself, and pray to the One who had sent Him (Mark 1:35). Although He came down from heaven, He did not rely on Himself. So remember that you are not a generator—you are a receiver and retransmitter. God is the great power source of the universe. Plug in and turn on the lights!

Lord, I am reminded of my dependence on You. Use me today according to Your will.

April 15

AND I SAW TO THE RIGHT OF THE ONE SITTING ON THE THRONE A SCROLL, WRITTEN WITHIN AND ON THE BACK, SEALED WITH SEVEN SEALS. *And I saw a powerful angel proclaiming with a loud voice, "Who is worthy to open the scroll, namely, to break its seals?" And no one in heaven or on earth or under the earth was able to open the scroll or to look into it. And I wept much because no one was found worthy to open the scroll or to look into it. And one of the elders said to me, "Do not weep!* THE LION OF THE TRIBE OF JUDAH, THE ROOT OF DAVID, *has overcome to open the scroll and its seven seals." REV. 5:1-5.*

Many translations of the Bible suggest that the scroll is in the right hand of the One sitting on the throne. But recent research suggests that the phrase "in the right hand" probably means "at the right side" instead.[41] This makes a lot of sense in the light of how the ancient world used thrones. People in those days generally felt that the right side of the king was the highest possible place of honor. Psalms 80:17 and 110:1 describe the king of Israel as sitting at God's right side, and he and God are corulers of the nation.

Many ancient thrones were large enough for three to four people to sit on. It has been suggested that the ancient reader may have understood the scroll to be lying on the throne at God's right side. If that is so, to take up the book is to sit on the throne at God's right side. In other words, when Jesus picks up the book with His hands, He also sits down at the right side of the Father, assuming His role as the new king in the line of David (Rev. 5:5).

In Old Testament times the Israelites had an extended period in which they had no king except God. The country had no clear central control. While putting a king on the throne could cause them to look away from God, in practice things were rather chaotic without an earthly ruler to give direction (Judges 17:6; 21:25). So God permitted them to institute a monarchy, first in the person of Saul (from the tribe of Benjamin) and then with David (from the tribe of Judah). David's reign was so blessed in comparison with Saul's that his reign, and the reign of his son Solomon, became models of ideal rulership for Israel.

So this concept of Davidic kingship lies behind the story of Revelation 5. The Lamb is "the Lion of Judah" and the "Root of David." Elsewhere in the New Testament Jesus sits down at the right hand of His Father on the throne in heaven (Matt. 26:64; Heb. 8:1, etc.). So when Jesus comes and picks up the scroll, He is taking His seat on the throne in the heavenly sanctuary.

Lord, this is wonderful news. The One in charge of earth and heaven is the Lamb that was slain. He knows what my life is like and has felt what I feel. I can trust Him to rule wisely, fairly, and compassionately.

And I saw to the right of the One sitting on the throne a scroll, written within and on the back, sealed with seven seals. And I saw a powerful angel proclaiming with a loud voice, **"WHO IS WORTHY TO OPEN THE SCROLL,** *namely, to break its seals?" And* **NO ONE IN HEAVEN OR ON EARTH OR UNDER THE EARTH WAS ABLE TO OPEN THE SCROLL** *or to look into it. And I wept much because* **NO ONE WAS FOUND WORTHY TO OPEN THE SCROLL** *or to look into it.* Rev. 5:1-4.

The scene in Revelation 5 builds on the one in the previous chapter. Revelation 4 describes the general realities of the heavenly throne room. The throne is in the center of the room, and everything happens in relation to the throne. The main thing going on, of course, is worship. Again and again in these two chapters the four living creatures break into song, and more and more worshippers chime in.

But a major difference exists between chapters 4 and 5. Whereas chapter 4 describes the general realities of the heavenly throne room, chapter 5 depicts a specific point in time. A crisis erupts in the throne room of the universe. All the praise suddenly stops, and everyone looks toward the center of the room with anticipation and silence, asking by implication, "What's going on?"

What is the problem? They see a scroll that no one can open. While this might seem at first to be a trivial problem, the silence in heaven and John's weeping suggest a life-and-death crisis. Someone *must* be found to unroll the scroll. What heightens the drama even further is the fact that the scroll is in the possession of God Himself, the one sitting on the throne. Why is it necessary to look for someone to open the scroll? Can't the Lord do that Himself?

The point of this scene seems to be that the universe has a huge problem, one so large that God Himself is reluctant to handle it on His own. It has to do with the right to rule. God is certainly powerful enough to seize control if He wanted to. But might does not make right. So ultimately only a "worthy" person can solve the difficulty.

The word "worthy" actually picks up from Revelation 4:11: "'You are worthy, our Lord and God, to receive glory and honor and power, for you created all things, and by your will they were created and have their being'" (NIV). To be "worthy" is to be qualified or suitable for a task or an office. Here the task is to open the scroll. Being God is not enough to qualify. The issue represented by the scroll requires a special kind of qualification. Nothing less than the death of the Lamb allows Him to unroll the scroll.

Lord, thank You for reminding me of how much my sin costs both You and the stability of the universe. Thank You, Jesus, for the painful road that qualified You for the greatest task in history.

April 17

And **I WEPT MUCH** *because no one was found worthy to open the scroll or to look into it.* Rev. 5:4.

W   e are often reluctant to identify with the positive characters in the Bible, assuming that people such as John were on a far higher spiritual level than we are. Yet the Bible invites us to model our lives on the characters in it (Heb. 6:12). Paul, for example, encourages the members of his churches to imitate him (1 Cor. 4:6, 7, 16; 11:1; 1 Thess. 1:6, 7). Although Jesus is the primary one to emulate (2 Cor. 3:17, 18; 1 Cor. 4:17), we can gain a great deal from the positive and negative examples we find in the stories about various Bible characters.

In this and other verses John becomes part of his own vision. And it is encouraging to realize that the prophet portrays himself not as a great saint, but as one who makes mistakes and is even a bit clueless at times. In Revelation 5:4 he weeps because he has no idea what is going on in heaven. He sees but doesn't understand. An elder asks him a question in Revelation 7:13, 14, and he has no idea how to answer it. Then in Revelation 19:9, 10, and 22:8, 9, he falls down to worship an angel, only to get rebuked for it. Now, to do this once might be understandable. But to do it a second time a short while later really looks foolish! Apparently prophets are not automatically smart in all areas.

I can be pretty clueless at times myself. I remember when I was in high school a college choir came by, directed by a Ph.D. in music. Not impressed with the choir, I figured the conductor must be no good, despite her high degree. So when I joined my friends at the water cooler after the performance, I began to expound about how Ph.D.s are usually less competent than people with lesser degrees because they get out of touch with real life, etc. Quickly I got on a roll about how bad this conductor was. In the middle of my monologue I turned around, only to discover her standing behind me, taking in every word. I have rarely felt so dumb!

The good news is that readers like me can identify with John and other biblical characters in their weakness. Elijah was easily discouraged and depressed, yet at God's command he could make it stop raining. David murdered at least 200 innocent people in his lifetime, yet the Lord found a way to forgive him. John the Baptist questioned whether Jesus was really the Messiah, yet Jesus called him the greatest of the prophets (Matt. 11:1-13)! Job and Jeremiah were "saints" who wished they had never been born (Job 3:3; Jer. 20:14, 15). "It is encouraging to our desponding hearts to know that through God's grace they could gain fresh vigor to again rise above their evil natures; and, remembering this, we are ready to renew the conflict ourselves." [42]

Lord, I was feeling down, but now I am encouraged to rise up and try again!

And one of the elders said to me, "Do not weep! **THE LION** *of the tribe of Judah, the Root of David,* **HAS OVERCOME** *to open the scroll and its seven seals."* Rev. 5:5.

A former student and good friend, Leslie Pollard, shared the following poem in the July 2002 *Adventist Review*. It powerfully sums up the victory of the Lamb:

> "The world cannot contain Him
> Universities cannot explain Him
> Circumstances cannot detain Him
> Prisons cannot restrain Him
> Because He won!
>
> Parliaments cannot unseat Him
> Armies cannot defeat Him
> Petitioners cannot deplete Him
> Lyricists cannot complete Him
> Because He won!
>
> Historians cannot erase Him
> Skinheads cannot deface Him
> Islam cannot displace Him
> Popes cannot replace Him
> Because He won!
>
> Philosophers cannot ignore Him
> Teenagers cannot bore Him
> Angels gladly adore Him
> Because He won!
>
> Time cannot diminish Him
> Death couldn't finish Him
> Because He won!"

Lord, You are the mighty king, the master of everything. When I contemplate You, my heart can sing!

April 19

And I saw, in the middle of the throne and of the four living creatures, and in the middle of the elders, **A LAMB STANDING AS IF IT HAD BEEN SLAUGHTERED.** REV. 5:6.

Think how shocking these images might have been to the first readers of this book. Revelation 4 and 5 portray God as the all-powerful Creator. It seems that He can do anything He wants. But when a seemingly insurmountable problem arises (Rev. 5:1-4), the solution is a stunner! God solves the greatest problem in the universe through a slaughtered Lamb!

Why doesn't an all-powerful God deal with such problems through His infinite power? Why doesn't He just *make* things happen? Why does He take such a huge risk by sending His Son to this earth, knowing that people will reject and brutally murder Him? Because good things happen when someone takes risks. The path may be harder or more dangerous than other options, but the results are worth it.

I think, for example, about how different my childhood was than it is for children today. Sometimes I wonder how my friends and I survived. We rode happily in cars with no seat belts or air bags. Some of my happiest memories involve riding in the back of a pickup truck on a warm day. In those days manufacturers painted baby cribs with bright-colored lead-based paint. We often chewed on the bars of the crib, enjoying the paint. And in those days there existed no childproof packaging on medicine bottles or anything else that could possibly hurt children (I prefer calling it "adultproof" packaging, since my children open such things just fine, while I tend to struggle).

I rode my bike all over town without a helmet on and drank city water from a garden hose instead of purified water from the grocery store. My friends and I escaped parental supervision during summers by simply leaving home in the morning and playing all day at the park or sometimes riding all over New York City on the subways. No one was able to reach us all day. With spare change from my allowance I would sometimes buy doughnuts and sugar-saturated soft drinks, but I never gained weight, since I was always outside playing. We learned to confront bullies with no adults to protect us.

You may be shocked at some of the risks that my friends and I took, but my generation produced some of the greatest risk takers and problem solvers the world has ever seen. We had freedom, failure, success, and responsibility, and we learned how to deal with it. While some of the changes in today's world are good, character develops when we take risks. In fact, every relationship is a risk, but there's no other way to have a rich and rewarding life. I somehow think God knew that when He sent Jesus to redeem us back to Himself.

Lord, thanks for taking the big risk when You came to save us. Give me the courage today to reach out to souls for whom You died, no matter the response.

And I saw, in the middle of the throne and of the four living creatures, and in the middle of the elders, **A LAMB STANDING AS IF IT HAD BEEN SLAUGHTERED,** *having seven horns and seven eyes, which are the seven spirits of God that have already been sent into all the earth.* REV. 5:6.

I have had the privilege of spending significant time in the Middle East during the past dozen years. Early in that period my oldest daughter chose to be baptized in the Jordan River. It was a special moment, whether or not it was near the place where John the Baptist actually baptized people. A pretty spot, it had trees on both sides of the river, and the water flows quietly at that point.

A few years later my youngest daughter began to show an interest in baptism. Reminding her of her sister's baptism, I asked if she had any special plans for her own. I wondered what she could possibly come up with that would top what her sister had done. "I'd like to be baptized in the Red Sea, at the place where the Israelites crossed!" she announced. I doubt she realized it at the time, but Paul associates the crossing of the Red Sea with Christian baptism in 1 Corinthians 10:1-4. My daughter could not have chosen the location more wisely.

Now, archaeologists are not exactly certain where the Israelites made their crossing. Some even suggest that it was not the Red Sea, but the "sea of reeds," which they identify with a lake north of the Red Sea near the Suez Canal today. Scripture states that the Israelites were "hemmed in" with a mountain to their right and the sea to their left (Ex. 14:1-4). The beach at Ain Sukhna in Egypt fits the description perfectly. So some friends and I took her there and baptized her during the summer of 2001.

The book of Revelation encourages Christians to see the experiences of ancient Israel as a model for Christian action and experience today. The Lamb in Revelation 5 is a slaughtered one, reminding us of the Hebrew sanctuary and its sacrifices. The plagues of Revelation are modeled on those that fell upon ancient Egypt. It was the blood of the Passover Lamb that protected the Israelites from the worst of those plagues. Similarly, the blood of Jesus shelters His people during God's judgments on humanity (Rev. 7:3; 12:11). Just as the original Israelites became a kingdom of priests at Mount Sinai, so the followers of Jesus are a kingdom of priests drawn from every nation, tribe, language, and people (Rev. 5:9, 10).

The Exodus is a model for Christian experience today. Our personal Exodus occurs when our old nature is buried in baptism and we rise to newness of life (Rom. 6:3, 4).

Lord, thank You for the newness of life that You have given me through the mighty action of Jesus Christ. May my appreciation for His sacrifice constantly increase.

April 21

And I saw, in the middle of the throne and of the four living creatures, and in the middle of the elders, **A LAMB** *standing as if it had been slaughtered, having seven horns and seven eyes, which are the seven spirits of God that have already been sent into all the earth. And He* **CAME AND TOOK IT FROM THE RIGHT SIDE OF THE ONE SITTING ON THE THRONE.** Rev. 5:6, 7.

One of the highlights of a cold Michigan winter is the arrival of a case of sweet juicy navel oranges. Several local schools bring in shipments as fund-raisers. When I carry the box home, I can't resist sliding the cover off and gazing on the orange-colored beauties. I take a sniff or two and sometimes even head straight for the kitchen to cut one up. The feel of orange juice squirting inside my mouth is almost as good as the flavor (don't you want one right now?).

But oranges have more than just the flavor and the texture. If we are to believe double Nobel prize-winning chemist Linus Pauling, a megadosage of vitamin C abundant in oranges would help prevent colds. While his theory has never gained wide acceptance, an integral part of North American culture is the belief that vitamin C can help fight colds.

When winter comes to the Northern Hemisphere, our body systems are more vulnerable to colds. At just the time when our systems need a boost, God has an abundance of vitamin C growing on citrus trees in the warmer climates. It is so like God to anticipate the needs of His children and provide resources in advance to keep them healthy and strong.[43]

Today's chapter describes the greatest of the resources God has made available. "While we were yet sinners" (Rom. 5:8), He has already provided a Lamb to remedy the crisis of sin in our lives. But even before the Lamb was slain on the cross, He had become worthy. The Lamb is one of the many symbols of the humanness of Jesus.

Since divinity cannot die, humanness was a prerequisite for opening the scroll. The Creator had to become a creature. Because the Lamb was human, He could also die to redeem the human race. But He needed a further qualification: *"To him who sits on the throne* and to the Lamb be praise and honor and glory and power . . . !"* (Rev. 5:13, NIV).

Jesus is worthy not only because He is human and He died, but also because He is divine. This combination of qualities makes Him unique in all of history. As God did with oranges, He carefully arranged the remedy for our greatest need long before we needed it. That's what makes the Lamb so special in the book of Revelation.

Lord, I am in awe as I realize all that Jesus went through in order to redeem me. I will praise Him today with all of my heart.

And when He had taken the scroll, the four living creatures and the twenty-four elders fell down before the Lamb, each of them having a harp and golden bowls filled with incense, which are **THE PRAYERS OF THE SAINTS.** Rev. 5:8.

The exciting message of this verse is that the worship of heaven includes the prayers of the saints. The prayers of the saints arise from a world very different from the scene John witnesses in heaven. In that world the saints seem to be defeated. Evil appears to reign. But the book of Revelation lifts the gaze of believers up to heavenly places. There the decisive victory has been won, forever crippling evil. Prayer is not just a nice thing to do—it is a link to the mighty, victorious power of heaven.

Before we had children, my wife and I each bought a 10-speed bicycle to enjoy the landscapes of our mountain valley. We rode quite often for a few years, but in the past couple decades the pressures of family and career turned our attention in other directions, causing us to neglect those bikes. They sit now under the elevated sunroom of our house, a place where they stay dry, but are a little too hard to get to.

Some time ago I crawled under the sunroom and pulled out my red racer, thinking it was about time to take it for a spin. I found that it had quite a bit of rust here and there and the tape had come off one of the handlebars. After 25 years it didn't look very good, but it did seem to roll OK. It still had that pleasant buzzing sound that high-quality bikes make when the wheels turn at a slow pace. While the tires were a little flat and I didn't know where the air pump was, they still had enough air to work.

Taking the bike out for a ride, I headed down the road. Since it was really quite hard to keep it going, I wondered if my leg muscles were out of shape. It just wasn't as much fun as I had remembered biking to be. After a bit I brought the bike back, thinking it might as well go back into hiding for another 20 years. But after some effort I located a pump, injected some new air into those old tires, and tried again. What a surprise! Everything went so much easier. A little air made a very big difference.

It has been said that "prayer is the breath of the soul." Prayer is like the air I put into my bicycle's tires. When we try to solve our problems by ourselves, life is truly hard. But prayer vaults our challenges into the throne room of heaven, where no problem is too big to solve, no battle is too hard to win. Thanks to the victory of the Lamb, prayer is the key to victory on earth. Don't leave home without it!

Lord, I don't ask for an easy life. But I do ask that Your mighty power will multiply my efforts to extend the victory of the Lamb to everyone I meet.

April 23

And they sang a new song, saying, "You are worthy to take the book and to open its seals, **BECAUSE YOU WERE SLAIN AND PURCHASED FOR GOD WITH YOUR BLOOD PEOPLE FROM EVERY TRIBE AND LANGUAGE AND PEOPLE AND NATION,** *and You have made them to our God a kingdom and priests, and they will reign on the earth."* REV. 5:9, 10.

The medical staff told the chaplain that he was in for a tough visit. A young couple had had a stillborn baby. The chaplain arrived on the third floor to see a crowd of people laughing in the hall. The desk nurse told him the room number, and he made his way through the crowd and entered a room completely dark except for the dim crack of light coming from the bathroom. In the bed he could see the mother. She was young and pretty, with blond hair and tired-looking eyes. "Hello," the chaplain said feebly. Words never mean very much at a time like that. "I'm the chaplain."

Despair filled her eyes, and she was clearly in pain, yet sleepy, as if she had been sedated. She was holding the lifeless child. Before he could say anything she handed him the infant. The little girl was wrapped in white blankets, her little face lifelike, her body limber. Looking at her, one could imagine her as just asleep. The father was slumped in a chair, staring out the window. He was in shock, not even able to communicate, and barely acknowledged the chaplain's existence. Sitting next to the mother was the grandmother, sobbing endlessly.

The chaplain stood there, holding the stillborn little girl. *Help me, Lord; help me,* he prayed silently, gently cradling the lost dreams of this young couple. He suspected that their house had a fully decorated bedroom, waiting for an occupant that would never come. How many times had her husband and she talked excitedly about their new child? How many gifts, good wishes, plans, and dreams had they shared in anticipation?

The chaplain couldn't hide his tears as he led them in the "Our Father." Handing the baby back, he told them he'd be there if they needed him.

In the hallway others were celebrating the arrival of their child. He quietly asked them to please try to keep it down a little, out of respect. They quickly did so, sensing the young mother's pain.

Either of the parents of the stillborn child would have done anything to make their baby live. They probably would have given their own lives if it meant saving their child. That's what Jesus did when He decided to give up His life rather than see us die. He had a choice between eternal life for Himself without us, or giving it up to save us. Jesus couldn't live without us—you and me. That's how much He loves us.[44]

Lord, thank You for loving me so much that You died for me. I want to feel the full impact of that sacrifice in my life today.

And they sang a new song, saying, "You are worthy to take the book and to open its seals, **BECAUSE YOU WERE SLAIN AND PURCHASED FOR GOD WITH YOUR BLOOD PEOPLE FROM EVERY TRIBE AND LANGUAGE AND PEOPLE AND NATION,** *and You have made them to our God a kingdom and priests, and they will reign on the earth.* REV. 5:9, 10.

A ccording to today's text the focus of the gospel is incredibly international. The death of the Lamb purchases people for God from every tribe, language, and nation. Such openness goes far beyond anything the contemporaries of early Christianity would have known. And its international welcome was so successful that no one today is surprised that the vast majority of Christians are Gentiles.

Nevertheless, the gospel's complete lack of prejudice can still teach us a great deal even today. The gospel embraced and still embraces people that we would not expect. This goes against the grain of our natural suspicion toward anyone who isn't like us. I remember meeting with a small body of Christians in a Muslim country. I shared with them my passion for bringing the good news of Jesus to everyone, regardless of their race, background, or religion. It stunned me to discover that they had no interest in Muslims. No matter what I said, they felt no call from God to reach out in love to their neighbors.

Although history gives Muslims plenty of reasons to hate Christians, I have found Muslims more open to relationship with Christians than vice versa. The actions of a few terrorists should not prevent us from seeing the great value in which God holds human beings of every race, language, and culture.

I have discovered that people of every nation and culture are open to the gospel if treated with respect and kindness. God is calling a new generation of Christians to discard the prejudices of the past and reach out to others in the spirit of Jesus. In our treatment of others we can offer a foretaste of the multicultural heavenly chorus of Revelation 5.

Imagine a choir filled with the saints of all ages: ancient Israelites worshiping with tambourine and joyful dance, African saints swaying and chanting, European Reformers with their majestic hymns, faithful monks with their medieval solos, messianic Jews dancing around the Torah, and maybe even Muslim followers of Isa (Jesus in Arabic) bowing with forehead to the ground. Do you think you could handle the complexity of that harmony? I'm sure that God will be able to teach us how to blend. Why not begin practicing God's harmonies right where you live?[45]

Lord, help me to see others through Your eyes. Fill my heart with the joy You feel in the infinite variety of the peoples You created.

April 25

And I saw and heard the sound of many angels around the throne, and of the four living creatures and of the elders, and their number was ten thousand times ten thousand and thousands of thousands, saying with a loud voice, **"WORTHY IS THE LAMB,** *who was slain to receive power and riches and wisdom and strength and honor and glory and blessing." REV. 5:11, 12.*

J esus is truly worthy. Not only was He the active agent in Creation (Rev. 4:11; John 1:3), but He powerfully intervened to redeem that creation at the cross, the event celebrated so loudly in this chapter of Revelation. What is exciting about this is that the value that He has by right can also become ours by redemption (Rev. 5:9, 10). We can join the angels in celebrating His worth when we see how it makes all the difference in our lives.

A fundamental need of all human beings is to have a sense of great value. But how much is a person worth? It depends on the context. If someone were to melt me down to the chemicals my body consists of, I'm told that I would be worth about $12 (make that $13, since I've gained a little weight in recent years). But the employer of the average American values him or her at a much higher level than that, something like $50,000 a year. But suppose you were a great basketball player such as Shaquille O'Neal. Suddenly the value jumps to tens of millions of dollars a year. And if you were the nerdy designer of the operating system on most of the world's computers, you would be valued at tens of billions of dollars (Bill Gates)!

You see, we are always valued in terms of others. But according to the Bible human value is infinitely higher than what we assign to each other. Scripture tells us that Jesus is worth the whole universe (He made it), yet He knows all about us and loves us as we are. His death on the cross established the value of the human individual. When the Creator of the universe and everyone in it (including all the great athletes and movie stars that people often worship) decides to die for you and me, it places an infinite worth on our lives. And since the resurrected Jesus will never die again, my value is secure in Him as long as I live.

Let's put it another way. A baseball in my hands is worth about $5. But a baseball in Alex Rodriguez' hands is worth about $25 million. A golf club in my hands is worth $50. A golf club in Tiger Woods' hands is worth millions of dollars. A stick in my hands will keep an angry dog from biting me, while the same stick in Moses' hands parted the Red Sea. Nails in my hands might produce a birdhouse. Nails in Jesus' hands led to salvation for the world. You could say it all depends on whose hands each of these objects is in.

Lord Jesus, You are the most genuinely valuable person in the universe. Help me to seek my true value in Your hands and not in the fickle affirmations of others.

"WORTHY IS THE LAMB, WHO WAS SLAIN *to receive power and riches and wisdom and strength and honor and glory and blessing."* REV. 5:12.

T hat Jesus overcomes by dying certainly challenges our way of doing things. We prefer to approach God from a position of strength. And we seek to win on the basis of our talents, not God's grace. Through the slain Lamb, however, we learn that true victory comes in sacrifice and weakness. The sacrifice of Christ compels us to depend on God's vindication rather than on our own abilities or efforts. Jesus sets the example of true victory, and heaven summons us to follow Him.

Most writers jealously protect their schedules and their privacy. But toward the end of his life Henri Nouwen broke down such barriers of professionalism. Trained in Holland both as a psychologist and a theologian, he spent his early years achieving. Nouwen taught at Notre Dame, Yale, and Harvard. Averaging more than a book a year, he traveled widely to give lectures. But in the process his own spiritual life began dying.

Ten years before his death he made a radical break with the past and became priest in residence at a home for the seriously disabled in Toronto. He lived in a simple room with a single bed, one bookshelf, and a few pieces of Shaker-style furniture. With no fax machine, no computer, no PDA or Daytimer calendar, he found spiritual serenity amid the castoffs of society.

Philip Yancey visited him one day and watched as Nouwen served Communion to Adam, a retarded 26-year-old man unable to talk, walk, or dress himself. Adam gave no sign of comprehension, drooled throughout the ceremony, and grunted loudly a few times. Nouwen confessed that it took him nearly two hours each day to bathe and dress Adam, brush his teeth, comb his hair, and guide his hand as he tried to eat breakfast. For Nouwen, those hours of "holy inefficiency" became a chamber of prayer and meditation.

Was this the best possible use of a great writer's time? Couldn't someone else take over the manual chores? Nouwen did not think of such acts as a sacrifice. "I am not giving up anything," he insisted. "It is I, not Adam, who gets the main benefit from our friendship."

It had been difficult at first. Physical touching, affection, and the messiness of caring for an uncoordinated person did not come easily. But he had learned to love Adam—to truly love him. In the process he had discovered what it must be like for God to love us—spiritually uncoordinated, retarded, able to respond only with what must seem to God as inarticulate grunts and groans. In Adam's face he learned that one did not have to achieve to be loved by God, that one could rest in His love. Nouwen followed the Lamb's path to victory.[46]

Lord, I am humbled as I realize how much I have bought into the culture of achievement and success. Help me to see others through the eyes of the slain Lamb.

April 27

And I heard every creature which is in heaven or on earth or under the earth or upon the sea, and all that is in them, saying, "To the One sitting on the throne and to the Lamb be blessing and honor and glory and strength for ever and ever." And the four living creatures said, "Amen." And the twenty-four elders fell down and worshipped. Rev. 5:13, 14.

The Lamb has now joined the Father on the throne, an action anticipated in Revelation 3:21. This is the last of a series of five hymns in Revelation 4 and 5.

1. In Revelation 4:8 the four living creatures sing a song based on the "Holy, holy, holy" of Isaiah 6. They direct their hymn toward the "One sitting on the throne," presumably the Father.

2. In Revelation 4:11 the 24 elders praise God on the basis of His acts in creation.

3. In Revelation 5:9, 10, the four living creatures and the 24 elders together praise the Lamb because of His death on the cross.

4. In Revelation 5:12 an innumerable host of angels join in the chorus of praise to the Lamb.

5. Finally, in our text above, the One on the throne and the Lamb receive praise together as the entire universe offers one single harmony of praise.

The last of the five hymns is the climax. The first two hymns are sung to the One on the throne and focus on creation. The next two hymns are sung to the Lamb and dwell on salvation. The fifth of the five hymns praises both of Them together. So we find a progression from the Father to Jesus and finally to both of Them together.

We also notice an amazing crescendo in the size of the groups that sing these hymns. The four living creatures present the first and the 24 elders the next. In the third hymn the four living creatures and the 24 elders join together in singing. In the fourth hymn a massive angel choir accompanies the four living creatures and the 24 elders. And finally, every creature in the entire universe proclaims the fifth hymn.

The whole sequence of Revelation 4 and 5 moves toward the great climax in which the Lamb joins the Father on the throne. The major point of this passage is the exaltation of the Lamb to equal status with the Father. It is a status He clearly had before the cross.[47] But after His death fresh praise declares the glory of Jesus Christ. His mighty self-sacrifice on the cross raises the acclamation of heaven to new heights never before seen. Never again will God be praised without mention of who the Lamb is, what He has done, and why He is accounted worthy. The joy and integrity of the universe now centers in the worthiness of the Lamb.

Lord, I place Jesus on the throne of my life today. It is my purpose to obey Him in everything, for He is worthy.

And I saw when **THE LAMB OPENED THE FIRST OF THE SEVEN SEALS,** *and I heard one of the four living creatures saying with a voice like thunder, "Come!"* Rev. 6:1.

The four horsemen herald the horrors of war, famine, and pestilence. The language seems to go back to Leviticus 26 and Deuteronomy 32, which list these three plagues among the consequences of breaking the Mosaic covenant. In Revelation 6 they express the results of rejecting Jesus and the salvation He provides.

In Western countries things such as famine and pestilence (contagious disease) may seem like distant realities. They occur mainly in "benighted" corners of the world that make the news but rarely get visited. If we are to truly grasp the dread that these images must have evoked when first written, we need to consider analogies that lie closer to home.

Many people, even in Western countries, are only a paycheck or two away from missing house or rent payments. With corporations downsizing and markets shifting, few jobs are secure, even in corporate America. It takes only a small downturn in the economy to bring a hint of apocalyptic dread into the lives of many people.

When I was 17 years old I started working for a temporary agency. It sent me with a couple other men to unload 1,100 doors from a boxcar. The workforce of the agency largely consisted of "drunks" and "college kids." My boxcar companions were of the former variety. One was 35 years old and the other 47. Both began to get the "shakes" by around 11:00 in the morning. The older man would often sneak away from the work site to get a beer.

Fascinated by the two of them, I did some investigating. I discovered that the younger man was a nuclear physicist and the older one an engineer. In fact, the latter had been a supervisor in the construction of Henderson Field on the island of Guadalcanal, one of the most famous Pacific battlefield sites of World War II.

Both men had started life with high hopes and great achievements. But then the riders of "war, famine, and pestilence" invaded their lives. The gruesome plague of alcohol shattered their families and reduced the men to miserable hulks of humanity. Eking out a bare subsistence in the midst of plenty totally consumed their lives.

Tragedy is no stranger to even the wealthiest of societies. We all need the Lamb to survive.

Lord, the seals and trumpets have baffled the best interpreters for 2,000 years. I have often wondered why You included material like this in Your Word. As we begin examining these "plagues," give me a clearer picture of Your purpose for these images. Use these plagues to enlighten my mind to the way You see our world.

April 29

And I saw when **THE LAMB OPENED THE FIRST OF THE SEVEN SEALS,** *and I heard one of the four living creatures saying with a voice like thunder, "Come!"* REV. 6:1.

I have always considered it a good idea to have a little extra cash around in case of emergencies. While it is dangerous to have a lot of cash, because that might end up rewarding thieves for no purpose, a couple hundred dollars is worth the risk and can come in handy on short notice. I have kept the envelope in my desk, in the refrigerator, in a dresser drawer, and in a couple other places. And no, I have no intention of telling you where it is right now!

One day I came home from a fairly long trip, needing to replenish my wallet in order to pay off some expenses that had accumulated in my absence from home. I went to the place where I kept the envelope and pulled it out. Something was wrong. It didn't have its usual bulky feel, with several ones and fives along with larger denominations. When I opened the envelope, the shape and color of the contents startled me.

You see, instead of good old "greenbacks," the envelope had several Post-It notes inside. One said, "$20 for birthday present." Another declared, "$15 to order pizza." And a third stated, "$3 to rent video." You get the idea. It reminded me of the scene in a funny movie in which a guy finds a briefcase full of cash and spends it on frivolity, accounting for every cent on little bits of paper. When the owner of the briefcase returns and opens it, he finds a useless pile of notes instead of the cash.

"What's this?" he asks.

"Oh, those are IOUs," comes the reply. "Don't worry, with me they're as good as cash!"

Right!

Needless to say I confronted my teens with the absence of "my" money. Their response was interesting. "Dad, it's not your money—it's our money. We got things we needed."

You see, my kids are OK with living on Dad's earnings. I was tempted to feel they had taken advantage of me, but when I stopped to think about it, I realized they were at least partly right—for the time being.

My experience illustrates something similar going on in Revelation. Because of the cross, the Lamb can open the scroll and provide everything necessary to redeem the universe. Salvation costs me nothing, but it cost Him everything. In a sense, "His money is our money." It is good to be the child of the King.

Lord, help me to remember today that everything I have ever had was a gift from You, the fruit of Your sacrifice on the cross. I choose to be generous with Your gifts today.

April 30

And I saw when **THE LAMB OPENED THE FIRST OF THE SEVEN SEALS,** *and I heard one of the four living creatures saying with a voice like thunder, "Come!" And I saw, and behold, a white horse, and the one sitting on it had a bow. A victory crown was given to him, and he went out conquering and in order that he might conquer.* REV. 6:1, 2.

I t is clear that Revelation 6 builds on the throne scene of chapter 5. The Lamb takes the book in chapter 5 and begins to break its seals in our passage above. But a question arises: are the seals the content of the book itself? Or do the contents get revealed only when the Lamb breaks all seven seals? Answering this is crucial for anyone who wants to understand the passage.

If the book is a scroll, shaped like a rolling pin, the seals would be placed outside the "book" and would have to be torn away before anyone could read the book. If the book is a codex (like the book you are holding now), with sheets of paper bound together on one side, you could conceivably seal or tape up the book into seven sections that you could free one at a time.

While the Romans invented the codex form around the time of the composition of Revelation, Jews still use the scroll form for their Bibles up to this day. Christians, however, immediately switched to the new form. Of the hundred or so earliest manuscripts of the New Testament (often existing today only as fragments), only four are in scroll form. We can tell when a manuscript fragment came from a scroll by the slight curvature in the paper that results from being rolled up for a long time.

Why did Christians switch to the codex form for their Bibles? Probably because of the four Gospels. Christians wanted to be able to include all four of them in the same document. A scroll that big would be too large to handle, but you could fit all four Gospels into a codex fairly easily. So shortly after the time of Revelation Christians switched to the codex form.[48]

Now back to our original question. Is the book being unsealed a scroll or a codex? Are the events of Revelation 6 a view of the content of the book, or are they the kinds of things that lead up to the opening of the book? Fortunately, John does not leave us in any doubt. In Revelation 6:14 he says, "The sky was split open *like a scroll being rolled up."*

According to this verse the sky opens like a scroll when someone rolls it up. The word for "scroll" in Revelation 6:14 is the same used for the sealed scroll of chapter 5. The sealed scroll, therefore, is clearly not a codex. With a scroll, you would have to break the seals completely before you could read anything inside. Since the author relates the events in Revelation 6 to the breaking of the seals, they do not describe the content of the scroll itself, but are things that have to take place before the scroll can be opened.

Lord, it's great to understand the deep things of Your Word a little better. Help me to trust You even when I don't understand.

May 1

And I saw when the Lamb opened the first of the seven seals, and I heard one of the four living creatures saying with a voice like thunder, "Come!" And I saw, and behold, **A WHITE HORSE, AND THE ONE SITTING ON IT HAD A BOW. A VICTORY CROWN WAS GIVEN TO HIM, AND HE WENT OUT CONQUERING AND IN ORDER THAT HE MIGHT CONQUER.** Rev. 6:1, 2.

Who is the rider on the white horse? The symbols seem consistently to point in the same direction. First of all, the horse is white in color. Throughout the book of Revelation the color white always refers to the things of Christ and His people. The same is true for the "victory crown" (Greek: *stephanos*) that the rider wears.

While the language of conquering might seem to reflect something negative, it is primarily a spiritual term in Revelation. In fact, up until chapter 6, the Greek word for conquering always refers to Christ and His people ("to the one who overcomes I will give . . ."). The word "conquer" in Revelation refers to victory in spiritual matters (Rev. 5:5; 12:11).

The rider on the white horse, therefore, represents the gospel of Jesus Christ, beginning with His enthronement in heaven (Rev. 5) and continuing until the very end. Passing on that gospel is now the major activity of God's people on earth.

I will never forget how the gospel came to me. Serving as a pastor, I wanted to please God and to reach other people for Him. Yet everything I did was to earn His favor. I had no assurance that I was right with Him.

One day I was walking down a forest path sharing the gospel with someone else (how ironic!). She looked at me with desperate eagerness.

"Could God ever accept me after everything I've done?"

"Oh, yes," I said with words that I truly meant, but that didn't seem to apply to me. I assured her many times that all sins could be forgiven. We prayed the "sinner's prayer."

Then she looked at me and said, "Do you think God is really here?" I replied, "Of course." Just then lightning flashed, thunder rolled, and a huge downpour soaked us to the skin. She looked at me with eyes shining. "I'm being baptized again!" And I could see that the gospel had truly struck home for her.

But when I saw the power of the gospel in her eyes, God touched me with a sense of my own acceptance with Him as well. They say that lightning never strikes twice in the same place, but the gospel struck twice that day!

Lord, I need to know that I am right with You. Touch my heart with anything that needs to be made right, anything that I need to understand. I want to be clean in Your eyes.

And I saw when the Lamb opened the first of the seven seals, and I heard one of the four living creatures saying with a voice like thunder, "Come!" And I saw, and behold, a white horse, and the one sitting on it had a bow. **A VICTORY CROWN WAS GIVEN TO HIM,** *and he went out conquering and in order that he might conquer.* REV. 6:1, 2.

The author of the book of Revelation carefully structured it, although many aspects of that structure elude most twenty-first-century readers. The first half of the book focuses on the general realities of the whole Christian age. One finds references to the cross, the preaching of the gospel, and the kinds of events that go on all the way from Jesus' day to the end of the world. The second half of the book, on the other hand, focuses almost exclusively on the final events of earth's history.

When you see parallels between the first and second halves of the book, therefore, the first part of the parallel tends to focus on the general realities of the whole age, while the second part looks back on the Christian age from the perspective of the end-time. For example, the first section of the book praises God for creation (Rev. 4:11) and for redemption (Rev. 5:9, 10, 12, 13)—events already in the past at the time of the writing of Revelation. Revelation 19:1-6, on the other hand, lavishes the same language of praise on God's deliverance of His people at the end of history.

In a similar fashion white horses appear in only two places in Revelation. The white horse of Revelation 6 parallels the white horse of Revelation 19. Both riders wear crowns, but John uses different Greek words for the respective crowns. The rider of our passage wears a *stephanos* crown, a crown of victory. The ancients used the term for the "Olympic gold medal," the token of victory received by Olympic athletes when they won a race. The rider in chapter 19, on the other hand, wears the *diadem,* the royal crown of rulership. The first half of Revelation repeatedly refers to Jesus and His people as overcomers, like Olympic athletes. The one who overcomes like Jesus will receive the crown of victory. In Revelation 19 Jesus puts an end to all opposition on the earth, and He can now wear the crown of royalty and sovereignty.

I will never forget the Olympics of 1980. The greatest moment for me and for most Americans was the victory of the American hockey team over the Soviet Union's. The high feelings elicited by the cold war raised the excitement of the game to unimaginable proportions. On top of this was the fact that the Russian team consisted of thinly veiled professionals, while the Americans sent college boys into the fray. Athletics fans will never forget the "miracle on ice."

Thank You, Lord, for the reminder that every thought and every decision I make today is at least as important as a gold medal Olympic hockey game. What I do today matters greatly in the ultimate scheme of things. May Your victory become mine.

May 3

And when he opened the second seal, I heard the second living creature saying,
"Come!" And another horse, a fiery red one, went out, and the one sitting on it
was given to **TAKE PEACE FROM THE EARTH, IN ORDER**
THAT THEY MIGHT SLAUGHTER ONE ANOTHER, *and*
a great sword was given to him. REV. 6:3, 4.

The root of all violence is the absence of peace. Where people reject the gospel, peace vanishes from the earth. Men and women get separated from spouses, parents, children, and friends (Matt. 10:32-36). Everyone seeks to secure their own personal peace at the expense of everyone else and their peace. The resulting chaos leads to violence. On the other hand, the presence of the gospel in one's life brings genuine peace. I don't need to assert my opinions or demand my rights, because I already have everything I need in Jesus Christ. Otherwise, even the smallest issues can lead to violence.

An example of this took place at a recent baseball game. The Chicago Cubs had not won the National League pennant since 1945, but they were only five outs from a trip to the World Series. The score was 3-0 Cubs in the eighth inning. A foul ball looked as if it would land right at the top of the wall separating the playing field from the spectators in the left field corner. Moises Alou, the Cubs' left fielder, raced toward the wall and leaped high into the air, extending his glove over the wall. It looked as if he would make the catch.

Just then a fan reached over with a glove of his own. The ball hit the fan's glove and fell into the stands. Alou landed on the ground and made an angry gesture toward the fan. Somehow the incident seemed to suck the energy out of the Cubs. Their opponent, the Florida Marlins, went on to score eight runs in the inning and would eventually win the World Series in place of the Cubs.

Things got ugly in the stands. Security officials had to escort the fan off the field, covering his head because of the objects thrown at him by other spectators. "Kill him!" cried some. "You cost us the World Series," others shouted. After receiving death threats, the fan, Steve Bartman, went into seclusion, afraid for his life. The irony of it all is that Bartman was not an anti-Cub terrorist, planted there to foil the team's chances to make the World Series. He was actually a Cub fan who was brokenhearted about the result of his own actions. When he saw the ball coming, he said, "I had my eyes glued on the approaching ball . . . and was so caught up in the moment that I did not even see Moises Alou."[49]

In the absence of the gospel, even the most trivial of pursuits can become the basis for human violence. A relationship with Jesus Christ is the only way to genuine peace.

Lord, help me keep things in their true perspective. May I extend to others the peace
that You have given me.

And when he opened the second seal, I heard the second living creature saying, "Come!" And another horse, a fiery red one, went out, and the one sitting on it was given to **TAKE PEACE FROM THE EARTH, IN ORDER THAT THEY MIGHT SLAUGHTER ONE ANOTHER,** *and a great sword was given to him.* REV. 6:3, 4.

Those who have never known war firsthand often glorify the image of war. But those who have experienced it tend to view it more realistically. The fear, the pain, the separation, the carnage, the loss of life—it has nothing pretty about it, except perhaps in the minds of armchair generals. In the words of General Robert E. Lee: "It is well that war is so terrible, or we should grow too fond of it."

War is not far from any of us today. Even without the use of weapons of mass destruction, terrorism has found ways to multiply suffering and garner worldwide attention.

And while international terrorism is an ongoing threat, we cannot ignore its domestic version. Timothy McVeigh's truck bomb killed 168 people in Oklahoma City, and he was not an isolated activist. He took the script for the bombing from the novel *The Turner Diaries,* which has sold 200,000 copies.

It is hard to use the word "civilization" in the phrase "twentieth-century civilization." That century witnessed the Nazi holocaust against the Jews, the genocides in Cambodia and Rwanda, and the ethnic cleansing of Armenians and Greeks from Turkey, Croats and Muslims from parts of Bosnia, and Serbs from Croatia. Less known is the "rape of Nanking," in which, after the city's surrender, soldiers gang-raped women and butchered men for bayonet practice. And we do not have space to talk about the millions destroyed by Mao, Stalin, and World War I.

In 1905 the United States approved Japan's annexation of Korea, often viewed as the nation's first subjugation in 5,000 years of recorded history. During World War II the occupying soldiers abducted about 200,000 Korean women for daily rape. After virgins became rare they seized married women. They abused the women from 20 to 70 times a day, and when the war ended, they left them to die in desolate areas or exterminated them to conceal the evidence of their war crimes. War brings out the worst in people of every ethnic group.

If John had received his visions in our time, the terrifying symbols might have been different, but the essential message would be largely the same. Humanity has not been evolving morally through the centuries—we have simply developed more efficient means of killing one another. In a world filled with terror and chaos, nothing is certain except that God is the one who is in ultimate control of history. The only solid ground we have to stand on is to trust in Him.[50]

Lord, I choose to trust in You, no matter what I see on today's news.

May 5

And when he opened the third seal, I heard the third living creature saying, "Come!" And I saw, and behold, a black horse, and the one sitting on it had a scale for weighing in his hand. And I heard, as it were, a voice in the middle of the four living creatures, saying, **"A QUART OF WHEAT FOR A DENARIUS AND THREE QUARTS OF BARLEY FOR A DENARIUS, AND DO NOT HARM THE OIL AND THE WINE."** REV. 6:5, 6.

A denarius was roughly a day's wage during this period, so the prices mentioned in the text represent a severe famine. A man would have to work all day to get enough wheat to feed himself. If he had a family to support he would need to buy the cheaper barley. Given the large size of families in those days, the children would likely die or be stunted by malnutrition.

Why does the text mention sparing the oil and the wine, items less necessary for life than grain? In Asia Minor of the first century A.D. this text would have connected with a hot issue. Wine trade at that time was more profitable than grain. The wealthy landowners of Asia were, therefore, switching from grain to grapes.

So property owners dedicated much of the land in the province of Asia (which included the seven churches) to producing olive oil and wine for profitable export. Meanwhile, the cities of Asia had to import grain all the way from Egypt or the areas by the Black Sea. So while landowners and shippers profited from their choice, the people in Asia had to pay higher prices for staple foods.

The problem was serious enough that the emperor Domitian tried to intervene and force the landowners to restrict vine production in such places as the province of Asia. His attempts were extremely unpopular and proved unsuccessful. If he had succeeded, it would have been quite a blow to the wealthy of Philadelphia, especially those who gained their wealth from wine production. As is often the case, the greed of the wealthy had serious consequences for the poor.

But we could also read the sparing of the oil and the wine as a token of God's mercy in the time of judgment. Ancient Mediterranean warfare included destroying the standing crops in the fields, but not the vines and the olives trees (which took more than 15 years to reach productive capacity). The loss of wheat and barley meant hardship for a year, but eradicating vines and trees would result in enduring disaster.[51]

While the judgments of God in our lives can be severe, they seek to redeem us, not destroy us. It is not God's purpose to prolong suffering, but to use difficulties to get our attention and bring us to a place that would be better for us. If everyone were more attentive to God's call much of the injustice in the world would disappear.

Lord, I want to be attentive to Your call in my life today. May I not need overwhelming difficulties before I am willing to listen to You.

And when he opened the fourth seal, I heard the voice of the fourth living creature saying, "Come!" And I saw, and behold, a pale horse, and the one sitting upon it was named DEATH, *and Hades followed after him. And they were given authority over a fourth of the earth, to kill with the sword, with famine, with pestilence, and by the beasts of the earth.* REV. 6:7, 8.

This seal is the third in a series of deepening disasters. While the language is literal, speaking of war, famine, and pestilence, the description reflects the progressive spiritual decline of those who reject the gospel. To reject the gospel is like removing sunshine and moisture from a plant's environment. Nothing can grow without water and light.

A friend recently took on a difficult project—a stable area in his family's back yard. He decided to begin repair work on the oldest section of the stable. The room was in dire need of repair. One wall was almost falling down, cobwebs hung everywhere, and the floor had almost wholly rotted out. The whole place was filled with junk of various kinds, and it was with some trepidation that he began the process of clearing everything out so he could begin the restoration process.

The first order of business, then, was to remove all the junk from the room and knock the one wall down before it collapsed of its own accord. That done, Jim had to decide whether to remove the existing floor or build on top of it. Finally he began to rip out the floor that had almost totally rotted out after decades of neglect.

The demolition of the floor exposed the ground underneath the stable. Jim was really surprised by the absolute "death" that existed underneath the floor after several decades. The soil beneath the structure had turned into a very fine powdery substance. Because no moisture or light had reached it for years, the ground almost completely lacked any kind of life. The only things living there were some nasty-looking bugs that spent their existence boring aimlessly through a maze of silver dust.[52]

Our spiritual life will rapidly decline unless nurtured by the water of the Word and the sunlight of God's love. The end result of spiritual neglect is a life full of "bugs" and the dry desert of discouragement. But we can grow spiritually when we open ourselves up to God and His Word. Spiritual renewal means ripping open the floorboards of sin that separate us from God and tearing down the walls of distrust and distraction that keep the Son from shining in. The One who created the world from nothing can then bring life even to the spiritually dead.

Lord, today I choose to open myself to the light and moisture of Your presence. Remove the spiritual obstacles in my life and fill me with Your refreshing Word.

May 7

And when he opened the fourth seal, I heard the voice of the fourth living creature saying, "Come!" And I saw, and behold, a pale horse, and the one sitting upon it was named Death, and Hades followed after him. And they were given authority over a fourth of the earth, **TO KILL WITH THE SWORD, WITH FAMINE, WITH PESTILENCE, AND BY THE BEASTS OF THE EARTH.** Rev. 6:7, 8.

The key Old Testament background to the four horses of Revelation 6 is the covenant and its curses. But we also find additional background within the New Testament. Revelation 6 has strong parallels with what scholars call the Synoptic Apocalypse, the end-time sermon of Jesus recorded in Mark 13, Matthew 24, and Luke 21. These three chapters, therefore, form the major New Testament background text for Revelation 6.

In the Synoptic Apocalypse Jesus moves through a series of events that will characterize the whole Christian age from the cross until the second coming of Jesus. They include wars and rumors of wars. Earthquakes, famines, and pestilences will strike various places. In addition, Christ speaks of deception, persecution, and a final climax in heavenly signs. All of these themes also occur in Revelation 6. The basic message of both passages is that God is in full control of history, even when bad things afflict God's people. The course of human history is the consequence of the Lamb opening the book.

After I had taught a class on Revelation 6, a young man, extremely upset, came up to question me. Taking issue with a couple things I had said in discussing the chapter, he seemed to have great difficulty with the idea that God was "in control" of human history. After some discussion he finally revealed that when he was a teen-ager he had been forced to watch the murder of his brother. The horrendous event forever marked him and the way he thought about God.

You see, he felt that if God could have intervened on that occasion, He should have. Since He did not, the young man was angry with Him. But that placed him in a dilemma. He didn't want to be angry with God. So his solution to the dilemma was to believe that God did not have the power to come to his brother's aid.

I affirmed his need to do theology in light of his brother's death. But I pointed out that for some people the thought that God was unable to intervene would be even more frightening than the idea that He sometimes chooses not to. On the surface the world seems completely out of control. But the message of Revelation 6 and the Synoptic Apocalypse is that even when things seem chaotic, God still rules and will set everything right in His good time.

Lord, I trust Your judgment and Your timing. Help me to have faith in You even when I think You should have intervened and You did not.

And when he opened the fifth seal, I saw under the altar **THE SOULS OF THOSE WHO HAD BEEN SLAUGHTERED ON ACCOUNT OF THE WORD OF GOD AND ON ACCOUNT OF THE TESTIMONY WHICH THEY HAD MAINTAINED.** Rev. 6:9.

T he sacrificial language of this text suggests that Christians will not fully proclaim the gospel to all nations (Matt. 24:14) until God's people become radical enough to die for the sake of the unreached. In the past many mission fields were pried open only in the wake of a multitude of Christian martyrs. Today's "difficult fields," such as the strongholds of Islam and Hinduism, may require similar sacrifice.

In the words of John Fischer: "Point a gun at each of the 60 million people who, according to [George] Gallup's poll, are born-again Christians. Tell them to renounce Christ or have their heads blown off, and then take a recount. I think George, like Gideon, would find his troops dwindling. Actually, the price probably wouldn't have to be so extreme today. Threatening to confiscate their TV sets might just produce the same results. When faith is cheap, it is easily pawned."

In the late nineteenth century Hudson Taylor sought recruits to help in his mission to China. He claimed that he needed "men and women . . . such as will put Jesus, China, souls, first and foremost in everything and at every time—even life itself must be secondary." Such a commitment was bound to be tested eventually. The Boxer Rebellion of 1900, a response to the insensitivity of many Westerners in China, slaughtered 188 Protestant missionaries and 30,000 Chinese Christians. Yet it led to threefold church growth in the decade that followed.

In 1986 on Flatbush Avenue in Brooklyn a minister urged a man to accept Jesus as the only way to be reconciled to God. The man became angry and announced that he had a gun and would kill the minister. "You talk about heaven," he charged. "We'll see how ready you are to die." How one responds at a time like that depends on the cumulative effect of many small decisions over the years. Most of us may never encounter a time when our lives are at stake on the basis of faith. But if we have proved faithful in the smaller tests that we face each day, we will be well-trained for the ultimate test if that should come.[53]

In the incident on Flatbush Avenue the man with the gun ended up walking away and the next night even returned to apologize and ask where the minister's church was. The faith of the martyrs always produces fruit, whether or not someone dies.

Lord, I have only a small idea of what "martyr faith" is like. I'd prefer to go on living for a while, but I pray that whether I live many years or few, I will be found faithful today.

May 9

And when he opened the fifth seal, I saw under the altar **THE SOULS OF THOSE WHO HAD BEEN SLAUGHTERED** *on account of the word of God and on account of the testimony which they had maintained. And they cried out with a loud voice saying, "How long, O Lord, the Holy and True One, do You not* **JUDGE AND AVENGE OUR BLOOD** *on those who live on the earth?"* REV. 6:9, 10.

Friedrich Nietzsche, the nineteenth-century German philosopher famous for the line "God is dead," became a serious opponent of Christianity. He claimed that it was a religion invented by the weaklings of the world to make themselves feel good about their unfortunate circumstances. By exalting humility, submission, and poverty as virtues while condemning pride, power, and wealth, the powerless in society could cast their condition in a positive light.

Nietzsche believed that this inversion of values was bad both for individuals and for society as a whole, and he ridiculed it as "the slave rebellion in morals." Taking offense at texts such as the above that exalt the powerless and the victims of oppression, he had no use for "blessed are the meek" or "turn the other cheek." The New Testament had much more to offend him: "Whoever wants to become great among you must be your servant." "If anyone would come after me, he must deny himself and take up his cross daily and follow me."

The philosopher scorned the entire Christian value system as a glorification of all that is weak and ineffective in life. And his objections have no easy answer, no simple way to prove that the Christian way of suffering and service is inherently superior to self-promotion and competition. The Bible does make clear, however, that when God asks His followers to follow the way of humility and suffering, it is only because He Himself has already set the example. He requires these characteristics in His followers because they are traits that He Himself exemplifies.

In the person of Jesus, God demonstrates that He is "gentle and humble in heart" (Matt. 11:29, NIV). Though He held the highest place in the universe, Christ "did not consider equality with God something to be grasped, but made himself nothing, taking the very nature of a servant (Phil. 2:6, 7, NIV)." Jesus not only became human, which would be humiliating enough, but submitted to unjust arrest and execution (Phil. 2:8).[54]

In Revelation 6:9 and 10 the souls under the altar recognize the injustice in their suffering. At the same time, they are following in the footsteps of the Lamb that was slain. The cross does not call us to do what is natural—it summons us to deny ourselves and follow Him, even to the point of death.

Lord, teach me the full meaning of the cross. I yield my plans and my ambitions to You today. Teach me Your ways.

And when he opened the fifth seal, I saw under the altar the souls of those who had been slaughtered on account of the word of God and on account of the testimony which they had maintained. And they cried out with a loud voice saying, **"HOW LONG, O LORD,** *the Holy and True One, do You not judge and avenge our blood on those who live on the earth?" And each of them was given a white robe and was told that they should* **REST YET A LITTLE WHILE, UNTIL THEIR FELLOW SERVANTS AND BROTHERS, WHO ARE ABOUT TO BE KILLED AS THEY WERE, SHOULD BE MADE COMPLETE.** REV. 6:9-11.

One can read the awkward sentence at the end of this passage in two different ways. Taken at face value, it seems to suggest that the future martyrs need to go through some sort of "completion" before their deaths. Most Bible translators, however, add a few words to fill out the picture. "Until *the number* of their fellow servants and brothers who were to be killed as they had been was completed." That is, the end will not come until history records a certain *number* of martyrs.

This was a popular idea in first-century Judaism. Statements similar to Revelation 6:9-11 occur in 1 Enoch 47:1-4 and 4 Ezra 4:35-37. The author of 4 Ezra wrote the book in reaction to the destruction of Jerusalem in A.D. 70, around the same time as the composition of Revelation. As a non-Christian Jew, the writer seeks to understand God's will and ways in the light of incomparable anguish and suffering.

Israel's history, from Old Testament times until A.D. 70, had more downs than ups. Magnificent promises and prophecies mingled with betrayals, apostasies, and disappointments. At the time of 4 Ezra's composition Jewish hopes for a national Israel seemed forever crushed. Thus "Ezra's" words ring through and through with sorrow.

In a "vision" Ezra wrestles with the vast number of faithful Jews who lost their lives in A.D. 70. How can God ever fulfill His promises when His own chosen people suffer such disasters? The angel Uriel responds that the whole current age is full of sadness and infirmity. Only in the age to come will the promises of God find their complete fulfillment.

"How long and when will these things be?" Ezra asks.

Uriel tells him, "Didn't the souls of the righteous in their chambers ask about these matters?" God's answer to them was: "When the number of those like yourselves is completed." Such an answer may not satisfy us today, but it expresses the idea that suffering does have a purpose, a limit, and an ultimate goal. We will never fully see justice in this world—only in the world to come.

Lord, I pray that I will not be distracted by my local and temporary perspective. Help me to trust in Your overall control of both the present and the future.

May 11

And when he opened the fifth seal, I saw under the altar the souls of those who had been slaughtered on account of the word of God and on account of the testimony which they had maintained. And they cried out with a loud voice saying, **"HOW LONG, O LORD, THE HOLY AND TRUE ONE, DO YOU NOT JUDGE AND AVENGE OUR BLOOD ON THOSE WHO LIVE ON THE EARTH?" AND EACH OF THEM WAS GIVEN A WHITE ROBE** *and was told that they should rest yet a little while, until their fellow servants and brothers, who are about to be killed as they were, should be made complete.* REV. 6:9-11.

Orenthal James Simpson, known commonly as "O.J." or "The Juice," was one of the most famous running backs in American football history. His coach at the University of Southern California, John McKay, said of his star player: "Simpson was not only the greatest player I ever had—he was the greatest player anyone ever had." His National Football League achievements included most rushing yards in a season, most rushing yards in a single game, and most touchdowns scored in a season.

After retiring from football, Simpson spent time working as a sports commentator, acting, and golfing. Interestingly, Simpson acted in the film *The Klansman,* in which he played a man framed for murder by the police. While still married to his first wife, Simpson met 17-year-old server, Nicole Brown. He married her in 1985. After what was described as a "rocky marriage," Nicole filed for divorce in 1992.

Prior to the murders of his estranged wife and Ronald Goldman, the relationship between the Los Angeles Police Department and Simpson was one of admiration for his celebrity. Right up to the time Simpson fled in his Bronco, the LAPD deferred to his celebrity status by allowing him to surrender voluntarily to save him the embarrassment of a public arrest.

While Simpson was acquitted at the murder trial of his estranged wife, his friends in large part seemed to melt away, especially in upper-class Los Angeles. Simpson still plays golf occasionally, but never at his former home course, the Rivera Country Club. Members of that club informed his business manager, Skip Taft, that Simpson was no longer welcome there.[55]

The O. J. Simpson trial was the story of a man whose closest friends seemed to think him guilty of murder, yet he was (rightly or wrongly) acquitted of the crime. This is the opposite of the situation in this text. "How long?" is a cry of protest. The saints are innocent, yet human courts have accounted them guilty. The good news is that a higher court reverses that ruling. While their vindication does not become public until the end, they are now on the winning side.

Lord, in a world of false accusations and unjust judgment, help me to hold my peace and trust in the ultimate vindication that You have promised.

And each of them was given a white robe and was told that **THEY SHOULD REST YET A LITTLE WHILE,** *until their fellow servants and brothers, who are about to be killed as they were, should be made complete.* Rev. 6:11.

The above translation reflects some puzzling aspects of this text. First, what are the "souls under the altar" (Rev. 6:9, 10) supposed to be doing? They are to "rest, wait, relax for a while." Instead of acting, they must remain passive until something else happens. In most translations that something else is waiting for a certain number of martyrs to be reached ("until the number . . . was completed" [verse 11, NIV]). But the word "number" isn't in the original. Instead, as mentioned yesterday, the translators have put it in to make sense of the passage. But the passage does make sense as it is. The "fellow servants" are being "completed," perhaps a reference to their character in the final crisis of earth's history (Rev. 19:7, 8). They are waiting for God to act in some special way for them.

Being told to "relax" is a bit surprising in a message from heaven. When I "relax," bad things often happen (read "procrastination"). For example, I have a sizable patch of grass not far from the septic tank at my house. I don't know if it is the type of grass planted there or the proximity to natural fertilizer, but it seems to grow twice as fast and twice as thick as anywhere else on my lawn. Particularly in the month of May we have plenty of both sunshine and rain, the grass is seeding itself, and the plants' metabolism is at peak efficiency. But what is good news for plants becomes bad news for me if I "relax" more than a day or two beyond my mowing schedule.

Other parts of the lawn are not as dense and grow more slowly. The grass there is not difficult to mow even if I skip a few days. But this patch in the back quickly becomes nearly impossible to cut down to size. If the grass is the least bit damp (and we have dew almost every day), the mower clogs almost instantly. I have the nasty task of having to raise the mower on all four wheels (and lower it later) and then mow a couple square feet at a time, stopping to clean out the underside of the machine every couple minutes. Not fun.

My point is that waiting or relaxing *can* be a foolish thing. Yet heaven instructs the souls under the altar to relax for a while in order to let God do His work. It would be nice to have a voice from heaven telling us when God *wants* us to relax or when relaxing would be procrastination. But wrestling with God's will and His timing can teach us valuable lessons. While relaxing may feel like procrastination, it can also be an expression of faith in God's action.

Lord, my day is already overfilled. I need Your guidance to know what things will improve if they don't get done today. Help me trust that You are working even when I am not.

May 13

And I saw, when he opened the sixth seal, there was a great **EARTHQUAKE,** *and* **THE SUN** *became black* **LIKE** *sackcloth of hair, and* **THE WHOLE MOON** *became* **LIKE** *blood, and* **THE STARS** *of heaven fell to the earth,* **LIKE** *a fig tree drops its unripe figs having been shaken by a mighty wind, and* **THE SKY** *was split open* **LIKE** *a scroll being rolled up, and* **EVERY MOUNTAIN AND ISLAND WAS MOVED** *out of its place.* REV. 6:12-14.

Today's passage lists a series of six items. The first and last of the six are earthquakes, the latter being so great that every mountain and island shifts position, a truly cataclysmic event. In between the two earthquakes occur four heavenly signs: the sun darkens, the moon turns bloody red, the stars fall to the earth, and heaven itself splits up.

The images are either literal or spiritual. I am not aware of a compelling case to treat the sun, moon, stars, and sky as symbolic here. So we should probably interpret them literally. In the Greek of this passage the word *hos* (in bold above translated "like") usually compares something literal with something figurative. The pattern is that the sun becomes black *"like* sackcloth of hair," the moon becomes *"like* blood," the stars fall *"like* a fig tree drops its unripe figs," and the sky splits open *"like* a scroll being rolled up." So we should take the sun, moon, stars, and sky literally and what happens to them figuratively.

Events like the first three have taken place in the past. In 1780 an incredibly dark day spread across North America in which animals came home early, thinking the day was already over, and roosters crowed at odd hours. That night the moon turned a dark red. The event was so unusual that many people took note of it. Then in November 1833 a meteor shower was so spectacular that many people wrote their local newspapers announcing that the end of the world must be at hand.

God used the events to stimulate tremendous interest in the prophecies of the Bible around the world. But interpretation of this text cannot stop with the nineteenth century. The descriptions in verse 14 go way beyond anything history records. The sky ripping apart and every island moving out of its place are events not yet seen. They point to the time just before the return of Jesus.

We find the spiritual message of this text when we examine the Old Testament passages it echoes. "Though the mountains be shaken and the hills be removed, yet my unfailing love for you will not be shaken nor my covenant of peace be removed" (Isa. 54:10, NIV). The assurance is that no matter what, God will never forsake His people.

Lord, I crave a calm confidence that my whole life is sheltered in Your caring hands, no matter what the circumstances I may face today.

And I saw, when he opened the sixth seal, there was a great earthquake, and the sun became black like sackcloth of hair, and the whole moon became like blood, and the stars of heaven fell to the earth, like a fig tree drops its unripe figs having been shaken by a mighty wind, and the sky was split open like a scroll being rolled up, and every mountain and island was moved out of its place. And the kings of the earth, the great ones, the captains of thousands, **THE RICH AND THE STRONG, AND EVERY SLAVE AND FREE PERSON** *hid themselves in the caves and in the rocks of the mountains.* REV. 6:12-15.

The sixth seal portrays the end of the cosmos as the ancients understood it. The seals begin with the four horsemen, who depict the kind of judgments that repeat themselves again and again in the course of history (Rev. 6:1-8). The passage above, however, includes the absolute dissolution of the heavens (verses 12-14) followed by the world's recognition of that event and its condemnation by the wrath of the Creator (verses 15-17). This seems to express the end of history as we know it.

The ancients used to sum up the totality of humanity in contrasting opposites, such as "rich and poor," "slave and free," "male and female." In our text John lists representatives of the entire social order. Absolutely no one, from Caesar on down, will escape final judgment.

How we relate to a passage like this could be influenced by the culture in which we were raised. The Shona of South Africa, for example, traditionally believed that earthquakes resulted from God walking around on the earth. Other tribes attribute earthquakes to the work of special deities. To them a passage like this expresses God's full control over everything that happens on earth.

God's ultimate power over earthquakes has proved comforting to Christians living near the San Andreas fault in California. "God just clapped His hands," announced one witness of the Bay Area earthquake of 1989, an earthquake that claimed more than 60 lives and billions of dollars in property damage. Because John's audience in Asia Minor knew and feared earthquakes (the Roman province of Asia was in the middle of an active seismic area), a passage like this would prove unnerving rather than comforting.

The overall impact of today's text is to terrify anyone who has too much confidence in the material things of this world. We have no security, no firm ground to stand on, nothing in the universe to depend on except God Himself. The creation, and everything in it, will one day collapse. If our confidence rests only on that which we can hear, see, and touch, our lives are tenuous indeed.[56]

Lord, teach me the uncertainty of money, land, education, and everything else I am tempted to trust in. I place my confidence today in You—and in You alone.

May 15

And they said to the mountains and the rocks, "Fall on us and hide us from the face of the One sitting on the throne, and from **THE WRATH OF THE LAMB.** *For the great day of His wrath has come, and who is able to stand?"* REV. 6:16, 17.

It was a defining moment of my life. Fifteen years and two months old, I was at a teen camp for boys and girls ranging in age from 13 to 15. While I'm not sure if I was the oldest in my group, if I was, it was by a couple weeks at the most. As our unit prepared for bed that first Sunday night, one thing was missing. We had not yet had a counselor assigned to us. That may sound like a teenager's dream vacation, but it was a bit unsettling nevertheless.

At 2:00 in the morning a group of counselors gently shook me awake, took me outside the cabin, and told me that the camp staff had chosen me counselor of my unit. What a daunting task! I was roughly the same age as my group, and they would wake up thinking I was just one of them. How would I assert any measure of authority?

The ultimate challenge occurred a couple days later. A 14-year-old locked me in the bathroom of the cabin at a crucial point of the day. When he refused to open the door at my request and then my command, I broke out with a crash. In a rage I ordered him to take off his shoes and run 10 times up and down a gravel path on a nearby hill. After a couple trips his feet were scratched and bleeding a bit.

I was mortified as I realized that I had overdone the punishment. But if I went back on my sentence no one in the unit would respect me. Instinctively I made a decision. I joined him in his punishment, finishing the 10 laps up and down the hill with him. That week I had no further trouble with my unit, and the camper who locked me in the bathroom became my most admiring and loyal subordinate.

The concept "wrath of the Lamb" sounds like an oxymoron. Can you really imagine a "raging lamb"? What would that look like? The slain Lamb, of course, represents the cross. The wrath represents God's unwillingness to compromise with sin. On a very small scale my experience with the camper mirrored the problem God had in the universe. The "campers" were rebelling. While He could back off on His authority, that would lead to chaos. But simply being the "Great Counselor" would mean everyone would serve Him out of fear.

So at the cross He joined us in reaping the consequences of sin. In so doing He won the love of the universe as well as its respect. And in the end a "raging Lamb" who brooks no compromise with sin, yet identifies with the sinner, proves able to heal a broken universe.

Lord, I respect Your integrity, and love You for Your sacrifice. I want to be like You in my treatment of everyone I meet.

And they said to the mountains and the rocks, "Fall on us and hide us from the face of the One sitting on the throne, and from the wrath of the Lamb. For **THE GREAT DAY OF HIS WRATH HAS COME, AND WHO IS ABLE TO STAND?"** Rev. 6:16, 17.

A friend of mine received an invitation to teach a class in Bangkok, Thailand. One of his students was a pastor in the northeastern part of the country, close to the Cambodian border and about 400 miles from Bangkok. Since one of his children had become sick, the pastor decided to head home for the weekend and invited his teacher to travel with him.

After an all-night bus ride, which was an adventure in itself, the two men arrived in the beautiful and tranquil rice fields of rural Thailand. The pastor's home was located on the same property as the church, and they had a delightful Sabbath school and worship service with the local people. After a refreshing potluck and conversation, the two men set out to visit some members in another district.

It was a most rewarding experience for Jim to see the homes of these hospitable people and eat a traditional Thai meal of sticky rice dipped in various sauces, which range from mild to painfully hot.

When he and his student got home, they were all preparing to get some rest. The pastor's wife was in the bathroom area where the family kept their washing machine, preparing a load of clothes. The floor was wet as she adjusted the electrical plug. Suddenly powerful jolts of electricity surged through her. She screamed for her husband. Fortunately he was not only near but had the presence of mind to shut off the current instead of touching her and adding himself to the shock treatment.

It took about an hour for the wife to recover from her almost deadly encounter. Although my friend didn't understand any Thai, he could tell the next day that she was excitedly telling everyone she met about the previous night's escape from certain death.[57]

In our text the very presence of God and the Lamb provides the equivalent of an overwhelming jolt of electricity to those who experience the coming of Christ. Without the mercy and protection of Jesus our Savior, sinners will not be able to endure the shock of God's presence. But Revelation 7 makes it clear that the 144,000 and the great multitude will be able to stand in that day. For those who are washed in the blood of the Lamb (Rev. 7:14), He functions as an insulator to the overwhelming power of God's presence. And even now His ability to save us is just a prayer away.

Lord, I am so grateful that You reckon the purity of Jesus' righteousness to me each day. Help me to be fully aware of my need for Him.

May 17

After this I saw four angels standing at the four corners of the earth, **HOLDING BACK THE FOUR WINDS OF THE EARTH,** *in order that the wind might not blow upon the earth, upon the sea, or upon any tree.* REV. 7:1.

Our text affirms God's ability to exempt people from judgment. He is able to hold back destructive winds and preserve His people in any circumstance. Not a deist God, who wound up the universe like a clock and then went on vacation, He is intimately concerned about His people and arranges for their protection.

The heavy shelling that occurred some time ago in Brazzaville, central Africa, demonstrated His ability to intervene. The bombardment ruined most of the large stores and hotels. Many Christians and others crowded into the large church building, and though everything around it was destroyed, the structure itself remained undamaged.

But life is not always that simple. What about the many situations in which the righteous do not get protected? For example, a pregnant woman in the Philippines and the child she carried miraculously survived several shots in the torso from a high-powered weapon at close range. But 17 other victims gunned down with her died. Emma Moss, the daughter of the founders of the Salvation Army and active in ministry work, was the only person to die in a train accident. Spencer Perkins, a strategic player in the racial reconciliation movement, died suddenly of a heart attack at the age of 43.

Sometimes we face death because of our own choices and actions. Other times we do so because we have ignored proper warnings. Perhaps we perish because we didn't realize the warning we received was from God. Occasionally death simply seems to be the result of the random course of events. But often God is at work in tragic circumstances in ways that we may not clearly recognize until much later.

William Wilberforce, for example, lost his father at age 9. His aunt and uncle were childless. But the combination of the two circumstances exposed Wilberforce to the evangelical preaching of the abolitionist John Newton. Ultimately Wilberforce became the leading champion of abolitionism in England until, on his deathbed, the entire British Empire outlawed slavery. So we must trust in God's ability to protect and deliver, knowing that in a given situation it may not occur. But even if death or tragedy does happen, we know that God can bring something good out of it in the long run.

Lord, thank You for the abundant evidences of Your protection in the past. I trust You and place myself in Your hands today. I know that You have my best interests at heart, no matter what happens.

And I saw another angel ascending from the rising of the sun, having the **SEAL OF THE LIVING GOD.** *He cried out with a loud voice to the four angels, to whom it was given to harm the earth and the sea, saying, "Do not harm the earth, the sea, or the trees,* **UNTIL WE HAVE SEALED THE SERVANTS OF OUR GOD** *upon their foreheads."* Rev. 7:2, 3.

The words for sealing in the New Testament have multiple meanings. First of all, you can seal a document to protect it from tampering. You can do the same with a tomb or a prison cell. When you seal a document or a place, you are concealing something or someone: examples in the Bible include the tomb of Jesus (Matt. 27:66); the heavenly scroll (Rev. 5); and Satan's confinement in the abyss (Rev. 20:3).

Second, sealing can certify that something or someone is reliable: certified letters have a seal indicating that the information inside is trustworthy or has been delivered without tampering (cf. John 3:33; 6:27; Rom. 15:28; 1 Cor. 9:2).

Third, sealing can indicate that God has accepted someone. The Lord knows who belongs to Him, and He gives them the Holy Spirit (2 Tim. 2:19; 2 Cor. 1:22; Eph. 1:13; 4:30). Sealing, therefore, became associated with circumcision in the first century (Rom. 4:11) and baptism in the second.

The sealing of Revelation 7 occurs just before the close of probation. From John's point of view, sealing involves how people relate to God at the end. In the broader sense, sealing is the indication that people are acceptable to God. "The Lord knows those who are His" (2 Tim. 2:19, NKJV). So the New Testament does not limit the concept of sealing to the end-time. But in Revelation 7 sealing occurs in an end-time setting. The final proclamation of the gospel results in a great last-day sealing work.

This kind of study doesn't make for light reading. Sometimes Christians need to do heavy, detailed investigations of Scripture in order to understand God's ways. We live in an age that prizes relevance more than learning, and many people have no patience with Bible study that doesn't have an obvious and immediate payoff.

But I suggest that such investigation can lead to great joy. If Christians want to understand the deep things of God, they must at times do detailed study, even though its immediate usefulness may not be clear. But the long-term reward for such study is an understanding of the big picture that transforms everything you read in the Bible.

Lord, thank You for the depth of the challenge in Your Word. Encourage me to take up that challenge and open my mind to comprehend the immensity of Your wisdom.

May 19

And I saw another angel ascending from the rising of the sun, having the seal of the living God. He cried out with a loud voice to the four angels, to whom it was given to harm the earth and the sea, saying, "Do **NOT HARM THE EARTH, THE SEA, OR THE TREES, UNTIL WE HAVE SEALED THE SERVANTS OF OUR GOD UPON THEIR FOREHEADS."** Rev. 7:2, 3.

The setting of Revelation 7 appears in the last verse of chapter 6. "For the great day of His wrath has come, and who is able to stand?" (Rev. 6:17, NKJV). The purpose of Revelation 7 is to provide the answer to this question at the end of Revelation 6: "Who [at the time of the end] is able to stand?" The answer comes in two parts: the 144,000 (Rev. 7:1-8) and a great multitude (verses 9-17).

This passage has a chilling background. The scene is Jerusalem, the year probably 586 B.C. In a vision Ezekiel's companion summons the guards of the city. The prophet watches as six terrifying men approach the Temple from the north with deadly weapons in their hands. A seventh man accompanies them, and he has a writing kit at his side. The seven men enter the Temple courts and stand by the altar of burnt offering (Eze. 9:1, 2).

Then a stunning thing happens. Visible to all, the shekinah glory of God rises up from the ark and exits the door of the Temple! God Himself calls out to the man with the writing kit and says, "Go throughout the city of Jerusalem and put a mark on the foreheads of those who grieve and lament over all the detestable things that are done in it" (verse 4, NIV). Then He orders the other six to follow him and slaughter old and young, male and female, without showing pity or compassion. "But do not touch anyone who has the mark. Begin at my sanctuary" (verse 6, NIV). And the men begin the slaughter among the elders standing in front of the Temple (verse 7).

The scene is one of the most frightening and sobering ones in all the Bible. It is a symbolic description of events that took place almost literally in the destruction of Jerusalem in Ezekiel's day. God drew a distinction between those who were on His side (sighing and crying for the abominations of the people) and those who would perish.

Revelation 7 seems to offer a glimpse of the last events of earth's history: a final proclamation, symbolic marks on the forehead, the world called into judgment, and God rescuing His people. In the end His discerning eye can tell who is committed to Him and who is not. His people have often suffered at the hands of others in His name. At the end God will make clear to all exactly who belongs to Him.

Lord, this scene of judgment is sobering. Help me not to respond in fear, but in the sober sense that every choice and every decision matters to You. I want Your seal even more than life itself.

And I heard the number of those who were being sealed, **144,000, SEALED FROM ALL THE TRIBES OF THE SONS OF ISRAEL.** Rev. 7:4.

One of the most fascinating puzzles in the book of Revelation is what to do with the eye-catching number 144,000. What or whom does this group represent and what difference might that make to those of us who read this text today?

The most obvious thing in the passage, perhaps, is that the number derives from multiplying 12 times 12 by 1,000. One 12 represents the 12 tribes of Old Testament Israel; 12,000 come from each tribe, thus reaching a total of 144,000. But the Old Testament uses the Hebrew word for "thousand" (pronounced *eleph*) in a variety of ways—it is not just a number. As a number, of course, *eleph* would represent 144 groups of 1,000 people each. Related to this, the word can also designate a military unit. We would call that unit a brigade or battalion. The Romans referred to it as a cohort. A Roman cohort had about 1,000 men, 960 soldiers plus their officers.

It appears that *eleph* ("thousand") could also apply to the administrative divisions of each tribe, something like counties or shires (Ex. 18:21, 25). Ancient Israel had rulers over ten thousands (the number of men in each tribe totaled five figures [Num. 26:4–62], rulers of thousands (this would be like the county administration), and rulers of hundreds (villages), fifties and tens (extended families).

Since the nation of Israel originally descended from a single family (see Gen. 49:1-28), such administrative divisions also represent a family tree: each of the tribes could be broken down into subtribes, clans, and families. The *eleph* then would not represent a number, but the leader of a major tribal subgroup or clan. The number 144,000 would stand for 144 heads of households, each ruling a clan numbered in four figures. What is the point? However you interpret the "thousand," the number 144,000 is a symbolic way of depicting the totality of Israel's people.

So the 144,000 depict the people of God as a whole. The book of Revelation expands Israel to include those who follow the disciples of the Lamb in their allegiance to the Messiah. In the New Jerusalem (see Rev. 21) each gate represents one of the 12 tribes of Israel and each foundation stands for one of the 12 apostles (see Matt. 19:28). So the 144,000 is not some elite group that leaves most of us out. It is a symbol of everyone who has ever been faithful to the God of Israel, no matter when or where (Rev. 7:9).

Lord, I am so grateful that everyone can be a part of the totality of Israel, no matter who they are or where they are from. I commit myself to be part of your faithful end-time people.

May 21

And I heard the number of those who were being sealed, **144,000, SEALED FROM ALL THE TRIBES OF THE SONS OF ISRAEL.** Rev. 7:4.

Revelation 7:4-8 echoes Old Testament passages that number the armies of Israel (see tomorrow's devotional). The 144,000 are God's end-time army. But it is a different kind of army. It doesn't win victory by forcing its will on others. Instead, the model of Christian warfare is the Lamb that was slain (Rev. 5:6). Christians overcome not by intelligence or human power, but by the blood of the Lamb (Rev. 12:11). In other words, Christian victory comes through weakness, not strength (see 2 Cor. 12:7-10).

Aleksandr Solzhenitsyn spent years resisting his captors in the Soviet gulag. He sought to achieve some semblance of control over his schedule, his food, and other matters. But when he became a Christian, he relinquished such attempts at control. In so doing he "became free of even his captor's power."

A Hezbollah leader reacted in shock when Brother Andrew offered his life in exchange for that of a prisoner. The Muslim official became Brother Andrew's friend. But observing the lack of commitment among most Christians, he later protested, "Andrew, you Christians . . . are not following the life of Jesus anymore. . . . You must go back to the book, the New Testament." What he meant was that the teaching of Jesus includes loving our enemies, something the Hezbollah leader had not experienced from Christians until he met Brother Andrew.

An army requires close cooperation to achieve success. So our lives together as Christians are an important part of our witness. The genuineness of our experience reveals itself in how we treat each other (John 13:35).

An army must be prepared for both offense and defense. Sometimes the Christian soldier can do no more than hold a position against the devil's schemes (Eph. 6:11-14). But God also issues Christians an offensive weapon: the sword of the Spirit, which is the Word of God (verse 17).

We are, therefore, called to do more than just worship and encourage each other in a church setting, waiting for the lost to come in. The 144,000 take the good news of salvation outside the walls of the church into the "highways and byways" of our communities. But Revelation makes it clear that every "offensive" takes place in weakness, trusting in the power and the presence of our Lord.

Lord, I wish I were bolder in witness. It is not that I am ashamed of You, but that I am afraid that people will think differently of me. Help me to remember that in humiliation and weakness I am following Your steps. I have nothing to fear, because Your path leads to victory.

And I heard the number of those who were being sealed, **144,000,** SEALED FROM ALL THE TRIBES OF THE SONS OF ISRAEL. *From the tribe of Judah 12,000 were sealed, from the tribe of Reuben 12,000, from the tribe of Gad 12,000, from the tribe of Asher 12,000, from the tribe of Naphtali 12,000, from the tribe of Manasseh 12,000, from the tribe of Simeon 12,000, from the tribe of Levi 12,000, from the tribe of Issachar 12,000, from the tribe of Zebulun 12,000, from the tribe of Joseph 12,000, from the tribe of Benjamin 12,000.* REV. 7:4-8.

Richard Bauckham, a British New Testament scholar, has argued convincingly that this passage echoes the Old Testament idea of a military census. Israel numbered its tribes to determine the nation's potential military strength. The count was limited to males of military age (Num. 1:3, 19-46; 26:1-51; 2 Sam. 24:1-9, etc.). The 144,000 in Revelation thus consist of males from the 12 tribes of Israel (Rev. 14:4).

The repeated formula "from the tribe of . . ." particularly echoes the census of Numbers 1 as Israel organized for the conquest of the Promised Land. That census provided the model for the eschatological war in the Dead Sea scrolls (1QM), as well as the book of Revelation. The number of the Israelite army in Revelation 7 is clearly symbolic, as are the dimensions of the New Jerusalem. The 144,000 represent the totality of Israel arrayed in opposition to the forces of evil (Rev. 9:16; 17:14; 19:11-21). In other words, Revelation describes the spiritual issues of the end-time in military terms.[58]

The 2003 invasion of Iraq was the most technologically advanced military engagement in history. With the wonder of stealth technology, cruise missiles, and GPS-guided munitions, it almost seemed as if one could wage battle with the push of a button. But territory is not considered taken until occupied with the very low-tech presence of infantry. They sleep on the ground, carry their own food, and find themselves closest to the fighting. Without their presence land would not change hands—there would just be the destruction of distant targets.

A similar principle appears in the spreading of the gospel today. While mass media and the Internet can play a role in reaching people, it is still the infantry, God's faithful people making disciples one by one, that proves to be the decisive difference. Just as no amount of bombardment can replace the soldier, so no amount of media can substitute for the faithful witness. If you have enlisted in God's infantry, you are irreplaceable. The Lord has commissioned you to go make disciples of the nations. Television and radio can't do that for you.

Lord, I want to make a difference in the real world. Touch my heart with someone's need today.

May 23

After these things I looked carefully, and a large multitude, which no one was able to count, from **EVERY NATION AND TRIBE AND PEOPLE AND LANGUAGE,** *was standing before the throne and before the Lamb, having dressed in white robes and having palm branches in their hands.* Rev. 7:9.

The people of God incorporate a wide variety of ethnic, racial, and national backgrounds. The presence in eternity of people from so many different backgrounds will certainly be a challenge. But this amazing melting pot will work because of the marvelous gospel of God's grace to all, without exception.

His people will model how they relate to others on His treatment of them. The redeemed will learn to appreciate the differences in others rather than feel threatened by them. In eternity such characteristics will produce joy and excitement rather than conflict and irritation. It is people who differ from me that bring unique and enriching things into my life.

A story tells of a water bearer in India who had two large pots, each hung on the ends of a pole that he carried across his neck.[59] One of the pots had a crack in it and always arrived only half full, while the other pot always delivered a full portion of water. For a full two years this went on daily, with the bearer delivering only one and a half pots full of water to his house. The perfect pot was proud of its accomplishments. But the poor cracked pot felt miserable that it was able to accomplish only half of what it had been made to do.

Finally the cracked pot spoke to the water bearer by the stream. "I am ashamed of myself, and I want to apologize to you," it said. "Because of my flaw the water leaks out along the path, I deliver only half a load, and you don't get full value from your efforts."

"Did you notice that flowers grew only on your side of the path," the man said, "but not on the other pot's side? That's because I have always known about your flaw, and I planted flower seeds on your side of the path. Every day while we walk back, you've watered them. For two years I have been able to pick these beautiful flowers to decorate the table. Without you being just the way you are, there would not be this beauty to grace the house."

Each of us has our own unique flaws. But God can use and even transform our cracks and imperfections to enrich others. And we can learn to appreciate their flaws as well. That's what heaven will be like. And heaven will begin for us here to the extent that we value the difference that God's variety makes in our lives. After all, if the Creator had made us all the same, how boring would that be?

Lord, may I recognize the beauty that You see in the incredible diversity of Your creation. Help me to transform irritations into joy and differences into blessings.

After these things I looked carefully, and a large multitude, which no one was able to count, from every nation and tribe and people and language, was standing before the throne and before the Lamb, having dressed in white robes and having palm branches in their hands. And they cried out with a loud voice, saying, **"SALVATION** *to our God, who is sitting on the throne, and to the Lamb."* REV. 7:9, 10.

Salvation is an issue Christians like to disagree about. While the subject should be our greatest delight, we find ways to argue about it. I recently wrote about the subject of forgiveness of sins in the Gospel of John. Someone called to tell me that I was wrong. Sins don't get forgiven—people do! She pointed to the text: "Your sins are forgiven *unto you*" (Mark 2:9). I pointed out that in another place (Matt. 26:28) Jesus did talk about the forgiveness of sins. I have no problem with her point except that the biblical witness is richer than that.

The word "salvation" in the Bible, for example, is not a precise term—it is a metaphor, an illustration. In fact, it is one of many biblical metaphors about getting right with God. Such metaphors usually describe a problem and a solution. For example, "salvation" is a metaphor from the world of rescue missions. Describing the sin problem in such terms as "lost" or "taken prisoner," it depicts the solution as being "rescued" or "saved." Anyone who has ever been lost in the forest can relate to this metaphor.

From the perspective of the medical world, if we speak of the human condition as being "sick" in sin, the solution is to find "healing" (Mark 5:34; Luke 7:50—in Greek the word for "healing" is the same as the verb for "salvation"!) And using imagery from the banking world, we portray sin as a "debt" that we owe. What we need, then, is "forgiveness." In sanctuary terms, the sin problem has to do with "defilement," being dirty. The solution, in that case, is "cleansing." To portray the sin problem as the result of unfulfilled hunger calls for feeding on the Bread of Life.

To state the problem in legal terms, sin is "condemnation"—a guilty verdict in court that requires "justification," a verdict of acquittal. And looking at sin as enmity with God calls for "reconciliation." Spiritual "slavery" demands freedom.

What God was doing in the Bible was not describing the matter of salvation in precise, Western, scientific terms. Instead He was inspiring people to use language from everyday life to illustrate His plan of salvation. The beauty of all this is that the Bible has a metaphor for every situation. It would be a tragic thing if we required everyone to be satisfied with our pet metaphor. The broader the biblical net, the greater the number of people that can find their way to God!

Lord, thank You for the wide variety of metaphors with which You reach out to us. You express Your love in so many ways that I can't miss it! I am so grateful.

May 25

And all the angels standing around the throne and the elders and the four living creatures fell down upon their faces before the throne and **WORSHIPPED GOD,** *saying, "Blessing and glory and wisdom and thanks and honor and power and strength to our God for ever and ever. Amen." REV. 7:11, 12.*

The seminary where I work has an annual retreat in which we head out to some country place, hear some things from a significant speaker, and just generally hang out and fellowship with each other. A couple adults usually accompany us to care for the children. Toward the close of one retreat a dozen years or so ago, the leader of the children's program came up to me and asked, "I understand that you are home-schooling your children."

"Yes," I replied.

"Are you teaching at the graduate level?" he asked (our oldest was 10 years old at the time).

"What do you mean?" I asked, somewhat flustered.

"Well, your 10-year-old keeps giving graduate-level answers to biblical questions," he responded. "I can't believe she's only 10." Music to a father's heart.

"Oh, and there's one more thing you need to know," he went on. "I asked the kids who their hero was, the absolutely greatest person they knew, and different ones said athletes or movie stars. Then your daughter said, 'My father.'"

It hit like a bullet in my chest. Do you think I was proud? Hey, what a great father I am! Not at all. I was humbled and felt so unworthy of such adoration. But the great thing about it was the way that report bonded my heart to my daughter. I love her so much. I don't ever want to disappoint her. Her adoration is food for my soul. Nothing else could take its place.

People sometimes wonder why God "demands" worship. Is He full of pride? Does He need constantly to hear praise in order to feel good about Himself? No, I think He longs for our adoration the way any father seeks to have his children admire and love him. God could be self-sufficient, but He has a tender heart. His love makes Him vulnerable to those He loves. He is like a mother delighted to receive her child's offering of dandelions. A cleansed leper who returned to give thanks, for example, especially moved Jesus.

Yes, God does want our worship, but not because of arrogance or pride. He seeks it because He has chosen to put His heart in a place where he needs us. He needs it because our love makes a difference within Him. As Augustine put it, "God thirsts to be thirsted after." [60]

Lord, I sense a bit of the joy You feel when I come to You in prayer and adoration. I choose to place Your need at the top of my agenda today.

And one of the elders asked me, "Who are these dressed in white robes and where have they come from?" And I said to him, "My lord, you know." And he said to me, "These are the ones who are coming out of **THE GREAT TRIBULATION,** *and they have washed their robes and made them white in the blood of the Lamb."* REV. 7:13, 14.

God's end-time believers overcome by the suffering and victory of the Lamb rather than by armed resistance. Christ reveals His power more clearly through the broken than through the powerful and the talented. The humility of a Saint Francis advances His kingdom further than the temporal power of the popes who promoted the Crusades. A Christian faith that stands up for the weak and the powerless is far more effective than one that brandishes its wealth and political clout.

Some homeless teenagers, who grew up on the streets of Philadelphia, beat a young Korean to death. He was a Christian doing graduate studies at the University of Pennsylvania. At the time of the crime the victim had just mailed a letter to his family at home in Korea. The parents traveled to the United States for the trial and sat silently throughout. As the trial drew to a close, they asked for one opportunity to speak. The judge granted their request right after the reading of the guilty verdict and before the sentencing.

The parents approached the judge's bench, and to the stunned amazement of the audience, they knelt down before the judge. They begged the judge not to carry out the penalty he had in mind, but instead to release their son's murderers into their custody, so that they could give them the home and the care that they had never had.

"We are Christians," they explained to the judge, "and we want to show something of the grace that we have received from God to these boys." The ones who had done so much evil to them and their son would now be on the receiving end of a grace that only God could possibly inspire.

The judge, whom newspaper reporters claimed had a reputation for being hard and unemotional, had tears in his eyes when he said, "I'm so sorry, but that is not how our system of justice works!"

By their forgiveness, these parents offered a powerful testimony of a kingdom that is utterly different from those of our world. It is a kingdom whose system of justice is radically unlike the ones we know, but a kingdom open to anyone who dares to believe in its existence and in its radical solution to life's problems.[61]

Lord, this example of forgiving grace deeply challenges me. Forgive my lack of forgiveness in far lesser situations. Transform my heart through the example of the Lamb.

May 27

And I said to him, "My Lord, you know." And he said to me, "These are the ones who are coming out of **THE GREAT TRIBULATION,** *and they have washed their robes and made them white in the blood of the Lamb."* REV. 7:14.

One night as a group of women met together they stumbled across the verse in Malachi 3:3 that declares that God "will sit as a refiner and purifier of silver" (NIV). They were curious about what God and a refiner of silver would have in common. After some discussion the women broke up for the evening, with one of them promising to find out more about the process of refining silver that week.

The woman made an appointment to go to a silver workshop. As she watched the silversmith hold the silver in the hottest part of the flame, she asked why he was doing it. "It is because the heat of the flame takes away all impurities," the man explained. "The hotter the flame, the purer the metal is when it comes out."

She noticed that he carefully held the silver in exactly the right spot, and he didn't once take his eyes off it.

The woman was still curious. "But how do you know when the silver is ready to come out of the flame?"

"Oh, that's easy," the refiner replied. "I know it's ready when I can see my reflection in it."[62]

The basic meaning behind the word translated "tribulation" is "pressure" or "hard circumstances." We can all relate to the idea of "great tribulation" since we have all experienced events in our lives that have brought us great stress, trauma, and pressure. When we pass through such times of tribulation it is nearly impossible to believe that anything good could come out of intense suffering. It is only with the perspective of time that we can often see God's refining hand reaching into our lives and using the pain of our hard experiences to purify us and bring us to a level of usefulness that could not have happened any other way.

Whenever I feel that I am in an unbearably "hot spot," I take comfort in the fact that my "Refiner" is holding me very carefully. Despite what it might feel like, I can be sure that He won't ever leave me alone, not even for a second. And I can rejoice in the fact that if the suffering continues longer than I think necessary, it is because He has a goal for me. By the time I am ready to be taken out of the "fire," He will be able to see His reflection in me! I don't care how hard things may become—nothing is more thrilling than the thought that when all is said and done, I will be more like Jesus!

Lord, I am tempted to ask You to take away the problems that make my life difficult right now. Instead, do whatever will best prepare the way for my future growth and usefulness.

And I said to him, "My lord, you know." And he said to me, "These are the ones who are coming out of **THE GREAT TRIBULATION,** *and they have washed their robes and made them white in the blood of the Lamb."* REV. 7:14.

I n the original language the word for tribulation *(thlipseôs)* refers to more than persecution and martyrdom. It includes such concepts as "trouble," "stress," "difficult circumstances," and "suffering" in general. Many have assumed that "the great tribulation" is a single event at the last days of earth's history. But one of the heavenly elders tells John that the great multitude of Revelation 7:9 are the ones who "are coming" out of the great tribulation. Whatever the text means by the phrase, it also pointed to something going on already in John's day, something that has continued throughout Christian history.

The book of Revelation makes a lot of sense here. No one ever gets through life without stress—without "great tribulation." Yet we often do all we can to avoid it. Because it looks like an enemy to us, we assume it can only hurt us.

The fear of tribulation reminds me of something that happened at my best friend's place. He lives in a hilltop house in the Iowa countryside. From its front steps you can see for miles in three directions. One day I drove up to the house for a visit and experienced quite a surprise. Bounding out of the house to greet me was the largest animal I'd seen running free since an elephant or two crossed the road in front of my car in Africa. Spotting it out of the corner of my eye, I thought a lion was heading for me! The beast opened its mouth and let out an immense roar that scared me half out of my wits. Upon closer inspection, however, I realized that I wasn't facing a lion—it was a 250-pound dog! The beast was Ed's St. Bernard named Gabe. Gabe turned out to be the sweetest, gentlest creature you would ever want to know. His bark is a shade short of thunder, but it is all noise and no bite!

That is what stress is like. Although we may perceive it as an enemy, what really matters is how we respond to it.[63] An automobile is useful for taking us from place to place, but out of control it is extremely dangerous. Stress out of control prematurely wears the body down and sets the stage for disease. But managed stress is actually something quite useful to our lives. Giving drive and energy to everything we do, it is the raw material that God uses to bring about His glory (John 11; 2 Cor. 3:18). Growth happens in our lives as we respond positively to the stresses of life. While we might prefer our existence to be more calm and peaceful, God knows that little growth and development will occur in the absence of stress and difficulty.

Lord, when my life seems out of control, I allow myself to get rushed and lose track of You. Help me to see the difficulties of life as pathways that You can use to help me grow and become more useful in Your service.

May 29

For this reason they are before the throne of God and **SERVE HIM DAY AND NIGHT IN HIS TEMPLE,** *and the One sitting on the throne will spread His tent over them.* REV. 7:15.

Many Americans have experienced the difference between shopping at Kmart and at Nordstrom. Merchandise clutters the aisles of Kmart, and looking for an attendant can seem like an all-day affair. On the other hand, Nordstrom is a store chain with a reputation for quality merchandise and exceptional service, even though its prices may not compare with other popular chains. The attendants are polite and knowledgeable and carry you through the shopping experience with aplomb.

A friend of mine recently moved from California, where Nordstrom and Kmart were two prominent choices, to the Philippines, where shopping is often a very different world than that of California. Shortly after his arrival in the Philippines he discovered the limitations of even the legendary Nordstrom. He described his experience in a very large Filipino department store called SM as almost "otherworldly."

South Mall in Manila has an SM store twice the size of most Wal-Marts. As Jim and his family entered the store they immediately noticed the extremely large number of uniformed attendants standing about every 20 feet throughout the store. At one point he counted 14 in about a 20-foot radius. If you even dared to approach the extremely well-stocked and organized merchandise, two or three of them would immediately converge to help you in every way possible. Such immediate attention was rather unsettling at first, but after recovering from the initial shock, Jim was able to purchase some much-needed items.[64]

The people of God will one day "serve" God day and night in the heavenly temple. But the best place to practice for that heavenly status is right here and right now. Scripture tells us that the acts of kindness and service that we bestow on others here and now God accepts as if done to Jesus Himself (Matt. 25:34-46).

Finding the balance between genuine, helpful service and annoying intrusiveness requires much experience and a strong dose of the Spirit's guidance. Does the person we wish to serve desire a Kmart, Wal-Mart, Nordstrom, or SM department store type of experience? But when the love of Jesus genuinely drives our service, we can be confident that much good will be done. And in the process of serving others we will learn how to serve God more fully.

Lord, I choose the attitude of a servant today. May others find joy and help in my presence.

For this reason they are before the throne of God and serve Him day and night in His temple, and **THE ONE SITTING ON THE THRONE WILL SPREAD HIS TENT OVER THEM.** REV. 7:15.

To truly appreciate what our passage today is saying you need a sense of the ancient setting. For me, spending time in a tent is "roughing it." I might do it for a change of pace, but I wouldn't want to live like that every day. My youngest daughter is different. As I mentioned in an earlier devotional, she recently spent eight straight days backpacking in the Upper Peninsula of Michigan—*in February!* During that month in Michigan most of us stay outside just for a moment. She was outside the whole time, sleeping in "tepees" at night with a small portable gas-burning stove. For me that's a little too much adventure! And I doubt that was the kind of tenting experience our text had in mind.

I came close to understanding the passage, however, when I visited Petra in the country of Jordan. It is a red rock area similar in appearance to the national parks of Utah. The visit begins with about a two-mile hike that includes a twisting trail through a narrow canyon. You come out of the canyon into a vast open space surrounded by cliffs with all kinds of ancient dwellings carved right out of them! The view is exciting, but the sun beats down on you, and water is rather scarce back in there. And visiting the sites involves some stiff up-and-down hiking.

After climbing 1,000 feet to the "high place," we returned to the central valley around noon, hungry and thirsty and at least a two-mile walk from the last sign of civilization. As we passed a Bedouin tent, a man at the front beckoned us in. At first we were reluctant, not sure what we were getting into, but when we saw some of our colleagues already inside, my family and I went in too. The tent itself consisted of black hides stretched over a frame, but beautiful carpets covered the ground, and we saw lovely cushions to lean on. The man offered us lunch and cold drinks. Believe it or not, I think I had a Sprite in the middle of nowhere! In that heat and dryness it was a joy to come inside for a cool drink and delicious food. But best of all was shade from the sun, and the most wonderful, soft cushions on which to rest aching muscles.

Revelation 7 tells us that God will "spread His tent over us" in the intense noonday heat of the troubles we face both now and when the end-time comes. This text offers us an image for hard times. When life gets tough, God provides a cooling tent in the knowledge that nothing happens to us that cannot serve a purpose in the larger picture (Rom. 8:28). And in the searing fires of the end, His cooling tent will be a comforting refuge.

Lord, at times I have thought that the hard things of my life meant that You didn't care. Help me to experience Your cooling shade in the challenges that I will face today.

May 31

THEY WILL NOT HUNGER ANYMORE, NEITHER WILL THEY THIRST ANYMORE. THE SUN WILL NOT BEAT DOWN ON THEM, NEITHER ANY HEAT, *because the Lamb who is in the middle of the throne will shepherd them and lead them to the springs of living water. And God will wipe every tear from their eyes.* REV. 7:16, 17.

I will never forget the Valley of the Kings! I was visiting Egypt with a group of graduate students. Since it rarely rains in Egypt, most parts of the country are lush and green within three to five miles of the Nile River, but beyond that stretches harsh desert. The soil is a fine powder with hardly even a weed!

To get to the Valley of the Kings we crossed to the west side of the Nile in a boat and then traveled several miles by bus until we were outside the irrigation zone. It was about 50°C (122°F) in the valley and dry as a bone. We visited the tomb of King Tut and several others that day.

Since the tombs are artificial caves it was a relief to enter them for a while. But we soon discovered that visitors bring their own humidity into the tombs. The high humidity overwhelms the cooler temperatures underground. So over several hours the combination of high heat outside and high humidity inside wore us down, until we were tired and extremely thirsty.

When we had gotten back onto our bus, we would have liked nothing better than to head straight back to our air-conditioned hotel. But it was not to be. The driver insisted on taking us to his favorite alabaster shop (no doubt for the kickbacks he would receive from every purchase we made). Grumpily we entered the shop.

Suddenly, in a dark corner of the shop, I spotted a small refrigerator with a Sprite sign on it. The glass top revealed dozens of bottles inside! I quickly purchased one and drank it down in an instant. Then I purchased another, and another, and still another. It seemed that I could not stop. Our group cleaned out the entire refrigerator in a matter of minutes.

Scholars have noticed that descriptions of heaven in the book of Revelation are mostly negative. Rather than explaining what heaven will be like, it tells us what it won't be like. It won't be a place where we will be tired, hungry, and thirsty. Nor will it be a place like the Valley of the Kings, where oppressive heat bore down on us. There won't be any more tears there. The life of heaven means the absence of everything that harms or makes us miserable. And if it doesn't have a Sprite machine in the corner when we need it, it will have something even better!

I pray, dear Lord, that You would keep my mind focused on the incredible future You have in store, and on the fact that my life can be different now in the light of that future.

June 1

AND WHEN HE OPENED THE SEVENTH SEAL *there was silence in heaven for about a half hour.* REV. 8:1.

This is probably the best place to review Revelation 4-7 and think briefly about the implications of the big picture.

Chapter 4—Here we have a general description of the heavenly throne room with no particular point in time in mind.

Chapter 5—The scene moves to a decisive event. A crisis gets averted in heaven when the Lamb that was slain proves worthy to take the scroll and break its seals.

Chapter 6—Seven further events, each tied to the breaking of one of the seven seals, closes with the climax of earth's history in the sixth and seventh seals.

Chapter 7—Two visionary groups depict the answer to the question of Revelation 6:17: "Who is able to stand?"

The best interpretation of these chapters appears in Revelation 3:21. It contains the essence of Revelation 4-7 in advance. Verse 21 mentions the Father's throne (cf. Rev. 4), Jesus joining His Father on His throne (cf. Rev. 5), and His people gathering with Jesus on the throne (cf. Rev. 7:15-17). God gives this incredible promise to all who "overcome." That is what Revelation 6 is all about—the struggle of God's people to overcome from the time of the cross until the Second Coming.

Sitting with Jesus on His throne implies power, but the image has something even more exciting in it. It is about squeezing together on a throne!

While my family has chosen to live without television reception, we do enjoy a video now and then. In the living room we have a TV monitor and the appropriate players that pipe the sound through six speakers. The room has a couch, a love seat, and an armchair available for family and friends. I love to cuddle up with my wife on the couch and watch a video together. The sense of shared experience and touch makes for real bonding.

But my wife has a strange preference (it seems to me). Every so often she wants us to squeeze together into the armchair. That is really, *really* close. Although my muscles cramp up and circulation gets cut off, it does wonders for our relationship!

I see something like that in the image of Revelation 3:21. Jesus not only offers us a place of importance and purpose, but holds out to us a relationship that is really close and will never end. The greatest Person in the universe wants to spend really intimate time with me at His place. That makes me want to "overcome" more than anything—motivation enough for a lifetime!

Lord, I am humbled by the awesome promise You have made to us. I will trust in You to see me through all the way to Your throne!

June 2

And when he opened the seventh seal there was **SILENCE IN HEAVEN FOR ABOUT A HALF HOUR.** . . . *And another angel came and* **STOOD UPON THE ALTAR, HAVING A GOLDEN CENSER.** **MUCH INCENSE WAS GIVEN TO HIM** *in order that he might add it to the prayers of all the saints upon the golden altar which is before the throne. And the smoke of the incense, along with the prayers of the saints, went up from the hand of the angel before God. And* **THE ANGEL TOOK THE CENSER AND FILLED IT WITH THE FIRE OF THE ALTAR AND THREW IT TO THE EARTH.** *And there were thunders and noises and lightnings and an earthquake. And the* **SEVEN ANGELS WHO HAD THE SEVEN TRUMPETS** *prepared to blow them.* Rev. 8:1-6.

It was a typical morning in the Temple of Jerusalem around the time of Jesus. The priests were sleeping in second-floor chambers above the colonnade surrounding the outer court of the Temple. Shortly after the rooster crowed, the officer of the day knocked on the door. He conducted the casting of lots to determine those who would do the various duties of the daily service.

At daybreak they brought a lamb to the outer court. While one priest prepared to slaughter the lamb, another entered the Temple to clear the ashes from the altar of incense and relight the lamps inside the holy place (cf. Rev. 1:12-16). The opening of the great entrance door into the Temple (cf. Rev. 4:1) was the signal to slay the lamb (cf. Rev. 5:6-10). Priests then brought the body parts of the lamb to the altar of burnt offering and poured out its blood at the base of the altar (cf. Rev. 6:9-11).

The appointed priest then took the golden censer (cf. Rev. 8:3-5). It was like a frying pan with a long handle and had a lid on it. The priest filled it with coals from the hottest part of the fire on the altar of burnt offering (cf. verse 3). He then entered the open door of the Temple and arranged the coals of fire on the altar of incense. At the time commanded by the officer of the day, he added incense to the fire on the altar (cf. verse 4).

At this decisive point in the service three things happened. Someone threw a shovel down (cf. verse 5) between the altar of burnt offering and the entrance to the Temple. A break in the singing of the Temple choir produced a moment of silence (cf. verse 1). And during that moment of silence seven priests would blow seven trumpets (cf. verses 2, 6).[65]

John based the first third of the book of Revelation on the *tamid*, the daily sacrifice in the Temple. The incense represents the righteousness of Christ applied to the prayers of the saints throughout the Christian Era. This scene assures us that the perfect righteousness of Christ covers our mistakes and even the inadequacy of our good deeds.

Lord, thank You for the assurance that I can be right with You today, no matter how inadequate I may feel.

And I saw the seven angels who have stood before God, and **SEVEN TRUMPETS WERE GIVEN TO THEM.** Rev. 8:2.

One day my friend Jim found himself in Beijing, China, desperately needing a size 11 shoe. Now, getting a size 11 shoe is not a problem in North America or Europe, but it can prove an almost hopeless task in China. Jim browsed around in a large open market that contained many stalls with brand-new shoes, but none of them fit.

At one particular shop Jim finally found a pair of shoes that did fit somewhat, but were not to his liking. The salesperson pleaded with him to buy the shoes and kept coming down in price. Politely Jim thanked him and tried to walk away. The salesperson grabbed his arm tightly and with another tremendous drop in price implored him to purchase the shoes.

After several minutes he escaped the man's grasp and went looking further down the aisle. To his mild amusement, the salesman followed him with the shoes in hand (which had now come down to about $8). Finally Jim bought another pair from the man to end the whole episode.[66] If the man had not been so persistent, Jim would not have bought the shoes. What does this have to do with the seven trumpets?

The concept of trumpets has a rich background in the Old Testament. Six Hebrew and two Greek words are translated as "trumpet" or "blow the trumpet." Of 134 uses in the Greek Old Testament, 75 are in the context of worship, 33 refer to battle situations, and 10 warn that an enemy is approaching (Eze. 33).

The most important of these references is Numbers 10:8-10. The passage tells us that trumpets were sacred instruments whether used in worship or in battle. They called on God to remember His covenant. When He heard the trumpet's call, He would protect and defend His people in battle (verse 9). And as priests blew trumpets over the sacrifices of Hebrew worship, God "remembered" His people and forgave their sins (verse 10).

Thus whenever the priests sounded the trumpets God acted. So the blowing of trumpets was a symbol of covenant prayer. When God's people pray on the basis of His promises, He will respond. He will deliver them from human enemies and also from sin.

On the surface the seven trumpets sound like a litany of war and disaster. But at a deeper level they portray a spiritual concept. They symbolize God's people calling for Him to right the wrongs on this earth. And like the shoe salesman in Beijing, it pays to be persistent.

Lord, help me to renounce retaliation in my everyday life. Help me, instead, to trust You to do what is right and deal with my "enemies" if that becomes necessary.

June 4

Another angel came and stood upon the altar, having a golden censer. And much **INCENSE** *was given to him in order that he might add it to the prayers of all the saints upon* **THE GOLDEN ALTAR** *before the throne. And the smoke of the altar went up, along with the prayers of the saints, out of the hand of the angel before God.* REV. 8:3, 4.

A pastor on vacation rented a sailboat in the Caribbean. He and his family greatly enjoyed the combination of heat from the sun and the bracing coolness of the ocean breezes. It was a wonderful respite from the daily pressures of ministry back home. One day they beached the boat on a small, sandy island with palm trees. Soon a couple who had anchored a gigantic air-conditioned yacht a few yards from shore joined them. After the initial pleasantries, the pastor identified his occupation. But while the couple was clearly secular, they didn't seem fazed by that. Instead they invited the pastor and his family to join them for supper on the yacht.

The minister looked forward to an opportunity to witness about the difference Jesus can make in life, even for those who seem to have it all. All through the meal he waited for the golden opportunity to share, but it never came. Soon the sun began to go down and he knew that he had to get back to the sailboat and return to the resort before it got dark.

The family said goodbye to the couple and went down the ladder to the sailboat tied alongside. After his wife and children made it to the sailboat, the pastor headed down the rungs of the ladder. Just at that moment the woman of the boat leaned over the rail, looked down at him and asked, "What does it mean to be a Christian?" He looked up, knowing that the timing of the question meant he'd better answer in one minute or less!

"Religion is spelled D-O," he replied. "Christianity is spelled D-O-N-E. Christian faith isn't about what we do for God—it is about what God has done for us." In other words, because of the cross, human beings become acceptable to God. They can find meaning and purpose in life because God has already acted to make it possible.

That's what the incense at the altar is all about. The incense originated from the altar of sacrifice. It is the sacrifice that makes the incense possible. The cross is the foundation of everything God does for His people. Because of what happened on the cross, Jesus can provide forgiveness. In the daily ritual of the Old Testament sanctuary the incense constantly hovered over the camp, covering the people and their sins. When we fall short of the glory of God, the incense of Christ's righteousness shields our lives as well.

Lord, thank You for the perfect acceptance available to me today in Christ. May I sense the presence of the "increase" of Your righteousness in all that I do.

Another angel came and stood upon the altar, having a golden censer. And much incense was given to him in order that he might add it to **THE PRAYERS OF ALL THE SAINTS** *upon the golden altar before the throne. And the smoke of the altar went up, along with* **THE PRAYERS OF THE SAINTS,** *out of the hand of the angel before God.* REV. 8:3, 4.

D oes God still answer prayers the way He used to? Does He talk to people the way He did to Abraham? Early one morning a voice awakened Abraham and said, "Take your only son up to that hilltop north of you, stab him to death, and then set fire to him." If you had been Abraham, would you have done it?

How did he know that the strange request had come directly from God? I suspect that Abraham, during his long life, had done a lot of walking and talking with the Lord. He had come to know when God was communicating with him and when it was simply his own inner feelings or some other influence. Abraham had experimented with God until he had figured out when it was God speaking and when it was not.

Does God still speak to people today? I have employed the following process. When I am ready to pray, I take a pencil and paper with me. Finished with my prayer, I remain in position and wait quietly. Then I write down whatever thoughts and ideas come to my mind. A large percentage of them are usually irrelevant to my life at that point. But some of them seem more promising. I pass these ideas through the filter of Scripture, as far as I understand it, and eliminate all ideas contrary to God's Word. I test the rest of the ideas in experience and observe the results. If I feel impressed to visit someone, I go! Or if I'm urged to make a phone call, I do it! Whether or not something is from God can be discerned by the results of trying out the impressions that come to us.

A student who heard my suggestion decided to try it. After prayer he felt impressed that a woman in Canada needed a phone call. Since his wife was in Canada at the time, he called her and asked her to contact the woman. She tried several times but didn't get through. My student urged his wife to keep trying. The next time she did, the woman picked up the phone.

"My husband died three days ago," she said, "and I just returned from the doctor who diagnosed me with cancer. I was just sitting here by the phone wondering if anyone cared!"

Needless to say, that student and I believe that God still answers prayer.

Lord, touch my heart today with anything You would have me do. I am open to Your leading.

June 6

Another angel came and stood upon the altar, having a golden censer. And much incense was given to him in order that he might add it to the prayers of all the saints upon the golden altar before the throne. And the smoke of the altar went up, along with **THE PRAYERS OF THE SAINTS,** *out of the hand of the angel before God.* Rev. 8:3, 4.

A ship wrecked during a storm, and only two men survived. They were able to swim to a small desertlike island. The two survivors, not knowing what else to do, agreed that they had no other recourse but to pray to God. They decided to make a contest out of it. To find out whose prayer was more powerful, they agreed to divide the territory between them and stay on opposite sides of the island.

The first thing they prayed for was food. The next morning the first man saw a fruit-bearing tree on his side of the island, and he was able to eat its fruit. The other man's parcel of land remained barren. After a week, the first man was lonely and prayed for a wife. The next day another ship sank just offshore, and the only survivor was a woman who swam to his side of the island. But on the other side of the island things remained the same.

The first man prayed for a house, clothes, and more food. Like magic, he received all of them. However, the second man still had nothing. Finally, the first man prayed for a ship, so that he and his wife could leave the island. In the morning he found a ship docked at his side of the island.

The first man boarded the ship with his wife and decided to leave the second man on the island. He considered the other man unworthy to receive God's blessings, since none of his prayers had received any answer. As the ship was about to leave, the first man heard a voice from heaven booming, "Why are you leaving your companion on the island?"

"My blessings are mine alone, since I was the one who prayed for them," the first man answered. "His prayers were all unanswered, so he does not deserve anything."

"You are mistaken!" the voice rebuked him. "He had only one prayer, which I answered. If not for that, you would not have received any of my blessings."

"Tell me," the first man asked the voice, "what did he pray for that I should owe him anything?"

"He prayed that all your prayers would be answered." [67]

Though we hate to admit it, selfishness often taints our prayers. The prayers of true saints demonstrate the self-sacrificing concern for others that Jesus showed on the cross.

Lord, purify my prayers today with the incense of Your righteousness.

And the angel took the censer and **FILLED IT WITH THE FIRE OF THE ALTAR AND THREW IT TO THE EARTH.** *And there were* **THUNDERS AND NOISES AND LIGHTNINGS AND AN EARTHQUAKE.** *And the seven angels who had* **THE SEVEN TRUMPETS** *prepared to blow them.* Rev. 8:5, 6.

At 8:00 p.m. on October 30, 1938, most American families gathered around their radios to listen to the number one program in the country, Edgar Bergen and his dummy sidekick Charlie McCarthy. But on another network others settled in to hear *Mercury Theatre on the Air.* Orson Welles began the program with a fake weather forecast followed by music from a dance band. He interrupted the music with a series of news flashes about explosions on the planet Mars, followed by the arrival of a strange cylinder just outside Trenton, New Jersey.

Ten minutes into his program Edgar Bergen needed a drink of water, so they took a break in the live broadcast. While a vocalist sang, many listeners turned their dials to see what else was on. Stumbling onto *Mercury Theatre on the Air,* they were drawn in by the seemingly live news flashes. The program included fake interviews with crowd noise and police sirens in the background. As if they were actually happening, news reports told of fearful creatures trashing New Jersey neighborhoods and fields, as well as the deaths of police and civilians. The aliens from Mars were attacking everything and everyone. Nothing seemed able to stop them.

The imagination of the listeners began running wild. Mass panic spread across the nation. Ministers interrupted and dismissed church services. People contemplated suicide rather than let themselves fall into the clutches of the invading monsters. The program duped even highly educated scientists.

In Fayetteville, Indiana, the Nickless family became concerned for their lives. They collected the children and drove the mile and a half over to Grandfather's house. Grandpa Nickless was a solid man with solid values. He would know what to do. By the time they arrived at Grandpa's they were almost hysterical. They shouted, "Turn on the radio!" Grandpa listened for a bit and then began to laugh. He told them that it was a hoax—that it was just a radio program.

"How do you know?" they shouted.

Picking up his Bible, he said, "According to this, the world won't end like that." Then he reminded them of Revelation and its outcome. After a while the Nickless family calmed down and returned home to put the children to bed. Grandpa was right.[68]

Strange things have occurred and will yet occur in this world. The trumpets of Revelation don't hide the premonition of disaster. But John did not write the book to terrify us. Instead it assures us that no matter how bad things get, it will turn out all right in the end.

Lord, calm my worries and my fears with assurance from Your Word.

June 8

And the first angel blew his trumpet, and it was that **HAIL AND FIRE MIXED WITH BLOOD WERE THROWN TO THE EARTH. A THIRD OF THE EARTH WAS BURNED UP,** *a third of the trees were burned up, and all the green grass was burned up.* Rev. 8:7.

If nuclear war ever breaks out, here's a suggestion on where to take cover. North of Yellowstone National Park, in a place called Paradise Valley, you will find a remarkable number of places to hide underground. In the splendid scenery of Paradise Valley one could easily overlook the clues: ventilation equipment, vaultlike doors in hillsides, a watchtower that could double as a machine gun nest. One of the shelters is called Mark's Ark, a sort of Motel 6 located 20 feet under the ground. When someone asked the builder, "Why don't you live down here?" he said, "Are you nuts? The only reason I'd come down here would be because I had to."

The first 90 feet of walking gets you through the entryway to Mark's Ark. It's cluttered with spare parts that might be useful in a long-term disaster. Next you go through a decontamination room and an engine room with a large amount of stored fuel. The main shelter is 32 feet across and 132 feet long. It has three floors and 40 bedrooms! They're individually furnished by families who plan to live in them someday, if things get really bad outside. The place even has an auxiliary shelter for pets. Dehydrated food, lentils, beans, and oatmeal pack the long corridors. The shelter also has a well-stocked clinic and a big community kitchen. "Easily feed 150," says the builder.

But why would 150 people want to go underground for a year? It started in the 1980s with predictions of nuclear war by a controversial local religious group, the Church Universal and Triumphant. The shelter craze spread to the church's neighbors. The area now has about 30 community shelters.

Today the same people talk less about the nuclear threat and more about natural catastrophes involving extreme wind, as when the earth tips on its axis. According to one potential resident, "Now if that happens, it throws the whole kilter of the air cycles off. The jet stream, instead of staying up there, could come right down on the surface, and man—300 mile-an-hour winds would just change your life entirely." In Paradise Valley they think the rest of America is woefully underprepared.[69]

A large percentage of these people are conservative Christians, who see in the trumpets natural disasters that will affect all people. But they misunderstand the text. According to Revelation, the trumpets are judgments of God that fall on unbelievers (Rev. 8:3-5; 9:4). So the best safety against the judgments of God is not a shelter in Montana, but rather obedience to the gospel of Jesus Christ.

Lord, whenever my world "caves in," help me to trust You rather than my own devisings.

And the second angel blew his trumpet, and it was that **A GREAT MOUNTAIN, BURNING WITH FIRE, WAS THROWN INTO THE SEA, AND A THIRD OF THE SEA BECAME BLOOD,** *and a third of the living creatures in the sea died, and a third of the ships were destroyed.* REV. 8:8, 9.

The fact that water turns into blood here strongly reminds us of the first plague of the Exodus (Ex. 7:19-21). Turning the Nile into blood would destroy Egypt's economy and comforts in an instance. The lifeblood of Egypt was and is the water of the Nile.

If you have ever traveled to Egypt, you know that it is a lush and productive country along the banks of the Nile, but just a few miles away from the river you will encounter some of the driest, most barren land you will see anywhere. It rains so seldom that the soil is as fine as flour and dusty in the extreme. You can hardly find a blade of weed, much less healthy crops there. In fact, the humidity is so low 10 miles from the Nile that it all but sucks the moisture right out of you. Every time I have had a chance to visit the Egyptian desert, I have had to drink a couple liters on my return or face a serious headache!

Our text contains a second clear allusion—one to God's judgment on ancient Babylon. "'I am against you, O destroying mountain, you who destroy the whole earth,' declares the Lord. 'I will stretch out my hand against you, roll you off the cliffs, and make you a burned-out mountain'" (Jer. 51:25, NIV). In Jeremiah 51 God pronounces judgment on Babylon because it has oppressed the people of God. So the second trumpet blends elements of the Old Testament judgments on both Egypt and Babylon. What is interesting is that both countries were and are flat, dry, and dependent on the great rivers that pass through them.

But if ancient Babylon was located in a flat river valley, why does this verse speak of a mountain? It is a symbolic reference. Daniel 2 depicts God's kingdom in terms of a great mountain. So Jeremiah's description suggests Babylon is a great counterfeit of God's true kingdom. This trumpet promises that God will destroy that counterfeit in the waters of its own "sea."

The symbolic judgments represented in the second trumpet may well reflect the collapse of the Roman Empire, an event still future at the time that John wrote the book of Revelation. From the point of view of the first readers the empire may have seemed invincible. But the vision assures the prophet that God marks the activities of oppressors on this earth, and He acts at the proper time.

Lord, give me the confidence that matters are still under Your control. May I not grow impatient at the pace of Your interventions.

June 10

AND THE THIRD ANGEL BLEW HIS TRUMPET, AND
A GREAT STAR, BURNING LIKE A LAMP, FELL OUT OF
HEAVEN. AND IT FELL UPON A THIRD OF THE RIVERS
AND UPON THE SPRINGS OF WATER. AND THE NAME
OF THE STAR IS CALLED WORMWOOD. AND A THIRD
OF THE WATERS BECAME WORMWOOD, AND MANY
MEN DIED FROM THE WATERS BECAUSE THEY HAD
BEEN MADE BITTER. REV. 8:10, 11.

The language of this trumpet echoes the Old Testament. The falling star, for example, reminds me of Lucifer tumbling from heaven in Isaiah 14. Lucifer, who claims to be like God, is cast out of heaven like a star falling from the sky (Rev. 8:10).

Scripture often associates a torch, or a lamp, with the Word of God (Ps. 119:105; Prov. 6:23). But here John connects it to a falling star, so it represents a counterfeit of the truth. The action of falling, then, represents spiritual decline (Rev. 2:5; Heb. 4:11). The falling star gives off light like the Word of God, but it is not the real thing.

These images are consistent with the embittering of rivers and springs that follows in our text. Rivers and springs symbolize spiritual nourishment. Just as we need physical water to keep from perishing, so we need spiritual water (the Holy Spirit— John 7:37-39; cf. Ps. 1:3) in order for our faith to survive.

When the falling star strikes the rivers and springs, however, it makes the water bitter. People come seeking the nourishing waters of the Spirit and the truth, but instead get poisoned by waters that have become bitter. In the Old Testament wormwood and bitterness are consistent symbols of apostasy and idolatry (Deut. 29:17, 18). Because the water of truth has been poisoned, that which promised life instead becomes the source of death. Bitter water cannot sustain life (Lam. 3:15, 19; Ex. 15:23).

Most of us know the frustration that comes when we buy computer software that doesn't do what we need it to do. Imagine purchasing a computer program that includes a software manual that is full of mixed-up information. It says, "If you want to accomplish this task, do thus and thus." But when you do what the manual tells you, nothing happens or the computer crashes.

Now, hopefully that has been pretty rare in your experience. But it happens frequently in the spiritual world. People encounter all kinds of false information about God and spiritual life. When they buy into it, their own spiritual software begins to malfunction, and the consequences are great.

Lord, help me to be more serious about what I believe. I don't want to have a casual faith—I want one that will survive whatever comes.

June 11

And the fourth angel sounded his trumpet, and **A THIRD OF THE SUN, A THIRD OF THE MOON, AND A THIRD OF THE STARS WERE SMITTEN,** *in order that a third of them might be darkened, and that a third of the day might not shine, nor a third of the night likewise.* Rev. 8:12.

It started as a routine trip home one night. As I came around the S curve and entered the straightaway that brings me to my street, I saw the strangest thing. There appeared to be a full moon rising above the horizon in front of me, but it looked as if someone had taken a big bite out of the left-hand side.

"Could that be a gibbous moon [the third quarter of the lunar month, when the moon begins to shrink after its full phase]?" I asked my wife, who was riding home with me.

"I don't think so," she said. "I've never seen anything like this."

Undeterred by her opinion, I tried to think of whether a gibbous moon was like a reverse crescent, or whether it "had a bite out of it," as this one did. I kept on pondering the significance of what I had seen, but when I arrived home I forgot all about it for a half-hour. Then I suddenly remembered the moon again.

"Hey, kids!" I called to my teens. "You've got to look out the front window. The moon has a bite out of it!"

They followed me out to the living room to look past the white birch in our front yard. I wasn't prepared for what I saw. No longer did the moon have a bite out of it. Instead I was looking at a half moon. ("What's the big deal, Dad?") Could the moon go through half a phase in a half hour? I ransacked the limited scientific knowledge in my brain and came up with a negative conclusion. Then I noticed that the dark part of the moon was a dull red, completing the full circle.

"I know!" I blurted out. "It must be a lunar eclipse. ["Told you so," grumbled the wife.] The earth has moved directly between the sun and the moon, and the shadow of the earth is moving across the moon." I continued watching until the white part of the moon completely vanished, leaving a dull red circle.

The best explanation of Revelation 8:12 is probably an image drawn from the eclipses of sun and moon that were widely known to the ancient world. The sun, moon, and stars symbolize the Word of God (Ps. 19; 119:105), the people of God (Dan. 12:3), and the things of heaven (Dan. 8:10) in the Old Testament. The rejection of God's Word and His ways results in spiritual darkness. But the darkness here is partial. We still have time to repent.

Lord, I want to live in the light of Your Word and Your ways. Keep me from choices that will lead me into spiritual darkness.

June 12

And the fourth angel sounded his trumpet, and a third of the sun, a third of the moon, and a third of **THE STARS** *were smitten, in order that a third of them might be darkened, and that a third of the day might not shine, nor a third of the night likewise.* REV. 8:12.

When I was 10 years old, I spent two years of savings on a telescope. I thought it was so cool to be able to look at the heavens and see such awesome things as the rings of Saturn, the craters of the moon, and the satellites of Jupiter and its colorful gas clouds. But the best thing I ever saw in my telescope was the Pleiades. In spite of the smoggy air in my neighborhood just outside New York City, the Pleiades knocked my socks off.

People sometimes refer to the Pleiades as the seven sisters. To the naked eye they appear as a small cluster of six or seven points of light. But in my telescope the Pleiades expanded to a cluster of several hundred stars sprinkled across the viewing area like so many jewels. The stars were visibly yellow, red, blue, green, and every shade in between. It was the equal of any of the royal crowns I have seen in the palaces of Europe.

After this experience I fully agreed with the psalmist, who said, "The heavens declare the glory of God" (Ps. 19:1, KJV). In viewing the heavens through my telescope I caught a glimpse of God's greatness and how much He is a lover of the beautiful. Stars also illustrated the infinity of God for Job. When Job was questioning why he had to endure so many problems, God pointed him to the stars. "Can you bind the beautiful Pleiades? Can you loose the cords of Orion? Can you bring forth the constellations in their seasons or lead out the Bear with its cubs? Do you know the laws of the heavens? Can you set up God's dominion over the earth?" (Job 38:31-33).

Our text for today speaks of a partial darkening descending over the stars and the other heavenly bodies. In a spiritual sense this would portray a time in history when events disguise or partially obliterate the true knowledge of God. Just as it is hard to imagine a world in which we can no longer see the stars, the author of Revelation is boggled by the thought of a world in which the spiritual light of God is no longer visible.

In the context of this passage we discover a God who hides Himself at times. When we take Him for granted, when we ignore the abundant blessings that He has scattered everywhere for us, He sometimes removes Himself from our view for a time. He hopes that we will remember what we are missing and long for a renewed walk with Him.

Lord, I don't want You to have to hide from me. Keep Your glorious greatness ever before me. I want to see You as You really are.

And the fourth angel sounded his trumpet, and a third of the sun, a third of the moon, and a third of the stars were smitten, in order that a third of them might be **DARKENED,** *and that a third of the day might not shine, nor a third of the night likewise.* Rev. 8:12.

Today's text speaks about a partial darkness, one that affects some people more than others and some parts of the day more than others. It is a good description of life as we experience it. The darkness of sin touches some people more than others.

A humorous story tells about two famous people. Jack Nicklaus was one of the greatest professional golfers of all time. Stevie Wonder is a popular singer distinguished by the fact that he is totally blind. The two of them supposedly got together one day, and it astounded Nicklaus to hear that Wonder was an avid golfer too.

"How can you possibly play golf when you're blind?" Nicklaus queried.

"Oh, it's not so hard, really," Stevie Wonder said. "When I tee up my ball, I have my caddie walk out the distance I usually drive and call to me from the center of the fairway. Then I hit the ball in his direction, and he calls me from where it lands. I walk over to the ball and then he moves further out in the direction I need to hit until he is standing in the center of the green. He tells me how far it is to traps and water hazards, and I hit the ball accordingly."

"That's amazing!" Nicklaus said. "But tell me something—how do you ever manage to putt?"

"Oh, that's the easy part for me. The caddie describes the tilt and speed of the green and then lies on his stomach, talking to me from right behind the hole. I just hit the ball to his voice. In fact, I think I could beat you if we played together."

"You're incredible. But there is no way you could beat me."

"Actually, I think I could," Wonder replied. "Why don't we play a round today?"

"I'm free," Nicklaus answered. "What time shall we get together?"

"How about 10:00 tonight?"

If you know anything about golf, you had a good laugh at that one. Golf is not a game most people would try at night. A teacher of mine loved to say, "In the land of the blind, one eye is king!" Well, in the darkness of night a blind man has a distinct edge over a sighted person. When the darkness of sin sweeps over the world, those who follow God will have the advantage—they will see with spiritual eyesight (cf. John 9:39-41).

Lord, help me not to limit myself to one or two ways of knowing You. Energize all my senses to be receptive to the signals You want to send me.

June 14

And I saw and I heard a vulture flying in midheaven saying with a loud voice,
"WOE, WOE, WOE, TO THOSE WHO LIVE ON THE EARTH, BECAUSE OF THE REST OF THE SOUNDS OF THE THREE ANGELS WHO ARE ABOUT TO BLOW THEIR TRUMPETS." Rev. 8:13.

The book of Revelation marks out the role of the trumpets more clearly than most people realize. The key to understanding them is Revelation 6:9-11. There the "souls under the altar" cry out, "'How long, Sovereign Lord, holy and true, until you judge *the inhabitants of the earth* and avenge our blood?'" (verse 10, NIV). The "inhabitants of the earth" are those who have persecuted and martyred God's faithful people. These "inhabitants" appear again in Revelation 8:13. The three woes of trumpets five, six, and seven fall on "the inhabitants of the earth." The seven trumpets, therefore, are judgments on those who have martyred and persecuted God's faithful people.

Revelation 8:2-6 tells us that the trumpets sound in response to the prayers of the saints, which rise up like incense from the altar (verses 3, 4). What are those prayers? They are the martyred saints (Rev. 6:9-11) calling out for justice. When those prayers reach heaven mingled with incense, judgments hurl down to the earth (Rev. 8:5, 6). The seven trumpets, therefore, carry a powerful message to those abused, neglected, and killed because of their faith. The trumpets assure them that God is actively confronting those who oppressed them. And those judgments begin already in this life.

A friend of mine was a professor at a school of medicine. A church officer pleaded with him to leave his job at great professional and financial cost to himself and work for the church, living in a small church-owned apartment. Out of love for Jesus he accepted without hesitation. He joyfully threw himself into the work of the church.

But one day my friend had a difference of opinion with the church officer. The latter felt that my friend had offended his dignity and challenged his authority. Without warning he arranged for my friend to be fired. Stunned, for several hours my friend dazedly cleaned out his desk and office. Having been a man of wealth and influence in his country, he now had no job and no source of income.

In discouragement he went home only to find the locks of the church apartment changed and all his belongings tossed out on the sidewalk, up for sale to anyone who would pass by. His wife had discovered them there and was sitting on a couch, sobbing uncontrollably. While revenge would be a thought on most people's minds, my friend decided to leave that up to God. The trumpets assure us that God marks the injustices of our world and will make them right in His time.

Lord, thank You for the assurance that everything that happens to me matters to You.

June 15

And I saw and I heard a vulture flying in midheaven saying with a loud voice,
**"WOE, WOE, WOE, TO THOSE WHO LIVE ON THE
EARTH,** *because of the rest of the sounds of the three angels who are about
to blow their trumpets." REV. 8:13.*

L adies and gentlemen, we got him," U.S. administrator Paul Bremer told
journalists in Baghdad, to loud cheers from Iraqis in the audience.
American soldiers had just found Saddam Hussein in a tiny cellar at a
farmhouse about 10 miles south of his hometown of Tikrit. Saddam was
the most wanted man on a list issued by U.S. authorities, but had not been seen
since Baghdad fell to American forces seven months before.

After receiving a tip from a member of Hussein's family, U.S. forces cordoned off
the area. Then they discovered the Iraqi strongman, responsible for the deaths of hundreds of thousands during a 24-year reign of terror, cowering in a "spider hole," a tiny
cellar. Access to the hiding place consisted of a narrow hole covered with a rug, bricks,
and dirt and about six to eight feet deep. In one last show of bravado, he announced
to his captors, "I am Saddam Hussein, president of Iraq, and I am ready to negotiate."
A quick-minded American soldier rejoined, "I bring you greetings from President
George Bush."

Video footage released by the U.S. military showed a disheveled-looking
Saddam with a long black and gray beard in custody, receiving a medical
checkup. Hussein emerged from his hiding place "very much bewildered" and
said "hardly anything at first," according to Major General Raymond Odierno.
Soon after, people began celebrating the capture of their former president in the
streets of Baghdad and the northern Iraqi city of Kirkuk by sounding their horns
and firing into the air.

The hut where Hussein had been living contained two tiny rooms. One was
a bedroom cluttered with clothes, some of them new and still in their wrappers,
and the other a kitchen with running water. In spite of his record, I felt a tinge
of sympathy for the man.[70]

Christians suffering at the hand of evil rulers should never envy the position of
those who persecute them. The seven trumpets are poured out on "those who live
on the earth," the very ones who afflicted the faithful, as described in the seals (Rev.
6:9, 10). Those who have hurt or killed the faithful people of God are marked in
the "books," and if they do not repent, they will suffer as much as or even more
than those they attacked. It isn't a pretty picture. I'd rather face the wrath of humanity than the wrath of God.

*Lord, help me not to judge reality by who is up or down in the power polls. Enable
me to see that human power is temporary and so is the suffering it causes. Lead me to trust
that You will soon make everything right.*

June 16

And the fifth angel blew his trumpet, and I saw a star, having fallen out of heaven to the earth, and the key to the pit of **THE ABYSS** *was given to him. And he opened the pit of* **THE ABYSS** *and smoke came up out of the pit, like the smoke of a great furnace. The sun and the air were darkened by the smoke from the pit.* REV. 9:1, 2.

This section of Revelation is one of the most terrifying passages in the book. A star from heaven receives a key to the abyss. The opening of the abyss results in darkness that completely blots out the sun and the atmosphere. The darkness turns out to be locusts, agents of Apollyon (Rev. 9:3, 10, 11).

We find a couple significant parallels to this passage in the Gospel of Luke. When a demon-possessed man confronted Jesus, the demons pleaded with Him not to send them back into the abyss (Luke 8:30, 31). Evidently the abyss is where the power of God confines demons, a place they don't want to go.

Further parallels occur in Luke 10:17-20. There Jesus sees Satan falling like lightning out of heaven. Nevertheless, He states, His disciples should not be alarmed. They will have authority to tread on snakes and scorpions, symbols of the power of the enemy. Their assurance of salvation will provide the confidence to confront Satan in the name of Jesus.

How far does demonic power go? Would it be wrong for Christians to worship in a place that once served for the worship of Satan? Is it always wrong to use forms of music previously employed in pagan rituals or worship?

Consider the dilemma of those who first translated the Bible into a language steeped in the worship of spirits, trees, and other magical creatures. The translators struggled to find ways to express the sublime truths of Scripture and salvation in words and expressions already loaded with profane and even demonic associations. Its pagan origins saturated every aspect of this language. But the translators went ahead anyway. I'm glad they did. That language was English.

We may feel disturbed to hear the gospel in language and musical forms that have had a checkered history. But we mustn't forget that God chose to be incarnated in human flesh in spite of all of its pagan, promiscuous, and perverted history. When the Word became flesh, however, He brought life and light to the human race. Wherever He went, the demons fled. It is not the presence of demons that condemns the human race—it is the absence of Christ.[71]

Lord, I choose to have Christ with me wherever I go. I praise You for overcoming the evil one at the cross. May the power of Satan be vanquished in my life as well.

And locusts came out of the smoke onto the earth. And they were given authority like **THE SCORPIONS OF THE EARTH** *have authority.* REV. 9:3.

I have seen only one scorpion in the wild. I was staying in a kibbutz at the edge of Jerusalem when one of them wandered through the wide-open outside door of the ballroom and headed across the floor. The fearsome stinger remained in full view the whole time, arched over the scorpion's back. A crowd gathered at a safe distance to watch its progress, wondering fearfully what to do. After a couple minutes a skittish but determined colleague of mine found a widemouthed glass, turned it upside down, and covered the scorpion on the floor with the glass. He then slipped a piece of paper between it and the floor. This way he could carefully return the creature back outside.

A story tells of a frog and a scorpion contemplating a swift river that they both needed to cross. The barrier was more of a problem to the scorpion than it was to the frog. So the scorpion asked the frog to permit it to ride on its back across the river.

"Why would I allow you to do that?" the frog demanded. "When we get halfway across the river you will sting me, and I will drown."

"Why would I do that?" the scorpion countered. "If you drown, so will I. It would be stupid for me to sting you."

Convinced by the scorpion's argument, the frog agreed to ferry the scorpion across the river. Halfway across the river the scorpion stung the frog. As both drifted down to their deaths, the frog protested, "Why did you do that? You promised!"

"I couldn't help it," the scorpion responded. "It's my nature to sting!"

While I was able to avoid it that day, I understand that the scorpion's sting is one of the most painful things a human being can endure. The excruciating pain captures one's full attention for some time. In this passage the scorpion represents the power of darkness and evil. Satan offers people enticing opportunities. He promises that if they will follow him they will have pleasures galore, wealth and fame, and everything their hearts desire.

His followers quickly discover, however, that while he may promise many things, it is his nature to torment those in his control. The enticing things he dangles—such as illicit sex, power over others, and the accumulation of things—all have consequences that lead to misery and pain. He seeks to hide their results behind a pleasant face, but let the tempted ones beware! Serving Satan leads to no joy and no future.

Lord, I am constantly bombarded with advertisements and other incentives to make choices that would lead me away from You. Share a good dose of reality with me today.

June 18

And it was told to them that they should not **HURT** *the grass of the earth or any green thing or any tree,* **ONLY THOSE WHO DID NOT HAVE THE SEAL OF GOD ON THEIR FOREHEADS.** *Rev. 9:4.*

The year was 1944. Continental Europe struggled under the domination of the Axis powers, who controlled everything from the shores of France to the plains of western Russia. The allies, mainly the United States and Great Britain, built up an enormous invasion force, filling up the southern part of England with men and equipment. Thousands of ships and landing craft assembled as an even larger number of aircraft moved into action.

On the shores of France, Belgium, and the Netherlands, German forces braced for the inevitable assault, not certain where the blow would strike. Weeks and months of bombing all along the coast preceded the invasion. Then on the sixth of June, forever to be known as D-day, the push got under way.

One of the key French cities in the path of Allied forces was Caen. The city's war museum graphically tells the story of the invasion and its impact. The British and American bombers dropped thousands of tons of bombs in and around the city. When the Allies finally marched into Caen, the bombardment had destroyed almost every building.

There were, however, a few notable exceptions. The churches of Caen, built during the Middle Ages, survived. Wartime photos attest to the fact that ancient spires still stood among the rubble. Apparently the careful construction of these ancient churches was so solid that the populace of Caen would use them as air-raid shelters during the terrible nights of bombing.

What is remarkable about Revelation 9:4 is that the locust/scorpions seem able to discern between the genuine followers of Jesus and those who only profess allegiance. The seal represents the living presence of God in His people (Eph. 4:30; 2 Tim. 2:19).

Satan's attacks will become more and more pronounced in the period before Jesus comes. The good news is that those who have their character solidly built on the foundation of Jesus Christ will not be harmed. In our own human strength we would have no chance against Satan, but those in living relationship with Jesus are shielded from the worst of the devil's devices.

We construct spiritual foundations through time spent each day with the Lord, in the study of His Word, and in prayer and in ministry to others. There is no more significant way to use our time as we approach the last days of earth's history.

You are the Master Builder, Lord. Strengthen my spiritual foundations today for the challenges yet to come.

And it was given to them [the locust/scorpions] that they should not kill them [the unsealed], but rather that they should be tormented for five months. And their torment was like **THE TORMENT OF A SCORPION, WHEN IT STINGS A MAN.** *And in those days men will seek death, but they will not find it.* **THEY WILL LONG TO DIE,** *yet death will flee away from them.* Rev. 9:5, 6.

Recently my wife and I were in Australia. She wanted some video footage of a new "down under" hairdo she had just received, and we decided it would be fun to put her behind a jungle bush and in front of a tree in which a kookaburra (the famous Australian "mocking" bird) was calmly sitting.

My wife posed like a model, the kookaburra visible just above her head. Suddenly she disappeared from view. I made some wisecrack or other into the camera and continued taping. Suddenly Pamella started shrieking.

"Ants, ants—they're biting me. Help! Get them off of me!"

Knowing my wife's tendency to joke for the camera, I sauntered unhurriedly in her direction. As I came around the jungle bush I suddenly noticed that the ground seemed to be moving. Ants swarmed between the bush and the kookaburra's tree. My wife raised one leg of her slacks and was swatting wildly at her shoe and the skin of her leg.

"Help! Do something!"

At last I went into action. "Get away from here! Quick! Get out of this spot!"

She started running with me half dragging her to the laundry room about 20 yards away. There we slammed the door for privacy and pulled the pants off. As I snapped the pants like a whip, ants scattered onto the floor, where we went after them with a vengeance. After we had finished off all the ants that appeared on the floor, we tended to six or seven large welts on my wife's right leg. Bull ants, whose bite burns like a flame, had attacked her. Only after the intensive application of anesthetic did the fire in her legs die out. For a few moments, at least, she experienced as severe a torment as she had ever known. Had the "fire" lasted for hours or days, she would probably have felt just like the tormented ones of Revelation 9.

The basic message of the text is that those under Satan's control may think that they have real freedom, but in reality they have submitted to a tyrant that makes Hitler or Idi Amin appear benign. The torment of stinging insects illustrates how enslavement to Satan sucks the joy out of life and eventually makes even death seem attractive.

Lord, help me to just say no to the attractions of sin. May I clearly see its potential enslavement and torment whenever temptation comes.

June 20

And the locusts were like horses prepared for war in appearance, and on their heads was something like golden crowns, and their faces were like the faces of men. Their hair was like the hair of women, and their teeth were like lions' teeth. And their breastplates were like breastplates of iron, and the sound of their wings was like the sound of horse-drawn chariots rushing into battle. REV. 9:7-9.

Careful study has unearthed no clear goal or theological purpose in this passage. It is as if John has piled one image onto another for the simple purpose of heightening the terror of the overall picture. So what, then, is the point? What spiritual lesson can we learn from horrific images such as the above? And what role can disasters possibly play in our daily walk with Him?

If nothing else, disasters turn our minds back to God and His Word. The Creator has designed us as human beings. The Bible, therefore, is like a software manual. It tells us where we came from, how we were made, and how we function the best. The best software manual, of course, comes from the mind of the one who designed the software. That's why the Bible is so important for us. The One who created us knows what we are like and how we should live.

Sin is like a "glitch" in the software of our minds and bodies. When your computer's operating system develops a glitch, you call Microsoft and say, "Look, I'm having trouble with Windows." Wouldn't it be comforting to hear the following: "I'm sorry to hear that. This is Bill Gates. How may I help you?" As the chair of Microsoft and one of the inventors of computer operating systems, he would be in a good position to make sure your problem gets solved!

Now, that is very unlikely to happen. Mr. Gates is far too busy to answer computer help lines. But the analogy I have offered may enable us understand the value of Scripture. As with software, many hands participated in creating the Bible, but God was personally involved in every part. When we study the Bible and pray, we put ourselves in direct touch with the Designer.

The divine judgments, in a most down-to-earth way, act as attention-getters. They are not vindictive, but rather wake-up calls to realign our software to the way God originally intended. The decision of how we relate to Jesus and His Software Manual is the most important decision we will ever face. Designed by God, we function best in relationship to Him. The worst possible disaster, therefore, would be to turn our face away from God and try to do things our own way. The trumpets are about the lesser disasters that turn our hearts away from the worst disaster.

Lord, I thank You for Your presence as we study the challenging images of the seven trumpets. I pray that I might clearly understand the consequences of falling away from Your purpose for my life. And I choose to give renewed attention to the divine Software Manual.

THEY HAD TAILS LIKE SCORPIONS AND STINGERS.
And with their tails they had the authority to harm the human race for five months.
THEY HAD A KING OVER THEM, THE ANGEL OF THE ABYSS. HIS NAME IN HEBREW IS ABADDON, AND IN GREEK HIS NAME IS APOLLYON. REV. 9:10, 11.

The fifth trumpet contains many images that would have been familiar to readers in the time of John. Darkness is the opposite of light. In the New Testament it would represent a philosophy that denies Jesus and the gospel (John 3:18-21). The abyss is a place in which God confines demons (Luke 8:30, 31). And the tail is a symbol of lying prophets (Isa. 9:15).

While many parts of this trumpet remain mysterious, the "plague" is a spiritual one that torments the followers of Satan but does not harm those who are sealed (Rev. 9:4-6). It leaves the wicked in suicidal anguish (verses 5, 6). The sun of God's Word is eclipsed but not destroyed (verses 2, 3). The symbolism fits well with the effects of secularization in our world today.

Secularization is a process by which people become less and less attached to religious organizations. Not atheists, secular people just don't make time for God and/or religion. Such secularization isn't all bad, however, as it often sets the stage for a deeper appreciation of human rights and religious liberty. The secular commitment to universal education also gives people the tools to search the Word of God for themselves. Bible societies, scientific progress, and archaeology are hard to imagine in a world without freedom of thought and faith. So the secularization of the Western world has had its positive points.

But secularization, of course, has also had a negative impact. Through the French and Russian revolutions it opened the way for Communism, which made the practice of faith extremely difficult in Communist countries. Secularization has also paved the way for the wrong kind of ecumenism. All other things being equal, Christian unity would be a good thing. But a certain type of ecumenism impoverishes faith and steals away certainty, implying, "Don't be a fanatic. It doesn't really matter what you believe!" Also secularization has led to unbridled materialism. Particularly if you believe there is no God, then life at its fullest is mainly about shopping and eating. People with such beliefs usually become obsessed with the things of this world.

Ultimately, secularization is a trend that God has used to judge oppressors and free up His people to serve Him without restraint. And the beauty of the fifth trumpet is that it does not harm those who know God. A bumper sticker I saw a while ago states the ultimate Christian response to secularization: "God is not dead—I talked to Him last night."

Lord, in a world that ignores You in its pursuit of possessions and pleasure, keep me focused on Your living presence.

June 22

They had tails like scorpions and stingers. And with their tails they had the authority to harm the human race for five months. They had a king over them, **THE ANGEL OF THE ABYSS.** *His name in Hebrew is Abaddon, and in Greek his name is Apollyon.* Rev. 9:10, 11.

I was a pastor in New York City during the year 1980. One of the perks of living in the big city is access to world-class culture. Our favorite part of that was the Museum of Natural History on the west side of Central Park in Manhattan. The museum has wonderful dioramas of scenes from all over the world, thousands of gems and minerals, and gigantic dinosaur skeletons that fill the eyes of children with wonder.

My wife and I enjoyed the place so much that we decided to become members, which introduced us to another level of New York culture. Members of the museum received special invitations to lectures and classes. Another perk was the opportunity to see special showings of new exhibits before they opened to the public.

On one occasion the museum hosted a display of artifacts from the ruins of Pompeii. It scheduled a members-only showing one evening. At a reception beforehand we rubbed shoulders with New York City's elite. Then, after viewing the exhibit, we were treated to a screening of the 1935 movie *The Last Days of Pompeii*. It absolutely stunned me. The movie was a powerful story of the gospel and its effect on the values of people in the first century, nothing like the secular fare Hollywood produced in the seventies and eighties. I realized for the first time what a powerful effect secularization has had on the Western world.

That impact multiplied at the conclusion of the movie. As the lights came on, the moderator of the program came to the podium and said in a voice dripping with sarcasm, "Well, we've just received a lot of moral instruction, haven't we?" I was amazed at how far we had wandered away from Christian values in just 45 years! The interesting thing is that we hardly noticed. Like a frog in a kettle, we experienced secularization's gradual increase in heat and never noticed when God ceased to play a major role in our lives.

The fifth trumpet warns us not to succumb to the flashing lights of materialism and technology. A life without God results in torment and anguish (Rev. 9:5, 6). It leads to a loss of meaning and direction and a frenzied emptiness that people may notice only in the still of the night. Although he hides behind the mask of fun and games, the angel of the abyss is a hard taskmaster.

Lord, help me recognize my own drift away from You. When I get too busy to read Your Word, too busy to pray, the current of today's world carries me where I don't want to go . . .

THE FIRST WOE HAS GONE AWAY. BEHOLD, TWO MORE WOES ARE COMING AFTER THIS. REV. 9:12.

Revelation 8:13 announced that three woes would fall on those who live on the earth. The fifth trumpet followed. Now in Revelation 9:12 we learn that the first woe has "gone away"—it is now past. Since a similar announcement occurs in Revelation 11:14, after the sixth trumpet, it seems clear that the three woes of Revelation 8:13 are the fifth, sixth, and seventh trumpets.

I received a major reality check about 15 years ago when I heard a particular preacher for the first time. He had an incredible impact on me. Whenever he spoke, my heart would burn within me. It was as if he could read my soul. But he was neither a prophet nor a mind reader, a point he made extremely clear. He was just an ordinary Christian speaking from the heart. And yet his words had prophetic power.

What was it that made his preaching so powerful? Ninety percent of his illustrations came from his own personal experience. And when he did speak from his own experience, he almost always talked about his failures and not his successes. That led me to think about my own sermons. When I gave illustrations from my own life, I always talked about my successes and almost never about my failures. It was a total reality check. I came to realize that I was using the pulpit to polish my image.

The church I serve also received a major reality check some time ago. Trying to understand better how to reach the lost, we learned that Hispanic congregations in southern California were doubling in numbers every three years or so. Assuming that they must be doing something the rest of us weren't, we wanted to apply those strategies to the broader situation in the United States. But investigation revealed a startling discovery. During a 10-year period not a single third- or fourth-generation (in America) Hispanic was baptized. Growth was there, but only immigrants and their children were being baptized. It was clear that the success among Hispanics was not transferable to the mainstream situation in the United States.

Each part of the Bible is useful for teaching (2 Tim. 3:16), but different passages apply to different circumstances. Passages such as the fifth and sixth trumpets do not particularly comfort the bereaved or encourage the lonely. But they are quite useful for shaking people out of their complacency. These trumpets provide a reality check. They summon us to face the illusions that relative prosperity can bring. We can all benefit from a reality check.[72]

Lord, I find that I fall so easily into the trap of complacency. Although I prefer for life to be peaceful, I need a serious reality check every so often. When it comes, give me the courage to learn and not to resist.

June 24

The sixth angel sounded his trumpet, and I heard a voice from **THE FOUR HORNS OF THE GOLDEN ALTAR** *which is before God saying to the sixth angel who had the trumpet, "Release the four angels who are bound by the great river Euphrates."* REV. 9:13, 14.

I n the fifth trumpet a demonic plague brings humanity to the point at which a great number of people seek death but cannot find it (Rev. 9:1-6). The sixth trumpet grants a third of humanity their wish. As horrible as the sixth trumpet is, the passage begins with a voice from the four horns of the altar. Scripture presents the horns of the altar as a place of mercy.

When David reached about 70 years of age, his health deteriorated and his control over the kingdom diminished. Instability threatened as his sons jockeyed to take his place as king. Adonijah, next-oldest son after Absalom, gained the support of Joab, head of David's army, and of Abiathar the high priest. Since both men had been loyal to David during Absalom's rebellion, Adonijah seems to have assumed that he had David's support. But key people in the army and among the priests did not join in Adonijah's "coronation" outside Jerusalem (1 Kings 1:5-10).

Nathan the prophet conspired with Bathsheba to get David involved (they alone seem to have known David's preference for Solomon, his son with Bathsheba). David decided to transfer the throne to Solomon immediately. So Zadok, the second-highest priest, anointed Solomon king, and, to great celebration, Bathsheba's son sat on David's throne in Jerusalem. After a blast of trumpets a mighty crowd chanted, "Long live King Solomon!" (verses 11-40).

The noise of this rival coronation drifted south to where Adonijah and his followers were also celebrating. "What's with all this noise coming out of the city?" Joab demanded (verse 41). At that moment Abiathar's son arrived with the news of David's action. In an instant Adonijah's guests fled for their lives. Left alone, Adonijah could think of only one thing to do. He went directly to the sanctuary and grabbed hold of the horns of the altar, invoking God's protection on his life. Solomon respected the action and let him live, on condition of good behavior in the future (verses 42-53).

As horrible as the sixth trumpet is, mention of the horns of the altar puts a touch of mercy into the plague. The door to salvation has not yet closed. As the earth slides into the final stages of self-destruction, it is still possible to hear the voice of Jesus and to repent. When life causes us to hit bottom the way Adonijah did, the only sensible thing to do is hang our helpless souls on the mercy of God.

Lord, "nothing in my hand I bring, simply to Thy cross I cling." I choose today to lay aside pride, achievements, status, and success. I look to You for all I need.

The sixth angel sounded his trumpet, and I heard a voice from the four horns of the golden altar which is before God. It said to the sixth angel who had the trumpet, **"RELEASE THE FOUR ANGELS WHO ARE BOUND BY THE GREAT RIVER EUPHRATES."** REV. 9:13, 14.

Our world is known as the blue planet, because of its extensive reserves of water. It covers three fourths of the earth's surface. Unfortunately, 98 percent of this surface water is in the oceans, with only 2 percent accessible as fresh water. To make matters worse, 90 percent of the fresh water supply is either at the poles or remains under the ground. So human beings have direct access to only a small fraction of 1 percent (.26) of the earth's water supply.[73]

The availability of fresh water supplies is one of the defining keys to a nation's success. Most of the "developing nations" occupy the world's arid or semiarid regions. Europe, on the other hand, contains half the running surface water in the entire world. So it is no surprise that the region has played a dominant role in recent world affairs. As earth's population increases, wars over scarce water supplies will increasingly break out.

In the Bible lands fresh water has always been in short supply. In such a place the abundant fresh water of the Euphrates River guaranteed power and wealth for those who controlled it. In this passage the river symbolizes the great power and resources of the final opposition to God in this world. His people, in ancient times, lived in a land with only one major source of fresh water, the Sea of Galilee. They had to rely, therefore, on heaven to provide moisture when they needed it.

Strong parallels exist between the sixth trumpet and two other scenes in the book of Revelation. Revelation 7:1-4 has four angels, a form of restraint, and the comment "I heard the number." So the 200-million-strong army of Revelation 9:16, 17, stands in contrast with God's end-time people, the 144,000. Also we observe parallels to the sixth bowl, in which you also have the river Euphrates, military language, and a demonic hoard (Rev. 16:13-16). So the sixth trumpet portrays the gathering of Satan's end-time army for the battle of Armageddon.

The book of Revelation contains many scenes of war. But it is less interested in the affairs of nations than it is in the progress of the gospel on earth. The war that truly matters to God is the battle going on in our minds every day. As we approach the end, even the smallest decisions of life have eternal consequences.

Lord, I feel the power of the battle that rages in me. I have no strength to defeat the overwhelming power of the enemy. Help me today to trust completely in the power of the cross for victory.

June 26

And the four angels [by the great river Euphrates], who were prepared for that very hour, day, month, and year, were released **IN ORDER TO KILL** *a third of the human race.* Rev. 9:15.

In the larger picture of the sixth trumpet these four angels call up an "army from hell," dressed in red, blue, and sulfurous yellow. The angels and their army have one purpose and one purpose only—to kill human beings in massive numbers. You could say that they are the ultimate agents of mass destruction. The powerful weapons they direct, emanating from the mouths and tails of 200 million cavalry horses, kill a full third of the human race. In the background of all this destruction lurks the "angel of the abyss" (Rev. 9:11). The urge to kill and destroy ultimately arises from the proud and vengeful heart of Satan himself.

A friend of mine, Gordon Retzer, tells the story of Frank Taitague, who knows this urge from personal experience.[74] A resident of Guam, Taitague was a teenager when the Japanese army took control of Guam during World War II. In an attempt to gain complete control of the island, the occupiers decided to kill all the residents. Taitague managed to escape to the hills, but not before he saw his 8-year-old niece thrown to the ground and brutally kicked. When the war ended and the Americans liberated his country, he remained a prisoner of hatred, determined to get revenge.

Taitague carried a rifle with him wherever he went. Like the four angels of Revelation he had a set purpose, and that was to kill. One day he came upon some Japanese soldiers who had not been able to leave the island when the war ended. Immediately he took aim, prepared to kill without remorse. But before he could pull the trigger someone grabbed his arm. It was perhaps the one person who could have stopped him at that moment—his father. A dedicated Seventh-day Adventist Christian, his father reminded Frank that he had always dreamed of being a pastor. The set purpose of the pastor is to bring life, not to kill. Together they decided that Frank would leave the island and go to Pacific Union College to study to become a minister.

But God was not finished with Frank Taitague. When he arrived at the college, the men's dormitory dean assigned him to a room and informed him that his roommate had already arrived. Frank reached his room and knocked on the door. A Japanese student opened the door! Instinctively Frank raised his fist, prepared to do serious damage. But God worked a miracle in his life. He and his roommate became the best of friends. God's purpose to love and give life replaced Satan's purpose to hate and kill.

Lord, You are the giver of life. You are the one who can change the way I think about others and behave toward them. Help me to see others through Your eyes of love.

And the number of the mounted soldiers was two hundred million. I heard the number of them. And this is the way I saw the horses and the ones sitting on them in the vision: They had breastplates the color of fire, hyacinth, and sulfur. The heads of the horses were like the heads of lions, and **OUT OF THEIR MOUTHS** *came fire, smoke, and sulfurous fumes.* REV. 9:16, 17.

Satan's army can be numbered only at the time of the end. They are the counterpart of God's end-time people, the 144,000. The wicked beg for the rocks and mountains to fall on them (Rev. 6:15-17) while the great multitude stands safely before the throne (Rev. 7:9). Two hundred million surge forth in the sixth trumpet in contrast to the 144,000 (Rev. 7:1-4) and the two witnesses (Rev. 11:3-6). A beast from the sea represents the wicked (Rev. 13), and a remnant symbolize the righteous (Rev. 12:17).

The visions of Revelation tend to blur the distinctions between good and evil. The reason for the ambiguity in the visions is the role of deception and counterfeit in the central part of the book. Toward the end of time the line between truth and error will be hard to distinguish.

I know a man who went out one evening to raise funds door to door for charity. At the corner of one street he noticed a large and angry-looking dog guarding the yard of a house a few doors down. He expressed his concern to a companion and indicated that he wanted to skip that house.

The companion offered a piece of advice. "No dog will ever bite you if you stare right into its eyes. It shows them you are the boss. Go ahead. Try it! You can do it. It isn't hard."

The first man was a bit dubious about the advice, but decided to accept it anyway. He banished his fears and approached the house. As he passed through the gate the large dog charged toward him. He fixed his eyes on those of the dog and followed them as the animal veered off course and circled behind him. And he kept on staring at the dog's eyes as the creature continued circling in closer and bit him in the back of the leg.

So much for the advice "No dog will ever . . ." It turns out that all the facts were not in. The dog had a brain tumor that prevented normal behavior. Sometimes things are not what they seem. As we approach the end, Satan will do all he can to deceive us. Just because something is religious doesn't mean it is right or honors God. The Word of God is our best safeguard against Satan's deceptive advice.

Lord, as I approach life's challenges today keep my head clear through Your Word.

June 28

A third of the human race was killed by these three plagues: by the fire, the smoke, and the sulfurous fumes that **CAME OUT OF THEIR MOUTHS.** *For* **THE AUTHORITY OF THE HORSES WAS IN THEIR MOUTHS AND IN THEIR TAILS.** *For their tails were like snakes, having heads, and with them they did harm.* Rev. 9:18, 19.

This description indicates that the plagues of the sixth trumpet have some kind of connection to those of the fifth trumpet. The power to harm in the fifth trumpet resided in the tail, while in this trumpet the danger lurks in both the mouth and the tail. So we observe an escalation of terror here. The good news is that the plagues of the trumpets focus on the wicked (Rev. 9:4, 20, 21). God is well able to protect His own.

In 1944 Nazi-held Belgrade came under assault from the Red Army and Yugoslav partisans. Martin's wife, Melanie, became sick in the aftermath of giving birth. As the battle wound down, Martin took many risks to bring needed supplies for her. But suddenly he felt impressed to leave his wife and go to church headquarters.

Heeding the call of God, he hurried through the desolate, bloody streets. Reaching the street where the church headquarters were located, he saw four people walking toward him. As he drew closer he realized that three soldiers in green uniforms were escorting his pastor, Joseph Vitner.

"Brother Vitner, where are you going?" he asked.

"Comrades are taking me," the man replied.

Martin realized that Vitner was of German descent and that the soldiers were Yugoslavs. The pastor now faced death as a "collaborator" with the Nazis. Instantly Martin felt impressed to plead with one of the soldiers to let him go in Vitner's place. "He's a better man than you and me put together," he said. The soldier said as he and his prisoner left several minutes later, "If he is a good man, not one hair will fall off his head. But if he's not, he's going to face the firing squad."

Feeling at peace about the matter, Martin assured church members that their pastor would be back in a few minutes. And he was! Vitner reported that the soldiers took him directly to the firing squad. But the young soldier interceded with his commander. "Sir, half the city of Belgrade is vouching for this man!" The commander responded, "We need more people like you. Go home and take care of your family."

We'll never know how one man's word became "half the city," but Martin's impression to go at that moment and then say exactly what he did seems exquisitely arranged by God. Like Pastor Vitner, we need not fear the fiery plague, because our lives are in God's hands.[75]

Lord, give me confidence today that my life is completely in Your hands.

And the rest of the human race, those who were not killed by these plagues, **DID NOT REPENT** *of the works of their hands in order that they might not worship demons or idols of gold, silver, brass, stone, and wood. Such idols are not able to see, hear, or walk. And the rest of the human race* **DID NOT REPENT** *of their murders, their magic arts, their acts of fornication, or their thefts.* Rev. 9:20, 21.

T his is truly an amazing passage. The people here have endured horrendous tribulations. Marauders numbering in the hundreds of millions have attacked them (Rev. 9:16). Fire, smoke, sulfur, and apocalyptic horses with snakelike tails that bite have assaulted them. One third of the human race has perished from all the various tribulations. One would expect that the rest of humanity would be far more traumatized by these events than were New Yorkers on September 11, 2001. Yet they refuse to repent. Amazing.

One day a chaplain received a request to visit George (not his real name) in the intensive care unit.[76] He learned that George was 47 years old, but when the chaplain entered the room he thought he was in the wrong place. The patient looked more than 60, yet the charts indicated that the chaplain was in the right place, and the man answered to the name listed on the charts.

George was under a sheet and talked as if he were freezing to death. Shaking and desperate, as if every breath would be his last, he spoke the way a drowning man would.

"Gonna . . . (pant, pant, pant) get my life together. I wanna . . . (pant, pant, pant) get my life together. . . . I wanna change."

God can work so easily with people like George. The man knew his need for God. He was on the fifth day of detoxification for alcoholism. His body had grown accustomed to being virtually "pickled" in alcohol. Body, mind, and soul all resisted the detoxification process with everything they had. George felt as if he were not going to live as he shook with pain. People like him clearly hear the call of God to repent and set a new direction for their lives.

The amazing thing about our text is that it describes a moment in earth's history when most of the human race is right where George was and yet still refuses to repent. It is possible to ignore the call of God, and do it again and again until one reaches the place that even hitting bottom is no longer enough for the Lord to get through to us. I'd rather pay attention to Him in the good times.

Lord, thank You for the many ways in which You call me to You every day. I have set my heart to hear You and repent today. Teach me what I need to do.

June 30

And the rest of the human race, those who were not killed by these plagues,
did not repent of the works of their hands in order that they might not worship
demons or **IDOLS OF GOLD, SILVER, BRASS, STONE, AND**
WOOD. SUCH IDOLS ARE NOT ABLE TO SEE, HEAR,
OR WALK. *And the rest of the human race did not repent of their murders,*
their magic arts, their acts of fornication, or their thefts. REV. 9:20, 21.

We set up images to honor people we admire or to extol causes we would gladly sacrifice time, effort, and money to uphold. As human beings we honor and celebrate what we admire. A friend's brother has spent much of his life openly proclaiming his admiration for drag racers and the magnificent machines that they create.[77] When he was growing up, Tom filled the bedroom he and his brother shared with pictures of dragsters. The photographs honored the likes of the "Melrose Missile," "Jungle Jim Lieberman," and "One-hand Willie Borsch." The photos depicted the famous racers trailing clouds of smoke as they blazed down the quarter-mile strip.

When he grew up, Tom turned out to be an excellent mechanic and earned the means to erect a memorial to his favorite sport in Rapid City, South Dakota. Today Tom's shop consists of a large metal building that houses a number of cars. It is immaculate, with clean concrete floors and room enough for all the tools and memorabilia that he has collected over the years. Almost every square inch on the walls is decked out with pictures, models, or some item from the sport of drag racing.

The centerpiece of the shop is Tom's own 850-horsepower Chevy Vega that does the quarter mile in the nine-second range. Fire up the beast, and you will hear thunder that shakes the entire building. Friends have even nicknamed Tom's garage "The Shrine," not an inappropriate title given his obvious devotion to the sport.

The images we erect are often literal: monuments, plaques, named cornerstones, and "shrines" such as Tom's fascinating celebration of American drag racing. But far more often these images remain hidden from view, buried deep in our hearts and minds. While many of these shrines, like Tom's, are interesting but harmless, we can erect other ones in our hearts to either great good or great evil. The German nation idolized Adolf Hitler to its own destruction. Youth often idolize celebrities who teach them self-defeating values. On the other hand, "we all, with open face beholding as in a glass the glory of the Lord, are changed into the same image from glory to glory" (2 Cor. 3:18). Idols not only reveal our innermost thoughts, but also help determine who we become.

Lord, I don't want to be like those in the sixth trumpet who refuse to give up their destructive idols. I choose to center my life's focus on Jesus today.

And I saw another mighty angel coming down out of heaven dressed in a cloud, and there was a rainbow upon his head, his face was like the sun, his feet were like pillars of fire. REV. 10:1.

For me, Revelation 10 and 11 have been as difficult to understand as any part of the entire book. A long interlude separates the seventh trumpet (Rev. 11:15-18) from the horrors of the sixth (Rev. 9:13-21). This section has a different character than the trumpet vision proper. Instead of horrific judgments, natural catastrophies, and the fate of the wicked, we find prophecy, preaching, and the experience of God's people.

Is the interlude of Revelation 10 and 11 connected in some way to the trumpets, or do the two visions have nothing to do with each other? We can answer that question with certainty. You may remember that Revelation 8:13 described three woes that would occur during the sounding of the last three trumpets. Then Revelation 9:12 said, "The first woe is past; two other woes are yet to come" (NIV). So the first woe obviously is the fifth trumpet (verses 1-11) and the second woe clearly begins when the sixth trumpet does (verse 13). But when does the second woe end?

"The second woe has passed; the third woe is coming soon" (Rev. 11:14, NIV). The ending of the second woe (the sixth trumpet) does not occur in Revelation 9:21, but rather in Revelation 11:14. That means that Revelation 10 and 11 are not something separate from the sixth trumpet. Revelation 10 and 11 deal with the same events as chapter 9, but from a different perspective. This is also the time of the sealing (Rev. 7:1-4) and the gathering for the battle of Armageddon (Rev. 16:13-16). The core of the sixth trumpet is just before the close of probation (Rev. 10:7).

You have, perhaps, heard the story of the six blind men who sought to understand what an elephant is like. One of them embraced one of the elephant's legs and declared that it reminded him of a tree. Another grasped one of the tusks and declared that the elephant was like a spear. The blind man who grabbed the elephant's trunk thought the creature must be like a giant fire hose. And so it went. What each blind man determined about the elephant depended on which part he had experienced.

So in the sixth trumpet John describes the same events from two different perspectives. Chapter 9 concerns the activities and fate of the wicked toward the end, and Revelation 10 and 11 offer a view of the righteous and what happens to them during the same period. While Satan's forces mass for the final conflict (Rev. 9:13-21), God at the same time prepares a people to counteract that threat (Rev. 10:1-11:13).

Lord, help me to discern clearly the difference between Your ways and the actions of the enemy as we approach the end.

July 2

And I saw **ANOTHER MIGHTY ANGEL** *coming down out of heaven dressed in a cloud, and there was a rainbow upon his head, his face was like the sun, his feet were like pillars of fire, and he had a scroll in his hand which had been previously opened. He placed his right foot upon the sea and his left foot upon the land, and he cried out with a loud voice like the roar of a lion. And when he cried out, the seven thunders uttered their own voices.* REV. 10:1-3.

Many commentators see this mighty angel as a reference to Jesus. We find here strong parallels to the one "like a son of man" of Revelation 1:12-20. The angel seems to be the same figure who appeared to John on Patmos. Like the Old Testament Yahweh, He makes the clouds His chariot (Ps. 104:3). His appearance also reminds us of the way Jesus looked at His transfiguration in Matthew 17:2. So this mighty angel represents Jesus Christ. As the Lamb, Jesus held the sealed scroll in Revelation 5, and now as a mighty angel here He clutches an open scroll. He is the most admirable person who has ever walked this earth.

As I write, the pro golfer Tiger Woods has excited considerable admiration. Spending three days of intense military training at Fort Bragg in North Carolina, he woke early for four-mile jogs, fired weapons, even jumped twice from a plane. Why? Because he wanted to appreciate the kind of sacrifice and service his father had contributed to his country while in the military. People were amazed that a multimillionaire celebrity would put himself through so much agony in order to experience how life looks in someone else's shoes.

But then another news headline put the admiration for Woods into perspective. Pat Tillman, a former NFL defensive back for the Arizona Cardinals, turned down a three-year, $3.6 million contract and joined the Army. When he made his decision, he refused media requests to cover his enlistment, basic training, or deployment. He wanted no special consideration or attention, preferring to be treated like any other soldier. Tillman was serving along the border of Afghanistan and Pakistan when insurgents attacked his patrol. At just 27 years of age, Tillman died in the firefight.[78]

The two stories put fame and heroism into perspective. We often glorify celebrities for their great success in relatively trivial matters. The real heroes risk their lives in support of causes far greater than themselves. The greatest Hero of all is the one who died that all of us might live. He deserves the highest place in our admiration and affection.

Lord, I am ashamed when I realize how often I have admired the achievements of others to the neglect of all You have done for me. Forgive my misdirected focus. I choose to place You first in my personal Hall of Fame.

And [the angel] cried out with a loud voice like the roar of a lion. And when he cried out, the seven thunders uttered their own voices. And when the seven thunders spoke, I was about to write, but I heard a voice from heaven, saying, "SEAL UP WHAT THE SEVEN THUNDERS SAID AND DO NOT WRITE THEM DOWN." REV. 10:3, 4.

J ohn experiences the seven thunders and finds much in them that he would like to record, but the heavenly voice tells him not to write it down. The thunders evidently reveal matters that are not yet ours to know. The hidden things belong to God alone (Deut. 29:29). No matter how much we study, no matter how brilliant we may be, we know only in part until Jesus comes (1 Cor. 13:9). We should be candid about our limitations of understanding and not speak dogmatically about uncertain matters.

Particularly with the book of Revelation, many teachers of prophecy like to fill in too many details on which the text does not directly comment. Prophetic speculation often takes the place of obedience to the clear teachings of the Word. Instead of hearing and obeying the text, we use the Bible to satisfy our curiosity about the future. In so doing we add to the message of Scripture (Rev. 22:18).[79]

Many put the blame for terrorism on religion. In the words of a protest sign that appeared on September 12, 2001: "No Religion, No War." The sign expressed the conviction that if you could get rid of religious authority and sacred texts, the world would be a better and safer place. In a world torn by division and hatred, any religion that adds to the divisions or fuels the hatreds is part of the problem rather than the solution.

But would the elimination of religion make the world a safer place? a more tolerant place? History offers a resounding no to both questions. The architects of the French Revolution and Russian Communism both saw the intolerance of the "Christian" West and sought to solve the problem by eliminating the Christian faith. But reaction against religion tends to create a new exclusion that breeds more violence in the future ("We have to stop those narrow-minded people"). To paraphrase the words of Aleksandr Solzhenitsyn: "The line between good and evil does not run between 'us' and 'them' but through the heart of every human being."

I believe that in a terrified world we don't need less faith but better faith. We don't need less spiritual guidance—we require better spiritual guidance. Instead of "no sacred texts" we could start with a lot more humility in how we handle the Bible. The very greatness of the God envisioned in the Bible warns us against the tendency to think we have gained absolute clarity in our understanding of Him.

Lord, open my eyes and my heart to the limitations in my understanding of You.

July 4

And [the angel] cried out with a loud voice like the roar of a lion. And when he cried out, the seven thunders uttered their own voices. And when the seven thunders spoke, I was about to write, but I heard a voice from heaven, saying, "**SEAL UP WHAT THE SEVEN THUNDERS SAID AND DO NOT WRITE THEM DOWN.**" REV. 10:3, 4.

When people come face to face with their limitations of understanding, they often find themselves tempted to give up trying to understand the Bible. Fortunately, most of us are too curious to quit. Something about the human spirit persists in asking questions and demanding answers. But as we study the Bible we face the further danger of making it say what we want it to. Struggling with the temptation to use its authority to promote our own opinions, we focus on evidence that agrees with us and ignore anything that disagrees.

A better way to approach the Bible is to take a big picture approach to the text. Read broadly through it rather than selectively focusing on any part of it. Try to discover what each Bible writer meant, rather than imposing ideas from our own time and place. Seek to be open to the whole text, rather than picking and choosing whatever looks good to us at first glance. As a result we will ground our understanding on what is clear, rather than trying to make the less-clear things say what we want them to.

How did I learn this method? One day in Brooklyn, New York, I had a visit from a Jehovah's Witness. I decided to spend some time studying the Bible with him to see what his group was all about. An interesting thing happened. We disagreed over every Bible text that we looked at. In frustration one day I suggested something radical. "If the Bible is the ultimate source of truth," I said, "then no organization should be allowed to control what the Bible says."

He agreed with that. So I suggested that we lay aside all books and articles about the Bible and just read the New Testament through from beginning to end. When we finished we asked ourselves the question, "Do my beliefs reflect the central themes of the New Testament, or do they represent what someone else has taught me?" We both discovered that the Bible, broadly read, was a very different book from what it seemed to be when you take a text here and a text there and put them together. His mind suddenly opened to Bible study as never before.

Now, I don't know what our encounter did for that Jehovah's Witness in the long term, but I know it changed my life. I learned to test every opinion I held about the Bible with the plain teachings of the text in its widest context. As I began to do this, I became amazed at what I had missed. As God says: "My thoughts are not your thoughts" (Isa. 55:8, NIV).

Lord, help me to read the Bible in such a way as to leave open the possibility that I might learn something! Feed me with all the truth I can handle, then help me to obey.

The angel which I saw standing on the sea and on the land raised his right hand to heaven and swore by the one who lives for ever and ever—who created heaven and the things which are in it, the earth and the things which are in it, and the sea and the things which are in it—"Time will be no more." But **IN THE DAYS OF THE SOUNDING OF THE SEVENTH ANGEL,** *when he is about to sound,* **THE MYSTERY OF GOD IS FINISHED,** *which He proclaimed as good news through His servants the prophets.* REV. 10:5-7.

My friend Jim was walking through the American cemetery overlooking the Normandy beaches in northern France. Thousands of American soldiers lost their lives on June 6, 1944, and during the days that followed. Young boys, full of hope and promise, would risk all in a land far away from their family, homes, and friends in order to liberate a distant country from the evil empire that was Nazi Germany.

As he walked among thousands of neatly lined white crosses, one in particular caught Jim's attention. It read:

Burnell W. Coolen
Pvt. 8 Inf. 4 Div.
Massachusetts, June 21, 1944

He realized with reverential awe that the soldier had died exactly six years before his own birth. Because Private Coolen was willing to die on Jim's birthday, Jim was born free instead of under the tyranny of the swastika. As Burnell W. Coolen lay dying in Normandy, he could not have possibly imagined that more than 60 years later his name and heroic deed would appear in a book read all over the world. But that is how acts of dedication often receive their reward. Long after the actor has passed from the stage of life, his or her acts of courage still inspire others.[80]

In the New Testament the "mystery of God" is the gospel, something hidden in ages past but brought to light through the proclamation of Jesus Christ (Rom. 16:25, 26). According to the book of Revelation, a great final proclamation of the gospel will take place just before the blowing of the last trumpet. That gospel tells us that another was willing to die for you and me, far away from His home, so that we could live in freedom and make a difference in this world.

Lord, I want to walk in the footsteps of the One who died for me. I take up His marching orders as I approach the final events of earth's history. Help me to keep in step with His cadence today.

July 6

"TIME WILL BE NO MORE." BUT *in the days of the sounding of the seventh angel, when he is about to sound,* **THE MYSTERY OF GOD IS FINISHED,** *which He proclaimed as good news through His servants the prophets.* REV. 10:6, 7.

When John wrote Revelation 10, he had Daniel 12 in mind. Daniel 12 talks about sealing up the words of the prophecy until the "time of the end" (Dan 12:4). Then in Daniel 12:7 someone lifts up his hands and swears by the One who lives forever and ever (see Rev. 10:5, 6) that there will be "time, times, and half a time." It sounds almost exactly like Revelation 10, except that in Revelation the phrase "time will be no more" replaces the cryptic time period.

The point of Revelation 10 seems to be that the time prophecies of Daniel have run their course. Revelation 10 brings us to the point when God would unseal the book of Daniel and God's final message (the "mystery of God") would go to the world. Both texts have a strong sense of an appointed time. So the sixth trumpet brings us to a period in earth's history in which the final events are about to take place.

During the nineteenth century students of the Bible ransacked the books of Daniel and Revelation, trying to understand where humanity stood in the course of human history. After careful study, some of them concluded that the time prophecies of Daniel would end around the year 1844. They naturally assumed that the phrase "time would be no more" meant the end of the world, the second coming of Jesus. However, they missed one tiny word in Revelation 10:7—"but."

In the Greek language this particular word for "but" portrays a strong contrast, even more emphatic than the English "but." It tells us that the time prophecies of Daniel did not bring the world to the very end, but only to the "time of the end." Since the close of Daniel's time prophecies we have been living in the final period of earth's history. We do not know when the end will come, but we do know that we are truly living in the "time of the end."

In a way this is nothing new. God has always portrayed the end as near (see Rev. 1:3). At the same time God's Word has always contained the seeds of an even deeper understanding. The disciples of Jesus, for example, thought that He would come immediately after His resurrection (Acts 1:6-8). But He then explained to them that the gospel had to go to the whole world first.

The Millerites in the nineteenth century, likewise, thought that the closing up of Daniel's time prophecies had brought them to the end of the world. But God's people still had a mission to accomplish first (Rev. 10:11; 14:6, 7). So the bottom line for the Christian life is not timing the end, but living the motto of the U.S. Marine Corps: "Semper Fidelis"—Always Faithful.

Lord, I want nothing more than to be found faithful when You come.

And the voice which I had heard from heaven spoke with me again: "Take the opened scroll which is in the hand of the angel standing upon the sea and upon the land." And I went to the angel and said to him, "Give me the scroll." He said to me, "Take it and eat it. It will make your stomach sour, but in your mouth it will be as sweet as honey." And I took the scroll out of the angel's hand and ate it. And it was as sweet as honey in my mouth, but when I had eaten it, it made my stomach sour. REV. 10:8-10.

This little acted parable expresses John's disappointment. He saw that his book would not bring the end. But at the time of the end, his book would prophesy again by means of another people (Rev. 10:11). In the context of Revelation 10:5-7, John's experience is also a forecast of another disappointment at the close of Daniel's time prophecies—a group of people who thought the end would come and it did not. To have hopes of Jesus' return raised and dashed would be a bitter experience for God's faithful people at any time.

Many people believe that second disappointment occurred in the year 1844. Thousands of Americans believed that Jesus would return on October 22 of that year. On that day they eagerly expected to see Jesus Himself approaching in the clouds, surrounded by all the holy angels. They looked forward to meeting all the dear friends that death had torn from them. With all their trials and sufferings over and caught up in the air to meet their coming Lord, they would inhabit mansions in the golden city, the New Jerusalem.

Feel the passion of the words of one of the participants, Hiram Edson: "Our expectations were raised high, and thus we looked for our coming Lord until the clock tolled twelve at midnight. The day had then passed and our disappointment became a certainty. Our fondest hopes and expectations were blasted, and such a spirit of weeping came over us as I never experienced before. It seemed that the loss of all earthly friends could have been no comparison. We wept, and wept, till the day dawn.

"I mused in my own heart, saying, 'My advent experience has been the richest and brightest of all my Christian experience. If this had proved a failure, what was the rest of my Christian experience worth? Has the Bible proved a failure? Is there no God, no heaven, no golden city, no paradise? Is all this but a cunningly devised fable? Is there no reality to our fondest hope and expectation of these things?' And thus we had something to grieve and weep over, if all our fond hopes were lost. And as I said, we wept till the day dawn." [81]

Lord, help me face the disappointments of each day in the knowledge that You have foreseen them and provided what I need to survive.

July 8

And the voice which I had heard from heaven spoke with me again: "Take the opened scroll which is in the hand of the angel standing upon the sea and upon the land." And I went to the angel and said to him, "Give me the scroll." He said to me, "Take it and eat it. It will make your stomach sour, but in your mouth it will be as sweet as honey." And I took the scroll out of the angel's hand and ate it. And it was as sweet as honey in my mouth, but **WHEN I HAD EATEN IT, IT MADE MY STOMACH SOUR.** *And he said to me, "You must prophesy again to many peoples, nations, languages, and kings."* REV. 10:8-11.

John is not the last person for whom everything turned sour. God's strategy with him seems to be a way that the Lord often uses to prepare people for a different kind of ministry.

When Gavin was a teenager he attended a prestigious private school. His classmates were the children of diplomats and the wealthiest people in the country. As a student he won scholarships, was captain of several sports teams, and received awards for many things. He never failed at anything he wanted to do.

When he became a pastor, however, everything seemed to turn upside down. Medical problems hospitalized him, and then he lost his job. He was continually tired. Gossip destroyed his reputation. His girlfriend of several years broke up with him. It was as if God were systematically taking away everything that he had learned to depend on.

When everything seemed the darkest, God completely restored his health and his energy. But sometime later he found himself complaining about his situation. From the moment that he began complaining, his renewed energy began to seep away. For two months he was angry with God. "Father, this is not fair," he protested. "You have taken everything away from me. I have nothing left!" The voice of the Holy Spirit was unmistakable: "Yes, that is the point."

The thought stunned Gavin. God wanted him to have nothing? Then he came to realize that he had been trying to do ministry in his own strength. He was "soured" because God removed his "strengths" so he could realize how much he needed to depend on the Lord. As with John in Revelation 10, God intended his disappointments to serve as stepping-stones to a different kind of ministry.

Gavin is back in ministry today. But the core of his service is not in his talent or strength—it is in intimacy with God. Just as the book of Revelation has had far more influence through the centuries than John could have imagined, so our work for God can exceed our expectations when we do it as the result of an intimate relationship with Him.

Lord, keep me open to new directions by whatever means You choose. Help me to recognize Your hand in the "sour" experiences of life.

A reed like a measuring rod was given to me, and I was told, "Rise up and measure the temple of God, the altar, and those who worship in it. But **THE OUTER COURT OF THE TEMPLE** *set aside and do not measure it, because it* **IS GIVEN TO THE NATIONS,** *and they will trample the holy city for forty-two months."* Rev. 11:1, 2.

A Gentile walking into the Temple at Jerusalem would have been awed by the huge size of the outer courtyard and the magnificent grandeur of its structure. He or she was free to circulate around the outermost courtyard (the word translated "nations" above is also the word for Gentiles). But close to the Temple building itself a stone fence announced, "Any Gentile passing beyond this point will be responsible for his own death, which will surely follow." It didn't take long to figure out that Gentiles' access to the God of this Temple was extremely limited.

Inside the Gentile barricade was the Court of the Women. All Jews were welcome here, but that was as far as Jewish women got. Only Jewish men could enter the innermost court in front of the Temple building itself. Even Jewish men, however, had limitations. Only priests could enter the Temple building itself, and even they could not go into the innermost room of the Temple, the Holy of Holies. Only the high priest could visit it, and then only once a year.

These levels of access taught important lessons about the holiness of God and the barriers that sin creates between Him and the human race. Relationship with God is not a "buddy-buddy" sort of thing for human beings. We must approach Him with a humility appropriate to sinners. Our relationship with God has no room for arrogance.

Amazingly enough, even these lessons in humility often get distorted into arrogance. People interpreted their right to closer entrance as a license to think of themselves as superior to others. To make matters even worse, in Jesus' day the Temple staff had turned the one part of the Temple complex that Gentiles could enter into a cruel and greedy marketplace. And Jesus reacted to the situation with fury, casting the sellers and money exchangers out of the Court of the Gentiles.

Nothing makes Jesus angrier than well-meaning religious people setting up unnecessary barriers to others who want to come to Him. Have you and I ever done this? Would you refuse to worship in a church building if the doors were red? Would you have a hard time worshipping with someone who was dressed shabbily or had on too much makeup? Is protecting the church carpet more important than welcoming children?

Lord, I repent of the many times I have tried to impose my personal preferences on others. Help me not to place unnecessary barriers in the way of those who need to find You.

July 10

"And they will trample the holy city for **FORTY–TWO MONTHS.**
And I will give to my two witnesses even that they will prophesy for **TWELVE HUNDRED AND SIXTY DAYS,** *dressed in sackcloth." Rev. 11:2, 3.*

This morning I went back to school. High school! Yes, I suppose I'm a little old for that (I graduated in 1967). But it involved a higher cause—one called parenting. One of my children was struggling with high school algebra, and when I looked at the textbook I could see why. The only problem was that my young person already knows more algebra than I do. So how do you help a kid who's struggling with a subject when you know less than he or she does about it? You go back to school!

The class was interesting. Adding and multiplying powers. Negative and zero powers. The subject has something incredibly elegant about it, even though it can be hard to learn—at least for some people. But what is mathematics? Is it simply a constructive form of intellectual play? Or is it a window into some deeper reality of the universe that already existed before we discovered it?

John Polkinghorne argues that mathematicians are discoverers, not inventors.[82] Through mathematics they explore a reality that already exists. The prime numbers (numbers that can be divided only by themselves and by 1—2, 3, 5, 7, 11, 13, and so on), for example, have always been "there," even before we noticed their existence. But where have they been? Polkinghorne argues that they are part of the fundamental structure of the universe, one existing at a deeper level beyond its physical reality. In other words, the universe involves more than objects that we can handle and observe. Research provides hints that fundamental principles, such as mathematics, truth, and beauty, have a reality beyond what human beings can observe and label. If the mathematicians are right, why can't there also be a God who transcends everything that science can observe and experiment with?

Polkinghorne's insight is fascinating when you realize that God's self-revelation in the Apocalypse is full of numbers, two of them visible in the above text. Forty-two months, 1260 days, five months, 10 days, and a time, times, and half a time represent some strange and unusual ways of describing the passage of time. We observe crowds ranging in size from 144,000 to 200 million (imagine what it would take to estimate the size of such a crowd!). In addition to these numbers we find the repeated use of basic numbers, such as three, four, six, seven, 10, 12, and 24. Rightly understood, the books of revelation and of nature both witness to the same God— a God of order in the midst of chaos, a God of mercy and justice, a God of both love and wrath.

Lord, this math stuff is way over my head. So are many of the numbers in the book of Revelation. Help me find Your order in the midst of my own personal chaos today.

July 11

"And they will trample the holy city for **FORTY-TWO MONTHS.**
And I will give to my two witnesses even that they will prophesy for **TWELVE HUNDRED AND SIXTY DAYS,** *dressed in sackcloth."* Rev. 11:2, 3.

Australia's first convicted terrorist was a man named Jack Roche. Accused of planning to bomb the Israeli embassy in Canberra in the year 2000, he reportedly had links with al-Qaeda and Jemaah Islamiyah (an Islamic terrorist group in Indonesia). Apparently he was in contact with representatives of both groups as he developed his attack plot. His trial was front-page news throughout Australia. A Perth court sentenced him to nine years in prison.

The unusual thing about the case is that Jack Roche did not actually carry out his bombing plan. The trial gave a glimpse of what might have been, but in actuality no buildings got blown up or damaged, nobody was killed or injured. Yet at his trial he faced a maximum prison sentence equal to the one he would have been liable for had he actually carried out his plot. One could say that the conviction was based on a prophecy. Given Roche's capabilities, his accomplices, and the quality of his planning, the court concluded that it needed to penalize even mere planning.

The verdict sought to send out a signal to other would-be terrorists in Australia that they could fail twice. They could fail to achieve the political goals of their action and at the same time they could lose their accustomed lifestyle. This raised the personal stakes in terrorist action and made it less attractive to people such as Roche.[83]

The events of Revelation 11 build on the close of chapter 10. Divine agencies tell John that he must prophesy again to "many peoples, nations, languages and kings" (Rev. 10:11, NIV). God gives him a glimpse into the future. While the message of the gospel is sweet, many traumatic events would occur before the end would come.

The time periods of 42 months and 1260 days recall Daniel's time prophecies (Dan. 7:25; 12:7). During that period the people of God will suffer at the hands of many enemies. At the end of the period the beast from the abyss would kill the two witnesses. But things do not end badly. God raises the two witnesses after three and a half days, and they ascend to heaven (Rev. 11:7-13).

Many aspects of these passages are difficult to understand. But the basic message is clear. God knows the end from the beginning even better than the Australian court system. He knows the thoughts of those who oppose Him and His people. Scanning the future course of history and seeing the consequences of evil action, He assures us in advance that He can deal with them. The Lord too has a plan, and the outcome is sure.

Lord, I want to be faithful to Your plan for the last generation.

July 12

"And I will give to **MY TWO WITNESSES** *even that they* **WILL PROPHESY FOR TWELVE HUNDRED AND SIXTY DAYS, DRESSED IN SACKCLOTH."** *These are the two olive trees and the two lamps which stand before the Lord of the earth.* REV. 11:3, 4.

The identity of the two witnesses is one of the most disputed issues in the book of Revelation. But whoever they are, one thing is clear. They represent the message of the gospel, a message that God intends will spread throughout the earth before the end comes (Matt. 24:14; Rev. 11:11, 12; 14:6, 7). John portrays the two witnesses as standing all alone, challenging the wrongs of their day and representing God in the face of great opposition.

We too sometimes find ourselves called to stand alone for God. Such occasions are not pleasant. Most of us prefer to be part of the "in" crowd, to be accepted in a group that believes and lives the way we do. But in hard times that may not be the case. The good news is that, as we make disciples for Jesus, our lonely influence multiplies and helps many others to receive Him in spite of the difficulties that following Christ can bring in this world.

In 1870 a Hindu Chuchra named Charles Ditt converted to Christ. The Chuchras, a subgroup among the untouchables of India, are part of the lowest caste among the Hindus. In places people treat them as of less worth than some animals. Charles Ditt added to his lowly caste position the social stigma of Christianity. Many Indians regard Christian converts as traitors to their country.

Ditt faced considerable persecution as he carried the message of Jesus Christ with him from village to village. In 11 years, however, more than 500 Chuchras became Christians in response to his ministry. By 1900 more than half of his caste had converted to Christ, and by 1915 all but a few hundred members professed the Christian faith. Certainly Ditt no longer stood alone in his relationship with Christ.[84]

In today's world God calls all of us to be witnesses for Jesus Christ. Three out of four people in our world do not believe in Jesus as their personal Savior, and half of the people in the world have yet to hear about Him in a meaningful way. While as individuals we can do little about the billions, we can each reach out to the one or two lost people closest to us. Even then we cannot know ahead of time which one will prove to be a Charles Ditt, someone specially gifted by God to reach large numbers for Christ.

The work of God will be completed under His supervision and in His time. Our personal part is to sense His direction and His call each day.

Lord, lead me to someone who needs You, or direct them to me, today. Touch me with the right words to say. Help me to be alert to recognize that person when he or she appears.

If anyone wishes to harm them, **FIRE COMES OUT OF THEIR MOUTHS** *and consumes their enemies. If anyone wishes to harm them, that is the way he must be put to death. These have the* **AUTHORITY TO LOCK UP HEAVEN** *in order that it might not rain during the days of their prophesying. And they have* **AUTHORITY OVER THE WATERS, TO TURN THEM INTO BLOOD,** *and to strike the earth with every kind of plague whenever they want.* REV. 11:5, 6.

At Pentecost God empowered the church with prophetic gifts (Acts 2:17, 18). The apostles exercised those gifts in conjunction with impressive signs and wonders (Acts 2:43; 5:12-16; 6:8; 14:3). Such events served as vehicles to draw attention to the gospel (Acts 3:6-12; 8:6, 7; 9:34, 35; 19:10-20). And parts of the world still have miraculous interventions accompanying the spread of the gospel.

In the Western church today, on the other hand, miracles rarely happen. And those that we *do* experience tend to be fairly trivial, not on the scale of the biblical record. Some have reinterpreted the Bible to suggest that God stopped the flow of miracles after the completion of the canon. But this text and others (such as Eph. 4:11-13) seem to assume that supernatural gifts will continue until the end of the age. History and international experience suggest God is still powerfully active wherever it will make a positive difference.

One possible reason for the lack of miracles in the Western world is secularization. The skeptical nature of Western thought picks miracles apart and attempts to show that they are the products of manipulation or wishful thinking. If a true prophet were to arise in the Western church right now, most believers would probably reject him or her on principle. The Western church, therefore, has a lot in common with the compromised Christianity of cities such as Laodicea, Thyatira, and Sardis, which were comfortable with their situation in the world. Jesus did not do miracles in Nazareth because they found Him too familiar to take seriously (Matt. 13:57, 58).

Another explanation for the lack of miracles in today's world is the sovereignty of God. In the Bible miracles tend to appear most frequently on the cutting edge of His new initiatives, especially in relation to spreading the gospel in new areas. Miracles are more likely to occur when believers are breaking new ground than when they are self-absorbed with their comfort this side of paradise. Only when the church is prepared to challenge society with the claims of Christ will we witness the power of God in its biblical fullness.[85]

Lord, I do not wish to get ahead of Your plans for this world. But wherever I am hindering the work You would like to accomplish in my community, do whatever it takes to get my attention. I choose to follow Your lead wherever it takes me.

July 14

And when **THEIR TESTIMONY** *is finished, the beast who comes up from the abyss will make war with them and kill them.* Rev. 11:7.

The concept of "testimony" has two basic meanings in the book of Revelation. It has the connotation of sharing one's faith, of telling others what Jesus has done for you and for the human race as a whole. But it also has the basic meaning of martyrdom, of witnessing for Christ even in the face of threat and death.

In a crisis people become martyrs because living without Jesus is more to be feared than dying with Him. The martyrs so cherished what Jesus had done in their lives that they could not conceive of living out of relationship with Him. When forced to make the choice, therefore, they opted for death rather than deny Him. And "the blood of martyrs became seed." No witness to Christ is greater than that of one who calmly goes to death instead of turning away from Him.

As I write these words, I have just completed a series of meetings for the public in Singapore. Local believers had been broadcasting recordings of my Revelation lectures on the radio there. When they advertised the meetings, hundreds of listeners came and wanted to hear more.

It was fascinating to meet people from such a wide variety of backgrounds. Christians from every denomination in Singapore were there, hungry for a deeper understanding of Revelation and of Jesus. Secular people, tired of an endless round of working, eating, and shopping, came looking for meaning in their lives. Hindus and Buddhists fascinated me by their openness to a deeper walk with God and eagerness to learn more about Jesus. In the process I encountered impressive elements of Indian and Chinese wisdom. We must not assume that people who have never heard of Jesus are necessarily ignorant.

I did not undergo martyrdom at the close of the meetings. Those who attended rejoiced in a deeper understanding both of Jesus and of the puzzling symbols in Revelation. I experienced all the joy of sharing my faith without the pain of the martyrs. My own life had been energized by contact with a large group of people who drank in every word and applied it to their lives eagerly.

Although genuine testimony in behalf of Jesus can cost us our reputations, our jobs, and even our lives, it always leaves the world a better place. To know Jesus is to know peace and to fill the emptiness that afflicts life without Him. It is a message worth dying for.

Lord, I want to know the Truth that is worth dying for. Give me a peace and a joy today that I cannot resist sharing with those I meet.

And when their [the two witnesses'] testimony is finished, **THE BEAST WHO COMES UP FROM THE ABYSS WILL MAKE WAR** *with them and kill them. And their dead bodies will lie in the street of* **THE GREAT CITY,** *which is spiritually called Sodom and Egypt, where also their Lord was crucified. And* **SOME FROM EVERY PEOPLE AND TRIBE AND LANGUAGE AND NATION** *will gaze on their bodies for three and a half days, and* **THEY WILL NOT PERMIT THEIR BODIES TO BE PLACED IN A TOMB.** *Those who live on the earth will rejoice over them, celebrate, and* **SEND GIFTS TO ONE ANOTHER** *because these prophets had tormented those who live on the earth. But after three and a half days* **THE BREATH OF LIFE FROM GOD ENTERED INTO THEM** *and they stood up on their feet.* **GREAT FEAR FELL ON THOSE WHO SAW THEM.** REV. 11:7-11.

A fter the close of the 1260 days a dying world receives a final message. The abyss is the home of demons, the place where God confines them (Luke 8:31). So the beast from the abyss is either Satan or some civil power controlled by Satan. Around the time of the French Revolution, many people saw the events of their day forecast in this text. They believed that the attack on the two witnesses represented the atheist onslaught against the Bible during the revolution.

Rejection is painful, especially when you care deeply about those who spurn you. In ancient times people considered it the ultimate rejection to be refused burial (1 Kings 21:23, 24; Jer. 8:1, 2 and 14:16; Ps. 79:2, 3) after one's death. And not only were the two witnesses left lying in the street, the wicked celebrated their humiliation by sending each other gifts, as the Jews did after their deliverance in the time of Esther (Esther 9:19, 22).

But God reverses this shame by breathing the breath of life back into the two witnesses. Their resurrection fills their enemies with great fear. One of the consequences of the French Revolution was a great revival of interest in the Bible. The great Bible societies organized during the following decades. So while the greatest attack against the Bible occurred in the 1790s, the 1800s saw the Word spread more widely than at any time in history.

It is interesting how enemies can become united in their common opposition to God's people. Lifelong enemies, Pilate and Herod, reconciled through their rejection of Christ (Luke 23:12). Sometimes parents are more willing to see their children become secular, or even criminals, than to join some other denomination. Nothing brings people together like opposition to God and His people, and that will certainly be the case in the last days.

Lord, I want to seek the kind of unity that draws people to You, unity in love and caring concern, not unity in opposition to others.

July 16

And their dead bodies will lie in the street of the great city, which is spiritually called Sodom and Egypt, where also their Lord was crucified. And some from every people and tribe and language and nation will gaze on their bodies for three and a half days, and they will not permit their bodies to be placed in a tomb. REV. 11:8, 9.

A t 4:00 p.m. on October 27, 1962, President John F. Kennedy met with his military leaders. The Joint Chiefs of Staff recommended that the U.S. attack Cuba within 36 hours and destroy the Soviet missiles that aerial photography had detected there. The CIA assured the leaders that the Soviets had not yet delivered the nuclear warheads to arm those missiles. What they did not know at the time was that the Soviets already had 162 nuclear warheads in Cuba. Fidel Castro had even recommended to Nikita Krushchev the use of nuclear weapons if the U.S. invaded. Events were spiraling out of control.

Krushchev had sized up the young president Kennedy as a weakling, considering him full of talk but timid in action. Knowing that getting nuclear missiles into Cuba would change the balance of power in an instant, he calculated that Kennedy would bluster but in the end do nothing. He was wrong.

Not only did Kennedy challenge Cuba, he threw down the glove to Krushchev's own Soviet Union. And he did it in spite of great danger to his people. When he asked Walter Sweeney, chief of the Tactical Air Command, if he was certain he could take out all the missiles, Sweeney replied, "We have the finest fighter force in the world; we have trained for this kind of operation, and they would destroy the great majority. But there might be one or two or five left."

On October 27 Krushchev gave no signs of backing down. Kennedy's advisors had split between those who wanted to attack and those who thought they should negotiate. At the last minute Kennedy took up an offer from Krushchev to withdraw the missiles if the U.S. promised not to invade Cuba. Worried that war might break out in the six hours it took to encode and transmit a message from the Kremlin to the White House, Krushchev decided to broadcast his response to Kennedy on Moscow public radio.[86]

The two witnesses in the book of Revelation seemed weak and helpless to their enemies. Evil is often emboldened by a "turn the other cheek" mentality. But those who assert their power and position against God's people in this life miscalculate as surely as the Soviet premier did in 1962. The book of Revelation teaches us that the triumph of evil is always short-lived. In the end God will vindicate His people in the sight of all who have despised and abused them (Rev. 20:7-10).

Lord, give me the patience to wait for Your vindication.

THOSE WHO LIVE ON THE EARTH WILL REJOICE
OVER THEM, *celebrate, and send gifts to one another because these prophets had tormented those who live on the earth. But after three and a half days the breath of life from God entered into them and they stood up on their feet.* GREAT
FEAR FELL ON THOSE WHO SAW THEM. REV. 11:10, 11.

I n April of 2004 I was flying from Hong Kong to San Francisco. A couple hours into the flight I took a casual look at the flight data screen. My head snapped forward with amazement. The screen said that our plane was traveling 775 miles per hour, well past the speed of sound. Thanks to a 200-mile-per-hour tailwind, we had smoothly broken the sound barrier.

On October 14, 1947, Chuck Yeager prepared for his ninth flight in the experimental rocket plane Bell X-1. Each previous flight had edged closer to Mach 1, the never-crossed barrier beyond which human beings would fly faster than the speed of sound. It was dangerous, he knew. A British test pilot had perished when his aircraft disintegrated at Mach 0.94. Yeager, the fearless test pilot who would one day pilot a rocket plane out of the earth's atmosphere, climbed down into the X-1 as it lay in the airborne belly of the huge mother ship, a B-29. He snapped the cockpit cover shut using a sawed-off broom.

At 20,000 feet the rocket plane dropped out of the bomb bay with a jolt. All four rockets fired, causing the plane to shake violently. The Mach needle edged up past 0.965, and then it went off the scale. Thunderstruck, Yeager realized that he was flying supersonic. "It was as smooth as a baby's bottom: Grandma could be sitting up there sipping lemonade," he said later. His X-1 had accelerated to Mach 1.06, or 700 miles per hour. He half didn't believe it— until the tracking crew ran up and reported hearing the world's first sonic boom, a sound that marked the end of the Wright Brothers' era and the beginning of the space age.[87]

According to our text, the emotions of "those who live on the earth" shifted suddenly from great rejoicing to great fear. In both cases the emotions were related to the future. When the two witnesses were dead, people foresaw no "torment" in their future. But the resurrection of the witnesses brought great fear. God's enemies had no idea what would happen to them.

Today we routinely break the sound barrier and hardly notice it, but Yeager had no way of knowing it would be that smooth. In an act of great courage he faced his fears and tried. Those who are on God's side don't have to be afraid of the future. We already know that the "sonic boom" at the end of time will not harm those who are sealed.

Lord, thank You for the assurance that we have nothing to fear for the future except we forget how You have led us in the past.

July 18

And **THEY** [**THE TWO WITNESSES**] *heard a loud voice from heaven saying to them," Come up here." And they ascended to heaven in a cloud, and their enemies saw them.* REV. 11:12.

One of the great issues of interpretation in Revelation is the identity of the two witnesses in chapter 11. Whoever they are, they have divine authority: they "prophesy" 1260 days in sackcloth (Rev. 11:3). Scripture also calls them the two prophets (verse 10). They deliver the prophetic message that John is required to "prophesy again" (Rev. 10:11).

In the Jewish legal system something had to be established by at least two witnesses in order to be accepted as true (Deut. 19:15). It was a good system because the two witnesses had to describe the incident separately in ways that agreed with each other. The court would not take it seriously if only one person said that so-and-so did it. The infamous O. J. Simpson trial was frustrating in that nothing could be established beyond a reasonable doubt since there were no witnesses. So the image of two witnesses suggests that the message is both serious and true (Rev. 11:3).

Who are these witnesses? Scripture depicts them as olive trees and as the lampstands of the sanctuary (verse 4). The description reminds us of the time of Zerubbabel, when the Jews were restoring the Temple after the exile to Babylon (Zech. 4). So the two witness are symbols of the power of the Holy Spirit to enlighten the earth through God's Word and His people. John further portrays the witnesses in terms of Moses and Elijah (Rev. 11:5, 6), who represented God despite great opposition. Although they suffer for the message, they are not powerless.

Students of Revelation through the centuries have offered two main explanations of who the witnesses are. The first is that they represent the Bible, the Old and New Testaments (also reflecting the law [Moses] and the prophets [Elijah] of the Jewish canon). The Old Testament scriptures bear witness to Jesus (see John 5:39, 40; 19:35, 37). So the concept of two witnesses to Jesus could be a reference to the Scriptures.

Equal evidence exists for a second concept. The presence of Temple imagery points to the church, often referred to as the temple of God in the New Testament (1 Cor. 3:17; 1 Peter 2:1-10). The church on earth is the light of the world (Matt. 5:14-16), because witnessing is the church's primary task (Luke 24:48; Acts 1:8).

In Revelation Jesus is both the faithful witness (Rev. 1:5) and the Word of God (Rev. 19:13). So the options are two sides of the same coin. Either way the point of the passage is the power of God's end-time message to change the world in spite of great opposition.

Lord, help me to keep my eye focused on the mission You have given Your church. Help me to use Your Word to make a difference in my world today.

And in that hour there was a great earthquake, and a tenth of the city fell. Seven thousand people were killed by the earthquake, and **THE REMNANT BECAME AFRAID AND GAVE GLORY TO THE GOD OF HEAVEN.** *The second woe has gone away. Behold, the third woe is coming quickly.* Rev. 11:13, 14.

The word "remnant" in this passage anticipates the use of the same word in Revelation 12:17. I believe it also foreshadows the work of the 144,000 in Revelation 14. Let me explain. Both the remnant (Rev. 12:17) and the 144,000 (Rev. 14:1-5) are the same group. And both concepts echo Joel 2:32, in which a remnant on Mount Zion calls on the name of the Lord. In Revelation 14 the 144,000, represented by an angel, proclaim: "Fear God and give glory to Him" (Rev. 14:7). Now, it is possible that the remnant of our text is merely "afraid." But I think it is more likely that they are responding to the message of Revelation 14:7. The remnant of Revelation 11:13 fear God and give Him glory, just as the first angel calls on the world to do.

There are at least three types of fear. The first is the fear of financial ruin. I remember March 14, 2000. On that day the financial markets in the United States reached a monumental peak. Many stocks and mutual funds had risen hundreds of percent from where they had been in 1995. But on that March 14 a slide began that lasted nearly three years, wiping out about half of all the money invested in the stock market. A magazine lamented, "Say goodbye to the all-powerful venture capitalists and dot-com millionaires and hello to bankruptcy lawyers, turnaround specialists, and liquidators."[88] The good news is that many failed investors found their true value, not in money and possessions, but in the kingdom of God.

A second type of fear is concern about physical harm. And such fear is legitimate. No amount of healthy living and safe driving can guarantee that earthquake, disease, criminal elements, or something else will not harm us. But God has promised to be with us when we pass through the "valley of the shadow of death" (Ps. 23:4, NIV). Knowing that He is in control gives us the confidence to live one day at a time, savoring each moment as a gift.

I believe that the third type of fear is the one illustrated in this text. It is the most important kind of fear, one that leads us to God. The Lord can use our natural fear (as when we confront things too big for us to control—such as a great earthquake) to lead us to an awareness of His presence and a desire to be right with Him. Paul talks about working out our salvation "with fear and trembling" (Phil. 2:12, NIV). Godly fear will lead us not only to a recognition of His presence, but to the appropriate awe and reverence.

Lord, help me to have a healthy appreciation of the fact that You are always watching me. I want to be accountable to You in everything I do.

July 20

The seventh angel blew his trumpet, and there were loud voices in heaven which were speaking, "The kingdom of this world has become the kingdom of our Lord and of His Christ, and He will reign for ever and ever." And the twenty-four elders, who are sitting on their thrones before God, fell upon their faces and worshiped God, saying, **"WE GIVE THANKS TO YOU,** *Lord God Almighty, who is and who was, because You have taken hold of Your great power and begun to reign."* Rev. 11:15-17.

One day the father of an extremely wealthy family took his son on a trip to the country with the intent of showing his son how poor people live. They spent a couple days and nights on the farm of what most would consider a very poor family.

On their return from their trip, the father asked his son, "How was the trip?"

"It was great, Dad."

"Did you see how poor people live?" the father inquired.

"Oh, yeah," the son replied.

"So, tell me, what did you learn from the trip?"

"I saw that we have one dog and they had four," the son answered. "We have a pool that reaches to the middle of our garden, and they have a creek that has no end. We have imported lanterns in our garden, and they have the stars at night. Our patio reaches to the front yard, and they have the whole horizon. We have a small piece of land to live on, and they have fields that go beyond our sight. We have servants who serve us, but they serve others. We buy our food, but they grow theirs. We have walls around our property to protect us, but they have friends to protect them."

The boy's father was speechless. Then his son added, "Thanks, Dad, for showing me how poor we are." [89]

In Revelation 4:9 we noticed the 24 elders giving continual thanks to God for Creation and for His mighty acts of salvation. In our text for today the elders are again worshipping and are offering thanks, but this time the object of their thankfulness is more specific. They praise God for His end-time invasion of the kingdom of this world, and for replacing it with His own kingdom, grounded in the mighty acts of Christ. When we fully grasp what Christ has done for us, it changes our attitude toward everything. This is one of the major functions of the book of Revelation. By raising our perspective from our own little world to the grandeur of God's universe, we become aware of how deeply grateful we should be. It's all in how you look at it!

Lord, whenever I am tempted to think that I have been shortchanged in this life, remind me of the treasure I have in Jesus Christ.

The nations were angry, and Your wrath has come, and **THE TIME TO JUDGE THE DEAD** *and to reward Your servants the prophets, and the saints and those who fear Your name, both the small and the great, and to destroy those who are destroying the earth.* Rev. 11:18.

This verse offers a summary of the final events of earth's history. They have five main parts or aspects. The nations are angry and the wrath of God has come, as well as the time to judge the dead, reward the righteous, and remove those destroying the earth. This text predicts that, just before the end, the nations will be angry. And we may be entering into just such a time. It is harder and harder to find common ground among the conflicting political agendas. The new world order proclaimed after the Gulf War of 1991 has turned into the new world disorder.

God responds in kind to the anger of the nations. The "wrath of God" here is a nutshell summary of the seven last plagues of Revelation 16 (see Rev. 14:10 and 15:1). The plagues soften up the forces of evil, preparing the way for the final victory of God. The Lord's final word in this trumpet is that of judgment. The judgment will make right the wrongs of this world. It will defeat oppressors and rescue and vindicate their victims. And it will be, not a time of pointless violence, but one of setting things straight.

I remember a meeting of secular Bible scholars. Many in the group studied the Bible for a living, but no longer believed that it was *the* answer to the great problems of life. In their comments they assumed that the Bible's promises of judgment and resurrection merely reflected the cultural hopes of the ancients.

But that day their assumption received a challenge from an unexpected direction. A hard-smoking, hard-drinking German scholar took objection to the proceedings. He protested that it was a waste of time to study the Bible merely as an academic exercise. "No matter how you paint it, the Bible is right about the injustices of this world. If this life is all we have to look forward to, nothing will ever change. If there is no such thing as judgment or resurrection, there will never be any justice in this world. The Bible writers believed that there was a judgment to come and a resurrection, and that is the only hope we have."

The resurrection and the judgment tell us that someday God will set everything right. While His justice may not be visible to many eyes just yet, we are nearer than ever to the time spoken of in this text.

Lord, I look forward to the day when You will correct all the injustices of this world. Help me to anticipate that time by doing the right thing today.

July 22

The nations were angry, and Your wrath has come, and the time to judge the dead and to reward Your servants the prophets, and the saints and those who fear Your name, **BOTH THE SMALL AND THE GREAT,** *and to destroy those who are destroying the earth.* Rev. 11:18.

T hose who face grief or hardship anywhere in the world can appreciate the message of the seventh trumpet. The world belongs to God, and He will take full charge of it at the appropriate time (Rev. 11:15). When He does, He will right all the wrongs of history, shattering all opposition to His rule (verse 18). Today's text reminds us that when the day of judgment comes God will reward both small and great (verse 18), just as He will punish both great and small (Rev. 6:15).

The hardships of the past have molded the Black church tradition of North America. Those who endured oppression in everyday life looked forward to church, where janitors could be deacons and street sweepers could be preachers. The Black church tradition follows the New Testament pattern in which slaves often rose to the office of bishop. There are no limits when God is on your side.

Rosa Parks was tired after a hard day as a seamstress in Montgomery, Alabama. She had to run a youth meeting later that night. Still she didn't jump right on the first bus that came by that Thursday evening. The bus stop was crowded, so she headed to a drugstore to shop for an electric heating pad, thinking that she could get a seat on the way home if she waited a bit.

When she finally deposited her 10-cent fare on the Cleveland Avenue bus, she found a seat in the first row of the "Colored" section in the back. But after a few stops the driver ordered her to get up so a White passenger could sit down. When Parks refused, the driver summoned the police to take her to jail. Two hours after the arrest she was released on $100 bail. By midnight Black leaders had formulated a plan for a citywide bus boycott. A young Baptist minister named Martin Luther King, Jr., became its leader.

The boycott lasted 381 days, until the Supreme Court ruled that segregation on buses was illegal. The success of the boycott ignited the modern civil rights movement. "When I declined to give up my seat, it was not that day or bus in particular," Parks said later. "I just wanted to be free, like everybody else." [90]

"Your will be done, on earth as it is in heaven" (Matt. 6:10, NIV). We don't need to wait until the kingdom comes to treat other people the way heaven does.

Lord, open my eyes to the injustice You see in my world and my community. Help me to be an agent of change today.

And **THE TEMPLE OF GOD WHICH IS IN HEAVEN** *was opened, and the ark of His covenant was seen in His temple, and there were lightnings, noises, thunders, an earthquake, and great hail.* REV. 11:19.

Today's passage offers an explicit view of the heavenly temple. In vision John's gaze lifts from events on earth (Rev. 11:18) to the heavenly temple. He receives the equivalent of a virtual reality tour into the temple, moving deeper and deeper until he gazes into the Most Holy Place itself. There he sees the Old Testament ark of the covenant, accompanied by flashes of lightning, loud noises, an earthquake, and heavy hail. What is going on here? What is the point of having an ark of the covenant in the gospel context of the New Testament?

It makes a lot of sense in the context of who Jesus is. One day He was standing in the outer courtyard of the Temple in Jerusalem. After casting out the moneychangers and stockyards, He finds Himself confronted by the Temple authorities. " 'Destroy this temple, and I will raise it again in three days' " (John 2:19, NIV), He challenges them. He must have been pointing to Himself when He said this, for John explains that He was referring to the temple of His body.

On another occasion Jesus said, "I tell you that one greater than the temple is here" (Matt. 12:6, NIV). For Jews there was only one thing greater than the Temple, and that was the Shekinah glory of God's presence inside the Temple. Putting both of these gospel texts together, we can see that the very presence of God was in Jesus' own body. The divine presence and character made the body of Jesus a temple. He carried the Most Holy Place with Him wherever He went.

So if Jesus represents the Shekinah glory, the temple is wherever Jesus is. Since Jesus is in heaven, according to the book of Hebrews, heaven has a sanctuary in which He ministers, intercedes, and judges. But Jesus is also present in the church (1 Cor. 3:17; 1 Peter 2:1-10). If believers gather in a living room or even a campsite, it is a temple of God. "For where two or three come together in my name, there am I with them (Matt. 18:20, NIV). Jesus also dwells in us by His Spirit. "Do you not know that your body is a temple of the Holy Spirit, who is in you, whom you have received from God?" (1 Cor. 6:19, NIV). When we receive Jesus, our bodies become temples as well.

The book of Revelation emphasizes the first of these three New Testament temples. But it also looks forward to the end-time restoration of the heavenly sanctuary (Rev. 11:1, 2, 19). That includes the full return of God's rule to the universe. When the character of God has been fully vindicated, universal peace and harmony will once again completely fill the universe.

Lord, I pray that everything I do and say today will vindicate Your character in front of a watching world. May I rightly represent You before everyone I meet.

July 24

And a great sign was seen in heaven, **A WOMAN DRESSED WITH THE SUN. THE MOON WAS UNDER HER FEET** *and* **UPON HER HEAD WAS A VICTORY CROWN OF TWELVE STARS.** *She was pregnant, and she cried out in pain as she labored to give birth.* REV. 12:1, 2.

The woman wears the sun, moon, and stars. Scholars believe the woman represents Israel, in part because her crown has 12 stars. The Old Testament often thinks of God in terms of Israel's husband. "For your Maker is your husband—the Lord Almighty is his name—the Holy One of Israel is your Redeemer" (Isa. 54:5, NIV).

While the woman symbolizes God's people on earth, Revelation depicts her as being in heavenly places. Our identity as His people is not determined by where we are on earth, but rather by our relationship with heaven. It is helpful, therefore, to build into our lives reminders of our higher relationship.

John McCain spent five and one-half years as a prisoner of war in Vietnam. In the early years of his imprisonment the NVA (North Vietnamese Army) kept him in solitary confinement or at times with one or two others in a cell. In 1971, however, the NVA moved its prisoners from isolation into large rooms with 30 to 40 men. One of the men in the larger room was named Mike Christian. A Navy flight officer, he had been shot down and captured in 1967.

As part of the change in treatment, the Vietnamese allowed some prisoners to receive packages from home. Some of the packages included handkerchiefs, scarves, and other items of clothing. Mike got a bamboo needle. During a period of a couple months he created an American flag and sewed it onto the inside of his shirt. Every afternoon, before they had a bowl of soup, the prisoners would hang Mike's shirt on the wall of the cell and say the Pledge of Allegiance. In that stark cell it was the most important and meaningful event of the day.

One day the Vietnamese searched the cell, as they did periodically, discovered Mike's shirt with the flag sewn inside, and removed it. That evening they returned, opened the door of the cell, took Mike Christian out, and beat him severely for the next couple hours in sight of the others. Then they opened the door of the cell and threw him back in. His cellmates cleaned him up as well as they could.

After the excitement died down, his fellow prisoners spotted Mike in the corner of the room, sitting beneath a dim light bulb with a piece of red cloth, another shirt, and his bamboo needle. With his eyes almost shut from the beating he had received, he was, nevertheless, fashioning another American flag. He was making that flag not because it made him feel better, but because it reminded him of home.[91]

Lord, help me to build into my life reminders of my heavenly citizenship.

And a great sign was seen in heaven, a woman dressed with the sun. **THE MOON WAS UNDER HER FEET** *and upon her head was a victory crown of twelve stars. She was pregnant, and she cried out in pain as she labored to give birth.* REV. 12:1, 2.

From childhood on, the moon has had a special interest for me. When I was 9 years old I bought a three-and-a-quarter-inch reflector telescope. With a special Barlow lens it was capable of bringing heavenly objects 270 times closer than with the naked eye. The telescope had a heavy, cast-iron base and was angled according to the tilt of the earth's axis, so one could follow an object as it moved across the sky because of the earth's rotation.

I set up the telescope in the front yard of my parents' home just outside of New York City. A half moon floated in the sky that night. I focused the telescope on the straight edge of the moon. The moon's craters were in sharp relief because of the long shadows near the lunar sunset. The view was magnificent. I stopped everyone walking by so they could have a look!

It should be no surprise, then, that I got up at 3:00 a.m. the night of the first moonwalk on July 20, 1969. Live television broadcast Neil Armstrong's first step onto the lunar surface. I distinctly remember the sound of his words: "That's one small step for . . . man, one giant leap for mankind." The words were so unexpected, yet so appropriate.

It turns out that Neil Armstrong meant to say, "That's one small step for a man," adapting the phrase from a children's playground game. Instead, because of intense radio static, Mission Control in Houston and the rest of the human race heard, "That's one small step for . . . man," one of the most famous sentences of the twentieth century.

Even on a grainy black-and-white television set the images were unforgettable. A camera mounted on the base of the lunar landing vehicle beamed back the otherworldly milestone. The 38-year-old Armstrong became the first earthling to stand on the moon. Since he was assigned to handle the portable camera, most of the pictures of that mission were of his fellow astronaut, Edwin "Buzz" Aldrin. We see Armstrong mainly as a reflection on Aldrin's faceplate. A total of 12 men have walked on the moon, the last in 1972.[92]

In another sense, though, Armstrong was not the first human to stand on the moon. The woman of Revelation got there first! Earth's final battle is the outcome of an earlier struggle in heaven. The two battles appear side by side in Revelation 12. What happens to the woman is determined by the outcome of the universal war between Satan and Christ. Whenever my life becomes a struggle, I look up at the moon and know that I am not alone.

Lord, help me not to be absorbed in my own difficulties. Keep me aware of the larger battle, of which I am only a part.

July 26

And another sign was seen in heaven: **A GREAT, FIERY RED DRAGON WITH SEVEN HEADS AND TEN HORNS,** *and upon his heads seven crowns. His tail dragged down a third of the stars of heaven and threw them to the earth. The dragon stood before the woman who was about to give birth, so that when her child was born he might eat it up.* Rev. 12:3, 4.

A strange-looking animal does extraordinary things here. At first glance, such stories seem totally out of touch with today's world. But that is not really the case. Take the Disney cartoon movie *The Lion King,* for example. Like Revelation, it appears to be a simple animal story at first glance. But it is much more. It is actually a parable about the way people and groups of people interact with each other. Furthermore, it is about taking risks, developing relationships, avoiding conflict, and confronting issues that make a difference in everyday life.

But *The Lion King* is even more than a sociological treatise in disguise. It derives from an African version of apocalyptic. The story involves the ruin and restoration of a paradise wherein all function in happiness and prosperity. *The Lion King* tells about an evil that arises from a dark place at the edge of paradise. And it is about the hope for the future that can result when a redeemer figure seizes their destiny with courage.

That's what makes the book of Revelation so powerful. Although it reads like an animal story (Rev. 11:7; 12; 13; 17), it's not really about animals. It is about people and their relationships, about interactions among groups of people—both good and evil—and how the course of human history will turn out. In other words, it is about the fundamental issues we all wrestle with from day to day.

Movies tend to be most successful when they intersect with the basic struggles, conflicts, and tensions within society's popular myths and fears. Such movies as *The Lion King* show that apocalyptic genre is as popular today as it was when John wrote the book of Revelation. The credibility of apocalyptic movies depends on whether their analysis of society and the human condition is believable. The same was true of ancient apocalypses.

No one knows whether anyone will remember *The Lion King* 100 years from now. But the book of Revelation has spoken powerfully for almost 2,000 years. It helps us understand both ourselves and the situation of the whole human race. Mirroring reality in a way that bypasses our psychological and emotional defense mechanisms, it strikes home with powerful force where we least expect it. And it helps us see the self-deception that lurks within each one of us.

Lord, give me eyes to see the truth about myself. May Your presence tame the dragon that lurks within me.

July 27

And another sign was seen in heaven: a great, fiery red dragon with seven heads and ten horns, and upon his heads seven crowns. **HIS TAIL DRAGGED DOWN A THIRD OF THE STARS OF HEAVEN AND THREW THEM TO THE EARTH.** *The dragon stood before the woman who was about to give birth, so that when her child was born he might eat it up.* Rev. 12:3, 4.

The psalmist said, "The heavens declare the glory of God" (Ps. 19:1, NIV). One of the best definitions of "glory" is as a representation of character. The psalmist tells us that the universe displays God's character in the things that He has made.

But the author of Revelation tells a slightly different story. Satan has done his best to obliterate the image of God that the Creator embossed into His creation. Sin has marred and defiled the earth, and it reflects God's glory in only the dimmest fashion. So it should not surprise us that the findings of honest science on this earth might not totally agree with the Scripture record. The evidence has been tampered with.

But shouldn't the condition of the wider universe be a different matter? After all, one would expect the ravages of sin to be located primarily on earth. Would not the wider universe remain unspoiled with clear traces of God's hand? Another psalmist begs to differ: "The heavens are the work of your hands. They will perish, but you remain; they will all wear out like a garment. Like clothing you will change them and they will be discarded" (Ps 102:25, 26, NIV).

Science bears out that the "perfection" of the universe is, at best, a very different one from what we might expect. Craters pock the moon, spots cover the surface of the sun, and planetary satellites have powerful volcanoes that alter their landscapes in destructive fashion.

Stars appear to go through life cycles in which they form, burn through a massive amount of fuel, explode, and then dwindle down to cold, lifeless spheres. Black holes suck in or destroy everything that passes near. Galaxies collide and cast debris here and there. It would seem that even in the heavens we find traces not only of God's hand, but also of the tail of the dragon, the old serpent, Satan.[93]

The safest course for the people of God is to stay close to His Word. The evidence of our eyes and ears can deceive us. The words of Scripture, on the other hand, guided by the illumination of the Spirit, give a picture of God that corrects the misconceptions inevitable in a universe marred by sin.

Lord, I purpose to seek You in all I do today. I want to be open to Your leading in research and experience, but help me to correct that understanding through Your Word.

July 28

And she gave birth to a son, a male child, who is about to shepherd all the nations with a rod of iron. And her **CHILD** *was snatched up to God and to His throne.* REV. 12:5.

The child in this verse clearly represents Jesus Christ. So in the middle of an apocalyptic vision we get a glimpse of something familiar—the Christmas story. John has the birth and ascension of Jesus Christ on display here.

Although we are familiar with the stories of the Christmas season, it is still hard to imagine Jesus as a child. Did He fall and scratch His knee at times? Did His mother put a bandage on the Son of God? How did Jesus get along with His playmates? When they grabbed one of His toys, did He demand it back, or did He simply let it go? Did they take advantage of Him as a result? Did His mother or father ever ask Him to do something that would have violated His conscience? How would He have handled that?

Some time ago I ran across a wonderful set of lessons that children learn in life. Reviewing them will give you a chuckle and also bring home the amazing truth that God did not send His Son to earth as an adult, ready to deal with adults, but as a child, subject to the lessons of everyday life. Here are some great truths about life that little children have learned:

1. No matter how hard you try, you can't baptize cats.
2. When your mom is mad at your dad, don't let her brush your hair.
3. If your sister hits you, don't hit her back. Parents always catch the second person.
4. Never ask your 3-year-old brother to hold a tomato.
5. You can't trust dogs to watch your food.
6. Don't sneeze when someone is cutting your hair.
7. Never hold a Dust-Buster and a cat at the same time.
8. You can't hide a piece of broccoli in a glass of milk.
9. Don't wear polka-dot underwear under white shorts.
10. The best place to be when you're sad is Grandpa's lap.[94]

Several of the illustrations would have been unfamiliar to Jesus as a child growing up in Nazareth. They do, however, give a delightful window into the world of the child and how life's lessons get experienced—and hopefully learned. It is moving to realize that God took the enormous risk of inserting His Son into a world He as a child could not control, an environment in which He was relatively helpless, facing the wrath of the dragon in full force. The measure of God's sacrifice is also the measure of His love for us.

Lord, thank You for sending Jesus to explore human life and its complications fully. I trust You to understand and meet my needs today.

And **THE WOMAN FLED INTO THE DESERT,** *where she had a place prepared for her by God, in order that she might be nourished there for a thousand two hundred and sixty days.* REV. 12:6.

Bible scholars generally agree that the woman of Revelation 12 represents the church suffering at the hands of Satan, particularly after the resurrection of Jesus. Persecution, of course, can come in many forms.

I was born on the Upper East Side of Manhattan when it was relatively poor (today that neighborhood contains America's most expensive real estate). My parents soon found affordable housing across the Hudson River in New Jersey. But while I grew up in another state, my family and I still thought of ourselves as New Yorkers. We went to church in Manhattan, and when we could afford it, my brother and I went to Adventist schools in the city as well.

It was tough growing up Adventist in New York City. Not only were most of the people on the street secular, but we didn't even feel at home with Christians of other denominations. We were a tiny, scattered community in the midst of an enormous world of skyscrapers and forbidden attractions. Like most New Yorkers, we hurried from one familiar place to another through a vast jungle of strangers with unfamiliar faces.

I can't say that anyone ever really persecuted me for my faith. I just knew I was different, even strange. I wanted to be liked, but the neighbor kids knew I was not one of them. I didn't go to the movie theaters with them and never showed up at the school dances on Friday night (I went to public school for five years). If my friends asked if they could come over on Saturdays I made some excuse or other. When offered a beer or a smoke, I declined as politely as I knew how (although I suffered many guilty struggles at the neighborhood candy shop). Persecuted? No. Abused? No. Scorned and rejected? Not really. My non-Adventist friends and neighbors were really nice people. A fish out of water? Yes. A stranger in a strange land? Definitely.

Growing up, I felt more at home in the book of Revelation than I did in my neighborhood. John seemed to understand my struggles with the world—the forbidden attractions, the sense of being different, even weird. He portrayed the kind of world I was living in. When I read about the woman in the desert, I felt she represented me. The Roman world as understood by Bible scholars was a lot like my world.[95] Christians in Asia Minor, even if no one persecuted them, still struggled with how to live in a pagan world.

Lord, train me in the relatively easy times to be faithful in the hard times that Revelation tells us are coming.

July 30

And there was war in heaven. Michael and his angels gathered to fight against the dragon, and the dragon and his angels also fought. And the dragon was not strong enough, neither was a place found in heaven for them. And the great dragon, the ancient serpent, the one called devil and Satan, who deceives the whole inhabited world, was thrown down into the earth, and his angels were thrown down with him. And I heard a loud voice in heaven saying, "Now have come salvation and strength, and the kingdom of our God and the authority of His Christ, for **THE ACCUSER OF OUR BROTHERS,** *the one who accuses them before the throne of God day and night, has been cast down." And* **THEY OVERCAME HIM** *by the blood of the Lamb and the word of their testimony, and they did not love their lives unto death.* Rev. 12:7-11.

The size of the known universe is dizzying. While the planet Earth is a large place, it is small compared to other planets circling a very average star. Our solar system is located at the fringe of a very average galaxy, which contains at least 100 million stars, many of them with solar systems of their own. We now know that there are billions and billions of galaxies in the known universe. This means that we are either very important—or very unimportant.

When you see how easily our planet could be lost in the limitless realms of the universe, you might begin to think we must be rather irrelevant. But when you read Revelation 12 you get a quite different impression. You begin to realize that what is going on here may be of greater significance to the universe than events anywhere else.

Revelation 12:4 tells us that the dragon threw down a third of the stars in heaven. In a symbolic-style story like this they are clearly not literal stars or galaxies. Revelation 1:20 interprets stars as angels, suggesting that the dragon (Satan) precipitated a conflict in heaven (the control center of the universe, wherever that is) that resulted in a third of the heavenly inhabitants becoming exiled to this earth. So our planet has become the ongoing location of an insurgency that began long ago in heaven.

This is the ultimate answer to the issue of evil, pain, and suffering on this earth. No doubt the angels who remained in heaven wondered if Satan's rebellion had any merit. The cross settled all their doubts. A God who would die for His creatures can be trusted to do what is right and fair. While Satan had some access to the heavenly courts before the cross (Job 1 and 2), his viewpoint has been banished from heaven since then (Rev. 12:10, 11).

Lord, I see the beauty of Your character at the cross. I choose to be faithful to You no matter what the cost.

And I heard a loud voice in heaven saying, ". . . THE ACCUSER OF OUR BROTHERS . . . has been cast down." And they overcame him by the blood of the Lamb and the word of their testimony. REV. 12:10, 11.

Satan here attempts to defeat God by accusing His people! He questions their standing with Him, their fitness to share in the victory that God won at the cross. But they can thwart Satan by applying the blood of the Lamb to their experience. When God's people truly understand what Christ did for them at Golgotha, even the threat of death cannot affect their loyalty to God. But what does all this mean in daily life?[96]

Satan's accusations are powerful weapons in an addictive society. Addictive behavior often traces back to abuse and rejection in the past. Careless parents traumatize children with words of rejection. Children from caring homes sometimes get abused in school or in the neighborhood. Even good parents can get trapped by the frantic pace of life. They may be physically there with their children, but absent emotionally and mentally.

So most youth grow up with a sense of rejection and abandonment, even though their parents never intended any such thing. Satan's accusations cause young people to blame themselves for their pain. He makes them feel worthless and helpless, tempting them to turn to alcohol, sex, and entertainment as emotional medicine for the soul. The more he can make them feel ashamed and alone, the stronger the chains of addiction become.

I knew a young man who responded to Satan's accusations with a vicious cycle of desperate sexual actions. After falling into sin a few times, he would try to pray his way out. Then he would slip into a few more episodes of sexual obsession, followed by still more prayer. Once he tried anointing. Nothing seemed to help, until one day others caught him in the act and he found himself thrown into jail. While Bill's sexual addiction was the result of abandonment by parents as a child, his inability to change led him to feel abandoned by God as well. Satan accused God in the man's mind. "You'll never get better. If God cared, He would cure you."

I suspect the apostle John also knew Satan's accusations from personal experience. "You've served God all your life, and all you have to show for it is a ticket to some God-forsaken island!" But the prophet doesn't buy into Satan's accusations, because he knows the blood of the Lamb. The blood of Jesus goes to the root of the addiction, the sense that we are worthless and alone. How? The "blood of the Lamb" means we are worth the whole universe to God. We are precious in His eyes. With that assurance we can enter into a process of healing that will affect the whole person.

Lord, I feel alone today, not because You don't care, but because the accuser trained me to believe that. Help me to see the value You placed on me at the cross.

August 1

And I heard a loud voice in heaven saying, ". . . The accuser of our brothers . . . has been cast down." And **THEY OVERCAME HIM BY THE BLOOD OF THE LAMB** *and the word of their testimony.* Rev. 12:10, 11.

The blood of the Lamb was shed already in the Garden of Gethsemane. Drops of blood fell to the ground (Luke 22:44) as Jesus battled to align His will with that of His Father (Matt. 26:39; Mark 14:36; Luke 22:42). The root of human self-will is found in the first garden. There Adam and Eve rejected God's will and asserted their own (Gen. 3:1-6). When Christ won the battle in another garden, He triumphed for the whole human race.

I don't know about you, but I face a battle with my will every day. While I don't have to combat alcohol, tobacco, or drugs, I often struggle with more "Christian" versions of addiction. I struggle to choose the right kind and right amount of food. I allow myself to get angry when things don't go my way. I let things at work affect the way I feel. And I allow negative and ungodly thoughts to linger in my mind. I'm glad I don't have to deal with alcohol or drugs, but frankly, the struggle to control my thoughts and my actions often goes hard.

Recently for health reasons I vowed to eat nothing in the evening except fruit. I set my mind and will to accomplish this goal. But I learned that many things can derail my will. My wife or daughter makes some delicious food in the evening, and I just have to have some! Or I don't want to hurt their feelings by saying no. Perhaps work or church has a special social. Or it's Christmas! Or Saturday night! The list goes on. Do you see my point? Weakness of will is deeply rooted in the human condition after the Fall in Eden.

Whether one's addictive behavior is life-threatening or of a more "vegetarian" variety, the path to victory is the same. Victory over sin is not really possible until we absorb into the very core of our being the triumph of the cross. Jesus completely exhausted all our sin and failure at the cross (1 Peter 2:24). When we realize that He blotted out our record of failure—our sense of shame and worthlessness—in Himself, we can begin to align our will with God's and break the chains of the past. Then we become freed from the past to become free in the present.

In my experience this victory comes in two stages. First, we need to grasp the *truth* of Revelation 12:11. The cross has already won the battle. Second, it takes time for battered and abused people to *feel* what they already *know*. Emotions are a "lagging indicator." Don't expect your feelings to change instantly just because you read this. You may need to assert the truth of the cross many times before your feelings and your will buy into that victory.

Lord, Your will has my best interest at heart. I say yes to Your will today—yes, no matter how I feel. I invite You to begin aligning my whole being according to Your will.

And they overcame him by the blood of the Lamb and **THE WORD OF THEIR TESTIMONY,** *and they did not love their lives unto death.* Rev. 12:11.

The book of Revelation usually associates the word "testimony" with Jesus. The "testimony of Jesus" is a vision that John saw (Rev. 1:2). It is the reason that the prophet is on Patmos in the first place (verse 9). A possession of the end-time remnant (Rev. 12:17), it is the spirit that inspires prophecy (Rev. 19:10). And it is the motivating force that encourages the martyrs (Rev. 20:4). Jesus offers His testimony to the churches (Rev. 22:16).

But the word "testimony" can also apply to believers. The souls under the altar were martyred because of the testimony they had (Rev. 6:9). The two witnesses offer testimony before they die (Rev. 11:7). And the overcomers become so in part through the word of their testimony (Rev. 12:11). Feeble and defective though we may be, our witness is modeled on His witness. As soon as we know something about Jesus, we start to tell others what we know.

In a way it is like the blind leading the blind! A friend of mine, Jim Park, visited St. Paul's Cathedral in London one day. After touring it, he needed to get back to the Waterloo train station during rush hour. A guide at the cathedral suggested that he ride the bus instead of the underground, and that seemed like a nice adventure.

It took him several minutes, however, to find out which side of the street he should stand on and which bus to board. Finally he got on what he fervently hoped was the right bus and settled down for a ride that would last 20 minutes—or so he had been told. A couple of stops later a well-dressed blind man got on the bus and sat close to Jim. The two men got acquainted, and Jim learned that Roger worked at a music publishing house and was on his way home. Since the blind man was not used to taking this particular route to Waterloo station, he asked *Jim* if he could guide him to the proper place.

Jim meekly stammered something about his own uncertainty, but offered to give the best help that he could. Fortunately for both of them, a third man guided them both off the bus and into the station. Roger said he could find his own train, but Jim insisted on being his eyes. Somehow they were able to quickly work through the confusion and rush of the station in record time, and Roger boarded his train just as it was leaving.[97]

God, of course, knows where He is going and where He wants us to go. We are wise to consult Him at every turn and submit our plans to Him. But as we learn more about His will and His ways, we become His eyes and ears on earth. As a result, we have the incredible privilege of being His witnesses here. In so doing we become like Him.

Lord, thank You for showing me the way. I want to be a "tour guide" for others today.

August 3

And they overcame him by the blood of the Lamb and the word of their testimony,
and **THEY DID NOT LOVE THEIR LIVES UNTO DEATH.**
REV. 12:11.

No aspect of human experience arouses our energies faster than the prospect of immediate death. The drowning man struggles desperately to keep his head above water. A woman who falls off a cliff frantically clings to the branch of a bush growing out of the rock near the top. The dying patient searches the Internet for some hope of a cure. Impending death sets the full powers of our being into action. Yet our best efforts are not good enough. While we can sometimes postpone death, the ultimate sentence will be canceled only in earth's final generation. Our only hope until then is to trust completely in God's power to save us even beyond death.

This text, therefore, implies that those who overcome do so on the basis of complete trust in God. They place their lives in His hands, do whatever He says, and rely on His power to accomplish those things that seem impossible in their own strength. A modern-day example of overcoming occurred in the beginnings of the 12-step movement during the 1930s.

Bill Wilson was a stockbroker who lived in Brooklyn, New York, and had a serious problem with alcohol. On a business trip to Akron, Ohio (May 1935), he found himself outside a bar, tempted and desperate. In the past he had fought the urge by talking to other alcoholics, who truly understood his struggle. That day he left the vicinity of the bar and began looking for a church. Through a local church group he found surgeon Robert Holbrook Smith.

Dr. Bob and Bill W., as Alcoholics Anonymous members know them, promised to keep each other sober. Bill developed a strategy: a simple set of principles later refined into 12 steps. Alcoholics, Bill said, must admit they are powerless against their addiction. Next they must fearlessly inventory the defects and weaknesses in their character. They must make amends to everyone they have harmed. And above all else, they must submit to God, however they understand Him, to provide the power that they do not have on their own.

The advice did not take immediately. Dr. Bob went to Atlantic City, New Jersey, for a convention. Several days later he showed up at the Akron train station, totally soused. On June 10, 1935, the dried-out but still jittery doctor was due in surgery. That morning Bill W. gave Dr. Bob a bottle of beer to steady his scalpel hand during the surgery. The beer was Dr. Bob's last. The two men pledged that day to bring Bill W.'s principles to other alcoholics, one day at a time.[98]

Lord, I admit that I am powerless in the face of (alcohol, food, sex, drugs, anger, overwork, laziness, whatever). I place my life under Your control today. I need the power only You can give.

For this reason rejoice, heavens and those who live in them! **WOE TO THE EARTH AND THE SEA** *because the devil has come down to you in a great rage knowing that he has only a little time. And when the dragon saw that he was thrown to the earth,* **HE PERSECUTED THE WOMAN** *who had given birth to the male child. The woman was given the two wings of a great eagle in order that she might fly from the presence of the serpent into the desert to her place, the place where she would be sustained for a time, times, and half a time.* REV. 12:12-14.

Commentators usually understand the woman to represent the experience of the church during the long years between the time of Jesus and the end. What the church goes through will not be a picnic. Much persecution befalls those who take the name of Jesus. Such suffering stands in startling contrast to the assertions of victory and power made in Revelation 5. How to relate Christian suffering to the victory of God has always been challenging.

No one noticed the smoke seeping from the windows of the rental truck as Timothy McVeigh pulled up to the Alfred P. Murrah Federal Building that gray morning. McVeigh had lit two fuses to the 7,000-pound fertilizer bomb in the truck and then parked beside the building's day-care center. The explosion vaporized the front of the building, leaving a yawning cross-section of cables and smoke.

The dead would number 168, including 19 children. At least six of the survivors or those who lost loved ones have since killed themselves. When McVeigh was executed in 2001, he remained convinced that he had punished the U.S. government for its 1993 siege of the Branch Davidian compound near Waco, Texas.

For America, the bombing was an introduction to mass-casualty terrorism. The enemy was no longer uniformed platoons but lone extremists in our midst. They could not be easily ferreted out or understood. But Oklahoma City also wrote the book on recovery. The survivors have become indispensable companions for the families of the September 11 victims. And the memorial to the tragedy shows that traumatized cities can unite to protest unimaginable evil.[99]

While this may be little comfort to those in the throes of loss or suffering, nothing is ultimately wasted with God. In His infinite wisdom even the greatest of tragedies can lay the foundation for healing and recovery. While hurt people often injure others themselves, many victims of tragedy find resources in God to become healers instead of hurters.

Lord, help me today to set aside bitterness and revenge as responses to the things and to the people who have hurt me. Help me to become a source of healing instead of pain.

August 5

AND THE SERPENT SPEWED WATER LIKE A FLOODING RIVER OUT OF ITS MOUTH AS IT PURSUED THE WOMAN, IN ORDER THAT HE MIGHT CAUSE HER TO BE SWEPT AWAY BY THE FLOOD. AND THE EARTH HELPED THE WOMAN. IT OPENED ITS MOUTH AND SWALLOWED UP THE FLOOD WHICH THE DRAGON SPEWED OUT OF HIS MOUTH. REV. 12:15, 16.

The story of the woman of Revelation 12 would have been familiar to many readers in the ancient Roman world. The ancient Greek writer Homer told the story of Leto, the bride of Zeus, king of all the Greek gods. Hera, queen of the Greek gods, was jealous and angry when she heard that Leto was soon to bear twins to Zeus. In her anger Hera forbade all the lands of the earth to give shelter to Leto, so Leto, heavy with twins, found herself forced to wander from place to place with nowhere to rest.

Python, a huge dragon that spat black venom, received a warning that Leto's son would one day destroy him. So Python chased after Leto as she wandered the earth, in the hopes of destroying her before the birth of the fateful child. Poseidon intervened, raising the island of Delos from the sea. Delos floated on top of the ocean, with only a single palm tree as its vegetation. Since Delos was free from the land, it was also free from Hera's bidding, so Leto could rest in the shade of the palm tree. When the dragon came seeking her there, Poseidon submerged the island temporarily to hide her from Python.

After Python left Delos, Hera was angry that Leto had found shelter. She ordered that Ilithyia, the goddess of childbirth, remain in Olympus and not allow Leto's twins to be born. As a result Leto suffered horribly in labor for nine days until Hera relented. Firstborn was Artemis, goddess of Asia Minor, and next came Apollo. Zeus blessed the twins with strong bows and magical arrows. Apollo came to the slopes of Mount Parnassus and slew Python with 1,000 golden arrows.

During the first century, coins reveal, some emperors linked themselves with Apollo. In Asia Minor Roman propaganda equated Leto with the goddess Roma. She became the mother goddess, and the Roman emperor was her child, the savior of the world.

In the vision of Revelation Jesus is the one who slays the dragon and its related beasts. Through the person of Herod, the dragon of Rome sought to destroy Jesus at His birth. Jesus' escape from Herod was a foretaste of His deliverance of the woman in this text and of the remnant in the text that follows. The vision takes over one of the great myths of the time to demonstrate the superiority of Jesus to all other claimants to divinity.

Lord, help me not to be distracted by modern claims to greatness and stardom. You are the true source of meaning for my life.

And **THE SERPENT SPEWED WATER LIKE A FLOODING RIVER OUT OF ITS MOUTH** *as it pursued the woman, in order that he might cause her to be swept away by the flood.* REV. 12:15.

The mouth of the serpent reminds the reader of the temptation in the Garden of Eden. While the devil certainly seeks to hinder the church by force, his most effective weapon is often deception. The attacks and the temptations come from unexpected directions.

The bomb went off shortly after noon and shook the entire building like an earthquake. The offices of Cantor Fitzgerald in the north tower of New York's World Trade Center went dark. No one knew what had happened, but within minutes the 700 employees calmly headed for the stairs. The stairway quickly became a traffic jam as 20,000 workers on lower floors also evacuated that cold February day, but the Cantor Fitzgerald people didn't panic. Some of them lashed their ties and belts to the wheelchairs of people with disabilities and carried them down the 105 flights of stairs. Others helped those who had difficulty walking until the firefighters, on their way up, took over around the twenty-fifth floor. Everyone made it out safely.

It was 1993, and a terrorist bomb had exploded in an unoccupied van in the Trade Center's underground parking garage. Six people died in the explosion, and many regarded the bombing as a warning to be better prepared the next time. Cantor Fitzgerald and the other tenants of the World Trade Center invested heavily to safeguard themselves against future incidents.

Among other security improvements, the Trade Center rebuilt stairways to make it easier for firefighters and police to enter. Security at ground level and below tightened. Cantor Fitzgerald and other businesses prepared detailed disaster-recovery plans. And life went on. Somewhere in the consciousness of those who worked at the World Trade Center was the belief that terrorists, like lightning, would not strike the same place twice.

No doubt the security improvements saved lives on September 11, 2001, but to a tragic extent, the Trade Center had erected its defenses primarily against the strategies of the past. No one fully foresaw the horror and destruction that was to come. Cantor Fitzgerald lost more than anyone—658 employees died when the first plane struck the north tower a few floors below, trapping them with no hope of rescue. For them the disaster recovery plan had no meaning.[100]

Just as terrorists constantly look for undefended targets, Satan studies us with great diligence, seeking points of weakness. In our own strength and wisdom we will be as helpless as the residents of the World Trade Center.

Lord, help me to "let go and let You" be my defense against temptation today. Give me divine discernment to make the right choices and to give You free reign in my life.

August 7

And the serpent spewed water like a flooding river out of its mouth as it
PURSUED THE WOMAN, *in order that he might cause her to be swept
away by the flood.* REV. 12:15.

I believe that the woman in this text represents the people of God throughout the Christian Age who have endured oppression at the hands of totalitarian governments and hostile majorities. Those persecuted for their faith always face the temptation to ask why. The suffering of the moment is usually incomprehensible. It is impossible fully to explain why God allows it.

What Revelation 12 does is pull back the curtain and show us the larger context for Christian suffering. A war rages across the universe, one that began in heaven (Rev. 12:3, 4) and climaxed after the death of Jesus on the cross (verses 7-12). The battles we face from day to day are a minuscule part of that larger conflict. It may not be possible to see how our experiences fit into the totality of God's plan. But Revelation reminds us that when bad things happen to His people it is because of a supernatural fury that must be allowed its moment in the sun, but will one day be destroyed forever (Rev. 20:7-15).

So we need to be patient and trust God no matter what happens. Justice is coming, but it will not take hold before I pass through serious trials. If I demand an explanation for everything that happens to me, I will not only lose faith in God but perhaps even my mind. I need to be content with the fact that in this life we "know in part" (1 Cor. 13:9).

This reminds me of a story about a lost marble. A man condemned to solitary confinement in a pitch-black cell had only one thing to occupy his mind with— a marble, which he threw repeatedly against the walls. He spent his time listening to the marble as it bounced and rolled around the room. Then he would grope in the darkness until he found his precious toy.

One day the prisoner threw his marble upward. It failed to come down. Only silence echoed through the darkness. The "evaporation" of the marble and his inability to explain its disappearance deeply disturbed him. Finally he went insane, pulled out all his hair, and died. When the prison officials came to remove his body, a guard noticed something caught in a huge spiderweb in the upper corner of the room. *That's strange,* he thought. *I wonder how a marble got up there.*[101]

Sometimes our experience poses questions the mind is unable to answer. But valid answers always exist. When it comes to the things we suffer, it is wise not to expect all the pieces to fit on the basis of our limited perception. God alone knows the big picture. The cross tells us that we can trust Him.

Lord, I trust the One who died for me. Give me endurance even when I don't understand.

And the serpent spewed water like a flooding river out of its mouth as it pursued the woman, in order that he might cause her to be swept away by the flood. And the earth helped the woman. It opened its mouth and **SWALLOWED UP THE FLOOD** *that the dragon had spewed out of his mouth.* Rev. 12:15, 16.

The book of Revelation uses the symbol of water in three different ways: it can represent (1) nourishment; (2) cleansing; and (3) flooding, or destructive power. The image of a great flood of water swallowed by the earth is not unknown in geography. This very thing occurs in the Kalahari Desert in southern Africa. It is a huge place called the Okavango Delta. There a large river pours into one of the driest deserts in the world. The water splits up into a delta full of plant and animal life, but the land is so dry that as the water continues flowing it disappears into the desert. Beyond the delta the land remains as dry as a bone.

The mouth of the serpent seems to be an allusion to the serpent's lying words in the Garden of Eden. If that is the case, the flooding waters here may mean powerfully deceptive errors as much as persecuting force. The flooding waters contain both deception and threat.

Satan has two main methods of leading people away from God: (1) deception and persuasion on the one hand, and (2) force, threats, and persecution on the other.

Flooding rivers and winged dragons are actually parallel images in the ancient world. From above, most rivers look a lot like snakes, meandering back and forth across the countryside. Now imagine that the river has overflowed its banks. From a vantage point looking down, that same river might now resemble a snake with wings. This is probably the root concept behind the ancient idea of a dragon. In that case, ancient readers or listeners would see the flood of waters as a natural way for the dragon to attack the woman in this story.

Many students of the Bible believe that this scene anticipated the situation of Europe in the Middle Ages. Faithful followers of God, such as the Waldenses in northern Italy and southern France, copied and studied the Scriptures. They often faced threats and destruction from armies sent out by the dominant Christian church. Their spread of the Scriptures posed too great a threat to the prevailing belief system.

In the final days of earth's history prayer will be a vital protection when God's people find themselves in distress. "Therefore let everyone who is godly pray to you while you may be found; surely when the mighty waters rise, they will not reach him. You are my hiding place; you will protect me from trouble and surround me with songs of deliverance" (Ps. 32:6, 7, NIV).

Lord, I know that I haven't persevered in prayer the way I need to. Energize my heart and soul to reach out to You more fervently than ever.

August 9

And the dragon was angry with the woman, and he went away to make war with the remnant of her seed, **THOSE WHO KEEP THE COMMANDMENTS OF GOD** and have the testimony of Jesus. And he stood upon the sand of the sea. Rev. 12:17, 18.

A few years ago our house had no windows on the south, the side where the sun shines most of the time. That made the public part of our house fairly dark. Since our garage is attached to the south side of the house, we couldn't do much about the situation as things were. So we decided to add on a sunroom to the west side of the kitchen and bring a flood of light into the house through it.

Since we had to have a lot of new wiring run to the sunroom, we thought we would add a couple outlets along the kitchen counter. The contractor warned us that if we did that, the code required us to upgrade all the kitchen outlets with a special push-button breaker system. We saw no problem with that and gave the order for him to redo the wiring in the kitchen.

For several months we were totally delighted with our new sunroom and the extra outlets in the kitchen. Then a strange thing happened. The lights and power went out in the garage. This was extremely annoying, as we now had to lift and lower the massive door to our garage by hand! I rushed immediately to the breaker box in our laundry room, fully expecting the red bar to show that the breaker to the garage had tripped. But I saw no sign of red anywhere on the breaker box. I couldn't figure out any way to get the power going to the garage again. We called in our handyman, and the problem stumped him as well.

After a couple of days I was frantic. What could be cutting off the electricity? I ransacked my mind for ideas and talked to everyone I knew about the problem. But no solution seemed in sight. On the third day I suddenly remembered the upgrade on our kitchen outlets. Could that have anything to do with the garage? It hardly seemed possible. But having tried everything else, I went into the kitchen and pushed the little breaker buttons on the kitchen outlets. Then I went to the garage and pressed the door opener. Immediately it responded! Somehow the new breakers in the kitchen were tied to the circuit in the garage!

It strikes me that being connected to Jesus is a lot like a breaker box. When I break one of His commandments, He does not permanently disconnect Himself and cast me away. By His grace I can be reset and offered a fresh start. Thanks to Him, the remnant will prove one day to be genuinely obedient to Him. In the meantime let's remember to push the button of repentance as often as necessary.

Lord, I thank You that I can be reset today for a fresh start with You. Give me the confidence to let Your power flow through me.

August 10

And I saw a beast coming up out of the sea, having **TEN HORNS AND SEVEN HEADS,** *and upon his horns ten* **ROYAL CROWNS,** *and upon his heads the names of blasphemy. The beast I saw was like a* **LEOPARD,** *his feet were like a* **BEAR,** *and his mouth was like the mouth of a* **LION.** *The dragon gave him his power and his throne and great authority.* REV. 13:1, 2.

The description of the beast in this passage has political overtones. The Old Testament frequently uses a horn as a symbol of political power. The beast wears the royal crowns (diadems) of political authority. The leopard, the bear, and the lion remind the reader of the great empires of the past such as Babylon, Persia, and Greece. Behind all this political power lurks the dragon, that old devil, the serpent Satan (Rev. 12:7-9).

One of the horrifying things about this passage is that the devil does not do his work alone, but has the active support of people. Human beings who follow Satan are capable of incredible depravity. It does not take long to come up with a Hall of Shame that includes Nero, Hitler, Stalin, Mao, and Pol Pot; the Arab and Western slave trades; terrorism; and genocide in Nazi Germany, Rwanda, Cambodia, Bosnia, and Armenian Turkey. No evil is impossible when demonic power removes all human restraint and amplifies the natural evil of human sin.

Human rights investigator Gary Haugen discovered in Rwanda that mass murder does not require "pathological" killers. "When all restraints are released, farmers, clerks, school principals, mothers, doctors, mayors, and carpenters can pick up machetes and hack to death defenseless women and children." Haugen concludes, "The person without God . . . is a very scary creature." [102]

The Nazis knew that almost anyone is capable of unspeakable brutality. Prospective SS officers received a German shepherd puppy at the beginning of training. The puppy grew up with the officer candidate. Working, playing, and sleeping together, they were constant companions for six months, the dog developing total trust for the budding officer. But the officer's final test before induction into the SS required him to strangle the dog to death with his bare hands. Those who couldn't do it were expelled from the SS. But those who did the deed had become capable of monstrous evil, and it had happened in only six months.

We certainly object to evil when it gets out of hand in a quantitative way. But are we as willing to acknowledge that the evil we exhibit each day is not substantively different from that which manifests itself on a large scale? But for the grace of God . . .

Lord, don't be afraid to confront me about the depth of my own depravity. I am willing to know the truth about myself so that You can purify me and make me more like You.

August 11

One of [the beast's] heads was as if it had been **SLAUGHTERED TO DEATH,** *but* **THE WOUND OF HIS DEATH WAS HEALED.** *And the whole world followed the beast with great amazement. They worshipped the dragon, because he gave his authority to the beast, and they worshipped the beast, saying,* **"WHO IS LIKE THE BEAST?"** *and* **"WHO CAN POSSIBLY MAKE WAR AGAINST HIM?"** Rev. 13:3, 4.

Verse 3 contains a clear allusion to the cross. One of the beast's heads was as if it had been slaughtered to death, then its deadly wound healed. The word "slaughtered" is exactly the same word found in verse 8: "The Lamb *slaughtered* from the foundation of the world." The wound of the sea beast is a clear parody of the death of Jesus Christ. Now, if the beast is slaughtered to *death,* what does it mean for the "wound of his death" to be healed? A resurrection! The sea beast has a death and a resurrection like that of Jesus Christ.

But this counterfeit has even more to it. Revelation 13:1 describes the beast as having 10 horns and seven heads. It looks just like the dragon! Jesus said, "Anyone who has seen me has seen the Father" (John 14:9, NIV). And anyone who has seen the sea beast has seen the dragon! Revelation 13:2 tells us that "the dragon gave [him] his power and his throne and great authority" (NIV). This reminds us of the saying of Jesus in Matthew 28:18: "All authority in heaven and on earth has been given to me" (NIV). Just as Jesus received His authority from the Father, the sea beast obtained its authority from the dragon.

The sea beast also has a ministry. According to Revelation 13:5 that ministry is 42 months long. Three and a half years! How long was Jesus' ministry? Also three and a half years. Thus the length of the sea beast's ministry is the same as that of Jesus! That makes the question of verse 4 quite interesting: "Who is like the beast?" The original readers who understood a little Hebrew would have known that the name Michael (the previous reference to Jesus in Revelation 12:7-9) means "Who is like God?"

The sea beast, then, is a clear counterfeit of God the Son, Jesus Christ. At the end of time as part of a great worldwide deception a counterfeit trinity stands in the place of God. The dragon, sea beast, and land beast form the three members of that trinity. In the last days of earth's history Satan brings in deception so carefully crafted that people will have difficulty telling which side is the right one.

What difference should that make in our lives today? As we approach the end of the world, we should pray and search the Scriptures as never before. Satan will seek to distort our understanding of them by any means possible.

Lord, I want the truth no matter what the cost. Help me to see what You desire for me to see in Your Word.

August 12

And a mouth was given to him [the beast from the sea], **SPEAKING GREAT THINGS AND BLASPHEMIES,** *and he was given authority to operate for forty-two months. He opened his mouth in order to* **SPEAK BLASPHEMIES AGAINST GOD, TO BLASPHEME HIS NAME AND HIS TABERNACLE,** *those who are in heaven.* Rev. 13:5, 6.

T he beast from the sea here behaves in a manner that makes perfect sense from a human perspective. If you want to be great and highly regarded by others, you "talk big things," as the beast does here. Let everyone know how spectacular you are. And it doesn't hurt your image to swear a little, making everyone think how tough and how cool you are. And don't forget to walk with a little swagger! Then people will conclude you're really something!

How the gospel goes against the grain! The sea beast is attempting to take the place of Jesus Christ in the hearts of earth's inhabitants. And to a degree he succeeds. But for the real Jesus, greatness does not appear in big talk, swearing, and swaggering. Real greatness is characterized by a basin and a towel (John 13). It humbles itself even to the point of death (Phil. 2:5-8).

I caught just a glimpse of real greatness on the golf course one day. The group a friend and I were playing with took the game very seriously. A string of profanities followed bad shots, as each desperately sought to show that he was better than the others. On the seventeenth hole the president of the club faced a crucial shot. The game was close, and every stroke counted. He studied the layout ahead, took a couple of practice swings, and carefully prepared to hit the ball. But his swing was a little high, and so instead of propelling the ball ahead, he drove it into the ground. I waited in silence for the inevitable. But he said nothing and prepared to swing again. This time he drove the ball even deeper into the ground! Once again he remained absolutely silent. I was amazed. It was like stubbing your toe twice on one trip across the room. Yet he said nothing (you could see on his face that it wasn't easy).

As my friend and I were leaving the clubhouse a little later, I stepped back in and went up to the man, put a hand on his shoulder, and said, "It took a really big man to do what you did on number 17 without swearing."

I learned that day that anybody can swear, but the person of really strong character is the one who can face bitter circumstances without letting loose. It is easier to become president of a golf club than it is to control your speech or humble yourself to serve others. True greatness does not come from following the beast, but rather from following the Lamb. What comes out of our mouth reveals our true character.

Lord, Your words are gracious and kind. You left heaven for me, to save me and to show me the path to true greatness. May You live that kind of greatness through me today.

August 13

And to him it was given to **MAKE WAR WITH THE SAINTS**
*and to conquer them. And to him was given authority over every tribe and people
and language and nation.* REV. 13:7.

D o you remember the long, hot, lazy days of summer when you were a child? I grew up in Little Ferry, New Jersey, an amazingly backwater community less than 10 miles from Times Square, New York City. Summers I spent hanging out with friends, playing board games and swimming on the hottest days, and playing stickball and Wiffle ball when the temperature was more conducive to being outside.

The part of summers that I least liked, however, was boredom. I was never bored on my own, because I had discovered the joys of reading and often had fun constructing games out of my imagination. The problem came when I was with other kids.

"Let's play Wiffle ball."

"I don't feel like it."

"How about a game of Risk?"

"I don't feel like it."

"What *do* you want to do?"

"I don't know—I'm bored."

The problem was that if I felt obligated to be with friends when they were bored, then I was stuck being bored too. Boredom today is something to avoid at all costs. No one wants a dreary day-in-and-day-out type of existence. When was the last time you heard "boredom" lauded as a major part of an "exciting" vacation?

Well, according to Revelation, Christian life is never boring. On the one hand, we have the excitement of Christian growth, of sharing the gospel, and of seeing what the Spirit will do next with our lives. On the other hand, Christian excitement involves the battle against sin and Satan, and the awareness that our faith will provoke opposition. Christian life has sometimes been termed "a battle and a march."

But the excitement of Revelation isn't always on the surface. Monotony and routine are underrated elements of the Christian life. Keep in mind that Jesus spent the first 30 years of His life toiling away as an unknown carpenter in a tiny village in northern Israel. The daily "monotony" of His existence allowed Him the time to sink His roots deep into the soil of God's wisdom and love. A healthy mix of excitement and monotony are at the core of Christian existence.

Whatever today will bring, Lord, use it to build character in me.

And everyone who lives on the earth will worship him [the beast], everyone whose name was not written in the book of life of **THE LAMB SLAUGHTERED** *from the foundation of the world.* REV. 13:8.

The picture never ceases to amaze me. The Lamb, so innocent and trusting, dies for the very ones who slaughter Him. He gives His life for the very ones who are taking His life. "Father, forgive them, for they do not know what they are doing" (Luke 23:34, NIV). A similar scenario played out again recently.

During the night of December 22, 2003, an intruder broke into the home of Ruimar DePaiva, a pastor in the island nation of Palau. The robber was intent on theft, but as members of the family got up, the man attacked them until they were all dead except 10-year-old Melissa. After abusing Melissa for 20 hours, he released her, and she told the story to the police. The authorities soon had him captured and put in prison. His deed stunned the whole nation, and the government ordered the country's flags lowered everywhere. A state funeral was held, hosted by the high chief of the island where the crime took place.

At the funeral Ruimar DePaiva's mother took the microphone without warning. She had already visited the prison holding the murderer, Justin Hirosi. Praying with the man who killed her son, daughter-in-law, and grandson, she assured him of her forgiveness. Then learning that Justin's mother was at the service, she asked Mrs. Hirosi to join her at the microphone. After hugging Mrs. Hirosi like a long-lost friend, she announced to the crowd that they were "both mothers grieving for lost sons."

Then she implored the community to remove any shroud of blame that they might place on Justin's mother or his family. She declared that parents raise their children and try to teach them right from wrong, but in the end they have their own minds.

The funeral reached another level of shock when the high chief announced that Justin's family, though of meager means, had sold many of their belongings and now desired to deliver $10,000 in cash to the surviving Melissa for her college education. But the greatest moment of all was yet to come.

When asked where she would like to live, Melissa said, "I'd like to stay here in Palau."

Her grandmother explained to her that that would not be possible.

"OK," the girl replied. "But I'll be back someday. I'll come back as a missionary!" [103]

Lord, help me to learn the full meaning of Your forgiveness so I can forgive others the way You have forgiven me.

August 15

And everyone who lives on the earth will worship him [the beast], everyone whose name was not written in the book of life of **THE LAMB SLAUGHTERED FROM THE FOUNDATION OF THE WORLD.** REV. 13:8.

I received quite a shock in Singapore recently. A meeting of all the Adventist churches in the city had been planned for Sabbath at a large public venue. To make sure that the members did not forget, the mission leaders sent out text messages on Sabbath morning to remind everyone of the times and the particulars. I thought they were talking about e-mails, but someone explained to me that these messages pop up on the screens of mobile phones and that nearly all the members in the city had such phones (I didn't)!

This novel way of reminding members of a major meeting caused me to pay attention to a report about text messaging in the Philippines.[104] It seems that the Manila area of the Philippines is the text-message capital of the world. Everyone there seems to have a cell phone—they are more ubiquitous than flies on a summer day. Even the poorest of people have cell phones, and they are constantly using them.

But because of limited resources, most of them cannot use the phone for talking—that is way too expensive. So they end up text-messaging one another . . . constantly. It is very common to see people everywhere waiting or walking, feverishly punching in their messages with some elaborate code and sending them off to all their buddies.

For a while text-messaging even affected the Catholic Church in the Philippines. It seems that instead of going to the priest in church to confess their sins, many Filipinos found a new and more time-effective way to confess their sins. They text-messaged their sins to the priest! The priest then sent the absolution back with the appropriate penance. The practice was convenient, but soon the horrified church issued a stern edict to stop it.

While we might chuckle a little bit at this convenience-store type of religion I wonder how many of us are "text-message Christians." Do we try to squeeze faith into our lives in order to meet the minimum daily requirement, or do we fit our lives around faith and seek God afresh every day with a personal and heartfelt devotion?

I am so glad that God is not a text-message Deity. He invested Himself in the person of Jesus. Instead of just punching in a few letters and hitting the send button, He gave of His time and sacrificed Himself in person. And that sacrifice affected things all the way back to "the foundation of the world." Such a God is worthy of more than just a casual response.

Lord, I see more clearly the depth of the investment You have made in me. I respond to You with a whole heart today.

If anyone has an ear, let him hear. If anyone leads into captivity, into captivity he will go. If anyone kills with the sword, with a sword he will be killed. Here is the **PATIENCE** *and the faith of the saints.* REV. 13:9, 10.

The word translated "patience" here literally means "remaining under." It depicts someone stuck for a time under a heavy burden or difficulty. He or she is in a position to escape the load but chooses not to for some higher cause than just avoiding a problem. Translators often render the word "patient endurance." Patience is about hanging in there for the long term, even when it doesn't feel great in the short term. In Revelation 13:10 the saints are willing to endure captivity and death because their hearts and minds are in heavenly places (note verse 6).

Few things are more frustrating than to have to wait for something you have prayed for. It taxes our patience. And it doesn't seem to make sense in the Christian scheme of things. Why should it take months or years for God to find you a good job when He spent only seven days creating the world? Why should people ever have to go hungry when Jesus fed the 5,000 in an instant? Why should it require months to be healed of some sickness when Jesus raised Lazarus with a word? What is the point of patient endurance?

One reason God asks us to do so is that waiting is a tremendous tool for personal growth. In Romans 5:3, 4, Paul tells us that suffering produces patient endurance (same word as the one in Revelation 13:10) and patient endurance creates character. So patience is not an option for Christians. In those times of waiting God reveals His plans and purposes to us in ways we would never discern in the hustle and bustle of everyday life. "Remaining under" develops strength of character in us.[105]

It seems, if you watch American television or Hollywood movies, that the American way is the one of instant gratification. If you need it, buy it; if you don't have the money now, borrow it; and if you want it but will never be able to afford it, steal it. But the easy and quick solutions don't serve long-term goals and don't produce long-term growth. In a sense Americans live in an adolescent culture. The main difference between an adult and a child is the ability to delay gratification. Real adults have the ability to wait. They can sacrifice immediate pleasures for long-term benefit.

It will take great strength of character to endure the trials of the end-time. "Remaining under" is never fun, but it's a lot easier when you keep your eye on things above!

Lord, I thank You for the visions of Revelation. They teach me how great You are, and how worthwhile it is to endure to the end. May my patience in the little things now bring the strength of character to endure the big things that lie ahead.

August 17

If anyone leads into captivity, into captivity he will go. If anyone kills with the sword, with a sword he will be killed. Here is the **PATIENCE** *and the faith of the saints.*
REV. 13:10.

A characteristic of the saints is patient endurance. Followers of God are persistent in well-doing and faithful in trial. Not content to live on the surface, they go deep into God's Word, willing to follow wherever it leads.
In 1938 the king of Saudi Arabia, Abd-al-Aziz ibn Saud, authorized a team of American engineers to explore the trackless desert bordering the Persian Gulf, an arid landscape marked only by the occasional palm-fringed oasis. He hoped they would find water. A tribal leader with precarious finances, Ibn Saud believed the Americans might discover places where he could refresh his warriors' horses and camels.

But the team, from Standard Oil of California, had something else in mind. Geologists had discovered oil in other countries in the region, and the engineers thought they would find more in Saudi Arabia. During a period of several years they drilled more than half a dozen holes without result. They could easily have given up in frustration. Instead, they decided to see if going deeper than normal might make a difference. So they set up their equipment again at well number 7 and dug deeper than they had ever done before. They burrowed all the way to a depth of 4,727 feet and finally hit the first sign of what would turn out to be the largest supply of crude oil in the world. A willingness to go a little deeper was all that stood between failure and unimaginable success.

Oddly enough, the king did not appear to appreciate the discovery at first. He ignored the news about the oil for an entire year afterward. Finally he and his retinue arrived in a caravan of 400 automobiles at the pumping station of Ras Tanura in time to witness the first tanker hauling away its cargo of Saudi crude. The discovery would change everything.

Up until then, the primary source of income in the Saudi kingdom came from servicing pilgrims in Mecca, Islam's holiest city. But even the first shipment of oil produced wealth beyond all expectation.[106] The lives and lifestyles of Arabian bedouin would never be the same. This isolated country with no other exportable product now became a major factor in global politics. The Saudi royal family became powerful players on the world scene. Their wealth became a crucial factor in Middle East politics and the bargaining over global energy supplies. Today their nation is at the center of world attention. All because a handful of American engineers were not willing to be content with a surface approach to their task.

Lord, give me the patience and the endurance of the saints. May I not be content with anything less than the deep things of Your Word.

And I saw **ANOTHER BEAST, THIS ONE COMING UP OUT OF THE EARTH.** *He had two horns like a lamb and spoke like a dragon.*
REV. 13:11.

An interesting feature of this part of Revelation is that beasts keep turning up, one after the other. The beast from the sea (Rev. 13:1-10) greatly resembles the dragon of chapter 12. The beast from the earth, on the other hand, looks very different. But all three beasts have something in common—they all behave badly. A serious indictment on the human race is that we learn very little from one generation to the next.

A beautiful, blond 13-year-old Austrian girl got on a train and said goodbye to her parents. Fifty years later she ended up in the hospital with high blood pressure. The physicians could find no explanation for the problem. Because she had no history of blood pressure problems, the doctors kept a close watch on her.

She told the chaplain that she was a Holocaust survivor. "I don't talk about it much—I mean, I didn't talk about it until my husband died. That's just how it was. We just didn't talk about it. But lately I've begun to . . . my parents were killed in Auschwitz. I was only 13. They sent me away on a train to Holland. From there I went to England. I never saw them again. I've always felt guilty that I left them there to die."

"You feel guilty?" the chaplain said.

"Yes, I still do. I never knew for sure if my parents were dead or alive until three years ago when they found the hidden files in East Germany. I was on a tour in Berlin when the news came to me about the date they perished in Auschwitz. The Germans kept very precise records, but they were hidden for many years.

"I have lived through things that are now part of the history books," she went on. "I don't understand why we [humans] don't learn. The genocides keep occurring. Look at Cambodia and Vietnam. Look what Saddam Hussein did to the Kurds. I watched a program last night about it. They showed pictures of the bones and things. That's probably why my blood pressure went so high."

A nurse came in. The chaplain told her the probable reason for the blood pressure surge, and she went off to tell the doctor.[107]

The book of Revelation places the blame for human misery squarely on Satan aided by human stupidity. Generation after generation we make the same mistakes, thinking we are solving our problems, when the only solution is to be found in the slain Lamb.

Lord, strengthen me to be part of the solution, not part of the problem, today. Help me to break the cycle of violence and oppression in my family first, and then everywhere else I go.

August 19

And I saw another beast, this one **COMING UP OUT OF THE EARTH.** *He had two horns* **LIKE A LAMB** *and spoke* **LIKE A DRAGON.** REV. 13:11.

Many students of the Bible have applied this beast to the United States of America. They point to a number of elements in the text. For one thing, this beast comes up out of the earth. Whenever the book of Revelation contrasts earth with sea (the first beast emerges from the sea), it is a positive element, not an enemy of God, an understanding further supported by the fact that the earth helped the woman in Revelation 12 when she faced attack from the dragon.

Its lamblike horns also suggest a positive beginning for this beast. Twenty-eight times the book of Revelation refers to Jesus Christ as the Lamb. The twenty-ninth use of the symbol of a lamb is in this text here. There is something lamblike about the beast when it first appears, but its opposition to the dragon fades and over time it begins to speak like the dragon. The land beast becomes the decisive player on the world stage, bringing about an end-time world unity in opposition to the true people of God (Rev. 13:12-18).

Twenty-five years ago the thought that America could become the dominant player on the world stage seemed ludicrous. From Vietnam to Watergate to stagflation to Jimmy Carter's apologies, America seemed in decline on the world stage. Before you can speak like a dragon you have to have a dragon's power and vocal cords!

But the scenario of Revelation is credible today. All it would take to trigger the "dragon" would be a terrorist event on a far larger scale than September 11. In the words of General Tommy Franks, who toppled Saddam in 2003: "The potential of a weapon of mass destruction and a terrorist, massive casualty-producing event somewhere in the Western world—it may be in the United States of America—[could cause] our population to question our own Constitution and to begin to militarize our country in order to avoid a repeat of another mass-casualty-producing event. Which, in fact, then begins to potentially unravel the fabric of our Constitution."[108]

If you remember the fear and helplessness that followed September 11, you know that Americans would be desperate to protect themselves if something far more deadly occurred. And if letting the attorney general read my e-mail, tap my phone, and peek in my bedroom window would save my family from getting nuked by terrorists, I'd be inclined to let him. But the end result would be the destruction of freedom and the emergence of the voice of the dragon!

That's why I'm glad this book is the "revelation of Jesus Christ" and not the revelation of the land beast or the dragon. Jesus promised to be with us always, and Revelation assures us that He will lead the winning side in the end.

Lord, thank You for providing solid ground in a terrified world.

And he [the land beast] exercised all the authority of the first beast in his behalf, **AND HE FORCED THE EARTH AND THOSE WHO LIVE IN IT TO WORSHIP THE FIRST BEAST,** *whose wound of death was healed.* Rev. 13:12.

Sharp contrasts seem to fill life. Jackie found herself drawn to a newspaper article about a recent massacre in Burundi. It seems that some rebel Hutus had attacked a United Nations refugee camp with machetes and automatic weapons. They shot and hacked to death some 180 men, women, and children. "Their charred remains lay among the cooking utensils and the smoldering remnants of their former homes. . . . The attack . . . resembled the killing during the 1994 genocide in Burundi's neighbor Rwanda."

While the article was fairly brief, Jackie felt compelled to place herself inside the story. What would she have been thinking had she been a survivor of this attack? Why is this happening to me? How can I live without my family? Whom can I turn to?

In startling contrast on the same page were ads that screamed out, "Cell phones that are cool and stylish. Buy one and get a second free." "Video mail . . . Free for 60 days! . . . Fun and easy to use!" "Fashion hits! Big summer clearance blowout! Up to 75 percent off."

Jackie struggled to find some correlation between the Burundi massacre and the need for video mail. Were the survivors of the massacre concerned about getting a more stylish cell phone? How many of them would be relieved to know that video mail even exists? Would they be excited that the latest fashions are now 75 percent off?[109]

In the last days God's people will be caught between two very contrasting worlds. The beasts of Revelation 13 counterfeit the work of Jesus and the Holy Spirit. Like the Holy Spirit, the land beast exalts the counterfeit Jesus, rather than itself. These two characters, along with the dragon of chapter 12, do a work of deception in the final crisis of earth's history.

The land beast has two horns "like a lamb." In the book of Revelation the true Lamb was willing to be sacrificed in order to redeem the human race (Rev. 5:6, 9, 12). The Lamb does not force His way into the affections of human beings. This self-sacrifice was not for personal advantage, but for the benefit of others.

By way of contrast, the beasts of Revelation 13 impose their will upon the people of the earth. Through economic boycott (Rev. 13:16, 17) and the threat of death (verse 15), the land beast forces human beings to submit to its authority and to worship the sea beast. The character of the beasts will be in sharp contrast to that of Jesus.

Lord, may I clearly see the contrast between the "beasts" of self-indulgence and the self-sacrificing spirit of Jesus.

August 21

And he [the land beast] does great signs, so much so that he causes **FIRE TO COME DOWN OUT OF HEAVEN TO EARTH** *in the presence of men.* Rev. 13:13.

At one time one could experience something similar to this in the Yosemite Valley of central California. Every summer evening national park personnel staged a "fire fall" from Glacier Point, which is more than 3,000 feet above the valley floor. People gathered before sunset for a short nature program at a campground near the base of the mountain. While this was going on, rangers tended a raging bonfire up at Glacier Point.

After the program below ended, someone would shout up the vertical granite wall: "Let the fire fall!" After a moment, there would come a response from the rangers high up at Glacier Point, "Let the fire fall!" They would then begin pouring hot coals over the side of the mountain to form an awesome glowing waterfall that disappeared several thousand feet into the darkness. It was truly a spectacular sight. Some people traveled thousands of miles for the chance to see the spectacle.

Bringing fire from heaven to earth reminds the reader of Acts 2:2-4. It tells of "a sound like the blowing of a violent wind came from heaven. . . . They saw . . . tongues of fire that separated and came to rest on each of them. All of them were filled with the Holy Spirit" (NIV).

The text of Revelation 13 warns us not to trust totally what we see with our eyes and hear with our ears. One day the fire of Pentecost will seem to be falling all around us, but it will not be the real deal. A great end-time agent of Satan will counterfeit the working of the Spirit and call people to give their allegiance to a counterfeit trinity.

But the best way to detect a counterfeit is to know the genuine. Those filled with God's Spirit will know when the counterfeit appears. And the true Spirit of God goes to those who seek God with all their hearts (Jer. 29:13) and are willing to do whatever He asks (Acts 5:31). God ministers His Spirit to us through His Word (John 6:63). As we treasure God's Word through faith in Jesus, we will be filled with the genuine Spirit. But this will not occur by means of occasional or casual attention to the Word.

Visitors to Yosemite Valley today will not see the fire fall. Years ago the valley was uncrowded and free from the masses that visit the place today. Nowadays, because of the popularity of the valley, the fire no longer falls. There are just too many people and too little space. Sometimes our lives can get too crowded to hear the voice of the true Spirit. Don't allow the press of people and things to keep the fire of the Spirit from spilling into your life.

Lord, clear some space for You in the events of this day. Tired and overwhelmed right now, I need Your Spirit as never before.

And he [the land beast] does great signs, so much so that he causes **FIRE TO COME DOWN OUT OF HEAVEN TO EARTH** *in the presence of men. And he deceives those who live on the earth because of the signs that he was given to do in the presence of the beast, saying to those who live on the earth that they should make an image to the beast who was fatally wounded by the sword and came back to life.* REV. 13:13, 14.

Emiko Okada was 8 and playing in the yard with her two little brothers when she saw the blinding light. Then came a loud boom and a blast that knocked her unconscious. As she came to, she recalls, "I felt like the sun was falling toward me." Her brothers wailed beside her, their bodies swollen with burns. Neighbors stumbled by, naked, skin hanging off them in shreds. Corpses littered the road.

It was August 6, 1945, in Hiroshima. No one in the southern Japanese city had paid much attention to the distant buzz of three American B-29 bombers overhead. But one of them was the *Enola Gay,* and at 8:14 a.m. it dropped a single bomb that unleashed the "rain of ruin" that President Truman had promised if Japan did not surrender.

An estimated one third of the city's 350,000 residents—including Korean conscripts and imperial army units—perished instantly. Many thousands more would die from its radioactive poison during the coming years. The bomb turned glass into liquid, buildings to dust, and people to mere shadows etched on the ruins.

A black rain fell. It looked like oil to Seiko Komatsu, then 9. The boy saw the rain soak his wounded grandparents. He had been having breakfast in their house when the bomb fell and gutted it. Three days later another atom bomb destroyed the city of Nagasaki. Japan announced its unconditional surrender on August 14.[110] Thus the greatest and most terrible of wars ended in an event that was far more horrible than the war it sought to end.

Nothing can minimize the horror of that day when fire rained down from heaven on an unsuspecting Japanese city. It would be easy to condemn President Truman and all others involved as the first mega-terrorists. But it is a historical fact that two atomic acts may have saved millions of lives and years of suffering for all involved in the war.

The land beast of Revelation 13 uses "fire from heaven" to assert the authority of the unholy trinity (dragon, sea beast, and land beast). That fire from heaven will increase evil and suffering rather than decrease it. But the One who did not shy away from the cross will find a way to end a war far more universal and more terrible than World War II.

Lord, I long to see an end to suffering and fear. As You wrestle with the end-game of the great controversy, help me to trust in You no matter what may come.

August 23

And he [the land beast] was permitted to give breath to **THE IMAGE OF THE BEAST,** *in order that* **THE IMAGE OF THE BEAST** *might speak and might cause whoever does not worship* **THE IMAGE OF THE BEAST** *to be killed.* Rev. 13:15.

Have you ever heard people say that you look just like your mother, or that one of your brothers or sisters strongly resembles your father? People who sit around examining baby books often exclaim over the similarity between one generation and another.

"Look who got Momma's nose!"

"Yeah, but notice who passed the dimple on!"

"I always wondered where the curly hair and the green eyes came from!"

Look-alikes are basic to the movie industry, and the Internet is full of advertisements for celebrity doubles and impersonators to cover any occasion. Saddam Hussein was known to have many doubles for security. The comedy film *Dave* explores what might happen if the president quietly had a stroke in the back room while a security look-alike was waving to the crowd. Power-hungry subordinates keep up the sham that the president is fine, all the while finding the double hilariously uncontrollable. This is nothing new. Charlie Chaplin look-alike contests were popular as far back as 1915. (Charlie himself failed to make the finals in one of them. How's that for an identity crisis!)

The image to the beast is a puzzling symbol of an entity who at the end of time will powerfully impersonate the sea beast of Revelation 13. Part of a pattern of deception, this image of the beast comes to life and seeks to convince the world that the beast is alive and well, even though out of sight (Rev. 13:12). The key to the deception is likeness—if the image did not look like the beast, the deception could not occur.

Whom do you look like? Can the people with whom you interact tell who your Father is? Do you have the mannerisms of your Brother? Do your reactions to difficult situations remind people of the Lamb or of the Beast? Whom do people think of when they really get to know you? Do you have your Father's eyes?

Should you not be proud of your image, ponder how you spend your time. By beholding we all become changed. If the major focus of the day is to follow the hottest celebrity, or download the latest hit song, or see the latest show, you are becoming a "look-alike" whether you know it or not. But here's the good news: While we had no control over our appearance in baby pictures, in the spiritual realm we get to decide whom we look like.[111]

Lord, I choose to become more and more like You. Help me to see through the deceptive alternatives today.

And he [the land beast] controls everyone; the small and the great, the rich and the poor, the free and the slave; so that he might place a mark upon their right hands or upon their foreheads, so that **NO ONE MIGHT BE ABLE TO BUY OR SELL EXCEPT THE ONE WHO HAS THE MARK,** *the name of the beast or the number of his name.* REV. 13:16, 17.

The economic temptation in this passage is not only an event of the end-time—it has been relevant to real life throughout Christian history. For example, John Chrysostom regularly criticized the wasteful use of wealth. He lived simply even as bishop of Constantinople. In the process he alienated other powerful bishops and the political elite, ultimately leading to his banishment and death. The wealthy Olympias freely gave her money to the poor despite opposition. Her continuing support for Chrysostom and his positions finally led to the seizure of the remainder of her wealth.

Economic compromises are common in our society. One *Christianity Today* interview suggests that bankruptcy rates are 18.6 percent higher in counties with casinos. Suicide rates are four times higher in heavy gambling areas. Nevertheless, the government gets major benefits from gambling, and the gambling industry gives money to churches and charities to keep them quiet. Money talks and many people listen, even to the compromise of their souls.

Local church boards in many denominations hire, fire, and pay ministers. In such an environment every sermon has financial implications. For example, a young man found Christ by talking with a street preacher. He went back to his home church and asked his pastor why he had never explained genuine conversion from the pulpit. The pastor noted that he had to be careful what he preached lest he offend the deacons. When our economic livelihood is at stake, it is hard to look the truth in the eye. It is easy to make adjustments to our message in order to keep the salary flowing.

Do we dare take this a step further? When we buy something we don't need because our neighbors have one, are we compromising with the world's value system? Can we be frivolous in our spending when we know that 40,000 people die every day of starvation? when we find out that 50 cents can provide food for a child for a whole day in some famine-stricken countries? when we realize that the overtime we worked for that squandered money we could have spent instead with our children or sharing Christ with a neighbor?

Revelation does not allow for divided allegiance. We have to decide between God and the world and between what each side values. As Christians we are citizens of a different kind of kingdom.[112]

Lord, I place all I have at Your disposal. Teach me how to use it to Your honor.

August 25

And he [the land beast] controls everyone; the small and the great, the rich and the poor, the free and the slave; so that he might place a mark upon their right hands or upon their foreheads, so that **NO ONE MIGHT BE ABLE TO BUY OR SELL EXCEPT THE ONE WHO HAS THE MARK,** *the name of the beast or the number of his name.* REV. 13:16, 17.

The time will come when a worldwide confederacy of religion and state will seek to impose its will on true believers. At that time it will not allow those who refuse to go along with the system to buy or sell. But what if this text provides a clue to how we should choose to live all of the time? What if our buying and selling gives tacit approval to a system that coerces and harms people? Are there times when *choosing* to buy and sell is like giving allegiance to the mark of the beast? Consider the following.

The beatings are routine. The supervisors allow only two bathroom breaks in a 14-hour workday and search every opening of the body before and after work. Pregnancy is grounds for dismissal. That's why Isabel has more than once found fetuses on the bathroom floor as women sought desperately to keep their jobs in this grueling and demeaning sweatshop. The jeans she and her colleagues make sell for more than $30 in popular clothing stores. The women, however, get paid 20 cents a pair.

This is not an isolated case. In a turbulent corner of Africa children as young as 3 years of age get lowered into the dark heart of diamond mines to harvest the expensive gems. Called *conflict diamonds,* the stones come from areas controlled by factions opposed to the government. They sell the diamonds to finance military insurrections.

Although the stones they find are worth thousands of dollars, the lives of these children are dispensable. Poor air and tainted water causes sickness, and rebel soldiers often maim, abuse, or kill the young workers. Children who do not work receive severe beatings or dismemberment. Such children trade in their brief lives to provide the world with the modern symbol of forever.

As children of God, we need to be aware of how our lifestyle choices affect others, particularly those who cannot speak up for themselves. God calls us to defend the defenseless. Sometimes a bargain for us gets purchased through the deprivation of others. Loving things more than people is not pleasing in God's sight. Perhaps the time has come to ask some hard questions about our buying and selling.[113]

Lord, I cannot solve all the world's problems, but I can make a difference. Open my heart to make a real difference today, one choice at a time.

Here is wisdom. Whoever has a mind, let him count the number of the beast, for it is a number of a man, and **HIS NUMBER IS SIX HUNDRED SIXTY-SIX.** Rev. 13:18.

Through the centuries teachers of prophecy have attempted to fit many names into 666. Nero Caesar was a popular choice during the early centuries of Christian thought. Hitler was certainly a character that many sought to tie to this prophecy. Some have even tried to associate this number with the name Ellen Gould White even though applying 666 to a person also requires that individual to be a "man."

Among the more creative suggestions was the recent association of the number with Ronald Wilson Reagan, because he had six letters in each of his three names. After leaving the presidency, he moved to a home in Los Angeles. Evidently the numerology bothered him enough that he had the address changed from 666 St. Cloud Drive to 668!

One recent favorite is the allegation that 666 appears on some international product codes. Since this relates to buying and selling (Rev. 13:16, 17), some think it significant. As far as I know, however, no one is talking about printing these codes on the forehead or the hand yet.

One California resident fought in court to prevent his daughter from being assigned a Social Security number. He somehow had the impression that Social Security numbers were associated with the 6-6-6. Since a couple each has a Social Security number of nine digits, together they have 18, which totals 6 + 6 + 6! Do you see how creative this gets? (Of course, the biblical number is *six hundred sixty-six,* not six plus six plus six.)

If we adapt the rules to make names conform (say multiply by seven, add four, then divide by three) we can eventually make any name fit 666. Bible scholars, scientists, and labor unions have all surfaced as candidates for the antichrist. Some have even speculated about the children's TV character Barney. If one adds up the Roman numerals of "Cute Purple Dinosaur" you get a total of 666. Hopefully, someone did that one as a joke!

More seriously, through the centuries many Christians suffering intense persecution supposed that they were experiencing the final tribulation before the Second Coming. It is not surprising that they wondered if Stalin, Hitler, or some Muslim ruler might not be the final antichrist. While they may have been wrong in thinking they were the last generation, they gained courage from grasping the larger principles of the book of Revelation. And in quality, if not in time, they tasted in part the final struggle with the forces of evil.[114]

Lord, I pray that speculation will never distract me from the challenge that Scripture presents to my way of life. Help me to be true to the realities of Your Word.

August 27

And I saw, and behold, the Lamb already standing on Mount Zion, and **WITH HIM ARE 144,000 HAVING HIS NAME AND THE NAME OF HIS FATHER WRITTEN ON THEIR FOREHEADS.** *And I heard a sound out of heaven like the sound of many waters and like the sound of massive thunder. And the sound which I heard was like the sound of harpers harping with their harps.* REV. 14:1, 2.

The chief characteristic of the 144,000 in today's passage is that they are a people in close contact with Jesus. They follow Him wherever He goes and have His name written on their foreheads, which means that they align their characters with His. In every way possible they seek to become like Him.

I have a friend who accepted an invitation to teach practical ministry at the Adventist graduate school in the Philippines. No sooner had he arrived in the Philippines than he began to take long bike rides through the beautiful countryside. The back roads wind through tropical jungles, open grasslands, and small towns.

Since the weather is almost always pleasant in the Philippines, he constantly sees the hospitable Filipino people hanging around outdoors, ready to greet anything and everyone that passes by. He imagines that he presents quite a sight to people. After all, the appearance of a rather tall White American lumbering up the road is an event to notice and remark upon. Almost everyone he meets will yell out one of two phrases: "Hello, Joe!" or "Where are you going?"

The "Hello, Joe!" greeting is a holdover from World War II when the GI "Joes" were in abundance in the Philippines. The "Where are you going?" greeting is far harder to respond to, because, unlike most Filipinos, Jim is not biking around to go anywhere in particular—he is out for the exercise and the fresh air. Not having a map of the area, he ends up taking whatever side road comes along in order to see what adventure it might hold. Since he really doesn't know where he is going, he generally responds to the question by shouting, "I don't know!"

Do you know where you are going with your life? Or do you think it doesn't matter so long as you just trust God? Yes, God certainly calls upon us to trust Him at every step, but this does not preclude us from making careful and concrete plans about our future that He can then bless or redirect. Not knowing where you are going on a bike ride is one thing. Leaving life to chance is another.

Lord, I'm grateful that You have provided a map for my life in the Bible. Beginning today, help me to pay it much closer attention.

And **THEY WERE SINGING, AS IT WERE, A NEW SONG**
before the throne and before the four living creatures and the elders, and no one was able to learn that song except the 144,000 who had been redeemed from the earth.
Rev. 14:3.

I'll never forget a dream I had as a teenager. I was at my parents' house near New York City. It must have been a fairly deep sleep, because, as I started dreaming, I was totally unaware of reality and was totally immersed in the dream. In it I found myself in the New Jerusalem. Looking around, I saw the streets of gold crowded with happy people and an aura of glory shining out of everything around me. As it sunk in that I was actually there—that the battle was over and that my salvation was secure—the first emotion that swept through me was a sense of total unworthiness. "I can't believe God accepted me—me of all people! Unworthy as I am!" A sense of amazement that this could actually happen to me washed over me.

Then a more powerful emotion replaced the sense of unworthiness. An overwhelming sense of joy and gratitude filled me. Wanting to shout and sing praises to God, I felt as if I would burst with thankfulness. I couldn't imagine doing anything else for all eternity! I just wanted to pour out my gratitude to Jesus, who made it all possible. Jesus, what a wonderful name! What a wonderful person. And I praised the glory of His grace until I woke up! Now I'm learning to praise Him in advance of heaven—for what He has already done for me.

The concept of a "new song" does not begin in the book of Revelation. It is a common theme in the psalms. But the interesting thing is that wherever the concept of a new song appears, it is always a response to God's great salvation.[115]

Psalm 40:3 declares, "He put a new song in my mouth, a hymn of praise to our God" (NIV). But in verses 1 and 2 he tells us what inspired the new song: "I waited patiently for the Lord; he turned to me and heard my cry. He lifted me out of the slimy pit, out of the mud and mire; he set my feet on a rock and gave me a firm place to stand" (NIV). That is what prompted the new song.

Psalm 98:1, 2 says, "Sing to the Lord a new song." Why? "For he has done marvelous things. . . . The Lord has made his salvation known and revealed his righteousness to the nations" (NIV). The psalmist sings a new song because of the wondrous things the Lord has done—particularly, making his salvation known throughout the world.

The psalms often repeat this pattern. Whenever the concept of a new song appears, it is always motivated by the mighty saving actions of God. When we arrive at the New Jerusalem, it is God's salvation that will inspire a new song. And we will sing that song with power because we will finally realize just how much we have been saved from.

May Your mighty works for me inspire the first notes of my "new song" today.

August 29

And **THEY WERE SINGING, AS IT WERE, A NEW SONG**
before the throne and before the four living creatures and the elders, and no one was able to learn that song except the 144,000 who had been redeemed from the earth.
REV. 14:3.

The song is new, not just because the experience is new, but because the people who sing it are also "new." Each of them has known sorrow and pain and abuse and rejection. They have struggled with physical, mental, and emotional handicaps. And they have known the bitter consequences of sin. But God will make all things new, including His people. He is the Master Craftsman.

Imagine a king who leaves his throne and goes down into the city in disguise. He enters the slums of the city and walks down a dark alley. There he sees an old, homeless man playing a beat-up trumpet, trying to raise a few coins by repeating the same old tune again and again. It sounds terrible. A broken song coming from a broken trumpet.

The king approaches the man and says, "I'd like to buy that trumpet of yours. I'll pay you enough money to live in a mansion."

"You mean this trumpet?" the homeless man replies. "This beat-up, rusty old thing, dents and all? You want this trumpet?"

"Yes, that trumpet." The king purchases it, takes it home, gives it to his son, and says, "I want you to fix this trumpet up for me."

The son takes the instrument to his workroom. He puts a new mouthpiece on it, hammers out the dents, and installs new valves on it. After scrubbing it clean, he then uses wax and a buffing cloth to polish it. The Bible says that God will make us like gold, polishing and refining us, cleaning us up, getting the dents out. He is working on us right now!

Finally the day comes when the trumpet is ready. The son brings it to his father with the father's name inscribed on the trumpet. The king accepts the trumpet and comments, "Looks great, son. I can't wait to try it out."

The king takes the trumpet, nice and shiny now, puts it to his mouth, and blows. And this time it is not the same old song—it isn't a broken melody. It isn't the kind of music this trumpet has played before. A new song emerges from that trumpet—a glorious and grand one. Both instrument and song have been made new!

Our lives today may be rusted with selfishness and pride or corroded with lust and envy. We may feel dented and warped. But the Master Craftsman already has us in His workroom. And when He's done with us, we'll be singing a new song![116]

Thank You for hope and a future, Lord. May that future shape my life today.

And **THEY WERE SINGING, AS IT WERE, A NEW SONG** *before the throne and before the four living creatures and the elders, and* **NO ONE WAS ABLE TO LEARN THAT SONG EXCEPT THE 144,000** *who had been redeemed from the earth.* Rev. 14:3.

The pastor of a congregation near Alexandria, Virginia, went to a music store to buy a digital piano for the youth chapel at his home church. The pianist of the youth chapel planned to meet him at the store to make sure he got the right piano. Arriving before the pianist did, the pastor noticed the piano he had seen in the magazine the pianist had given him. He decided to go over and test it out on his own, to see how it would sound.

His hands moved over the keys for a bit, but he didn't hear anything special. The pianist had praised the instrument, and the reviewers in the magazine had rated it highly. But the pastor's ear suggested that the piano might be overrated. As he stood there hitting some of the notes, the pianist walked in. Coming over, he began to play. Instantly the sound changed! The pastor blurted out, "Man! That's a good piano!" What made the difference was the masterful hands of the musician.[117]

The difference between the two men that day was one of experience. The pastor had little experience with pianos. He was just making random sounds. The pianist, on the other hand, was not sitting down in front of a piano for the first time. Having played for years, he had taken lessons and spent countless hours practicing without an audience so that when the pews were filled, God would be praised in the music.

Our text says that the 144,000 had to *learn* the new song. What qualifies them to sing in heaven is what they went through while on the earth. While the song is new, it wasn't thrown together on the spur of the moment—they had been practicing for years already while on earth.

Life today is a rehearsal. We are practicing this song. If the boss is getting on your nerves, remember that it's a rehearsal. You don't have to respond in kind. When you find out that people are talking about you behind your back, you can hold your peace, because it's a rehearsal for that new song. And when something has hurt your feelings, you don't need to strike back—make a rehearsal out of it instead!

When you sing this song in heaven, you will be harmonizing with people who hurt you, people who lashed out at you in their own pain, people who were difficult for you to get along with. If you can't "bury the hatchet" today, how will you sing then? Remember, rehearsal starts now!

Lord, help me to start rehearsing today. As I keep my eyes on You, I can let go of the hurts that bind me to this earth and begin learning that new song!

August 31

These are the ones who have not been defiled with women. They are virgins.
THESE FOLLOW THE LAMB *wherever He goes. They have been redeemed from among men as firstfruits to God and to the Lamb. And no lie was found in their mouths; they are blameless.* REV. 14:4, 5.

If God has redeemed the 144,000 from among humanity, they are certainly not blameless in the absolute sense. Every human being, except one, has sinned in the past and continues to fall short of the fullness of God's glory (Rom 3:23). The community they have achieved is not based on a perfect record from the past, but rather on the way God relates to their record and the way they respond to each other's past.

Brennan Manning tells the story of a Catholic woman rumored to have had visions of Jesus.[118] These rumors eventually reached the archbishop in that area, and he decided he had better check her out. It seems that often a fine line separates the genuine mystic and the lunatic fringe. The archbishop asked her, "Is it true, ma'am, that you have visions of Jesus?"

"Yes," the woman replied simply.

"Well," he said, "the next time you have a vision, I want you to ask Jesus to tell you the sins that I confessed in my last confession."

The woman was stunned. "Did I hear you right, Bishop? You actually want me to ask Jesus to tell me the sins of your past?"

"Exactly. Please call me if anything happens."

Ten days later the woman notified her spiritual leader of a recent apparition. "Please come," she said. Within the hour the archbishop arrived. He trusted eye-to-eye contact. "You just told me on the telephone that you actually had a vision of Jesus. Did you do as I asked?"

"Yes, Bishop. I asked Jesus to tell me the sins that you confessed in your last confessional."

The bishop leaned forward with anticipation. His eyes narrowed.

She took his hand and gazed deep into his eyes. "Bishop," she said, "these are His exact words: *I can't remember.*"

Whether or not the story actually took place, it still illustrates a great truth. When we accept Jesus as our Savior, God treats us as if we had not sinned (Isa. 43:25). Genuine community can happen when people gather in the name and spirit of the one who cannot remember the sins of the past. When we learn to do the same with each other, our communities will become places of healing that truly "follow the Lamb."

Lord, help me to forgive others as I have been forgiven.

September 1

And **NO LIE WAS FOUND IN THEIR MOUTHS;** *they are blameless.*
Rev. 14:5.

The 144,000 are noted for their truthfulness (the opposite of Laodicea in its self-deception). Their mouths pass on no lie. One of the key characteristics of God's people at the end of time is a thorough commitment to the truth and to telling it in every circumstance of life.

It is one of the ultimate goals of God's plan of salvation. Understanding and accepting the truth is the secret to freedom and a satisfying life, because whatever you choose to believe will determine what you will do and how you will behave.

A gifted high school student graduated at the top of his class. When he took the exam for entrance into the university, he received a grade of 98. The student thought that the 98 referred to his intelligence quotient, and since 98 is a low IQ, he began to think he was not intelligent. At the end of his first semester at the university, the previously bright and gifted student had failed all his classes.

One of his teachers called him in and said, "I'm just a bit mystified as to why a person with your brilliant high school record could suddenly do so badly at the university." The young man replied that he had discovered that he was dumb, and so was quite justified in doing badly.

Further discussion revealed the real truth. The grade of 98 was a percentage mark. In other words, the student had actually scored 98 percent out of 100. He was, in fact, one of the highest achieving students in the nation, one of the best that had ever attended that university. The next semester the student was back at the top of the class. What made the difference? The difference was in what he believed—in this case, what he believed about himself.

Wise Solomon once said, "As a man thinks in his inward parts, so is he" (Prov. 23:7). What we believe directly influences not only our performance but also how we behave. So if a large variety of conflicting truths fill the world, it is no wonder that unrest, trouble, and strife plague the societies we live in.

God's ultimate goal is to restore the human race to the perfection it originally enjoyed. The new earth will have no place for error and confusion. The problems we currently face originated with the "father of lies" (John 8:44, NIV). The solution is found in the truth as it is in Jesus (John 14:6). Scripture, therefore, describes God's end-time people as being without lies (Rev. 14:5). They are united in truth.

Lord, I commit myself today to three things: knowing You, knowing the truth, and practicing the truth that I know.

September 2

And I saw another angel flying in midheaven, having the everlasting gospel to preach to those who live on the earth, **TO EVERY NATION, TRIBE, LANGUAGE, AND PEOPLE.** Rev. 14:6.

Today's text shows God's caring concern for people from every nation, every language group, every ethnic type, and every family lineage. No matter how much they oppose Him, no matter how perverse their behavior may seem, Jesus died for them (Rev. 5:9; 2 Cor. 5:14). He values them in terms of the infinite cost of the cross. God shows a breathtaking lack of prejudice. Multiculturalism is not just a politically correct fad—it is fundamental in God's attitude toward people in all their infinite variety. Revealing no partiality, He cares for all peoples.

I grew up in New York City and figured that gave me a head start on appreciating God's great variety. The high school I went to was one-third White, one-third Black, and one-third Hispanic. All of my closest buddies were Hispanic. Once I captained an all-Black basketball team and didn't realize that fact until someone mentioned it halfway through the season. Prejudice, I thought, was a remote problem in my life.

I started college just as the Black Power movement got its start and also witnessed the first Black History Week. After the murder of Martin Luther King I heard all kinds of anger directed toward me that I didn't think I deserved, given my pristine behavior back in high school. *Why are these people so angry?* I wondered. *This is America. We all have equal rights and equal opportunities.*

And then I met Greg. Forcefully but patiently he introduced me into the world of African-Americans. Helping me to see the world through his eyes, he told me what it is like to be looked at with suspicion wherever you go. To be stopped by the police on a regular basis, simply because you are Black and driving a nice car. To be ignored in a clothing store while others get lots of help. To face a glass ceiling on the job with certain positions open only to the "right kind of people." And to be unwanted even in some churches simply because of skin color and other differences.

I realized that the world wasn't as simple as the one I thought I knew. And in the process I also came to understand that I was learning to see not only through Greg's eyes, but also through God's eyes. He who chose to create human beings in all their variety dwells inside people of every nation, tribe, and language. It is Jesus who died for everyone. How they feel and how they live matters to Him.

Lord, open my eyes to the pain in the lives of others. Help me to look past the differences and see a soul for whom Jesus died. Enable me to stand courageously against injustice whenever I run into it.

And I saw another angel flying in midheaven. . . . He said with a loud voice,
"Fear God and give glory to Him, because the hour of His judgment has come,
and WORSHIP HIM WHO MADE THE HEAVEN, AND
THE EARTH, AND THE SEA, AND THE FOUNTAINS
OF WATER."* REV. 14:6, 7.

T he fascinating story of Revelation is that God established a universe in which it is possible for beings He created to deny that He made it. In other words, the fact that people are invited to worship the Creator indicates that God does not force anyone to acknowledge His role in Creation. Human beings are like crickets who question whether a builder constructed the house they are living in, thinking perhaps that it somehow came into existence on its own. God is not only powerful, as nature can teach us (Rom 1:18-20), but He is infinitely patient with the intellectual limitations of His creatures.

Does it make sense in today's world to worship the One who made heaven, earth, sea, and the fountains of waters? Clifford Goldstein found a number of compelling reasons to believe in *The Book of the Cosmos,* edited by Dennis Danielson.[119] The volume contains the account of a scientist who specializes in probability theory. He estimated the chance that our universe could arise without a designer at one in 10^{229}. That's one chance in 1 followed by 229 zeros, a number too large for me to imagine! What makes the number even more awesome is the fact that the estimated number of all the protons and neutrons in the visible universe is only 10^{80} (1 followed by 80 zeros)! If your head is spinning as you read this, mine is spinning as I write it! These numbers suggest that it is virtually impossible that the universe as we know it could have arisen apart from divine design.

An astronomer, Owen Gingerich, adds his own testimony. "I cannot prove that God exists or that God's claims on our lives is what makes life meaningful. But do the heavens declare the glory of God? I think so. The universe is so full of such wonderful things that I can hardly think otherwise."

Goldstein goes on to paraphrase Cicero, the ancient orator. If flutes playing a tune were sprouting on an olive tree, you would have no doubt that the olive tree had some knowledge of flute playing. Isn't it obvious, then, that a world full of intelligent creatures points to an intelligent Person behind the design of our universe? But whether or not this should be obvious to us, God does not compel anyone's worship. In the last days He invites all one last time to acknowledge that we live and move and have our being because of Him.

Lord, thank You for making me one of Your incredible designs. Fill my heart today with a sense of Your greatness and a desire of worship and serve You with all my heart.

September 4

WORSHIP HIM WHO MADE THE HEAVEN, AND THE EARTH, AND THE SEA, AND THE FOUNTAINS OF WATER. REV. 14:7.

The last phrase of Revelation 14:7 contains language from the fourth commandment. "For in six days *the Lord made the heavens and the earth, the sea,* and all that is in them, but he rested on the seventh day. Therefore the Lord blessed the Sabbath day and made it holy" (Ex. 20:11, NIV). Careful research indicates an intentional allusion here to the fourth commandment of the Decalogue. In the last days of earth's history, when everything is on the line, God calls people to give attention to the Sabbath command. Does this make any sense? Isn't that kind of arbitrary on His part? The following is helpful to me in wrestling with this idea:[120]

Imagine a country (let's say some warm recess of Antarctica) in which the people have a culture different from ours. The women can have 60 husbands each. They communicate with their 60 husbands by building a statue of a man and then addressing their comments to the statue. Listing all 60 names before this statue, then they build an altar, light candles, and set fruit before the statue. I come along on a vacation tour of Antarctica. During it I fall in love with one of its women and offer to marry her. After she says yes, I explain to her how things are different in my culture.

First of all, I say, I will be her one and only husband. Second, anytime she wants to talk to me, all she has to do is dial my number on her cell phone. I will be there for her, no matter what I am doing. I am available 24 hours a day. Third, I tell her that where I live I am very famous and powerful. In fact, I am so famous and powerful that if she goes into any store and simply mentions my name, she will get whatever she wants.

And, finally, I tell her that every week, from Friday sundown to Saturday sundown, we will have our special time together. For that one 24-hour period I will be with her, she will be with me, and nothing will distract us.

"No problem—sounds great!" she replies. But soon she wants to see a marriage counselor.

"It's too hard," she says in frustration. "I'm tired of following your rules. I want to go back to my statue, have extra husbands, and change the day of our date. But I'd still like to keep your name, because it comes in handy whenever I need something, or when I get into any trouble."

What would I say to my new wife then? Would I still give my life for her, even though she has shattered my heart by breaking her vows? Would I let her go her own way? Or would I continue to pursue her, even though she is off with other men, never keeping our date, never calling me on our cell phone? Is our weekly date with God really such a difficult rule?

Lord, help me to put You first, even in my daily and weekly schedule.

September 5

WORSHIP HIM WHO MADE THE HEAVEN, AND THE EARTH, AND THE SEA, AND THE FOUNTAINS OF WATER. REV. 14:7.

Some friends of mine had their first child about 15 years ago. They were elated at the prospect. With great excitement they began to think of how best to prepare for the baby's arrival. At that point they discovered that they had rather different ideas on the subject.

The prospective mother had focused on the kind of bed crib to purchase, the color of the room, and the figurines for the wall. She knew the child would need a mobile to develop focused eyesight, and she selected the best in linens for the baby's nest. Spending more time than usual at the mall, she examined soft, subtle clothing and examined blankets and other necessary warm wraps for the cold climate where they were living at the time. Shoes, booties, socks, undergarments—the list was seemingly endless and grew by the minute.

The dad, on the other hand, knew that babyhood would wear off sooner or later, and when it did, he/she would be headed for high school, the first date, the college years—and then? He realized that the kind of life he had known before marriage was now truly gone forever—he was going to be a father! While he put up a brave front, he was a lot more scared than he was willing to let on! The wedding day and marriage itself were nothing in comparison to this.

Although they had two different perspectives and two very different roles, both were headed for the same destination: they were preparing for the arrival of a divinely appointed gift! Then it came, a baby boy. Nine pounds and some ounces later, the young couple forgot about the mobile, the room color, the blankets and wraps, the undergarments and cuddly clothes, the bassinet, or even the crib. The reality of the child's birth caused them to forget everything that they had invested in preparation, because they now focused on the event itself.[121]

The Sabbath comes after a day that Scripture identifies as the preparation day (Matt. 27:62; Mark 15:42; Luke 23:54). Friday is a day to get ready for worship, a day to prepare the mind, body, and environment for the weekly date that we should never forget, because it is a date with *God!* The right kind of preparation enables us to set everything aside so that we can concentrate our attention on Him.

The One who made heaven and earth, the sea, and the fountains of waters is worthy of our worship. His day deserves the kind of preparation and anticipation that young couples go through when anticipating their little gift from God!

Lord, help me to get the most out of Your weekly gift. I want to know You more, so I will be ready for the special date You have planned for us this week.

September 6

And another angel, a second one, followed, saying, "FALLEN, FALLEN IS BABYLON THE GREAT, *who has forced all the nations to drink from the wine of the wrath of her fornication."* REV. 14:8.

The Chinese people, being northern Asian, are highly efficient, businesslike people. At Chinese airports the planes leave and arrive early and the service is always quick and efficient. Chinese tend to be quiet in public and do not usually approach or talk to those they do not know. Once the ice is broken, though, the Chinese people are friendly and eager to talk to foreigners.

In contrast to northern Asians, the southern Asians tend to be more relaxed and always ready with a quick smile and pleasant hello. They are not so time-conscious but are more relationship-oriented. Despite living in deprived circumstances most of the time, they almost always possess a sweet spirit.[122]

An exception to this general rule is Singapore, a steamily tropical place with several million transplanted Chinese. Although most Singaporean Chinese were born and raised in the country, they retain the businesslike efficiency of their northern relatives.

While it may take centuries, it does seem that the latitude that people live in deeply affects their culture. The colder latitudes produce a more reserved people, while the warmer latitudes have nurtured the development of a more relaxed culture. Different circumstances produce different responses.

We discover two sides to the God of the Bible. In the Old Testament climate we find at times the stern God who dealt with Uzzah and the Gibeonites. Then in the climate of New Testament times God comes as a gentle lamb. But the book of Revelation portrays both pictures of God together. The Lamb is also a Lion (Rev. 5:5, 6). The gospel of Jesus Christ has two sides to it. On the one hand is the free offer of full acceptance with God. And on the other hand is a penetrating analysis of human depravity and its consequences. While God desires the salvation of all, the climate of the end will require corrective action.

The message of our text goes against the grain. The whole world worships the beast (Rev. 13:8). The message of God's angels (Rev. 14:6-12) will counter the voices of Hollywood, CNN, and the major universities. The good news is that God proclaims judgment before He actually completes it (verse 7). Each person still has an opportunity to avoid its personal consequences. The condemnation of Babylon is not so much bad news as a last opportunity to hear and to follow the good news! God cares enough to give us every opportunity to repent before it is too late.

Lord, help me to lay aside everything that keeps me from hearing Your voice today. I choose to submit to Your will without reservation.

And another angel, a third one, followed them, saying with a loud voice, "If anyone worships the beast or his image, and receives a mark upon his forehead or upon his hand, **HE WILL BE TORMENTED WITH FIRE AND SULFUR BEFORE THE HOLY ANGELS AND BEFORE THE LAMB. THE SMOKE OF THEIR TORMENT RISES UP FOR EVER AND EVER** *and no one has any rest, day or night, if they worship the beast or his image or receive the mark of his name." REV. 14:9-11.*

Many images of violence fill the book of Revelation. We find violence against Jesus (Rev. 1:5, 7; 5:6; 12:11); violence against His followers (Rev. 2:10, 13; 6:9, 10); and violence acted out by the enemies of the Lamb (Rev. 13:7; 16:6; 17:16; 18:7, 20, 24). But what bothers some people the most is the divine violence in the book, of which Revelation 14:9-11 is the most graphic. How can the Lamb be, on the one hand, the victim of violence and on the other hand the one who torments and destroys?

What people often overlook is that any truly good government must at some point exercise some kind of violence in order to restrain evil. Governmental force is not always graphic and bloody, of course. It may simply involve the kind of restraint that occurs when a policeman pulls you over at a speed trap or the IRS sends an agent to audit your taxes. You don't consider that violence? Well, let me ask you some questions. How fast would you drive if the police did not exist? How much taxes would you pay if they were voluntary? How eager are most convicts to stay in jail? Good governments provide a necessary restraint so we can all live together in peace. Not every citizen stops to consider what is good for others or for the whole when they act.

Most people are used to this level of governmental violence. When dealing with an Adolf Hitler or a Saddam Hussein, however, just violence becomes necessarily more brutal. Oppression demands justice (Rev. 6:9-11; 16:6; 18:7, 8), but evil never gives way voluntarily. And the greater the power and brutality of evil, the more force needed to undo that evil.

The images of Revelation are not pretty, but they assure us that God will do whatever it takes to end violence and oppression. The fact that destructive power of God occurs in the presence of the Lamb does not mean He enjoys such horrific images. To me it means that God has placed the One who has suffered much in charge of the process. While God's use of force is necessary, the Lamb oversees and limits it. Why the Lamb? Only He fully understands the cost of suffering and can be trusted to be merciful in the exercise of divine justice. The Lamb that was slain will undo evil without overkill. Divine justice will cause suffering, but not one iota more than necessary.

Lord, the mysteries of Your wisdom in the governing of this universe are beyond my understanding. Help me to trust completely in the Lamb that was slain.

September 8

Here is the **PATIENCE** *of the saints, those who keep the commandments of God and the faith of Jesus.* REV. 14:12.

In his book *Pure Desire* Ted Roberts defines the Greek word for patience as "integrity in the midst of personal pain."[123] It is one thing to maintain integrity when things are going well, and quite another to do so in the midst of personal pain or opposition. Integrity is about being who you really are, even when no one's looking or when the consequences are severe. The opposite of image, integrity is about being consistent and being real no matter the outward circumstances.

Integrity often gets lost in the little things. A man says, "I love my wife," and then flirts with the girls at work. A woman acts like a saint at church, but flies into a rage at the kids when she gets home. A husband's primary goal should not be respect on the job or with his friends, but respect from those who know him best. It takes a lot of integrity for anyone to retain their family's respect year after year.

As with the saints of Revelation 14:12, integrity happens when we keep ourselves constantly aware of God's kingdom and His presence. "Who will know if I do this?" Joseph knew the answer to that. God will know. But when we lose that sense of His presence, little impurities creep into our lives and compromise integrity. And without integrity disaster lurks just around the corner.

In 1912 the *Titanic* sailed for America from England. A new method of construction led its builders to declare it unsinkable. But when it struck an iceberg in the middle of the Atlantic, it took only a couple of hours for the ship to sink, carrying more than 1,000 passengers into the depths with it.

For years people wondered, *Why did the ship go down so rapidly? How could the unsinkable ship have sunk so quickly?* Some answers finally came when searchers discovered the wreckage at the bottom of the ocean. They were able to recover some of the steel plating from the hull, along with the rivets that had held the steel plates together. Analysis of those objects indicated that the steel contained a high level of impurities. This weakened the hull and the rivets, and in the icy waters of the Atlantic, the metal became brittle. The small impurities in the steel helped compromise the integrity of the ship and led to disaster.

When God's saints pass through the icebergs of the end-time, they will have an integrity not shattered by opposition or even personal pain.

Lord Jesus, You endured the cross for me because You had Your eye on the big picture (Heb. 12:2). Keep my eyes on You when I'm tempted to let the little things slip.

Here is the patience of the saints, those who **KEEP THE COMMAND-MENTS OF GOD** *and the faith of Jesus.* REV. 14:12.

W hen people hear about "keeping the commandments of God," they often have a negative impression. They think that God is an arbitrary taskmaster who loves to tell people what to do and wants to keep them from having any fun. But God's commandments are not designed to make us miserable. He designed them to help us achieve life at its best. So don't do what I did. Don't wait until someone else proves the benefits of obedience before you try God's ways.

You see, based on the Bible and other good counsels that have come my way, I've always been convinced that a consistent program of walking is part of God's plan for my life. But I was always too busy, or I didn't feel like it, or I just had more important things to do (or so I thought). Then one day I read an article in a magazine for over-50 types.[124]

John Stark told how, at age 52, he was the fittest person in a workplace that included many in their 20s and 30s who went to fitness clubs, jogged often, and did weekend activities such as skiing and kayaking. For him it started with a Japanese scientist who found that most people take 3,000-5,000 steps a day. American researchers built on that work by determining that to stay healthy and fight off disease, the average person needs 10,000 steps a day, a distance of about five miles.

Through the use of pedometers (devices that count steps), Stark discovered that he was averaging 20,000 steps a day and that few of the "weekend athletes" were even close to 10,000 steps a day. What was Stark's secret? Walking had become part of his life. He lives in Boston without a car in a fourth-floor walk-up apartment with no buzzer. He is, therefore, constantly up and down stairs to answer the door (38 steps each way) and walks to the subway (607 steps), the grocery store (3,000 steps round-trip), and the bank (8,000 steps round-trip). His two dogs require two or three walks a day (2,200 steps each), and often have to go "out" as well.

The article inspired me to change my life. I bought a pedometer (I'm fairly competitive and love watching the steps accumulate each day). While I drive to work, I walk home each day for lunch (5,000 steps). I scamper to the library, administration building, or the post office for every detail, instead of having my secretary do it for me (hope she's OK with this). And I dash around the building to drop stuff off, instead of using intercampus mail. The result? God knows what He is doing, and His commands are not grievous. Having lost 10 pounds and 20 years, I have energy I don't remember having since I was in college (don't ask when). My mind fills with inspirational thoughts as I walk, often with a book. I can't remember when I felt this happy. God's ways are the best after all. Next time I'll just take Him at His word.

Lord, I want to walk with You today. Help me to know the joy of obedience.

September 10

And I heard a voice from heaven, saying, "Write: **BLESSED ARE THE DEAD WHO DIE IN THE LORD** *from now on." "Yes indeed," says the Spirit, "so that they might rest from their labors, for* **THEIR WORKS FOLLOW AFTER THEM."** Rev. 14:13.

Dja-Dja was the only Christian in the village of Tangouroubi. All the others continued in their ancestral worship of the spirits. To all outward appearances, her witness was totally fruitless. As old age took its toll on her body she was no longer able to attend her church, which was some distance away.

One day Dja-Dja collapsed unconscious outside her hut. Her family brought her inside. Everyone knew that the time of her death was near. According to the Lobi tradition in Burkina Faso, they cradled her in their arms to assist her passage into the next existence. They believed that by doing that they could manipulate the spirits to assure her a blessed existence in Paradise.

As Dja-Dja's family held her, she regained consciousness. Taking in the scene and its animistic implications, she blurted out, "I don't want any of you pagans touching me. I want to die in the arms of Jesus."

In amazement her family put her down and backed away. While they had often heard her speak of Jesus, they wondered how she could trust her soul to someone she couldn't even see. Her dying moments were her supreme witness. It was the ultimate denial of ancestral animism with its fearfulness and its attempts to appease the spirits. And it was the greatest testament to her faith in Jesus.

While some of Dja-Dja's family may have felt offended, her simple statement of faith in a God they could not see overshadowed the offense. They knew she was speaking from her heart in this, her greatest time of need. Jesus was real to her. He was there comforting and holding her. She was at peace, safe and secure in the arms of Jesus—and they could see that it was so. When she died in the Lord, the blessedness of such a death was evident to all.

Since Dja-Dja's death, four individuals in her village have accepted baptism in the name of Jesus. More than a dozen now meet every week to worship the God of heaven in a village where Dja-Dja's witness had appeared fruitless for so long. Her death was blessed, she rests from her labors, and her works most certainly are following after her![125]

Lord, the specter of death haunts every human being. We hope against hope that an exception might be made in our case, but as the years go by we increasingly realize the limitations that death places upon our lives. Today, more than ever, I need a foretaste of the blessedness You have promised in Revelation.

September 11

And I looked, and saw a white cloud, and upon the cloud ONE LIKE A SON OF MAN *was sitting; He had a golden victory crown on His head and a sharp sickle in His hand.* Rev. 14:14.

When all is said and done in the book of Revelation, everything ends up with the Son of man, Jesus. He is the Lamb, the Bright and Morning Star, the Ruler of the Kings of the Earth. But in a secular, postmodern world people like to say, "Show me the money!" They want to know why they should follow Jesus in the midst of all the excitement and distractions of life in this world. The following may help to put things into perspective.

Can you name the man who won the Oscar for best actor in 2002? How about the best player in the championship game of the past five World Cup tournaments? Do you remember the name of Miss America or Miss World for the year 2000? Can you name even five people who have won a Nobel Prize in the sciences? What about the name of the team that won the World Series or the Super Bowl for each of the past 10 years? While I am interested in what is going on in the world, I can't answer a single one of those questions. Can you?

The shocking thing is that none of the above occurred on the sidelines. The answers to these questions filled headlines all over the world for at least a week. We are not talking about ordinary people. And yet most of us have already forgotten them. Why? Because as famous as they may have been, what they did didn't truly change our lives. Their achievements caused headlines, but did not make a difference over time.

Let's try this game once more. Can you name three teachers or mentors whose ideas changed your life? Can you name three friends who have been with you in hard times, who have made you feel valuable and appreciated? Can you name the person you most enjoy spending time with? Can you name a couple people whose stories have inspired you to be a better person than you might otherwise have been? How did you do on this quiz? Was it easier to supply names this time around? It certainly was for me. Why? Because these people have all made a difference in my life. I would not be what I am today if it had not been for them.

That's why the book of Revelation is so obsessed with Jesus. For nearly 2,000 years, no one has changed this world more than Jesus. Through His death, resurrection, and heavenly reign He has altered the world and transformed my life. I may care about who will win the World Series this year, but Jesus is the one that will still matter to me 10 years from now. If you are spending time with this book, you probably know what I'm talking about.

Lord, I am placing Revelation's picture of You at the center of my attention today. Thank You for the difference You are making in my life.

September 12

And another angel came out of the temple, shouting with a loud voice to the one sitting on the cloud, "Swing your sickle and reap, because the time to reap has come, since the harvest of the earth is ripe!" And **THE ONE SITTING ON THE CLOUD SWUNG HIS SICKLE OVER THE EARTH, AND THE EARTH WAS HARVESTED.** Rev. 14:15, 16.

The "Son of man" sitting on a cloud (Rev. 14:14) represents the second coming of Jesus. Although the passage does not employ terms such as wheat or grain, the imagery implies a grain harvest. Later the chapter (verses 17-20) depicts a grape harvest, with the subsequent juicing of the grapes. The grain harvest of this text represents the gathering up of the righteous to be with Jesus. They are "the 144,000 who had been redeemed from the earth" (verse 3, NIV). For the human race, the second coming of Jesus is the ultimate "way out" from its painful condition.

Growing up in New York City, I quickly learned that the best way to get around town was to ride the subway. Driving is slow, parking is expensive, and it sometimes takes longer to find a place to park than it would have required to walk the entire trip! And then you still have to get from the parking place to wherever you really want to go.

The subways, on the other hand, are noisy, crowded, and sometimes smelly, but they take you rapidly to wherever you want to go for a reasonable fee. The underground caverns are vast, often several levels deep, with shopping and eating places along the way. For the first-time visitor it can be extremely confusing. The various subway lines employ all kinds of symbols, and a division exists between express and local trains. I have often wowed visitors by walking them through the seemingly impenetrable labyrinth without difficulty or incident.

While entering and making your way around the subway system can be confusing, the way out is very clear if you read English. No matter how deep you go, you can always look for the words "to street" or "exit to street." If you follow those signs you will find your way to outside air and light eventually. For visitors, getting back to the street can be as joyous as a resurrection! You have risen up, as if from a vast underground tomb, to the bustling life of the New York streets. As soon as you get off the train, and at every possible juncture, the words "to street" point the way to the freedom of sunlight and open air.

Life today can be as confusing as finding your way around the subways of New York. But no matter how complex our lives may have become, the Word of God points us to Jesus. He is always there. If you take time to connect with Him, He will be there to guide you where you need to go. Jesus will bring your day into His light. And if you make it a habit to look for Him each day, He will one day lead you out to the streets of gold!

Lord, show me the way out of the problems and difficulties I am facing today.

Another angel came out of the temple that is in heaven. He also had a sharp sickle. Yet another angel came out from the altar, having authority over fire. He called with a loud voice to the one who had the sharp sickle, saying, "SWING YOUR SHARP SICKLE AND GATHER THE GRAPE CLUSTERS FROM THE VINEYARD OF THE EARTH, because its clusters of grapes have ripened." REV. 14:17, 18.

We find a major structural parallel between the end-time scene of Revelation 13 and 14 and Joel 2:28-3:21. If you want to understand Revelation, you need to know something about the book of Joel. 1. Joel depicts the Spirit being poured out. 2. He notes the appearance of heavenly signs. 3. The nations of the world who gather outside Jerusalem attack "the remnant." 4. Finally, God pronounces judgment from Mount Zion and "threshes" those opposed to His people. The story of Joel 3 is about a double worldwide gathering. The remnant assemble on Mount Zion (Jerusalem—Joel 2:32; 3:1). The wicked gather in the Valley of Jehoshaphat, just outside Jerusalem, where they meet their fate (Joel 3:2, 9-17).

The book of Revelation matches the story line of Joel: 1. God pours the Spirit out (Rev. 5:6). 2. Heavenly signs occur (Rev. 6:12-7:3). 3. The nations of the world attack the remnant on Mount Zion (Rev. 13:8-10, 12-18; 14:1-3). 4. The nations are trampled and destroyed outside Jerusalem. So Revelation 13 and 14 seem to build on Joel 2 and 3.

Both passages picture the final battle of earth's history in local and literal terms. Jerusalem stands on a hilltop and is surrounded by valleys on three sides. God's people are huddled together inside the fortress, encircled on all sides by enemy forces. In the interpreting of Revelation this local picture has become worldwide and spiritual (notice the word "earth" six times in this part of the chapter). Israel huddled in the fortress of Jerusalem becomes the worldwide church in hiding during the final crisis. John spiritualizes the double gathering of Joel into those who follow the three angels' messages and those who do not.

The images of warfare in Revelation are a spiritual matter for the Christian (see 2 Cor. 10:3-5 and Rev. 16:15). The weapons of the Christian's warfare are not the kind that tear you to pieces, such as AK-47 rifles, M1A1 tanks, and F-16 warplanes. Christian warfare is a battle with one's own thought processes, ideas, and attitudes. It is a struggle for the mind. Sin is so attractive and deceptive that God has laid out its consequences graphically in this text to get us to take the battle seriously.

Lord, in this vision You have given us a small glimpse of two contrasting groups at the end of the world. Help me to firmly align myself with the wheat, the remnant, and the 144,000 of this chapter.

September 14

And the angel swung his sickle into the earth and gathered the grapes of the earth and threw them into the great winepress of the wrath of God. **AND THEY WERE TRAMPLED IN THE WINEPRESS OUTSIDE THE CITY, AND BLOOD FLOWED OUT FROM THE WINE-PRESS UP TO THE HORSES' BRIDLES** *for about 1,600 stadia.* REV. 14:19, 20.

It was my first day in ministry. The personal witness mentor of the church organization that had hired me offered to spend the day with me. Not having a high degree of confidence in how to approach people, I was delighted to accept. He suggested that he would take the lead at first in showing me how to knock on doors and engage the people in conversation. We would be distributing health magazines the first day.

The magazine he brought that day had information about the dangers of smoking. On the cover were two pictures, one of a healthy lung and the other of a lung seriously corroded by decades of smoking. When a person came to the door, he would show them the front of the magazine and ask, "Do you smoke?" If the person did, he would point to the pictures and say, "Here is a healthy lung, and here is a smoker's lung." The people we visited would invariably react with horror and disgust. They eagerly accepted the free magazine.

The next week I returned with him to follow up the visits. Every person who had accepted a magazine had quit smoking! The view of the pictures and the accompanying text had motivated them to drastic action. Most of them thanked us profusely for drawing this information to their attention. They were confident that our visit had led them to increased control over their decisions and choices.

I kept visiting the homes and bringing more magazines on various subjects. But a surprising thing happened a couple weeks later. All the people who had quit smoking sheepishly admitted that they had started up again about two weeks after the initial contact. Evidently fear is a powerful motivator, but its effect seems to last only about two weeks!

The image of the winepress in this text is truly horrific. John seems determined to scare anyone sitting on the fence of indecision into radical obedience to Christ. The lines are clearly drawn, the wicked will be destroyed, and those who are wise will choose Christ now and reorder their lives now. Fear as a motivator is powerful—but it doesn't last. If reading Revelation has motivated you to a changed life, don't hesitate or make a halfhearted decision. You need to go all out while the motivation lasts. By committing yourself fully to Christ and re-orienting your life, new habits may form, and you may break through the wall of weakness when the fear wears off. "Today, if you will hear his voice, do not harden your hearts" (Heb. 3:8, NIV).[126]

Lord, help me not to shy away from drastic action today.

September 15

And I saw another great and astonishing sign in heaven, seven angels having **THE SEVEN LAST PLAGUES,** *because in them* **THE WRATH OF GOD** *has been brought to completion. And I saw, as it were, a sea of glass mingled with fire, and* **THE ONES WHO HAD OVERCOME THE BEAST AND HIS IMAGE AND THE NUMBER OF HIS NAME STOOD UPON THE SEA OF GLASS** *having the harps of God.* Rev. 15:1, 2.

As we have seen, this passage introduces the great final plagues of earth's history. They fall on those who have rejected God and hurt His followers. But like the original Exodus from Egypt, the mighty power of God delivers His people. While terrible things happen in the name of God, Revelation teaches us that even His plagues are acts of compassion to warn the unrepentant and to deliver the faithful.

David Kosoff tells the story of a famous rabbi who swapped places and clothing with his driver, Samuel, before visiting a synagogue. Upon their arrival the members of the synagogue immediately gathered around Samuel, thinking he was the renowned scholar. During refreshments the leaders of the synagogue flattered him and hung on his every word.

Relishing his newfound fame, Samuel refused to abandon the charade when it came time for the lecture. With misplaced self-confidence, he sauntered into the synagogue to expound upon the Talmud, one of the most important of Jewish writings.

The elders opened the book to an extremely difficult passage and asked Samuel to explain it. But he couldn't even read the Hebrew script, much less interpret it! It looked as if the ruse was up. But desperation sharpened Samuel's wit, and after examining the text for a moment, he said, "I'm surprised that you ask me to explain such a simple passage. Even my uneducated driver could deal with this!" Then he waved the "driver" forward to interpret the text, which he, of course, did with ease.[127]

Most of us occasionally find ourselves in difficulties that are beyond our ability to fix. At such times it is good for us to have a "driver" who is far smarter and stronger than we are. One of the major purposes of the book of Revelation is to convince us that God is able to handle any problem, and that no matter how bad things get He will win the victory in the end. In spite of our weaknesses, we can move ahead with confidence, knowing that a great God will see us through.

Lord, I resonate with the story of the rabbi and his driver. So often in my life I have allowed myself to get into situations that are bigger than I can deal with. Thank You for the assurance that there is no problem too big for You to handle. Help me to trust myself completely to Your care today.

September 16

And I saw another great and astonishing sign in heaven, seven angels having the seven last plagues, because in them **THE WRATH OF GOD** *has been brought to completion.* REV. 15:1.

The book of Revelation depicts a lot of emotion. The characters in the book are angry (Rev. 12:17; 18:3), are afraid (Rev. 11:13), rejoice (Rev. 18:20; 19:1-6), and become extremely sad (Rev. 18:9-19). But such emotions are not limited to the earthly realm. John portrays God as angry, furious, or wrathful (for example: Rev. 11:18; 14:10, 19; 15:1, 7; 16:1), and so is the Lamb (Rev. 6:16, 17).

Depending on how one tries to catalog them, there are four to six primary emotions. I think all would agree that the primary emotions include (1) happiness, (2) sadness, (3) anger, and (4) fear. Denying ourselves and our loved ones the ability to express our *true* feelings increases the severity of physical, mental, and emotional conditions. Children who fear expressing their sadness or their anger grow up unable to develop healthy and honest relationships.

God intended feelings of anger, sadness, fear, and joy as a protection and a release. They are part of His design for us. When we deny the reality of what we feel, we force ourselves to live a form of self-deception. It also results in consequences for others. Families fall apart when members suppress feelings for fear of hurting or breaking the relationship. It produces either dishonest relationships or no relationships at all.

A woman in her late fifties had just had an extensive mastectomy. Not only was she frightened, fearful that she might die—she was also extremely sad, grieving for the parts of her body she no longer possessed. In addition, she felt angry that such a terrible thing had happened to her. Emotional, mental, and physical pain flooded her world. Although she wanted desperately to talk about her feelings to her husband, a typical "strong" American male, he would have none of it.

"You'll be fine," he says. "Everything will be all right."

Her husband couldn't express his own fear and anger, so he wouldn't let her do so either. When the chaplain came, he dominated the conversation so the painful emotions couldn't come out. In the process, he robbed his wife of the chance to unburden her soul in the mistaken conviction that strong Christians bear their suffering quietly.[128]

We can begin to achieve God's design by expressing our feelings to God. Jesus did that on the cross (Matt. 27:46; Mark 15:34). God can take it. He prefers an honest disagreement to a dishonest submission! And He already knows how you feel, so it is safe. Feelings can hurt, but they can also bring us healing, togetherness, and love.

Lord, here's how I really feel inside today . . .

And I saw, as it were, **A SEA OF GLASS MINGLED WITH FIRE,** *and the ones who had overcome the beast and his image and the number of his name stood upon the sea of glass having the harps of God.* REV. 15:2.

M any commentators have noticed the slight difference between the two references to the sea of glass in Revelation. In Revelation 4 the sea of glass is clear as crystal, while here in Revelation 15 it is "mingled with fire." The reference to fire (same word as the "fiery" horse of the second seal) may suggest the bloody red color of the Red Sea after the destruction of the armies of Pharaoh. Exodus 14:30, 31, says, "That day the Lord saved Israel from the hands of the Egyptians, and Israel saw the Egyptians lying dead on the shore. And when the Israelites saw the great power the Lord displayed against the Egyptians, the people feared the Lord and put their trust in him and in Moses his servant" (NIV).

Sight is a blessing. It allows us to obtain a perspective that hearing and touching alone cannot give. One of the five senses, sight involves what photography refers to as "depth of field." Depth of field places the object focused on in a larger context that helps us to discern clearly what we are truly seeing.

For 430 years the Israelites lived in a foreign culture, subject to an oppression that altered their view of God. As a world power Egypt was unsurpassed, and the Israelites struggled with the temptation to think that their God was as weak as they were. The awesomeness of Egyptian polytheism had confused their minds. They needed the plagues to set them free spiritually as much as physically.

To see the Egyptian corpses on the seashore meant not only that their oppressors were dead, but that everything that Egypt stood for—wealth, splendor, intellectualism, military superiority, and religious influence—was now washed up on the sands of the Red Sea. For so long Israel had been impressed with a mirage. But now they could clearly see that what the Egyptians represented was inferior to the God who cared about Israel.

Since the fall of His creation, the Lord has been seeking to show us His hand in the world. All along God has permitted evil to coexist with the good, so that we might appreciate the significance of the good. But He has also promised that, if we obediently follow Him to the Land of Promise, He will put behind us all that has sought to deceive and destroy us. He will one day erase sin, death, and the grave (Rev. 20:6-15), and we will "see" our "spiritual Egyptians" dead on the seashore.[129]

Lord, I need spiritual depth of field so that I can clearly discern truth in the midst of distracting alternatives.

September 18

And **THEY SANG THE SONG OF MOSES,** *the servant of God, and* **THEY SANG THE SONG OF THE LAMB,** *"Great and marvelous are Your works, Lord God Almighty, righteous and true are Your ways, O King of the nations."* REV. 15:3.

T he sound of singing breaks into this scene completely unexpected, especially since rivers of blood anticipate even further plagues (Rev. 14:19–15:2). It would seem like a time to ban music and rejoicing. But sometimes the most powerful singing occurs when nobody plans on it. It was only an audition. That's why the session had no drums, no backup singers, and no expectations. Sam Phillips had heard about a good-looking local boy who favored ballads, knew a few guitar chords, and was blessed with the ostentatiously original name of Elvis Presley. In his search for a new kind of sound, Phillips had run nearly every singer in Memphis through his Sun Records studio. On that summer evening, the day after the Fourth of July, 1954, the 19-year-old Elvis was merely the next in line.

Phillips asked two trusted session musicians, guitarist Scotty Moore and bassist Bill Black, to provide backup. At 7:00 p.m., after a few minutes of small talk and nervous laughter, Phillips arranged the trio in a circle. Then he asked Elvis what he wanted to play. More nervous laughter. Elvis knew only a few songs, and most of those he couldn't play from start to finish. Somehow the group fumbled through "Harbor Lights," which had been a 1950 hit song for Bing Crosby. From the control room Phillips piped up, "That's pretty good," although it wasn't. Elvis sounded boring and mechanical. As a result, Phillips called for a break.

With the formalities suspended, Elvis picked up a guitar and started goofing around, playing an old blues song by Arthur (Big Boy) Crudup called "That's All Right." Except that Elvis was not singing the blues. He sounded almost euphoric, and the rhythm was all wrong—far too frenetic, almost wild. With no drums, Black began slapping his bass to keep time while Moore's guitar leaped in and out of the melody line. Sticking his head out of the control room, Phillips told the threesome to pick a place to start and keep playing. Two nights later "That's All Right" went on Memphis radio. Phillips had his new sound, and the era of rock and roll had begun.[130]

If Elvis Presley had not been recorded in an informal session, no one might ever have heard about him (I leave you to decide whether that would have been good or bad). But music is most powerful when it reflects the depth of a person's unique experience. That's the kind of song the redeemed will unexpectedly burst forth with after the plagues—the spontaneous song of deep experience.

Lord, deepen my experience in ways I would never expect. I want to be able to sing the Song of Moses and the song of the Lamb.

270

And they sang the song of Moses, the servant of God, and they sang the song of the Lamb, "Great and marvelous are Your works, LORD GOD ALMIGHTY, righteous and true are Your ways, O King of the nations." REV. 15:3.

S everal times the book of Revelation describes God as the "almighty." The English word translates a Greek compound of "all" with "powerful" or "strong." If God is truly all-powerful, then we don't need to worry. He can do great things with our small efforts, if we put ourselves in the place where He wants us to be. An amazing story that comes out of Philadelphia around the year 1900 illustrates this point.

A sobbing little girl stood near a small church. She had been turned away because it was "too crowded." "I can't go to Sunday school," she sobbed to the pastor as he walked by. Seeing her shabby, unkempt appearance, the pastor guessed the real reason for her rejection and, taking her by the hand, led her inside and found a place for her in the Sunday school class.

Some two years later the child died, and her parents called for the kindhearted pastor who had befriended their daughter to handle the final arrangements. As her poor little body was being moved, the child's family found a worn and crumpled red purse that seemed to have been rummaged from some trash dump. It contained 57 cents and a note, scribbled in childish handwriting, which read: "This is to help build the little church bigger so more children can go to Sunday school."

For two years she had saved for this offering of love. When the pastor tearfully read that note, he knew instantly what he would do. Carrying the note and the cracked, red pocketbook to the pulpit, he told the story of her unselfish love and devotion. He challenged his deacons to get busy and raise enough money for the larger building.

But the story does not end there. A newspaper learned of the incident and published an account. A wealthy real estate agent read it and offered them a parcel of land worth many thousands of dollars. When told that the church could not pay so much, he offered to sell it to the little church for 57 cents. As a result, church members made large donations. Checks came from far and wide. Within five years the little girl's gift had increased to $250,000—a huge sum for that time. Her unselfish love had paid large dividends.

When you are in the city of Philadelphia, look up Temple Baptist Church with its seating capacity of 3,300. And be sure to visit Temple University, which educates thousands of students. That girl's dying gift inspired others to establish both of them. It goes to show what the Almighty can do with 57 cents.[131]

Lord, help me not to hold back in serving You because the task seems small or the outcome meager. Give me faith in the Almighty today!

September 20

Who will not fear You, O Lord, and glorify Your name, for You alone are holy.
**ALL THE NATIONS WILL COME AND WORSHIP BEFORE
YOU,** *because Your righteous acts have been brought into the open.* REV. 15:4.

T he basis for worship offered in this text is the public display of God's mighty and righteous acts. At the end of history everyone will see that God has ended sin and oppression and has delivered His faithful people. God's saving action will be so overwhelming that the redeemed will break out into the kind of spontaneous devotion best known in games of football around the world.

In America the greatest act of worship occurs once a year at an event known as the Super Bowl. The widely celebrated occasion garners the full attention of the media for at least a week. While it is a sporting event, it has all the trappings of a grand religious festival.

When it comes to the Super Bowl, the "worship committee" seeks the largest and best "church" in the country to hold the proceedings. Millions more assemble in small groups all over the country to watch the ritual on television. This "worship service" is so popular that people actually *pay* to get in!

The opening music is stellar, and every single second of this "worship service" is planned like a Hollywood production. It has no cheap PowerPoint tricks, dead spots, or boring intervals. In fact, some people say that the special announcements scattered throughout the entire service are really the best part of the proceedings! People carefully watch everything and everyone, and absolutely nobody sleeps during the nearly four-hour ordeal.

A wonderful "Communion service," often consisting of chips and dip as well as various kinds of drinks, usually accompanies the affair, particularly when small groups watch in private homes. People have also been known to get quite excited during certain parts of the meeting, and fitful seizures of clapping, shouting, and high-fiving are considered most appropriate behavior by the worshippers. And long after the titanic struggle between good and evil has subsided, people from all over the country continue witnessing about the experience to their family and friends.

Although this is an age of widespread unbelief, no one seems surprised to learn that the majority of Americans set aside a whole four hours to celebrate the mighty achievements of two football teams. While God's mighty acts have not yet entered public consciousness, the Bible helps us to know and to celebrate what He has already done for us in Christ. So pass the chips and the dip and let the worship begin![132]

Lord, how often I allow the visible achievements of those around me to overshadow the admiration I should have for You and for what You have done for me. I'm sorry for offering You a secondary place in my acts of worship.

After these things I looked, and **THE TEMPLE OF THE TABER-**
NACLE OF THE TESTIMONY IN HEAVEN *was opened. And the*
seven angels who had the seven plagues came out of the temple dressed in clean and
bright linen, wearing golden sashes around their chests. Rev. 15:5, 6.

T his mention of the temple in heaven is one of many references to the
sanctuary in the book of Revelation. Each of Revelation's seven main
sections begins with a scene based on the sanctuary. Let me summarize
them briefly.

Revelation 1:12-20. Jesus walks among seven golden lampstands (verses 12-
20). He is not in the heavenly sanctuary, but on Patmos (verses 9-12). The lampstands represent the churches on earth (verse 20). So God's church is a temple in
its own right (1 Cor. 3:17; 1 Peter 2:1-10).

Revelation 4; 5. Revelation 4 and 5 contain a thorough mix of images from
every part and service of the sanctuary. The scene probably represents the inau-
guration of the sanctuary itself, when every item in the sanctuary was dedicated
to God.[133]

Revelation 8:3-5. The focus of this passage is intercession. The prayers of the
saints combine with incense to enhance their effectiveness before God.

Revelation 11:19. Here is a view of the Most Holy Place, containing the ark
of the covenant. It appears in the context of judgment.

Revelation 15:5-8. In Revelation 15 and 16 the temple empties and is not
put into use again. The heavenly sanctuary, inaugurated in Revelation 4 and 5,
went through phases of intercession and judgment, and is here shut down. Its services have ceased.

Revelation 19:1-10. We note a total absence of sanctuary furnishings in this
text: no building, no censers, no altar, no ark of the covenant, no lampstand.
Worship is taking place, just as it does in Revelation 4 and 5, but without any
direct reference to the sanctuary and its furnishings.

Revelation 21:1-8. In Revelation 21:2, 3, the "tabernacle" is actually the
New Jerusalem descending to earth. The city is shaped like a cube, just like the
Most Holy Place of the sanctuary. God and the Lamb Themselves become the
temple of the city.

The book of Revelation displays a completed sanctuary cycle. The cycle begins on earth (Rev. 1) and ends on earth (Rev. 21). Scenes 2-6, on the other
hand, focus on the heavenly sanctuary throughout the Christian Era. The sanctuary is inaugurated, goes through phases of intercession and judgment, then is
abandoned. When the plan of salvation comes to an end, the sanctuary will no
longer be needed.

Lord, help me to take advantage of every provision You have made for my salvation.

September 22

After these things I looked, and the temple of the tabernacle of the testimony in heaven was opened. And the seven angels who had the seven plagues came out of the temple dressed in clean and bright linen, wearing golden sashes around their chests. And one of the four living creatures gave the seven angels **SEVEN GOLDEN BOWLS,** *full of the wrath of God, who lives for ever and ever. Rev. 15:5-7.*

John often echoes the language of the Old Testament in writing out his visions. But he does not point the reader to specific Old Testament texts. We will understand his meaning only by going back to the Old Testament and digging out the echo in its original context.

Here's how echoes work: What is a lemon? Well, it certainly is a citrus fruit with a fairly sour taste. But the term has an extended meaning in American culture. A lemon is a new car that doesn't deliver on its promise. While it may be brand-new, it gives its owner far too many troubles and spends much too much time in the repair shop.

Now, if you live in the United States, you are familiar with this symbolic use of "lemon." In the context of automobiles, a lemon is a bad new car. But you are probably not aware of how this meaning became popular. About 35 years ago Ralph Nader published a book entitled *What to Do With Your Bad Car.* The cover of the book had a picture on it of a lemon with four plastic wheels. Reading the title and then seeing the photo had immediate impact. "Lemon" as a symbol with automotive connotations became widespread.

But most Americans don't need to know that piece of history to understand the extended meaning of "lemon." You pick up that piece of information "in the air" of American culture. And if you are writing or talking about lemons, your audience would automatically understand, whether or not they have ever heard of Ralph Nader.

The seven bowls of wrath are a terrifying piece of Revelation's legacy to the world. Along with the seven trumpets, they pile up images of suffering, assault, and unrepentance. But "in the air" of John's Jewish world, bowls would have had a strangely positive ring. The word for "bowls" appears repeatedly in texts describing the implements of the sanctuary in the Old Testament (Ex. 27:3; 38:3; Num. 4:14; 2 Kings 25:14, 15; 2 Chron. 4:8, 22). They are also mentioned in Revelation 5:8 as containing the prayers of the saints. When the wrath of God strikes the earth, He will still be listening to the prayers of His people.

Lord, in the midst of tragedy I want to pray all the more, to link up with You in Your purpose to save everyone. You can, while limiting the sorrow and the dying. Give me a heart to act as Your agent of mercy in the world, one person at a time.

September 23

After these things I looked, and the temple of the tabernacle of the testimony in heaven was opened. And the seven angels who had the seven plagues came out of the temple dressed in clean and bright linen, wearing golden sashes around their chests. And one of the four living creatures gave the seven angels seven golden bowls, full of the wrath of God, who lives for ever and ever. And **THE TEMPLE WAS FILLED WITH SMOKE FROM THE GLORY OF GOD** *and from His power, and* **NO ONE WAS ABLE TO ENTER INTO THE TEMPLE** *until the seven plagues of the seven angels were finished.* Rev. 15:5-8.

In contrast to the smoke of the world's torment (Rev. 14:10, 11), we have here the smoke of God's glory. It reminds us of the scenes that accompanied the dedication of both the wilderness tabernacle (Ex. 40:34, 35) and of Solomon's Temple (1 Kings 8:10-12). God filled both places with His glory to celebrate their dedication. Here in Revelation 15 He does so in response to the worship of His saints (Rev. 15:3, 4), who suffered at the hands of the wicked ones who will now taste His severe judgments.

After the Exile in Babylon, Zerubbabel raised up a more modest Temple (Hag. 1:12-2:9) to replace Solomon's, which Nebuchadnezzar had destroyed (2 Chron. 36:18, 19). It too had a ceremony of dedication (Ezra 6:13-18). A similar service occurred nearly 100 years later to celebrate the completion of the walls of Jerusalem under Nehemiah, which safely enclosed the holy precincts once more (Neh. 12:27-47).

The Feast of Dedication as we know it (called Hanukkah today), however, did not originate in Old Testament times. It celebrates the rededication of the Temple in Jerusalem after its defilement by Antiochus Epiphanes (165 B.C.). Among other things, Antiochus sacrificed a pig on the Temple altar, forbade observance of the Sabbath, and compelled many Jews to eat pork. After the Maccabees, a group of Jewish insurgents, liberated Jerusalem from the clutches of Antiochus, they cleansed and rededicated the Temple. The celebration that followed became an annual feast of Judaism (one that Jesus Himself attended—John 10:22).

In our text we actually have something along the lines of an "undedication." The glory of God drives out the angels. But instead of returning in a short while to resume their temple duties, as would be the case for a dedication service, they move on to other, more painful tasks.

God marks the unpleasant turns of life as well as the pleasant ones. For the next few chapters of Revelation things will become very unpleasant indeed.

Lord, hold Your sanctuary open if that is not contrary to Your will. I feel unprepared for the events of the end. Bring me to a place of readiness for the close of history.

September 24

And I heard a loud voice from the temple say to the seven angels, "Go, pour out **THE SEVEN BOWLS OF THE WRATH OF GOD** *into the earth." And the first angel went away and poured out his bowl into the earth, and an ugly and painful boil broke out upon the men who had the mark of the beast and had worshipped his image.* REV. 16:1, 2.

A re the plagues literal or figurative? It is difficult to know. Images in the book of Revelation normally call for a figurative reading. Most of the book, particularly the seals and trumpets, makes sense only in a symbolic way.

Figuratively, the plagues could represent the consequences that come as a result of sin. The Old Testament calls them the curses of the covenant. The boils of the first plague resemble leprosy, a symbol of the putrefying effects of sin on the soul. The waters turning to blood could conceivably be taken literally. But it would take the total abandonment of law and order or a universal war to cause so much bloodshed that the ocean waters turn a bloody red. If you take the image symbolically, it may represent that those whose hearts are set on sin lose access to the water of life. The scorching sun could represent the intensified glare of God's Word as it points out sin and calls for judgment on those who oppose Him.

But in the end, the plagues may simply be a fairly literal outline of the terrible experience of the wicked in the last generation. They will suffer sores and diseases, extreme pollution, and weather now completely out of control. Everything designed to make life worth living gets taken away.

People today don't want to talk about God's judgment. They feel that judgment is not what a deity is for. But Santa Claus theology cannot cope with the reality of evil or seemingly senseless suffering. To make God kind but never firm is to deny His Lordship over a world full of suffering. Facing hardship without some sense that God has a purpose in it leads only to a fatalistic resignation. A God who never inflicts corporate judgments on the world is not the God of Scripture—He is an idol of our own making.

It is not to say that anytime someone suffers it is a divine judgment of some sort. Some may experience suffering as a judgment, while others may encounter the same suffering as a test of faith. Suffering rarely reveals its purpose to us, but it always summons our attention to the God who can help us understand the purpose in our suffering. With all the wrongs that happen in this world, we should not find it hard to believe that our world needs God's judgments to bring about justice.[134]

Lord, I thank You for the firmness of character that will right all wrongs in this world someday. Give me the confidence to trust Your Lordship of this world until then.

And **THE SECOND ANGEL POURED OUT HIS BOWL ON THE SEA, AND IT BECAME LIKE THE BLOOD OF A DEAD MAN.** *And every living thing which is in the sea died.* Rev. 16:3.

This text portrays a worldwide, devastating environmental disaster. The waters in the oceans, bays, and inlets of the world transform into a bloodlike substance that kills the creatures of the sea. The plagues of Revelation 16 carry out the promise of Revelation 11:18 that God will "destroy those who are destroying the earth."

The earth is the Lord's (Ps. 24:1), so those who abuse it challenge God's rule whether they realize it or not. God has placed us on a planet finely tuned to our comfort and support. When we abuse His creation, we heap judgment on ourselves. An example of this is the current situation of the earth's oceans.

The human race is devastating them. In the nineteenth century codfish were so numerous off the coast of the northeast United States that European visitors reported catching them simply by lowering baskets into the water. "In relation to our present modes of fishing," the eminent biologist T. H. Huxley said in 1883, "a number of the most important sea fisheries, such as the cod fishery, are inexhaustible." Today the abundance Huxley extolled is on the verge of disappearing. Unless something changes soon, biologist Daniel Pauly recently warned in the New York *Times,* the next generation will have nothing left but "plankton stew."

Twenty-eight percent of fish stocks worldwide are either overfished or nearing extinction, while another 47 percent are near the limits of sustainability. The waters off New England and Newfoundland are by some measures the worst in the world. A University of British Columbia team led by Pauly predicted recently that many large species "will be all but gone from the North Atlantic region within a few decades." Humanity is setting off the aquatic equivalent of a neutron bomb, leaving the marine environment intact but killing off all its inhabitants.

Meanwhile, the demand for fish continues to soar. Population continues to grow, and rising standards of living lead more people to seek meat in their diets. Fish consumption doubled between 1973 and 1997. By 2020 the catch will have to increase again by nearly half just to keep up with demand. The greatest demand comes from developing nations in Asia, whose citizens can hardly be told to eat less protein than their counterparts in the West.[135]

In His mercy God has created the earth to be self-cleansing and self-renewing. It has taken much abuse and continues to treat us well on the whole. But this life has no free lunch. What we sow we will eventually reap.

Lord, teach me how to exercise stewardship in my relation to the earth. I want all of my actions to exhibit my recognition that the earth belongs to You, not me.

September 26

AND THE THIRD ANGEL POURED OUT HIS BOWL ON THE RIVERS AND SPRINGS OF WATER, AND THEY BECAME BLOOD. *And I heard the angel of the waters, saying, "You are righteous, who is and who was, the Holy One, because you have judged in these ways. For they have poured out the blood of saints and prophets, so* **YOU HAVE GIVEN THEM BLOOD TO DRINK, FOR THEY ARE WORTHY."** Rev. 16:4-6.

We have seen that before the plagues are poured out onto the earth, the temple of heaven ceases to function (Rev. 15:5-8). The glory of God is so intense that the seven bowl angels leave the temple, never to return. The closing up of the temple in heaven suggests the end of human probation. From now on there will be no more conversions. Sinners will no longer come to Christ, and saints will no longer fall away from God. So the sufferings experienced in the seven last plagues are not designed to bring anyone to repentance.

What is the point of the plagues, then? If they take place after the close of probation, why add to the world's suffering? If people can no longer repent, it seems vengeful and capricious to torment them further. But the answer may lie in the major underlying theme. God is just when He executes judgment on the wicked, because they are receiving in kind what they have done to others (Rev. 16:5-7). In other words, the punishment fits the crime.

"Is God's judgment always perfectly accurate?" some might ask. "Wouldn't the wicked change if they knew God better or had the same kind of opportunities as the righteous?" The plagues will answer such questions. They show that the wicked will continue to oppose God no matter the circumstances. The worse things get, the more they resist Him. Earlier plagues had brought people to repentance, but now the wicked refuse to return to Him, regardless of what He puts in their path (Rev. 16:9, 11, 21).

The righteous also suffer many things in the last days (Rev. 13:9, 10; 17:14). But these sufferings do not turn them away from their course either. They remain righteous, and the wicked stay wicked (Rev. 22:11). The close of probation is not an arbitrary decree on God's part. It is simply a time when world affairs reach the point that everyone makes a settled decision for or against Him at the very same time.

The plagues also are not arbitrary, even though they come after the close of probation, because they also serve God's purposes. The turning of the rivers and springs to blood corresponds in a natural way to the crime that is in view. Those who have shed the blood of saints and prophets receive blood to drink as a just reward.

Lord, whenever I am tempted to put immediate pleasure ahead of Your will, keep me mindful of the horrible consequences of sin.

And **I HEARD FROM THE ALTAR,** *saying, "Yes! Lord God Almighty, true and righteous are your judgments."* Rev. 16:7.

This is something new—an altar that talks! A lot of strange creatures speak in Revelation, but this beats them all. It reminds me a little of Jesus' comment about the stones crying out to honor Him if the people would not do it. But why is the altar before the throne of God making a proclamation about God's justice?

We find a clue in Revelation 8:3, 4. There it tells us that the golden altar is the place from which the prayers of the saints arise, mingled with the incense of the altar. The "prayers of the saints" is actually an echo of the souls under the altar in Revelation 6:9, 10. These souls plead to God because of the unjust treatment they have received from those who live on earth.

So the altar is the place that stores, so to speak, the prayers of all the saints who have been treated unjustly, killed, or tortured for their faith. It is the place in heaven where all the requests for justice that have ever ascended from earth gather together. Coals of fire, which symbolize God's anger regarding such injustice, fill the altar. The book of Revelation portrays the time when the fire of God's judgment erupts against every perpetrator of injustice.

But the altar represents something else as well. It is also the place where the blood of sacrifice is brought, sanctified in a cloud of incense. So the altar also symbolizes forgiveness. Every sinner can go to it to have the weight of sin removed. Even those who have done heinous crimes can come to the altar in repentance and receive forgiveness.

The horrors that are poured out on the wicked are not inevitable for you and me. God has made provision for every sinner to be forgiven and cleansed. He forces no one to face His wrath. The Lamb has died for those sins. Christ has allowed Himself to experience the fires of divine wrath so that no one else need to, except by their own choice.

If we lay our sins on the altar, they will be burned up there. But if we choose not to repent—if we insist on clinging to our sins—the altar will draw those sins to itself, consuming us along with them. Those who feel they are "good enough on their own" will not be separated from their sins or from the ultimate consequence of those sins.

That's why we find so many plagues and so much bloodshed in the book of Revelation. It is picturing the full, natural outcome of our daily choices. Revelation gives us God's call to come back to Him before it is forever too late. In order to get our attention, it portrays the consequences of not returning to our Creator and Savior. The choice is ours.[136]

Lord, I see more clearly the reality of sin in my life and the consequence of not seeking Your forgiveness and cleansing. I choose to come to You today.

September 28

And the fourth angel poured out his bowl upon the sun, and he was authorized to scorch the human race with fire. And **THE PEOPLE WERE SCORCHED WITH GREAT HEAT,** *and they blasphemed the name of God, who had authority over these plagues, and they did not repent in order that they might give Him glory.* REV. 16:8, 9.

One of life's great miseries occurs when the temperature swings way out of normal. And this is particularly the case when you aren't used to one or the other extreme. If you have always lived in Singapore, 90°F (32°C) with 80-90 percent humidity seems rather normal. And those from Siberia can find 20° below freezing balmy. But both places can feel miserable to those not adapted to the climate.

A friend of mine had spent his whole life in southern California. When he moved to Andrews University, he experienced real winter for the first time. Cold waves of air swept over the windshields of the cars every night and covered them with ice. Michigan locals all have ice scrapers handy to remove the ice off the glass in their cars. But Jim had a "better" plan of attack. On "cold" California mornings in his youth he had seen his father go out and put water on the windows, and that would melt the ice instantly.

Feeling more than a little smug, Jim headed out to his frigid car one morning with a pan of cold water. Imagine how dumb he felt when the water he poured onto the windshield immediately froze and added to the problem. He discovered a major difference between the "cold" of California and the "freezing" of Michigan.

But Jim confesses that he was slow to learn about the differences in climate. When his family moved to the Philippines, people warned him that clothes and leather goods would get mildewed in the high heat and humidity. He checked the closets after a couple days and everything seemed all right, so he did nothing about the advice he had received. A few weeks later enough mold had grown on everything that he could have performed scientific experiments with it! He learned that he needed to rig up some low-powered lights in the closets to make the air a little drier. Now his closets emit a soft glow at night, and the clothes are nice and fresh.

Jim has learned from such experiences the importance of a teachable spirit.[137] A great big world lurks out there, and most of us know very, very little about it. The Lord "guides the humble in what is right and teaches them his way" (Ps. 25:9, NIV). The victims of the seven last plagues are those who have consistently resisted the Lord's teaching in their lives. The plagues prove that no matter what God does for them, they refuse to learn and refuse to repent.

Lord, I want to have a teachable spirit today. Instead of complaining when things are not comfortable, help me to see each discomfort as an opportunity to learn.

And the fourth angel poured out his bowl upon the sun, and he was authorized to scorch the human race with fire. And the people were scorched with great heat, and they blasphemed the name of God, who had authority over these plagues, and **THEY DID NOT REPENT** *in order that they might give Him glory.* Rev. 16:8, 9.

Some people believe that television programs, television ads, and movies are lessening the quality of real life. Real life can't seem to compete with Hollywood. A single hour of television usually has more moments of suspense, more odd twists, and more romantic incidents than most people experience in a decade. And that is not even counting the 15 minutes or so of commercials that remind everyone how inadequate real life is.

Because of such human-made images people find it hard to look at the sky, the sea, or the forests with the wonder each deserves. The media images seem a lot more interesting. In real life, funny, heartfelt, profound, and even miraculous things happen. But they occur in God's time, scattered in the midst of run-of-the-mill, everyday activities. Compared to the dazzling array of experiences people have on TV, real life just doesn't seem worth writing home about.

It makes one wonder what it would take for God to get through to most people in today's world. Would it require something as big as the seven last plagues? Or would even that hardly faze the hardened devotees of visual fiction? But the above text reminds us that God will do whatever it takes to bring us back to reality.

You see, the glitter of those false images rubs off sooner or later. As that happens, we have to create more spectacular ones to produce the same impact. Eventually we become disillusioned with the race for bigger and better images that really can't get any bigger or better. When we tire of the things that "pacify" us, we will begin to look for something "real" that cannot be topped. That is where we begin to search for God.

People who have everything will eventually run into despair. Their relationships become a wreck, because they have spent their lives pursuing things that don't give life true meaning. They come face to face with the reality that the death rate is 100 percent. At some point we have to get a grip on our limitations and look for something eternal. But in a world filled with "virtual reality," it is that much harder to find the real—or even want it.

God sometimes lets us experience everything that we think will make us happy, so that in desperation we will seek the only One who can truly make us happy. The sad thing is that some have allowed themselves to become so hardened that even God's loudest megaphone (the plagues) will not get their attention. I'd rather start paying attention now.

Lord, do whatever it takes to get my attention today.

September 30

The fifth angel poured out his bowl upon the throne of the beast, and his kingdom became darkened, and they gnawed their tongues on account of the pain. And **THEY BLASPHEMED THE GOD OF HEAVEN** *because of their pains and their sores, and they did not repent of their works.* Rev. 16:10, 11.

My children constantly remind me that I'm now an "older person." One of the things I have noticed about such "older people" is that they become more and more like whatever they have been before. The person who has spent a lifetime being sweet and blessing others tends to become a really, really sweet old person. On the other hand, a person who has lived for self and felt that the world owed him or her a living will increasingly grow more and more selfish and difficult as the years wind down toward the end.

I remember bringing my wife along on a pastoral visit to an older woman. The woman was bedridden that day and asked if my wife could feed her something. My wife agreed and put some hot cereal together. She then began to spoon the cereal into the woman's mouth. Hungry, the woman ate with enthusiasm. But at one point my wife didn't get the food to the woman's mouth as fast as she expected it, and so she bit my wife harshly on the wrist!

I remember telling my brother about the incident and saying, "I want to get rid of all my hang-ups as soon as possible. I don't ever want to become like that when I get old!" As I said, as we age we tend to become more and more what we have been all along. This has implications for what happens on earth after the close of human probation.

In the face of the overwhelming judgment in this text, one would expect everyone to repent. But that is not the way it will be at the end of time. One survivor of a plane crash recounts that he had always expected people facing death to cry out to God for mercy in their final moments. Instead, as the plane headed downward, out of control, he heard many respond with cursing. In their "last moments" they were merely following habits that they had spent their lives developing.

It doesn't matter whether God responds with judgment or mercy, because some will refuse to believe, refuse to repent, refuse to bless the name of the Lord (Rev. 16:9, 11, 21). They are like the wicked in Sodom who laughed at Lot when he warned them of judgment to come. And so in the end the wicked die unrepentant in the face of divine judgments. In doing so they reveal a deep-seated obstinacy and a depth of human rebellion against God.[138]

Lord, I realize that it would be a big mistake to wait until the end to repent. I want to build qualities into my life now that will reveal themselves when the crisis comes.

October 1

The sixth angel poured out his bowl on the great river Euphrates, and its water was dried up in order that the way of the kings from the rising of the sun might be prepared. And I saw, out of the mouth of the dragon and out of the mouth of the beast and out of the mouth of the false prophet, three unclean spirits like frogs. For **THEY ARE THE SPIRITS OF DEMONS, DOING SIGNS,** *which go out to the kings of the whole inhabited world to gather them for the battle of the great day of God Almighty.* Rev. 16:12-14.

Harvey got a call from a friend of his. "Have you heard what's happening to Joe?" he asked.

"No," Harvey said. "What's wrong?"

"Well, I think you'd better give him a call—he may need a little encouragement right now."

Since he and Joe had been friends for many years, Harvey quickly made the call. He found out that Joe had been accused of sexual harassment and was about to lose his job in a church administrative office.

The news really puzzled Harvey, because he had always known his friend to be especially careful in the way he treated the women around him. In fact, Harvey's wife told him that Joe was one of the few pastors she knew that didn't look at her the wrong way.

Upon further investigation it became clear that no one had ever properly confronted the accuser. People had just taken the charges at face value. They were willing to believe a story simply because it had got passed around so long that it sounded true.

At the end of time deception will be a major factor in the world. But it is not only the beasts of Revelation that cause it. Sometimes even Christians are too willing to believe slander or gossip. All it takes is the barest hint of sexual impropriety to ruin a pastor's reputation. At other times sexual predators use deception to cover up their crimes and appear to be spiritual mentors. Because false accusations are devastating even at a local level, imagine what it will be like when deception is a universal phenomenon!

It is imperative, as we approach the end, that Christians strive to be as transparent as the sunlight. We should never believe accusations without clear evidence and without hearing both sides of the story. If we do not learn to deal in truth now, while things are relatively calm, we will be in grave difficulty when the final crisis comes.

Lord, I want to commit myself to operate in truth at all times. If I cannot speak what is clearly true, help me at least to remain silent. Give me a passion for the truth.

October 2

And I saw, out of the mouth of the dragon and out of the mouth of the beast and out of the mouth of the false prophet, three unclean spirits like frogs. For they are **THE SPIRITS OF DEMONS, DOING SIGNS,** *which go out to the kings of the whole inhabited world to gather them for the battle of the great day of God Almighty.* REV. 16:13, 14.

This passage parallels Revelation 13:13, 14, in which the land beast calls fire down from heaven to deceive those who live on earth. Here the deceptive trinity (dragon, beast, and false prophet) sends out unclean spirits to perform miraculous signs in order to deceive the leaders of the world so that they can enlist them on their side in the final battle of earth's history.

For many, deception seems to imply that those deceived are somehow not responsible for what they didn't see or understand. But the reality is that people open themselves to deception because of greed or envy or some other selfish motivation. Being deceived, then, is not an excuse—it is a consequence, a fact illustrated by an entertaining Jewish joke.

The story relates that in the early 1900s an old Jew was traveling alone in his compartment on the Trans-Siberian Railroad. The train stops, and an officer in the czar's army gets on. He and the Jew travel for a while in silence. Suddenly the officer grabs the Jew by the lapels and demands, "Tell me, why are you Jews so much brighter than everyone else?"

Silent a moment, the Jew then responds, "It's because of the herring we eat."

The officer quiets down, and the trip resumes. Soon the Jew takes out a piece of herring and starts to snack on it. The officer asks, "How many pieces of herring do you have?"

"A dozen."

"How much do you want for them?"

"Twenty rubles." It was a large sum of money.

The officer takes out the money and gives it to the Jew. The old man hands him the herring, and the officer takes a bite. Suddenly he stops. "This is ridiculous," he exclaims. "In Moscow I could have bought all this herring for a few kopecks."

"You see," the Jew replies, "it's working already." [139]

Now, obviously we laugh at this joke because of where it stops. Had the situation continued, the Russian officer would probably have attacked the Jew or thrown him off the train. But in the story we see how the old man exploited the other's envy and greed to relieve him of his money. In the last days Satan will employ our weaknesses to deceive us away from our faithfulness to God.

Lord, I don't want to give Satan even the slightest point of entry into my life. Guard me with the infinite power of Jesus' blood.

Behold, I come as a thief! Blessed is the one who **STAYS AWAKE** *and hangs on to his garments, in order that he might not walk naked and they see his shame.* REV. 16:15.

F alling asleep is the perfect metaphor for the way many of us live our faith. We go through the motions of religion, make it through worship songs without remembering a word, and sometimes even pray and read our Bibles in a daze—as if a fog prevented any of it from making an impact on our lives. But we don't have to stay in a fog spiritually. God has a ready antidote.

A lifelong Catholic named Dan found Vicky Nelson to be extremely irritating. He could hardly stand to be with her on the job. Why? Because she was so calm all the time. She emanated a rare glow of serenity. Peace radiated from her like a spiritual tranquilizer! To him it seemed as if she were on drugs or something.

"Why are you so calm all the time?" he asked her one day.

"My faith," she answered peacefully.

"What faith?" he stammered. "I have faith—I'm Catholic!" (He claims to have been the world's worst Catholic at the time.)

"My faith," she repeated.

"What do you mean?" He'd always believed in God but felt that anyone who called themselves "born again" must be nuts. When Christians called his radio show he played the theme from *The Twilight Zone* behind their voices.

Vicky dragged him down to a Bible bookstore. He bought a Bible and took a little yellow pamphlet called "The Four Spiritual Laws" from her. Among other things, the booklet had a drawing of a throne with a little man sitting on it. The caption said: "Take yourself off the throne, and put the One who made you on it."

H'mm, Dan thought. *Makes sense so far.* He got down on his knees and said, "OK, God, if You're really up there, come into my life and do Your thing! Amen." He then crawled into bed and read most of the book of John. But he fell asleep before he finished, because he already knew how it ended.

The next morning he woke up feeling as if he had drunk 10 cups of coffee or something. The reason was simple. He realized that he now *believed* in God! Suddenly he had a craving to read the Bible. And it made sense to him! Only the Lord could do a miracle like that.[140] The antidote to being asleep spiritually is to "ask and it will be given to you" (Matt. 7:7, NIV). It is simply to "taste and see" (Ps. 34:8). God is real and is waiting to show Himself to us.

Lord, I invite You on the throne of my life today. Let nothing separate me from You.

October 4

T his is a very important text because it demonstrates that the battle of Armageddon (Rev. 16:14, 16) is a struggle for the hearts and minds of real people. It is not about Middle Eastern oil or the kinds of fighting we have seen in that part of the world recently. Right in the middle of the passage describing the battle of Armageddon is a call to the people of God to stay watchful and faithful as the end-time approaches.

What is particularly interesting is the connection between this text and the message to Laodicea in chapter 3. We find four words in this passage ("garment," "naked," "see," and "shame") that appear together in only one other place in the Bible, Revelation 3:17, 18. At the decisive end-point of history God reminds us of the letter to Laodicea.

The key problem with Laodicea is inauthenticity. What she says about herself and what she is are two different things. According to the text, Laodicea has put on a mask of riches but lives in poverty. She dons a disguise of beautiful clothing but cannot escape the reality of her nakedness. And she claims to be living on easy street, but she is actually wretched and homeless. I can relate to her condition.

Some 30 years ago I was visiting the Riverside Church in New York City one Sunday with a couple friends. It has one of the five largest classical organs in the world. Being an organist myself at the time, I never got enough of it. The organist that day was Frederick Swann. Internationally famous, he had dozens of recordings.

When the worship service concluded, I took my friends up on the platform to get a closer look at the organ. And since I knew quite a bit about such things, I began to explain some of the organ's different features. As I talked about the organ, the audience began to grow. It was fun having a bigger audience. So I began to expand on the story a little. And the audience got even bigger. Then suddenly I began to realize that the people weren't looking at me anymore. They were watching something behind me. When I turned around I stood face to face with Frederick Swann himself. Looking me in the eye, he said, "You'd better get your facts straight, sonny, before you open your mouth." Then he turned and walked away. I wish I could have been teleported to another planet instantly! That day I learned a very painful lesson in authenticity.

Lord, I confess that sometimes I don't even know how much I try to be something that I'm not, or attempt to polish an image of me that isn't real. Help me to find my security in You so that I can give an authentic witness to the reality of Your presence in my life.

October 5

And **HE GATHERED THEM TO THE PLACE** *that in Hebrew is called* **HAR-MAGEDON.** Rev. 16:16.

The word "Armageddon" has become famous because of its role in the King James Version as the location of the final battle of earth's history. The word appears only once in Scripture, right here in Revelation 16:16. The Greek has a little breathing mark above the *a* that indicates an *h* sound precedes Armageddon. So the actual word in the Greek is "Harmagedon." According to the text, it is a word with a Hebrew background.

In Hebrew the word *har* means "mountain" and *magedon* is a frequent translation of the Hebrew *Megiddo* in the Greek Old Testament (Joshua 12:21; Judges 1:27; 2 Chron. 35:22). So the most natural understanding of this enigmatic term is "Mountain of Megiddo."

The region of Megiddo was an ancient battleground. There the armies of Deborah and Barak defeated Sisera and his Canaanite army (Judges 5:19). Later the same place was the scene of the fatal struggle between Josiah and Pharaoh Necho (2 Kings 23:29, 30; 2 Chron. 35:22). This was such a memorable event in Israel's history that Scripture recalled the mourning for Josiah years later (Zech. 12:11). If the author of Revelation was alluding to this ancient battleground, it is an appropriate background to the final battle of earth's history.

The problem with the text is the reference to the "mountain" of Megiddo. The Old Testament speaks several times of a city of Megiddo (Joshua 17:11; Judges 1:27, etc.), a king of Megiddo (Joshua 12:21), a valley of Megiddo (2 Chron. 35:22), and waters of Megiddo (Judges 5:19). But it never mentions a "mountain of Megiddo." Scholars have offered a number of solutions to this problem but most don't work unless you alter the text in some way.

The best understanding of the phrase, therefore, would seem to be as a reference to Mount Carmel, a 20-kilometer-long ridge running from Haifa southeast toward the Jordan River. The high point of the ridge is in view from the ruins of the ancient city of Megiddo. There on Carmel Elijah the prophet precipitated a showdown with the prophets of Baal (1 Kings 18:16-45). He called fire down from heaven to prove that Yahweh rather than Baal was the true God (cf. Rev. 13:13, 14). And there he defeated the false prophets of Baal (cf. Rev. 16:13-16).[141]

By alluding to the Mount Carmel showdown, John indicates that the Battle of Armageddon is a spiritual conflict over the issue of worship (Rev. 13:4, 8, 12, 15; 14:7, 9-11). It is a struggle for the mind (Rev. 16:15, 17:14). Everyone in the world must make a fateful decision with permanent results.

Lord, I know that every day a battle is going on in my mind. Help me to recognize the decisive moments of that conflict in my life and in the lives of those around me.

287

October 6

And **HE GATHERED THEM TO THE PLACE** *that in Hebrew is called* **HAR-MAGEDON.** REV. 16:16.

Texts such as Matthew 24, 2 Thessalonians 2, and Revelation 13 speak about a great end-time deception. According to Revelation 16:16, the place where it occurs is Har-Magedon, Mount Carmel. In the original event at Mount Carmel Elijah takes on the prophets of Baal. It was a showdown between two claims as to who was God—Baal and Yahweh. After a time of failure by the prophets of Baal (and a whole lot of mocking from Elijah), Yahweh responds to Elijah's simple prayer and sends fire from heaven to confirm that He is the one and only true God.

But the end-time version of the Carmel confrontation has one problem. The fire from heaven falls on the wrong altar! Instead of confirming the identity of the true God, the evidence of the senses will imply that the counterfeit trinity is the real thing. It will be a devastating shock to the human race.

Imagine the following scenario, one that many believe today. You get up from a restless sleep and peer past the living room curtain into the street. A jet-black 2007 Corvette has jumped the curb across the street, skidded across the lawn, and wiped out most of Charlie's prize petunias before embedding itself into a retaining wall. Homer is out inspecting the wreck and the damage to the retaining wall. But he can find no sign of Charlie or of any occupants of the Corvette, which is too heavily damaged for anyone to have extricated themselves from its remains.

It turns out that this is only one of several such mishaps on your block. As neighbors cluster around the wrecks you notice that none of the born-again types are around. Charlie talked a lot about a "rapture" in which all the born-again Christians vanish, leaving chaos behind. You remember him telling you to watch some TV evangelist, but you never got around to it.

Now is a different story. You flip on the satellite TV and turn to the Christian Broadcasting Network. Chaos fills the screen, people milling back and forth. Finally one of them comes to the anchor desk to inform you with a trembling voice that apparently the "rapture" has come. One of the televangelists vanished in midsermon. Airplanes have been crashing in midflight, minus pilot and/or copilot. The entire world has come to a standstill!

Would an event like that get your attention? Would you wish that you had spent a little more time studying your Bible and a little less on soap operas and the latest game shows? And this scenario is probably mild compared to whatever the real thing will be. However it turns out, the end-time Mount Carmel experience will be very disorienting. It will deceive many.

Lord, help me to trust Your Word rather than my feelings. I want to be prepared for whatever may come.

And the seventh angel poured out his bowl upon the air, and a loud voice came out from the temple, from the throne, saying, "It is done!" And there were lightnings and noises and thunders and a great earthquake. It was such a terrible and massive earthquake that none like it has ever happened since humanity has been on the earth. And the great city disintegrated into three parts, and the cities of the nations fell. Babylon the Great was remembered before God to give her the cup of **THE WINE OF THE FURY OF HIS WRATH.** REV. 16:17-19.

The concept of a raging God doesn't always sit well with people today. But one thing we have to keep in mind is that John wrote Revelation primarily to people who were suffering as they heard the book. In a time of ease language like this can seem inappropriate, but in desperate situations the thought of a mighty avenger can seem almost sweet to the abused and the downtrodden.

But more than this, God uses such language as a motivator in some circumstances. He knows that we often want to do the right thing, but we need some sort of prompting to pull it off. The sense of negative consequences can go a long way toward changing our behavior.

A high school principal faced a problem of motivation one day. It seems that a number of the girls thought it was great fun to coat their lips with lipstick and then plant a big kiss on the mirror in the girls' bathroom. The sight of all the lip marks seemed too hilarious for words. This, however, increased the janitor's workload greatly, as the oil-based substance was quite difficult to remove.

So the principal made it a rule: no kissing of mirrors in the girls, bathroom. Did it stop the practice? Of course not! Now there was not only the fun of smudging the mirror, but also the thrill of breaking a rule. So the lip imprints on the bathroom mirror increased rather than decreased.

The principal then levied a fine on the behavior, which made it even more attractive. Not only did the girls have the excitement of breaking a rule, but also the challenge of avoiding punishment. So that didn't work either.

Finally he came up with an idea. Clearing the girls' bathroom one day, he called in 10 of the most talkative female students for a demonstration. He would show them how hard it was to remove all the lip smudges. So with the girls looking on he called on the janitor to wipe down the mirror in front of them. The janitor dipped a sponge in the toilet and began to wipe the mirror. Needless to say, within two or three days the kissing of mirrors had stopped in that school.

Lord, I need a little extra motivation today. Help me to apply the principle of consequences to everything I do. May my choices result in a brighter future.

October 8

Every island fled away and mountains were not found. **GREAT HAIL**
weighing as much as a talent [90 pounds] **FELL FROM HEAVEN** *upon
men, and men blasphemed God because of the plague of hail, since the plague of hail
was so severe.* REV. 16:20, 21.

When natural disasters come, people always ask why. Usually there
is no simple answer. But a major cause of natural disasters are actions we thought would be to our benefit. Something done from
the highest of motivations may still have negative consequences.
"What I am trying to do is make the whole world safe for Jews," Harry
Truman wrote as he wrestled over the decision whether or not to recognize a
Jewish state in Palestine. Deeply affected by the Holocaust, the American president sympathized with Jewish aspirations for a homeland. In November 1947 he
lobbied for a United Nations resolution that divided Palestine into Jewish and
Arab states. Britain announced that it would hand authority over Palestine to the
U.N. by May 14, 1948.

Secretary of State George Marshall advised against recognition. He warned
Truman that Arab countries would unite in an attempt to destroy the Jews. On
the eve of the British withdrawal he told the American leader that "the office of
the president" was at stake. But Truman had made his mind up. At 4:00 p.m. on
the fourteenth of May, David Ben-Gurion read a 979-word declaration of inde-
pendence in front of a small audience at the Tel Aviv Art Museum. At midnight
British rule over Palestine lapsed. Eleven minutes later the U.S. announced its
recognition of Israel.

"God put you in your mother's womb," the chief rabbi of Israel later told
Truman, "so you would be the instrument to bring the rebirth of Israel." With
Truman's decision, the hopes of the Jewish people were realized, but so too were
Marshall's fears. Arab opponents of the new nation immediately declared war,
prompting a bloody struggle over Israel's existence that continues until this day.[142]

The plagues at the end are horrible. In a perfect world God would never
choose to destroy and devastate as described here. But this is not a perfect world.
His people are in danger of destruction, and He intervenes to deliver them from
end-time Babylon.

Like President Truman, God once faced a fateful decision. He could create beings programmed only to obey Him or He could fashion ones that were truly free.
But free beings would be able to reject God and plunge the creation into great misery. It was a God-sized decision with pluses and minuses either way. The Lord
chose freedom, and the rest is history. One day the universe will clearly see the wisdom of His choice. For now we live with the unavoidable consequences.

*Lord, thank You for the freedom we have to live and love and choose our way. Help me
to freely choose the best way—the way that You designed me to go.*

One of the seven angels who had the seven bowls came and spoke with me, saying, "Come, I will show you the judgment of **THE GREAT PROSTITUTE** *who sits on many waters. With her the kings of the earth have committed fornication, and those who live on the earth have become drunk with the wine of* **HER FORNICATION.** Rev. 17:1, 2.

One of my favorite old movies is *Samson and Delilah,* with Victor Mature and Hedy Lamarr. The long drawn-out scene in which Lamarr entices "Samson" to reveal the secret of his strength is one of the great moments in cinematic legend. On the one hand, you find yourself absolutely charmed by the attractiveness of Lamarr's Delilah and on the other hand absolutely infuriated by her duplicity and cunning.

In this kind of dynamic it is easy to put the blame entirely on the woman. She is the seducer. Samson's great strength doesn't seem to affect one iota of his brain. In her hands he is all but helpless (especially since he is too distracted by her to call on God to get him out of there). Delilah is the stereotypical femme fatale.

But this kind of dynamic is falling out of favor in today's world, and the book of Revelation has received a great deal of criticism as a result. Some commentators complain that John's portrayal of Babylon as a prostitute represents a sexist stereotype no longer appropriate in today's world. They worry that Revelation's great popularity in the Christian world will translate into even more abuse and hatred of women than already exists.

The women of Revelation do appear in stereotypical roles, but such images were already current in John's day. Gentile writers of the first century often personified their homeland in female terms. Coins and other artwork typically depicted a city as a goddess enthroned by a river. So the book of Revelation was adopting images that communicated effectively within the culture of its time. While Westerners may be uncomfortable with such language today, it can be explained in terms of its context. To condemn John (or God) for using the concepts of the prophet's day is culturally insensitive and anachronistic.

When sharing the message of Revelation, we should be prepared for some objections from modern audiences. God meets people where they are. That means Revelation was well designed to communicate truth in the first century. But not every aspect of the way that truth was presented will be culturally familiar today. God is not on trial in the logic or the style of the Bible's writers.

Lord, help me to discern the contemporary meaning of these ancient symbols. Enable me to interpret them in ways that will not hurt other people.

October 10

[The angel] carried me away **INTO THE DESERT** *by the Spirit. And I saw* **A WOMAN SITTING ON A SCARLET BEAST,** *which was full of the names of blasphemy,* **HAVING SEVEN HEADS AND TEN HORNS.** Rev. 17:3.

The writers, director, producer, and actors all sat down before a 12-inch black-and-white television to watch the first episode of *I Love Lucy*. It was October 15, 1951. All but one of the group had participated in the filming of the show, so the only laughter came from the single person who hadn't seen it before, the husband of a secondary actress. He laughed so hard he almost fell out of his chair. The others hoped that his reaction was a good omen.

When the reviews appeared, they were mixed. The *Hollywood Reporter* raved about the show. *Daily Variety,* on the other hand, indicated that it needed some work before it would be successful. The New York *Times* thought the show had "promise." *Time* called it "a triumph of bounce over bumbling material." But when the ratings came out, *I Love Lucy* stood in the Top 10, and six months later it reached number one. *Time* magazine quickly had a change of heart, featuring Lucy on its cover in May 1952. The more-than-50-year success of the show is a credit to the comedic genius of "Lucy," Lucille Ball.

I Love Lucy established all kinds of records. More than a billion people have seen it. But one of the show's greatest contributions to the entertainment world was something that happened before it ever went on the air. In the early 1950s most TV shows performed live for broadcast from New York City. Stations around the country then played a kinescope, a copy of the show filmed from a TV screen, which left a lot to be desired in terms of quality.

But Lucy and her husband, Desi, were expecting their first child, and they didn't want to move to New York. So Desi suggested shooting the show with three movie cameras in front of an audience. CBS said it would cost too much, so the couple took a cut in salary and in return received the rights to the negatives of the films. Thus the three-camera film system, still used for situation comedies today, came into being—as well as the rerun.[143]

Revelation 17:3 is also a rerun. We have seen the woman previously in the desert (Rev. 12:6, 13-16). The same applies to the beast with seven heads, 10 horns, and the names of blasphemy (verses 3, 4; Rev. 13:1-6). These characters also echo characters from the Old Testament (Eze. 23; Dan. 7; Hosea 1-4). "What goes around comes around" and "there is nothing new under the sun." Satan's strategies tend to be fairly consistent. The problem is not that he surprises us, but that we tend to fall for the same tricks again and again.

Lord, help me to learn from the spiritual mistakes I have made in the past. Teach me to recognize the wiles of Satan and enable me to be faithful in all things today.

And the woman was **DRESSED IN PURPLE AND SCARLET AND ADORNED WITH GOLD, PRECIOUS STONES,** *and pearls, having a* **GOLDEN CUP** *in her hand filled with abominations and the unclean acts of her sexual immorality.* **A NAME WAS WRITTEN ON HER FOREHEAD,** *"Mystery, Babylon the Great, the mother of prostitutes and of the abominations of the earth."* REV. 17:4, 5.

Many years ago I was attending a professional conference in Boston during the late stages of my wife's final pregnancy. My flight home to Andrews University was scheduled for 2:00 in the afternoon on a Tuesday. At 6:00 in the morning the phone rang in my room at the Sheraton Boston. It was my wife. "Jon, come home quick—the contractions have begun!"

I dressed and packed with uncommon speed. Hurrying through checkout, I grabbed a cab and sped off to Logan Airport. Arriving at the United Airlines desk a little after 7:00, I breathlessly announced the blessed event and asked if there was some way I could get home immediately. The woman behind the counter smiled and quickly put me on the 8:00 flight to Chicago, with a two-hour layover before the next flight to South Bend.

Arriving in Chicago a little after 9:00, I went to the departure board and noticed that the earlier flight to South Bend was not scheduled to take off for another 10 minutes. But the gate was about a mile away in the vastness of O'Hare Airport. With the help of moving walkways and accommodating pedestrians (it's amazing how accommodating people can be when a man runs wild hollering, "My wife is having a baby!"), I covered the mile in six minutes flat.

Racing up to the gate, gasping for air, I waved my ticket and shouted, "My wife is having a baby! Can I get on this flight?" The attendant waved me on, glancing quickly at the ticket as I thundered by (the good old days before elaborate security).

I arrived in South Bend 10 minutes before 11:00 Boston time (an all-time record for Boston to South Bend, I suspect). Heading straight to a phone and still breathing hard, I called my wife. "False alarm!" she announced cheerily! "They were false contractions and stopped a couple hours ago." Slumping into a chair, I decided to wait until my baggage arrived that afternoon.

Things are not always what they seem! A beautiful woman is dressed in clothing reminiscent of Israel's high priest (see highlighted text above). But the appearance deceives. She is Babylon the Great, the mother of prostitutes. Not everyone who declares the name of God really serves Him. We should never place our full trust in human beings and institutions. God's Word is our safest guide.

Lord, give us clear discernment to know the difference between truth and error.

October 12

And **I SAW THE WOMAN** *drunk with the blood of the saints and with the blood of the martyrs of Jesus.* **AND I WAS AMAZED, GAZING AT HER WITH GREAT AMAZEMENT.** *The angel said to me, "Why are you amazed? I will tell you the mystery of the woman and of the beast who is carrying her, the one who has the seven heads and the ten horns. The beast which you saw was and is not and is about to come up out of the abyss and go to his destruction. Those who live on the earth, those whose names are not written in the book of life from the foundation of the world, will be amazed when they see the beast that was and is not and yet is.* REV. 17:6-8.

It should not surprise us that John is astonished when he sees the woman (Rev. 17:6). The fact that she is in the desert recalls Revelation 12. There God's faithful woman fled to the wilderness to escape the dragon. Here is the next appearance of a woman, and she is also in the desert. And as we noted in the previous devotional, her dress echoes that of the costume of Israel's high priest.

Although the woman of Babylon resembles the true woman of Revelation 12 and dresses like a high priest, she clearly represents a power that opposes the true people of God. She is the enemy of God's end-time saints. The passage parallels the death decree and economic boycott imposed on those who do not worship the beast or his image (Rev. 13:15-17). Has the woman of Revelation 12 been transformed? Or is she some sort of new entity? John's reaction strongly suggests the former. The great end-time opponent of God's people is a power that at one time was the true people of God. End-time Babylon has a Christian face.

The vision ends with verse 6, and a confusing series of interpretations begins with verse 7. This may be the most difficult single part of Revelation to interpret. Riding on the beast portrays a position of dominance. The woman represents a worldwide union of religion. The beast symbolizes worldwide political union. So Revelation predicts that the world will be more united than ever in its history just before the end. At that time, interestingly, religion will be in control of the political agenda, something that has not been true until recently.

Not only was John astonished at the prostitute—the beast amazes the end-time inhabitants of the earth. In today's world, worldwide political union is not yet a reality or even close to it. But as we give careful attention to the message of Revelation, we will be prepared for future developments.

Lord, many things in this passage leave me a bit puzzled. I pray for clarity on the points that will see me through the crisis to come.

HERE IS THE MIND THAT HAS WISDOM: *The seven heads are seven mountains, on which the woman is sitting.* Rev. 17:9.

One of the great pastimes of the human race is laughing at the foibles of other human beings. It is amazing the stupid things that human beings can say when under pressure. And we laugh, perhaps, because deep down inside we recognize that we are equally capable of such stupidity in a crisis. Consider the following calls to a hospital emergency room.[144]

Caller: "If my mom is supposed to take her prescription every six hours, is it OK for her to take it now?"

"When was her last dose?"

Caller: "At 5:00 p.m."

"And what time is it now?"

Caller: "It's 11:00 p.m."

"Well . . . ?"

Caller: "Well, is it OK?"

Caller: "I've had sore ribs for maybe a month now. I think they're broken. I've been drinking for pain control, but it's not working. Is there anything else I should be doing?"

Caller: "I just drank an Odwalla beer that's been sitting out for four days. Should I go get some medicine to throw up?"

"Did the Odwalla taste bad?"

Caller: "Yes, awful. I drank the whole thing."

"Why did you drink it if it tasted bad?"

Caller: "Well, I was in a really big hurry."

Human stupidity can be so funny that even God gets a good laugh over it sometimes (Ps. 2:4; 59:8). But the humor has a powerful spiritual message embedded in it. True wisdom belongs to God (Rev. 7:12) and to anyone willing to receive it from Him (Rev. 17:9)! Without a heart that is open to receive God's wisdom, every one of us is just a crisis away from being a joke!

Lord, once again I am reminded of my deep need for the wisdom only You can give. Teach me today.

October 14

Here is the mind that has wisdom: **THE SEVEN HEADS ARE SEVEN MOUNTAINS,** *on which the woman is sitting, and they are* **SEVEN KINGS.** *Five have fallen,* **ONE EXISTS NOW,** *and one is yet to come, and when he comes it is necessary that he remains for a short time. And the beast, who was and is not, he is an eighth, but he is one of the seven, and he will go to destruction.* REV. 17:9-11.

In Greek the word for hills and mountains is the same. So the author may have had Rome, the city of seven hills, in mind as a model for this beast. On the other hand, since the hills appear one after the other rather than together, this may not be the intention of the text. Whatever their meaning, the hills in our text represent secular and political power in support of Babylon. With these "kings" behind her, the Babylon woman will have great power at the end.

The pedigree of this end-time beast is in the seven kings. Commentators have made many attempts to identify them. But the basic principle to follow in Bible study is that God meets people where they are. When a prophet gets an explanation of a prophecy, the Lord always presents it in terms of the person's time and place (Dan. 2:37-40; 7:19-25). Thus the one who "exists now" would be the Rome of John's day.

The five who "have fallen" would presumably be the great empires of the Old Testament: Egypt, Assyria, Babylon, Persia, and Greece. Each of them functioned as an enemy of God's people for a time. The "king" that is "yet to come," from John's perspective, would be a future power that would become an enemy of God's people after the fall of Rome. But the seventh "king" is not the last. Beyond the seventh is an eighth, who is also one of the seven! Can you see why this text has puzzled many through the centuries? And when you look more closely at the Greek, the imagery becomes even more confusing!

The best explanation seems to be that the seventh head is the sea beast of Revelation 13. It too came up after the time of John and the Roman Empire (Rev. 13:2) and is resurrected for the final conflict (verses 3, 12). The "eighth head" then would be the final manifestation of political power in support of Babylon at the end (Rev. 17:3).

But it may not be necessary to understand all the details here. What we have in this passage is the pedigree of a worldwide end-time political power. It functions at the end the way the seven previous powers in earth's history did. Worldwide political union was a reality in John's day and previous to it. Such worldwide union is not a reality at the present time, but will be restored in preparation for the battle of Armageddon (Rev. 16:14-16). This will be the last challenge of earth's history for God's people.

Lord, help this picture of end-time events to energize my decisions and actions today. I want to be faithful even when everyone else is not.

And the beast, who was and is not, **HE IS AN EIGHTH, BUT HE IS ONE OF THE SEVEN,** *and he will go to destruction.* Rev. 17:11.

This text is a monumental puzzle. First of all, the seven heads are seven mountains, then they are seven kings. Then an eighth head comes at the end but is also one of the seven heads, mountains, and kings! Not only that, all of these symbols are also equivalent to the waters on which the woman also sat (Rev. 17:1)!

But we find a practical principle in all this. The earlier kings are like the family tree or pedigree of the beast. He acts just like them. It follows a pattern that we can also recognize at the personal level. The sins of the fathers get passed on to their children. We all tend to repeat the mistakes of the past—our family history.

Once I had a chance to sit down with a great psychologist on the beach. I asked him what insight he had that might make my life better. He brought up the concept of "life commandments," explaining that everyone tends to internalize certain "laws of life" from their home situation around the ages of 9-13. Such laws are as unchangeable to us as the Ten Commandments, no matter how silly they may seem to others. Identifying our "life commandments" and reshaping them according to God's Word will bring positive change into a person's life.

After some discussion we identified three life commandments that governed my life in a major way. They were (1) the need to always be on time, (2) the need for fairness in all situations, and (3) a passionate dislike of dogmatism.

Now, all of these seem like good things, don't they? It is courteous to be on time and not make other people wait. The problem is that I can be pretty ugly to people who get in my way while I am trying to be on time! Often they are the ones I love the most, and they don't deserve to be trampled by someone else's obsession.

Being fair and rooting for the underdog are also good qualities to have. The trouble comes whenever I perceive that someone else isn't being fair with me. While I try to extend fairness toward others, I can get pretty upset if I do not receive a similar fairness in return. This has caused a lot of mishaps around my house!

Unless we act decisively with God's help, we are all prisoners of the rules that circumstances hammered into us in the past. So I've made some decisions. I consider it a courtesy to others to be on time, but not at the expense of courtesy toward my family and significant others. And I choose to be as fair as possible in my dealings with others, while letting go the pain of when others have been unfair to me. I'm happy to report that I'm making progress.

Lord, open my eyes to the truth about myself, no matter what the cost.

October 16

THE TEN HORNS THAT YOU SAW ARE TEN KINGS.
These have not yet received a kingdom, but they receive authority as kings for one hour with the beast. **THESE HAVE ONE PURPOSE, AND THEY GIVE THEIR POWER AND AUTHORITY TO THE BEAST.**
REV. 17:12, 13.

P reviously we have encountered the seven kings. Now John mentions 10 kings! What is going on here? The 10 kingdoms are end-time characters without a pedigree. Receiving their dominion along with the beast in the final period of earth's history, they exist in the time of the "eighth king" (Rev. 17:11).

If the beast represents the combined political and economic powers of the world, the 10 horns symbolize a significant subgroup of the world's nations. Crucial to the final events is a worldwide unity of political and economic power. In order for that unity to happen, this powerful subgroup has to sign on. Only time will reveal the identity of the 10 kings. Those who observe this prophecy with care will want to watch for a move toward world unity by a major subgrouping of the world's nations, possibly in the context of the United Nations or some similar organization.

If such an action occurs in the reasonably near future, two major candidates for the role described in this passage might be NATO and the G8 nations. NATO is a military alliance made up of the United States, Canada, and 24 European countries (including Turkey, which is partly in Europe). It was the outgrowth of the North Atlantic Treaty signed on April 4, 1949. The treaty's initial purpose was to provide a political and military counterbalance to Soviet power in Europe. With the collapse of Soviet Communism, NATO has become the chief military and political power in the world. Worldwide union would be inconceivable without its support.

The G8 nations, on the other hand, are more of an economic group than a political or military one. Since 1975 the leaders of the major industrial democracies have been meeting annually to deal with significant economic and political issues. The six countries at the first summit were France, the United States, Britain, Germany, Japan, and Italy. Canada joined in 1976 and Russia in 1998. While NATO is the more powerful organization on paper, the G8 countries together can dominate NATO.

Whatever the makeup of the 10 kings, the giving of their authority to the beast results in war with the Lamb (Rev. 17:14). The good news is that the end is not in doubt and that the outcome is clear. The Lamb wins, and the powers of the world lose.

Lord, I feel confident knowing that in relationship with You I am on the winning side at the end of history. May this confidence motivate me to live boldly for You today.

THESE WILL MAKE WAR WITH THE **L**AMB, *but the Lamb will overcome them, because He is Lord of lords and King of kings*—**AND THOSE WITH** **H**IM **ARE CALLED AND CHOSEN AND FAITHFUL.** REV. 17:14.

Recently Hollywood portrayed the social reality of a typical military unit as a "band of brothers." Why don't soldiers run for their lives in the heat of battle? Usually out of a sense of responsibility for their colleagues in the unit, who may become closer to them than family ever was. Something about going into battle together creates bonds of friendship between people the way few other things can.

A couple friends of mine—Ed Dickerson and Bill Underwood—developed the idea that friendships come in seven stages. First, people exchange greetings and comments about the weather. The second stage involves the swapping of facts and reports. When friends move on to the third stage, they will risk sharing opinions and judgments. Friends reach stage four when they are willing to communicate feelings as well as facts. In stage five, people begin to share their failures and mistakes with each other. With stage six, the level of trust has become so high that one allows the other the right to point out faults. Stage seven is the level of total intimacy, something rarely achieved on earth.

After outlining the seven stages of friendship with a group, Ed likes to ask, "If we apply them to our relationship with God, at what stage does conversion occur?" Ed believes that it happens when we reach level five with God, the stage where we are willing to share our faults with Him—what we usually call confession of sin. Ed goes on to point out that many, if not most, congregations seem to be stuck in stage three of human relationships, the exchange of opinions and judgments. If so, the average Christian would seem to have a closer relationship with God than with other Christians.

But that creates a problem. According to the Bible, one cannot have a closer relationship with God than one has with fellow Christians! "If anyone says, 'I love God,' yet hates his brother, he is a liar. For anyone who does not love his brother, whom he has seen, cannot love God, whom he has not seen" (1 John 4:20, NIV). When we cannot say, "I was wrong," to a fellow human, it calls into question our confession of sin to God.

As the final battle of earth's history approaches, God invites the church to truly become a "band of brothers and sisters." Those who are with Jesus then will be on intimate terms, not only with Him, but also with each other.

Lord, shield me from my relational blinders toward others. Help me today to grow in my capacity to know and love others, even as I know You and am known by You.

October 18

THESE WILL MAKE WAR WITH THE LAMB, *but the Lamb will overcome them, because He is Lord of lords and King of kings*—**AND THOSE WITH HIM ARE CALLED AND CHOSEN AND FAITHFUL.** REV. 17:14.

Native American culture is strongly centered in storytelling, not unlike the Hebrew culture that we find in the Old Testament. The elders of the tribe pass on stories about the ancestors that they had heard from their parents and grandparents. And the grandparents had learned those same stories from their own parents and grandparents.

One time a group of children approached a tribal elder. As most children will, they begged him to tell them a story. He shared one that personalizes the war described in our text for today.

According to the legends of the tribe, every person at birth receives two wolves who reside within. The wolves grow with each child and affect human behavior throughout a person's life. One wolf is the source of everything evil in life. It promotes unkind, hurtful, deceitful, hateful, and cruel behavior. The other wolf prompts acts of kindness, truthfulness, love and mercy. The two wolves constantly battle each other inside, and a person's behavior reflects the wolf winning that day.

The children, enthralled with the story, asked, "Which of the two wolves will win?"

The wise elder paused dramatically for a few seconds and then answered, "The one that you feed."

The war described in Revelation 17:14 is the global conflict of the end-time, called Armageddon in Revelation 16:16. It will involve every nation on earth and every economic and religious power. But that battle also has personal dimensions. The New Testament is fond of describing the personal battle against sin and Satan in military terms (see Eph. 6:10-17, for example). In the New Testament "the weapons of our warfare are not fleshly weapons" (2 Cor. 10:4). Fleshly weapons, such as assault rifles and tanks, rip you to pieces. But spiritual warfare is different. It is about "tearing down false arguments, and every pretension that lifts itself up against the knowledge of God, and taking captive every thought, to make it obedient to Christ" (verses 4, 5).

A battle rages inside every one of us. And our part in this conflict is real. The question is "What are you feeding your mind?"

Lord, I will have many opportunities today to choose between Your ways and the promptings of our common enemy. I submit my choices to You today.

[The angel] said to me, "The waters that you saw, where the prostitute sits, are peoples and crowds and nations and languages. The ten horns, that you saw, and the beast, these will come to hate the prostitute, and **SHE WILL BE MADE DESOLATE AND NAKED, AND THEY WILL EAT HER FLESH AND BURN HER UP WITH FIRE.** Rev. 17:15, 16.

Texts such as this disturb many readers of Revelation—and understandably so. A woman is brutalized, cannibalized, and left naked and desolate. That sounds like a major atrocity to contemporary ears. While the Babylon represented here was herself certainly brutal and violent, does that justify the use of such violent images in a biblical book? If television depicted such a scene, we would rush to turn it off so it would not scar our children.

But perhaps we are not seeing the whole picture in this text. I am reminded of a business establishment in Philadelphia that put up a scandalous sign: "We would rather do business with a thousand Arab terrorists than with a single Jew." Now, Philadelphia is the city of brotherly love and has plenty of sensitive people in it (including many Jews). You would think that crowds of people would have come to protest that sign. I would have expected the governor of Pennsylvania to call out the National Guard in case of rioting. Yet not a single person protested the sign, not even in the Jewish community! What was going on?

You had to see the sign in its larger context to understand. The business establishment was Goldberg's Funeral Home. If anyone was outraged, it was Arab terrorists, and they weren't talking! The sign was not an expression of hostility to Jews, but rather a wish that Jews would have long life.

The violence in Revelation is also a matter of context. On the surface it appears that God overcomes evil by the use of forces just as brutal and violent as those Babylon employed. Does that mean He is in the right because He has the might? Only if you ignore the larger context in the book of Revelation. You see, the agent of God's power is the Lamb (Rev. 17:14, 17) that was slain (Rev. 5:6). The violence by which Jesus conquers Babylon is ultimately the violence done to Him.

Although images of battle appear in the book of Revelation, God never calls His people to use violence in His behalf. They are summoned instead to suffer as the Lamb did, overcoming not with the sword, but by the word of their testimony (Rev. 12:11). In the end Babylon's violence leads to her own destruction (Rev. 13:10; 18:5-7). But the sacrifice of the Lamb and His followers results in a world without any violence at all (Rev. 21:4).

Lord, I am in awe as I consider the self-sacrificing path You took to end hatred and violence in the universe. I want to be more like You.

October 20

The ten horns that you saw, and the beast, these will come to hate the prostitute, and she will be made desolate and naked, and they will eat her flesh and burn her up with fire. **FOR GOD HAS PLACED IT IN THEIR HEARTS TO DO HIS PURPOSE,** *and to be of one purpose themselves, and to give their domain and power to the beast until the words of God are brought to completion.* REV. 17:16, 17.

God retains sovereignty over the choices that His enemies make. While evil is self-destructive in nature, God's guiding hand limits the harm that evil powers can do. In the end, not only the beast but even Satan will do God's bidding (2 Thess. 2:11).

In 1935 Karl Doenitz (born 1891) became the commander of the reconstituted German submarine command under Adolf Hitler. Derisively referred to as "Admiral Doughnuts" by the Allies, he considered the problem of defeating Great Britain in a war. The fact that Great Britain was an island nation was both an advantage and a vulnerability. It was an advantage in the sense that an enemy could not attack it unless it had overwhelming air and sea superiority. On the other hand, it was a vulnerability in the sense that the shipping lanes needed to remain open for Britain to survive a war.

Doenitz had an idea and presented it to Hitler. With careful planning and focused resources, he could have factories producing 40 submarines a month by the year 1938 (well in advance of the war that eventually broke out). If Germany targeted merchant shipping instead of military vessels, it might strangle Britain's military and economy in a matter of months. Hitler considered the plan but rejected it. He did not see the brilliance in a tactic that would surprise the enemy. Instead, enamored with "the big stuff," he wanted to match the British in the ego-boosting arena of naval warfare—battleships and aircraft carriers.

Hitler authorized a construction level of one or two subs a month in 1936. Then he placed massive resources into battleships such as the *Bismarck* and *Tirpitz* and aircraft carriers that would not have come on line until 1950! When war broke out in 1939, Doenitz's handful of subs sank 3 million gross tons of British shipping in the first year. Imagine the havoc 500-800 subs around Britain might have wrought! It is very possible that Britain would have found itself forced to surrender within a year after Dunkirk.

Hitler belatedly authorized Doenitz's plan. By 1944 the Nazis reached a production level of 40 submarines a month. But by then the Allies had discovered radar and broken the Nazi Enigma code, so they destroyed the submarines as fast as they came from the shipyards. While His hand is often invisible at the time, history reveals that God is always in control. It is sometimes the smallest deviations from plan that lead the enemies of God to disaster.

Lord, help me live in the assurance that You are in control of my life today.

The woman that you saw is **THE GREAT CITY** *that has rulership over the kings of the earth.* Rev. 17:18.

The image of the "great city" clearly has universal application. The book of Revelation calls it Sodom, Egypt, Jerusalem, and Babylon (Rev. 11:8; 14:8). It is still a factor in the world at the end of history (Rev. 17). So it is likely that early readers of Revelation would have identified this image with Rome. The great city "has rulership" (present tense) over the kings of the earth. The beast the woman rides is also seven mountains, which would probably remind first-century readers of the seven hills of Rome. First-century Jews and Christians often referred to Rome as Babylon, etc. There may be a lesson for us in this identification.

Around the time of the composition of Revelation the legal standing of Christians in the empire had begun to come under threat. Jews were taking action to isolate Christians from the synagogue. But Judaism was the only religion that was exempted from Roman religious law. To be seen as separate from Jews, therefore, put Christians in real peril.

A second problem that Christians began to face were accusations from their Gentile neighbors. As Gentiles came to see a distinction between Christian faith and Judaism, they often examined Christianity with hostile contempt. They accused Christians of being "haters of the human race." Pagan rituals and rhetoric saturated public events in Asia Minor. Christians, therefore, usually avoided them so as not to compromise their faith. Pagans began to think of them as antisocial.

The general population, on the other hand, took a smorgasbord approach to religion. They felt free to pick and choose among a variety of ideas. Much like today, they did not appreciate people who thought that they were right and that everybody else was wrong. As a result they accused Christians of "atheism" because they would not worship any god but their own. The peoples of the empire each had their own religious preferences, but added worship of the state gods as a token of their allegiance to the state. But Christians would not accept the state gods as objects of worship. So pagans considered them "atheists."

Christians, oddly enough, also faced charges of "cannibalism." It had to do with Gentile perceptions of the Lord's Supper, in which Christians were "eating the body and drinking the blood" of their Lord. Although Christians understood such statements in a spiritual way, apparently their pagan neighbors did not. So stories circulated that Christians sacrificed children and others in order to eat them at their Lord's table. Such accusations combined to create an insecure world for Christians to live in.

Lord, I am grateful to live in relatively sheltered times. Keep my faith strong when life is good.

October 22

After these things I saw another angel coming down out of heaven, having great authority. The earth was illuminated with his glory. He cried out with a loud voice, saying, **"BABYLON THE GREAT HAS FALLEN!** *It has fallen! It has become a dwelling place for demons, and* **A CAGE FOR EVERY KIND OF UNCLEAN SPIRIT AND EVERY KIND OF UNCLEAN AND HATEFUL BIRD.** REV. 18:1, 2.

Babylon is more than just an end-time power. As the "great city" it symbolizes all the evil powers that have ever dominated the earth. In the Greek of Revelation 17:18 Babylon "is" the great city that "has rulership" over the kings of the earth. This combination of a present tense verb with a present participle ("has rulership") is one of the most continuous expressions possible in the Greek. It means that Babylon rules constantly and ceaselessly over the kings of the earth. The principles of Babylon lie behind all the powers in earth's history that try to coerce and exploit people.

Babylon can rear its ugly head in surprising places. Israelite law required slaveholders to provide freed slaves with resources so they could build their own lives (Deut. 15:13, 14). But freed slaves in America never received the promised "forty acres and a mule." While the Northern states ended slavery through the Civil War, the freed slaves themselves lacked the land to become self-sufficient in the agricultural South. Many freed slaves became virtual debt slaves on the same estates on which they had once worked in bondage.

In the early twentieth century millions of rural Southern Blacks moved to Northern cities, hoping to find employment and to escape segregation. What they met instead was a new kind of segregation known as "White flight." As the Whites left the inner city they took their money with them, resulting in today's urban ghettoes. While slavery ended nearly 150 years ago, those born into the ghetto have automatic educational and economic disadvantages. Such disadvantages stem from conscious choices made by our ancestors on economic rather than ethical grounds.

Am I responsible for the sins and injustices of my ancestors? The Bible seems to answer yes (Rev. 18:4-7; Matt. 23:29-36). To ignore these disparities because "I had nothing to do with it" is like a baseball team cheating into the ninth inning and then saying, "OK, we'll play fair for the rest of the game!" Christians must be willing to do something, but what is it?

Race-based reparations may not be the answer. As John Perkins (an African-American preacher) jokes: "Many poor people would immediately buy an expensive car, and the rich people would have their money back!" But we can invest our time and money in needy communities. We can find ways to empower the poor to build their own lives.[145]

Lord, give me a heart to see the need of another the way You view it. Fill me with the courage and the sacrificial willingness to do something about it.

After these things I saw another angel coming down out of heaven, having great authority. The earth was illuminated with his glory. He cried out with a loud voice, saying, **"BABYLON THE GREAT HAS FALLEN!** *It has fallen! It has become a dwelling place for demons, and a cage for every kind of unclean spirit and every kind of unclean and hateful bird.* **FOR EVERY NATION HAS DRUNK FROM THE WINE OF THE WRATH OF HER FORNICATION. THE KINGS OF THE EARTH HAVE COMMITTED FORNICATION WITH HER AND THE MERCHANTS OF THE EARTH HAVE BECOME RICH BECAUSE OF HER LARGE CAPACITY FOR LUXURY."** REV. 18:1-3.

This passage will be directly fulfilled just before the second coming of Jesus. But the principle of Babylon can be found at many times and in many places. Babylon is more than just a dangerous outfit in another time and place. So we're glad that we are with the good guys! But at the risk of seeming unpatriotic, let me explore a few considerations that may bring this passage a little closer to home for Americans.

The United States today is not an evil empire in the sense of a totalitarian or repressive state such as Assyria or Nazi Germany. Such nations automatically invite judgment unless they repent. But this text seems to apply to America in other ways. We live in a world today in which the dominant trading partner of most countries in the world is the United States of America. And while many of the goods traded are fairly neutral in a spiritual sense, much of American trade contributes greatly to the evil in the world.

America has become one of the primary exporters of immorality. One of the most widely watched television programs in the world for years was *Baywatch*. Is it any wonder that some Muslim nations, who try to guard against public exposure of the human body, have regarded the United States as the "Great Satan"? After all, American priorities in the Middle East seem quite clear. When the Saudi government demanded that the U.S. embassy close down both worship services and nightclubs for American citizens, the embassy compromised. If they could keep the nightclubs open, they would terminate the worship services.

The export of American-style democracy seems like an improvement over oppression, but often a dramatic rise in Mafia-style crime accompanies it. Popular songs in newly minted democracies glorify drugs and rape, courtesy of the American entertainment industry. Alarmed by a younger generation that is getting its values from Hollywood and MTV, Chinese officials have sought stricter controls on public morality.[146]

If John were alive today, would he apply the term Babylon to the United States?

Lord, give me eyesalve to see clearly the sin that lies in my own backyard. Help me to clear the beams in my own eyes before I criticize the specks in the eyes of others.

October 24

And I heard another voice from heaven, saying, **"COME OUT FROM HER, MY PEOPLE, IN ORDER THAT YOU MIGHT NOT PARTICIPATE IN HER SINS AND IN ORDER THAT YOU MIGHT NOT RECEIVE ANY OF HER PLAGUES.** *Because her sins have accumulated up to heaven and God has remembered her crimes. Treat her the way she treated others. Pay her double according to her works. Mix double for her in the very cup in which she mixed."* REV. 18:4-6.

I t is easy to look at the residents of Babylon and say, "What's the matter with them? Why are they supporting the evil city with their presence? Don't they see what she is doing?" But the reality is that it is hard to recognize the corporate sins of an organization when you are a part of it. Since groups of people tend to share the same blind spots, it is easier to see corporate sin from the outside rather than from the inside.

God's end-time people will need a great deal of discernment to recognize clearly the deceptive webs of Babylon when the end comes. To avoid getting sucked into Babylon's deceptions, we need to develop a prayerful knowledge of God's Word. And we will want to combine that study and prayer with a healthy dose of self-distrust, so that we can discover our personal blind spots as we approach the end. One way to discover blind spots is to study the Bible in groups and do a lot of listening to others. Safety rests in many counselors.

I express my self-distrust with the following prayer from time to time: "Lord, I want the truth, no matter what the cost—even the truth about myself." Such truth can be costly. One Christian prayed two hours a day, telling God passionately that he loved Him so much that nothing else mattered. It was not until his wife died suddenly that he truly understood what it was that he had been praying about.

When we see corporate abuse and exploitation, we need to speak out against it. But eventually a society becomes too corrupt to listen. At such times God tells us to withdraw from it before it self-destructs or gets destroyed from the outside. We hear echoes of Sodom and Lot in the call of Revelation 18:4. When Sodom's time for destruction came, Lot had to leave Sodom or perish with it.

It is easy to condemn anyone belonging to an organization that operates contrary to Scripture. Our text, however, shows that many connected with "Babylon" are not doomed until the very end. God has His saints in every place and in every organization today. In a world with many shades of gray, it takes discernment to know right from wrong.

Lord, I see the need to study, stretch, grow, and learn. I invite You to be my constant guide and support along the way.

Just as **SHE HAS GLORIFIED HERSELF AND LIVED LUXURIOUSLY,** *so give to her torment and pain. Because in her heart she says, "I sit as a queen, I am not a widow, and I will never know pain."* Rev. 18:7.

The book of Revelation portrays Babylon as a queen dressed in fine garments and decked with jewels (Rev. 17:4, 5). Her wealth is also the commercial engine that prospers the merchants of the entire world (Rev. 18:9-19). She gained her wealth and standing, however, at the expense of others (Rev. 17:6; 18:2, 3, 5). So this text contains a call for reversal. In contrast to her luxurious life, she now stands condemned to the kind of torment and pain she inflicted on others. Scripture even lists her luxury as one of the grounds for her condemnation (Rev. 18:3).

Is a luxurious life a sin against God, then? If so, how luxurious? Is the mere possession of riches cause for censure? And if that is so, would not most of us stand condemned in today's world? After all, what ancient person would not have been awed at the wealth of a "poor" person today, many of whom own aging but self-propelled vehicles, live in apartments with central heat, and own electronic boxes that bring news and entertainment from afar! All of these would have been unimaginable luxuries in the Roman world. Is wealth a sin? And if so, how much wealth?

The answer lies in the first part of Revelation 18:7. It is not just that Babylon has lived luxuriously—it is that she has "glorified herself" in her possessions. The possessions themselves do not condemn her, but rather it is her selfishness in the use of them that is the crucial thing. Her goal in gathering possessions was not for the benefit of others or even humanity as a whole, but to glorify herself and make her own life comfortable and secure.

I suspect that God is less concerned with the size of your house than with your hospitality or lack of it. He is less worried about the kind of car you drive and more as to whether or not you use it to transport people who don't have a car. The size of your social circle does not bother Him so much as how many people consider you a friend. And He has less interest in the neighborhood you live in than He has with the way you treat your neighbors.?

I suspect that God doesn't mind if you have a high salary as long as you didn't compromise your character to obtain it. God will not condemn you for working overtime, but He will want to know if you did it for your own sake or for the sake of others. It doesn't bother the Lord if you gained advancements on the job, as long as you worked equally hard to promote others. And He is less concerned with the quantity of your possessions than He is with the degree to which they rule your life. Babylon thus isn't about what you have, but about how you live.

Lord, open my eyes to the Babylon within me. Forgive my blindness to the needs of others and help me to see others through Your eyes.

October 26

Just as **SHE HAS GLORIFIED HERSELF AND LIVED LUXURIOUSLY,** *so give to her torment and pain. Because in her heart she says, "I sit as a queen, I am not a widow, and I will never know pain." For this reason,* **IN ONE DAY HER PLAGUES WILL COME: DEATH AND MOURNING AND FAMINE,** *and she will be burned with fire, for strong is the Lord God who has judged her.* REV. 18:7, 8.

It is clear from our text that Babylon is not only wealthy—she is fully self-absorbed in her wealth. Her full attention is on her own pleasure, and she will defend that position at all costs. She has ignored the teaching of Jesus: "Give, and it will be given to you" (Luke 6:38, NIV). This suggests that if you want to be wealthy you have to give your riches away. To hoard them will cause you to lose them.

The fate of the Vanderbilt fortune illustrates the principle. The Vanderbilts differed with their wealthy peers in two respects. First, they had more money. William H. Vanderbilt, president of the New York Central Railroad, left his heirs $200 million upon his death in 1885. That sum had made him the wealthiest person on earth. Second, the family seemed beset with a great reluctance to share any of its wealth with those less fortunate. Shortly before his death the Commodore, as people referred to William H., responded to a Chicago *Tribune* reporter's question about social conscience with the expletive "The public be ——— ."

William Vanderbilt was not a total skinflint. He did give $1 million for the founding of Vanderbilt University and once allowed his wife to persuade him to donate $50,000 for the building of a church, as long as it was specified that the gift was a secular gesture, not a religious one.

The example of the Commodore seems to have been passed on to his descendants. What gifts they made to charity tended to be one-shot affairs, often after death. As was the case with the Commodore's church donation, they had no personal involvement in the few projects that they supported. Compared to the monumental contributions of the Morgans, the Fords, and the Rockefellers, the bequests of the Vanderbilt family were relatively small. Yet in spite of this careful hoarding of wealth, the Commodore's fortune is essentially gone today.

It seems that giving provides the sense of purpose that families need to keep the spirit and vigor of the founder alive for later generations. Where wealthy families have no such sense of purpose, they tend to dissipate their wealth in the pursuit of social status and self-gratification, leading to the dissipation of the family fortune.[147] To paraphrase Jesus again: "It is more blessed to give than to receive" (Acts 20:35, NIV).

Lord, touch my heart and the hearts of my children with the joy of giving.

THE KINGS OF THE EARTH, WHO COMMITTED
FORNICATION WITH HER AND LIVED LUXURIOUSLY,

will weep and mourn over her when they see the smoke of her fiery ordeal. They stand at a distance, for fear of her torment, saying, "Woe, woe is Babylon, the great city, the strong city, because in one hour your judgment has come." REV. 18:9, 10.

The situation of end-time Babylon would have rung a bell with people in first-century Asia Minor. They probably would have seen the "kings of the earth" here as the client kings (such as Herod in Palestine) that ruled in Rome's behalf in the provinces. Such rulers would keep their distance from the destruction out of self-preservation. Both then and now, love for "Babylon" is a self-interested thing and not self-sacrificing love.

In the first century Rome was the engine that drove the prosperity of the empire. Rulers in the provinces profited greatly from Roman rule. Many would not have risen to power and status were it not for the emperor's patronage. Rome provided security and prosperity for its friends. And Asia, where John was located, was the richest of the provinces.

But one reason Rome was so prosperous was that its luxury came at the expense of many. Four hundred thousand tons of grain came annually to the capital from Egypt, North Africa, and the Black Sea region. While provincials paid inflated prices for grain and sometimes had none, 200,000 families in Rome received a regular dole of free grain from the government.

Rome's appetite for luxury and wealth lured many wealthy provincials to invest in products they could export to Italy rather than what the locals needed. Landowners in Asia Minor used so much land for export items such as wine that Asia's cities had to import grain from Egypt and other areas. So the landowners profited from their relationship with Rome, but the common people had to pay high prices for their basic food needs (see Rev. 6:5, 6).

Roman commercial interests also propagated its religion, so people who wanted to buy and sell to the empire had to worship in exchange for the privilege. John no doubt enjoyed the irony of this vision. It is no wonder that the merchants and rulers in the provinces lament. They had sold their soul to the system that pampered them, and now that system had collapsed!

Jews were exempt from the religion of Rome, so they were able to buy and sell around the system. But Christians of the first century who were kicked out of the synagogue would have to choose between participating in pagan worship or losing their access to income. In the last days, similar challenges will take place in the world.[148]

Lord, help me see the degree to which wealth and power, rather than faithfulness to You, motivate my actions.

October 28

The merchants of the earth will weep and mourn over her also, because no one buys their cargoes anymore, cargoes of gold and silver and precious stone, of pearls, linen, purple, silk, and scarlet. Every kind of scented wood and objects made of ivory, costly wood, brass, iron, and marble. [Cargoes] of cinnamon, spice and incense, perfume and frankincense, wine and olive oil, wheat flour and wheat grains, pack animals and sheep, horses and carriages, and the bodies and souls of men. "The fruit of your soul's desires have gone away from you, and everything that was luxurious or radiant has perished from you. They will not find these things anymore." REV. 18:11-14.

Though luxury means as much to people today as it did then, this list is largely strange to us. When God revealed Himself to John, He spoke in the language of the prophet's time and place.

Nearly two decades ago I received a package from a pastor (let's call him George) whom I respected a great deal. It contained a letter asking me to read the accompanying notebook on a most difficult passage in the book of Revelation. He wanted my feedback on his research. A couple nights later I was tossing and turning, completely unable to sleep. So I decided I might as well get up, go to the other end of the house, and look at George's notebook.

The clarity and passion of his presentation fascinated me. Yet for some reason he saw something in each symbol and in each verse that my research indicated was not possible. It appeared to me that he was stringing a series of zeros together, believing that it added up to something. I thought it would not be difficult to set him straight.

Correspondence revealed that we didn't agree on a thing in this text! Finally it dawned on me what was happening. I was reading the book of Revelation as if written around A.D. 90. He was reading it as if composed around A.D. 1990! George wrote as if John were familiar with the works of modern religious authors. He viewed the book of Revelation as if John were alive today and through it speaking directly to the issues that drive certain Christians in today's world.

But the reality is that John did not compose the book of Revelation today or during even the past century. He wrote it during the first century, and it spoke powerfully to that time and place. It is true that it has a message for us at the close of the cosmic conflict, but to read the Apocalypse from one's own point of view is to end up where you begin—with ideas of your own making. God's message for us today is best discerned when we first pay attention to His message to John.

Lord, help me to be patient as I wrestle with the messages You gave to John. Help me not to assume that the first thing I see in the text is the very thing You intended for me.

[Cargoes] of cinnamon, spice and incense, perfume and frankincense, wine and olive oil, wheat flour and wheat grains, pack animals and sheep, horses and carriages, and the bodies and **SOULS OF MEN.** Rev. 18:13.

How do you buy and sell the souls of men, as Babylon did? What is a soul, anyway? The Hebrew philosophy of the Bible makes no division between body and soul. Unlike the ancient Greeks, who thought the soul could exist apart from the physical body, the Bible understands the human person to be a unified whole. In Hebrew thinking you cannot separate a person's thoughts from the chemical reactions in the brain. What happens to the body affects the mind, and what happens to the mind has an impact on the body.

Phineas Gage was an efficient and capable construction foreman in 1848.[149] Then a premature explosion on the job drove an iron bar through the front of his brain and out the top of his head. Amazingly enough, not only did he survive the terrible accident, but doctors declared him physically healthy two months later. But he was not able to return to his job. The accident had totally altered his personality. His actions were fitful and completely unpredictable. You never knew what he would do next. The damage to the physical tissue of the brain had completely changed the kind of person he was.

Such stories confirm the biblical view of soul. The basic meaning of "soul" is actually the whole person: mind, body, emotions, and spirit. As at the creation of Adam, Scripture calls the whole person a "living soul" (Gen. 2:7, KJV). When the Bible contrasts soul with body, as in Revelation 18:13, the word particularly emphasizes the mental, emotional, and spiritual side of the whole person. It is one thing to control human bodies, as occurred in the case of slavery. Slavery commands a person's body, but cannot dominate the mind and heart. But Babylon's power goes beyond slavery. She rules the whole person. So Babylon is even more dangerous than the slave trader—she can trade in the "souls of men."

This is why Jesus said, "Do not be afraid of those who kill the body but cannot kill the soul. Rather, be afraid of the One who can destroy both soul and body in hell" (Matt. 10:28, NIV). The "One" Jesus spoke about is God. In Revelation 18 Babylon takes on a Godlike role, part of the great end-time deception. We don't, however, need to submit ourselves to any power but God Himself. Oppressors may try to compel us, but we can refuse them our inner allegiance. We are citizens of another kingdom, the one that wins in the end.

Lord, my daily life often seems completely out of control. I choose to accept Your rulership over my life today, no matter how I feel.

October 30

The merchants of these things, who had become rich because of her, were standing at a distance for fear of her torment, weeping and grieving, saying, "Woe, Woe, the Great City, dressed in fine linen and purple and red garments, and adorned with gold and precious stones and pearls. **FOR IN ONE HOUR SO MUCH WEALTH HAS BEEN LAID WASTE."** *And every captain, and everyone who sets sail for any place, and sailors and whoever makes a living from the sea, they all stood at a distance.* REV. 18:15-17.

As we have seen, Babylon was not only wealthy, but fully self-absorbed in her prosperity (Rev. 18:7). She was willing to do almost anything to preserve her wealth and position. But the statement of Jesus "Give, and it will be given to you" (Luke 6:38, NIV) suggests the ironic principle that if you want to be truly wealthy, you have to give your riches away.

It seems that the one who creates a family fortune finds meaning and purpose in assembling it. But that kind of motivation will not work for later generations. They will inherit more than they can ever use, and unless they have learned to serve a higher purpose with that wealth, they lose any sense of meaning and goal. They will focus instead on the pursuit of social status and will be willing to spend enormous sums on self-gratification. This leads to the dissipation of the family fortune.[150]

In contrast to the Vanderbilts (see October 26), the Rockefellers early sensed the need to give back to the society that made the family's wealth possible. As his wealth began to skyrocket, founder and oil magnate John D. Rockefeller found himself besieged with requests for help. Spurred on by his Baptist faith, he had been generous before he became wealthy. Years before, while a dry-goods clerk in Cleveland, he had given funds to an African-American man to free his wife from slavery. Rockefeller came to believe that God had given him his wealth because He knew that he would "turn around and give it back." The more he gave, the more money seemed to come in. With Standard Oil generating massive dividends, John D. donated more than $500 million in his lifetime, a sum larger than the Vanderbilt fortune (the world's biggest at the time) just 30 years before.

John D. wisely included his children in helping him to evaluate and process requests for aid. With John D's example to follow, five generations of Rockefellers have continued to devote their lives to charity.[151] And all this giving does not seem to have reduced the family's wealth. The Rockefeller Foundation alone is worth more than $3 billion today. And that is only the tip of the iceberg.

Lord, help me give all I can, not just because it is the smart thing to do, but because it makes me more like You.

Seeing the smoke of her fiery ordeal, they cry out, "Who is like the Great City?"
They threw dust on their heads and cried out weeping and mourning, "Woe, woe,
the Great City, by which **EVERYONE WHO HAD SHIPS ON THE**
SEA PROSPERED ON ACCOUNT OF HER WEALTH, *for in*
one hour it was laid waste." REV. 18:18, 19.

Kings, merchants, and sailors all take their turns mourning the passing of Babylon. Revelation 18:9-19 contains the longest extant list of products from the Roman period. John adapts Ezekiel's list of more than 40 products that Tyre traded in his day (Eze. 27:2-24). Ezekiel arranged his list geographically while John structured his topically—by type of cargo (see Rev. 18:12, 13). The focus in Revelation is largely on luxury items, not trade in general.

Rome's newly rich in the first century flaunted their gold and silver. The empire imported the metals from Spain, where it owned a number of mines, but the human cost was high. Slaves who worked these mines rarely lived more than a few years. Merchants brought in precious stones mostly from India, and divers retrieved pearls from the Red Sea and the Persian Gulf.

Fine linen came from Spain, Asia Minor, and Egypt. Purple and scarlet cloths served as symbols of affluence and luxury. Silk had to travel from China, so only the ultrarich could afford it. Citron wood, imported from North Africa, was rare enough that a table made with it could cost as much as a large estate. Elephants became virtually extinct within the Roman Empire because of the ivory trade.

Cinnamon originated from Somalia and southward in East Africa. The voyage to there from Rome was a two-year round trip (that means expensive). Other spices had their origin in India, and incense and perfumes came from Arabia and Somalia. Sicily and Spain provided the best wine. In John's day the empire experienced a grain shortage at the same time as it had a wine surplus (cf. Rev. 6:6), because the wine trade was more profitable than grain. "Fine flour" was definitely a luxury item compared to coarse grain. The best flour had to be shipped all the way from Africa.

Even the rich rarely ate beef, since farmers used cattle more as work animals. Herders butchered some sheep for mutton, but most were used to produce wool. Italy did not have sufficient pasture for horses, so the promoters of chariot races brought horses from Africa and Spain in order to provide public entertainment.

John concludes his list (Rev. 18:12, 13) with the "bodies and souls of men." Since the empire was at peace, it had no steady supply of slaves from captives of war. So slave traders rescued babies discarded by the poor. Other slaves were "imported" from Asia.

Lord, help me understand the true cost of self-indulgence. I want to develop a spirit of service instead.

November 1

REJOICE *over her, O heaven, and also the saints, apostles, and prophets, because God has judged her in the same way she has judged you.* REV. 18:20.

An interesting feature of this text is that Scripture commands the saints to rejoice, orders them to be happy. Most of us think that we can be happy only when things are going well. But evidently happiness is a choice—one that God's people can make even in the hardest of times.

Recently my mother had to spend some time in a nursing home. Ninety-one years old at the time, she got her foot caught in a blanket while she tried to get to the phone, and she fell down hard, breaking the upper part of her left leg, right next to the hip. After the doctors set the break, she spent several weeks in the hospital. The time came when she still needed 24-hour care but Medicare would no longer pay the high costs of hospital rehabilitation. So she moved into a room at a nursing home with three other women at a reduced level of care.

While visiting her from day to day, I noticed that the residents of the nursing home seemed to have very different reactions to their situation. Some of them seemed angry all the time, demanding things of the attendants and complaining about everything from the food, to the quality of the mattress, to the location of the television, to the nurses' reaction time. They seemed to be suffering a great deal.

Others were just the opposite. Constantly cheery, they greeted everyone who walked by, thanked the nurses for their efforts even when things didn't go well, commented on the beautiful sunshine out the window, and complimented the doctor for taking time out of his busy schedule to visit with them.

Someone asked one of the residents about her unfailing cheerfulness. I thought you might be interested in her response.

"Happiness is something you decide on ahead of time. Whether I like my room or not doesn't depend on how the furniture is arranged. What counts is how I arrange my mind. Every morning I have a choice: I can spend the day in bed recounting the difficulty I have with the parts of my body that no longer work, or get out of bed and be thankful for the ones that do.

"Each day is a gift, and I try to make things as pleasant as I can for everyone around me. It seems that if I think more of others than I do of myself, I can make a difference in my world, even though much of me doesn't work anymore. This sense of purpose keeps me going. It's just a lot more fun to be happy and cheerful than it is to be angry and resentful."

Lord, I choose to be happy today. Help me to change my world and the attitude of the people around me.

A mighty angel picked up a stone the size of a large millstone and threw it into the sea, saying, "Thus with violence the Great City **BABYLON WILL BE THROWN DOWN, AND IT WILL NOT BE FOUND ANYMORE.** *The sound of harpists, musicians, flute players, and trumpeters will not be heard in you anymore. No craftsman of any craft will be found in you anymore. The sound of a millstone will not be heard in you anymore."* REV. 18:21, 22.

As we have seen, economic exploitation and negligence are a major part of Babylon's pattern of sin. As the world's largest economy, the United States of America can largely dictate trade policies in its own interests. While many of the problems in developing countries are self-inflicted, that is no excuse for taking selfish advantage.

Today more than 1 billion people live on the equivalent of less than $1 a day. The richest 20 percent of the world's people use 86 percent of the resources, while the poorest 20 percent employ only 1.4 percent. Eight hundred million people are malnourished or facing starvation. A quarter of a million children die every week from malnutrition and easily preventable diseases. Eighty percent of brain development occurs by age 2, yet 150 million children in the world lack the protein intake necessary for adequate brain growth, leading to permanent retardation.

The average annual income in the U.S. is about $20,000, while in Bangladesh it is less than $400. So one would think that the U.S. could afford to provide much help to less fortunate countries. After all, one's location at birth is not because of merit. Yet in assisting developing countries, Norway ranks the highest (1.12 percent of gross national product) and the U.S. is next to last (0.25 percent) among the wealthier nations. In any given year the U.S. budgets 20 times as much for defense as for foreign assistance, and even two thirds of the latter is for military aid. On top of that, protectionist trade practices cost developing nations twice as much as the total value of aid they receive. One day we will have to give an account.[152]

Advertising makes us think that we must have more things and makes us forget the needs of others. How tragic! We find much more satisfaction in relationships than in accumulating possessions. While possessions are not evil in themselves, their value is minimal compared with the needs of brothers and sisters in Christ.

Revelation 18 reminds us that God does not look the other way in the face of economic injustice. He will bring down every empire in time. When we squander money on things we do not need, will we somehow escape Babylon's judgment?

Lord, I am sobered as I contemplate the personal implications of Babylon's fall. Open my eyes to how You view my stewardship of the resources You have given me.

November 3

The light of a lamp will not shine in you anymore, the voice of a bridegroom and a bride will not be heard in you anymore, because your merchants were the great men of the earth, because with your sorcery all nations were deceived. **IN HER WAS FOUND THE BLOOD OF PROPHETS AND SAINTS AND OF ALL WHO WERE SLAUGHTERED UPON THE EARTH.** REV. 18:23, 24.

The injustices of Babylon are many (Rev. 18:1-7) and her doom, therefore, is sure. But an even greater tragedy lurks in all of this. Those who identify with Babylon in any way perish with her (verse 4). Many, like the kings, merchants, and sailors of this chapter, are not committed to Babylon's agenda in their hearts. They cooperate with her simply because they hope to better their own short lives on this earth (verses 9-19).

The choice is foolish but understandable. We simply want what is best for ourselves and our families. Yet the consequences of even casual participation in "Babylon" are catastrophic. How does God expect us to respond to the injustices of today's Babylons? Is it enough to live quiet and simple lives? Or do we need to "come out of Babylon" in more significant ways?

At its height the West Indies slave trade employed 5,500 sailors and 160 ships. It was a massive and socially accepted practice. But William Wilberforce and his allies, acting out of Christian conviction, fought in the British Parliament until slavery was abolished throughout the British Empire. In America the voices of abolitionists gave legitimacy to efforts to free the slaves in the South.

While our ability to transform our nation's behavior is often limited, that is not true of our capacity to change our own behavior. Jesus told His disciples not to value possessions. As Christians we should be ever ready to give them up (Luke 14:33). James tells us that failure to care for fellow Christians in need may indicate a lack of saving faith (James 2:14-17). Paul's central mission was preaching the gospel, but he did not forget the needs of the poor (2 Cor. 8:13-15; Gal. 2:10).

Sometimes our hearts are hard until we have firsthand exposure to human need. Tony Liston, a young pastor from Oklahoma, spent two days in a private hospital room in the Philippines at a cost of $47. As he entered the hospital he barely noticed a beggar woman near the outside entrance. When he left two days later, he saw her naked corpse stuffed into a nearby dumpster. She had died of the same affliction for which he had just received treatment. "She had no money," the nurse replied in a matter-of-fact tone. The experience so shook Tony that he has never been the same since.[153]

Lord, help me prioritize my resources according to what matters most to Your heart.

IN HER WAS FOUND THE BLOOD OF PROPHETS AND SAINTS AND OF ALL WHO WERE SLAUGHTERED UPON THE EARTH. REV. 18:24.

One day I found myself in court, sitting in the gallery with a church member who had gotten himself into a bit of trouble. As we waited for his case to come up we watched a drunken driving case playing out in front of us. The scene had four main players: the judge, a policeman (the accuser in the case), the defendant, and the defendant's lawyer.

It seems that the policeman had discovered the man, "drunk as a skunk," pinned behind the wheel of a car and asleep. The front of the car was embedded into the concrete abutment of a bridge. Behind the car, tracks in the snow indicated the car had driven along the sidewalk for about 130 feet (40 meters) before its impact with the bridge.

The outcome of the trial seemed obvious. The defendant clearly (as far as I could see) had been operating under the influence of alcohol when he wandered through town, barely missing shops and entryways before coming to a jarring stop upon impact with the bridge. The defendant, unable to extricate himself from the car, fell asleep (it was about 2:00 in the morning) behind the wheel. The policeman found him there and wrote up his summons.

The defense lawyer, however, was not intimidated by the apparent facts in the case. Pacing back and forth, he argued, to the thinly veiled amusement of the judge, that his client was not the driver of the car, but had wandered upon the scene after the accident. Finding no one in the car, he climbed into the driver's seat and fell asleep!

The judge wasted little time on deliberation. He pointed out how difficult it had been for the policeman to extricate the man, proving that he had been in the driver's seat at the time of impact. Then he referred to the tracks in the snow as evidence that the driver was not in normal control of his faculties. As a result he levied a stiff fine and a six-month revocation of license as a penalty.

The defense lawyer then jumped up and cried out, "We appeal the decision!" The judge responded immediately with a time and place for the appeal hearing.

Although justice was probably already done in this case, a healthy court system includes the concept of a higher court. Injustice at one level can get corrected at another. According to Revelation 18, the decisions of all earthly tribunals, including the U.S. Supreme Court, can be appealed to the higher court of God's end-time judgment. There God will reverse all the injustices of this life. Saints treated as criminals by earthly courts will then be vindicated.

Lord, thank You for the assurance that You will reverse the unfairness of life when You finally take full control. Give me the patience to await Your final verdict.

November 5

After these things I heard, as it were, the sound of a great crowd of many people in heaven, saying, "Hallelujah! Salvation, glory and power belong to our God. HIS JUDGMENTS ARE TRUE AND RIGHTEOUS BECAUSE HE HAS JUDGED THE GREAT PROSTITUTE WHO CORRUPTED THE EARTH WITH HER FORNICATIONS, AND AVENGED THE BLOOD OF HIS SLAVES OUT OF HER HAND." REV. 19:1, 2.

Hollywood loves a good revenge story, such as that of the Count of Monte Cristo. In it the count suffers injustice at the hands of an evil antagonist, but in the end he gets even and comes out on top. Many people must like such stories, as the movie industry keeps producing them. Revenge stories conclude when the hero rides off into the sunset, having brought justice into an unjust world. It is human nature to want to see the tables turned on those who have taken advantage of others.

Well, that is exactly what the book of Revelation is all about. Babylon has unjustly judged the people of God (Rev. 18:4-8), and at the end of the book she receives the same kind of punishment that she meted out on them. In Revelation the hero doesn't head off into the sunset—He returns to the New Jerusalem, where justice and peace will reign for all eternity.

But gaining the upper hand against Babylon is not a pretty picture in the Apocalypse. It requires powerful earthquakes and giant hailstones, battles and flaming fire, and a great sword that comes out of the mouth of the One who died for the human race. Christ now returns as an avenger against those who refused to repent, but instead have tormented others.

The greater the strength of evil, the greater the force needed to destroy its power and undo the damage it has caused. I have visited places in Africa and South America where people live in cardboard and tin shacks, where gangs roam and pillage at will. In other places rebel armies sweep back and forth, destroying the very people they claim to be fighting for.

I'm not sure what kind of rating Revelation would get if it were a movie—it certainly has plenty of violence and illicit sex in it. The Bible does not mince words when it describes the cesspool of sin that our world has fallen into. God wants us to know just how bad it has been since Satan took over our world. He also desires that we recognize that He is not going to allow things to go on like this forever. An end is in sight. Yes, the book of Revelation is all about turning the tables and evening the score. Soon God will banish evil from the universe and the prayers for justice will all be answered. What a relief![154]

Lord, thank You for going out of Your way to speak our language so we can know that our troubles will soon be over. Give us courage to endure until that day.

[GOD'S] JUDGMENTS ARE TRUE AND RIGHTEOUS

because He has judged the great prostitute who corrupted the earth with her fornications, and avenged **THE BLOOD OF HIS SLAVES** *out of her hand.* REV. 19:2.

In the end-time setting of Revelation 15-19 God acts in judgment against Babylon, the great power that has oppressed His people. It is interesting, however, to note that He calls His people "slaves." They are not Babylon's slaves, but God's slaves. Though redeemed by the blood of the Lamb (Rev. 5:6, 9, 10) in one sense they remain "slaves" in this life.

We find an interesting analogy to this language in American history. The American Civil War began as a battle over the relative rights of states verses the national government. But in the course of time a higher cause came into focus—freedom for the slaves in the Southern states. Many who were reluctant to die for national union were willing to give their lives so that all might be free.

Abraham Lincoln, the American president, longed to liberate the slaves, but knew it would be a pointless act if people believed the South would win the war. The Union armies marched from defeat to defeat until September of 1862. Then at Antietam Creek in Maryland, 3,600 men died on the battlefield in a single day (the largest casualty count of any day in American history, including September 11). As a result of the carnage, the Southern army withdrew to Virginia, and Lincoln made the Emancipation Proclamation, declaring the southern slaves free.

All over the South slaves heard the news and cried out, "I am free at last!" But were they truly free? Yes and no. Though many slaves fell to the ground, weeping tears of joy as they heard the news, the daily routine did not change. Husbands, wives, and children continued to be sold away from their families. Slaves still endured beatings, whippings, and hangings when they did not comply with orders. Many continued to be treated like cattle.

But something had changed. People were dying to set them free. Governments now acknowledged their right to freedom. Though they were slaves to the master's lash, their hearts and minds had been set free. They knew that the day of liberation was coming, because it had already been proclaimed. Though they remained slaves in one sense, in another they were already free!

In Christ all human beings have been set free. The story of Revelation is full of carnage and anguish because the battle rages to implement what Jesus has already done. No matter what you are going through now, the decisive event has already taken place. It is not too early for God's slaves to proclaim, "I am free at last."

Lord, help me today to live in the freedom that Christ has already won for me.

November 7

And a second time they shouted, "Hallelujah! Her smoke goes up for ever and ever. The twenty-four elders and the four living creatures fell down and **WORSHIPPED GOD,** *the one sitting on the throne, saying, "Amen, Hallelujah!"* Rev. 19:3, 4.

It must be easy to worship God when you are face to face with dazzling glory! Flashes of lightning, thunderous sounds, and blazing torches almost force you to fall on your face and worship One who possesses such glory and such power. But does it really take thunder and lightning and dazzling jewels to inspire people to worship the Lord? Or is it more about being attuned to His presence, wherever we are?

I remember the time my daughter and I climbed up the traditional site of Mount Sinai in the dark. At 5:00 in the morning we reached the top. Along with about 500 other people, we sat or lay down on rocks to await the sunrise. We battled to stay warm in a freezing wind atop the 7,400-foot peak.

Although we might have been on the very spot where Moses encountered the living God Himself, the crowd seemed to exhibit no awe or reverence. Locals were making money, loudly offering food, hot drinks, and blankets that they had transported to the mountaintop on the backs of donkeys and camels. Tourists cursed the cold and the wind and carried on conversations about sports, relationships, politics, and what they had eaten yesterday. They had no sense of God's presence on the mountain. All were consumed with the concerns of the moment.

That began to change with the first rosy glimmer at one end of the blackened sky. People began to stir from their places. A buzz of conversation all over the mountain banished the mundane details of everyday life and anticipated the appearance of the golden orb that lights every day. For an instant everyone forgot the cold, sports, and politics. As the red in the eastern sky gradually spilled over onto the peaks to the west, all sounds of human presence began to die down until an amazing hush gripped the whole mountaintop.

As the sun itself began to peek over the mountains to the east, no one raised up a sign or anything, yet everyone in the crowd either remained silent or at most talked in whispers. It seemed as if everyone had suddenly realized that we were in God's sanctuary—and what a sanctuary it was! The roof was the heavens and lit by the sun. It was fittingly huge as befits a King of His stature. Everyone responded in quiet awe. There was no thunder or lightning and no sparkling jewels. Yet for a moment all were attuned to God's presence.

Lord, I need a sense of Your presence today. I need to be awed by the mighty works You have done for me. Give me a glimpse of You in the midst of today's distractions.

The twenty-four elders and the four living creatures fell down and
WORSHIPPED GOD, *the one sitting on the throne, saying, "Amen,*
Hallelujah!" And a voice went out from the throne, "Praise our God, all His
servants, and those who fear Him both small and great." And I heard, as it were,
the voice of a great multitude, and the sound of mighty waters, and the sound of
loud thunderings, saying, "Hallelujah, because the Lord God Almighty has begun to
reign." REV. 19:4-6.

The worship in this text has its basis in God's marvelous deliverance of His people from end-time Babylon (Rev. 19:1, 2). In Revelation 4 and 5 worship takes place in response to creation and the cross, just as in the Old Testament, worship responded to God's mighty action in the Exodus. True worship is always about an awareness of the mighty things that the Lord has done for you. And the result of true worship is tangible. When we remember and recite what He has accomplished, it rekindles His mighty power in us and changes our lives.

One Old Testament passage especially unpacks this in detail: 2 Chronicles 20:1-23. The Israelites are under attack, outnumbered three to one. The enemy army has advanced to less than 30 miles from Jerusalem. King Jehoshaphat proclaims a fast and goes to the Temple courts to lead the prayers.

Now, if you were in his shoes, what would you pray about? "O Lord, help us! Do something, please! We're in big trouble!" Prayers get real focused when you are about to die. But Jehoshaphat's actual prayer doesn't sound desperate at all. Instead of whining and begging, he just recounts God's actions in the past. He reminds God of the Exodus and how He had promised the land to the Israelites forever (2 Chron. 20:6-9). Then the king puts God on the spot. "These nations wouldn't even exist if You hadn't spared them at the time of the Exodus!" (see verses 10-12). Through a prophet God assures him not to worry about the battle. The Lord will fight for them.

So what does Jehoshaphat do next? He sends out the Temple choir to lead the army into battle (verses 22, 23). And the enemy perishes. What did the choir sing that day? It wasn't "Trust and Obey"! Rather, they sang, "Give Thanks to the Lord, for His Love Endures Forever." Focused on God, not the problem, they were rehearsing His mighty acts.

And what happened when they did that? It reignited the power of the original act in their midst. The power of the Exodus became a living presence among them. And the result was another mighty act of God to celebrate in the future!

Lord, I'm grateful for all that You have done for me in Christ. I desire to experience His resurrection power in my life today.

November 9

Rejoice, be abundantly glad and give glory to Him, because **THE WEDDING OF THE LAMB HAS COME** *and his wife has made herself ready. And it was given to her to be* **DRESSED IN FINE LINEN, BRIGHT AND CLEAN** *(for the fine linen is the righteous actions of the saints).* Rev. 19:7, 8.

This text brings us to a much-anticipated point in history. Jesus Christ comes face to face with His people! John portrays the encounter as a wedding. Everybody loves a wedding, and this will be the greatest one of all time. When we understand a few characteristics of ancient biblical weddings, the description in Revelation will mean even more to us.

Ancient Hebrew marriage began with a betrothal, something like our concept of engagement. The prospective groom and his father would come to the house of the bride and her father for an engagement ceremony. In biblical culture the engagement was more than just a promise. People treated it as seriously as a marriage itself, even though the couple did not yet set up a joint household.

Then the groom would return to his father's house and prepare the place where the couple would reside. It was usually somewhere on the father's property. In a rural setting the couple would receive a piece of land on which the groom and his bride would live and farm. The groom would work with other members of his family to build a suitable house for the new family on that land. But in more urban areas they might construct an extension onto the family home. While this went on, the betrothed woman remained at her father's house, preparing herself to be a fit and honorable bride. She would also be shopping and packing things that would go with her to her husband's house.

On the wedding day itself, the groom collected his bride at her father's house and took her to the wedding celebration at his father's house. John 14:1-3 describes the second coming of Jesus in terms of this third stage of the biblical wedding sequence. The first advent of Jesus was like a betrothal. He left His Father's house in heaven, came to earth, and became engaged to His bride, the church. Then He returned to heaven to prepare a place for His bride while she remained on the earth, preparing herself. At the Second Coming Jesus will return to earth for His bride and escort her back to His Father's house.

In the ancient tradition the wedding occurs when the place and the bride are both ready. The bride is dressed in the righteousness of Christ and the righteous acts that she has done. Its brightness and cleanliness distinguishes her dress from that of Lady Babylon.

Lord, I want nothing more than to be pure and clean when You come. Take me and mold me to that end.

Rejoice, be abundantly glad and give glory to Him, because the wedding of the Lamb has come and **HIS WIFE HAS MADE HERSELF READY.** *And it was given to her to be* **DRESSED IN FINE LINEN,** *bright and clean* **(FOR THE FINE LINEN IS THE RIGHTEOUS ACTIONS OF THE SAINTS).** REV. 19:7, 8.

The brother of a friend of mine, Jim Park, asked him to buy a 1972 Ford Mustang Mach I in Los Angeles and drive it to Rapid City, South Dakota (a distance of more than 1,300 miles) for the brother's girl-friend. The Ford Mustang Mach I was one of those "muscle cars" that were popular back in the 1960s and 1970s in the United States (the 1964 Pontiac GTO started the genre). Such cars had massive engines and, usually, elaborate and distinctive decorations of some sort.

Driving the powerful Mach 1 made Jim the center of attention wherever he was in the western United States. People would look and point and treat him as if he were a member of some sort of "muscle car" royalty.

1. *October 10, 8:35 p.m., Monrovia, California.* Heading home from the place of purchase, Jim saw a man driving a 1960s Chevy Malibu muscle car. The man glanced over Jim's car and quickly gave him a thumbs-up. Jim felt as if he were now part of an exclusive club.

2. *October 11, 8:00 a.m., El Monte, California.* Jim's son, Jimmy, was 13 years old at the time. Jimmy begged Jim, Sr., to take him to school or to pick him up after school in the Mach 1 so all his friends could see him in it. In no time at all Jimmy was also part of the club.

3. *October 13, 3:45 p.m., Provo, Utah.* Jim was registering in the lobby of a motel on his way to Rapid City. A person in the lobby at the motel was very ex-cited to see the type of car he had once driven as a teenager in high school. The appearance of the car was definitely feeding the memories of anyone more than 45 years of age.

4. *October 14, 2:00 p.m., Rawlins, Wyoming.* As Jim was pulling out of a gas station, two young people made a signal for him to "rev up" the engine. Jim gunned the engine, and the couple smiled in response.

The wife of the Lamb is dressed in "the righteous actions of the saints." Like the sound and appearance of a "muscle car," something distinctive about her com-mands attention. As we walk and talk and drive around the block of life, what do people notice in you and me? Do they see the "fruit of the Spirit" or are the "works of the flesh" more in evidence? The constant abiding in Christ by faith is the re-quirement to be in the heavenly club.[155]

Lord, people know that I have chosen to serve You. They are watching to see if it makes a difference. Make me mindful today that everything I do and say sends a positive message about You.

November 11

And it was given to her [the wife of the Lamb] to be **DRESSED IN FINE LINEN,** *bright and clean* **(FOR THE FINE LINEN IS THE RIGHTEOUS ACTIONS OF THE SAINTS).** Rev. 19:8.

The bride of the Lamb at the end of history wears "the righteous actions of the saints" like a garment. While visible on the outside, they represent something deeper and even more important—character. The outward actions arise from within. When all is said and done, success will prove to be more a matter of character than skill or luck.

This reminds me of Jesse Owens, the famous Olympic athlete. While he certainly had great physical ability, the 1936 Olympics revealed his character as much as his skills. Said his mother, "Jesse was always a face boy—when a problem came up, he always faced it."

He grew up as a young Black man in a world dominated by Whites. Overcoming many barriers, he made the Olympic team, only to encounter the greatest challenge of his career. Adolf Hitler had proclaimed that Nazi Germany, the nation of the "master race," would prove its superiority on the sports field before it did so on the battlefield. Owens could not just concentrate on the sports—larger issues were at stake.

John Kelley was the captain of the U.S. marathon team in the 1936 Olympics and a good friend of Jesse Owens'. On the boat to Germany Owens told him, "I want to go up to the deck and exercise, but I don't have any shoes." Kelley responded, "I don't think my shoes will fit you." But that didn't stop Owens. He tried to get one of Kelley's shoes on, but his foot was so large, it split the shoe in half! Owens apologized, and Kelley had the shoe sewed up for 50 cents, a small price for what would become a treasured souvenir.

When Kelley finished the marathon, Hitler waved at him, and the American thumbed his nose in return. That became his greatest claim to fame. It stunned him later when Owens told him, "Kelley, Hitler waved at me, and I waved back." Talk about character! When Owens won his fourth gold medal, however, he became the hero of the games to everyone but Hitler. The dictator looked unbeatable at the time, and German athletes dominated the 1936 Olympics on the whole. But one African-American was all it took to expose the lie of a master race.[156]

Character is the sum total of many choices and actions over a long period of time. Crises do not make character—they expose it. The behavior of Jesse Owens at the 1936 Olympics was a beautiful garment that bore witness to the character developed during a lifetime.

Lord, thank You for the reminder that every small decision and action today sets the stage toward the larger purpose for which You designed me.

And it was given to her [the wife of the Lamb] to be dressed in fine linen, bright and clean **(FOR THE FINE LINEN IS THE RIGHTEOUS ACTIONS OF THE SAINTS).** Rev. 19:8.

The word translated "righteous acts" occurs only two times in the book of Revelation. First it appears in Revelation 15:4, which puts the righteous acts of God on view. The nations at the end of history worship before God, because His righteous acts "have been revealed." The total focus is on divine action. But in Revelation 19:8 the saints are the authors of the righteous actions. I suspect that John wanted the reader of Revelation to connect the dots between the works of God and those of the saints.

Wishing to encourage her young son's progress on the piano, a mother took her boy to a Paderewski concert. After they were seated, the mother spotted an old friend in the audience and walked down the aisle to greet her. Seizing the opportunity to explore the wonders of the concert hall, the little boy rose and eventually wandered through a door marked "No Admittance." When the house lights dimmed and the concert was about to begin, the mother returned to her seat and discovered that the child was missing.

Suddenly the curtains parted and spotlights focused on the impressive Steinway piano onstage. In horror the mother saw her little boy sitting at the keyboard, innocently picking out "Twinkle, Twinkle, Little Star." At that moment the great piano master made his entrance, quickly approached the piano, and whispered in the boy's ear, "Don't quit. Keep playing." Leaning over, Paderewski reached down with his left hand and began filling in a bass part. Soon his right arm reached around to the other side of the child, and he added a running obligato. Together the old master and the young novice transformed what could have been a frightening situation into a wonderfully creative experience. The audience was so mesmerized that they couldn't recall what else the great master played that night. Only the classic "Twinkle, Twinkle, Little Star."

Perhaps that's the way it is with God. What we can accomplish on our own is hardly noteworthy. We try our best, but the results aren't always graceful flowing music. However, with the hand of the Master, our life's work can truly be beautiful. The next time you set out to do something really great, listen carefully. You may hear the voice of the Master, whispering in your ear: "Don't quit. Keep playing." God sometimes "calls" those He has already equipped, but more often He equips those He has already "called."

Lord, it often seems that things won't work right unless they are done my way. Thank You for the reminder that whatever "greatness" I may achieve in this life, it is based primarily on what You add to my feeble efforts.

November 13

And he [the angel] said to me, "Write: **BLESSED ARE THOSE WHO HAVE BEEN CALLED TO THE WEDDING BANQUET OF THE LAMB.** *" And he said to me, "These are the genuine words of God."* REV. 19:9.

S cholars of Revelation often debate whether the bride of the Lamb is the New Jerusalem itself (Rev. 21:9-11) or the people of God. Today's passage does not mention the city here, but it does refer to the saints. The wedding dress that the bride of the Lamb wears is "the righteous actions of the saints." So the people of God certainly must have something to do with the bride. A city without inhabitants is not much of a city, so in a real sense the answer to the question of whether the bride is the city or the people must be yes.

These days we find an increasing interest in a vegetarian diet. And it involves much more than just the issue of health. For many, foregoing a meat diet is an issue of justice (another word for righteous). If so, it ought to be of concern to those thinking about marrying the Lamb.

Depending on what they eat, the amount of land it takes to sustain two meat-eating individuals can feed 20-60 vegetarians. It means that if Americans alone reduced their meat consumption by 10 percent, it would result in 12 million tons of grain for human consumption. If distribution were not an issue, that would be enough to feed the 60 million individuals who starve to death each year.

A plant-based diet also benefits the earth. One researcher argues that animal production uses more than a third of all raw materials and fossil fuels consumed in the United States. The fuel needed to produce a single hamburger patty would power the average car for 20 miles.

While water consumption has become a major concern in the age of pollution and conservation, few American consumers realize that beef production alone uses more water than that required for the nation's entire fruit and vegetable crop. One author estimates that you would save more water by not eating a pound of California beef than you would by not showering for a year.

Everything we do touches others. From our food and clothing choices to the automobiles we drive and the vacations we take, we are affecting others, either for good or for bad. We need to evaluate all of our actions in the light of what Jesus would do. The righteous actions of the saints include taking only what we need, giving as much as we can, and living honestly and simply. As those awaiting the call to the wedding banquet of the Lamb, we will seek to arrange our lives in light of the righteousness of Christ. This will include attention to what we eat.[157]

Lord, I hear the call to practical godliness in every aspect of my life. I am open to a deeper and more righteous walk with You today.

November 14

And he [the angel] said to me, "Write: **'BLESSED ARE THOSE WHO HAVE BEEN CALLED TO THE WEDDING BANQUET OF THE LAMB.'"** *And he said to me, "These are the genuine words of God."*
REV. 19:9.

When people brought lambs to the Temple for sacrifice, the animals had to be absolutely spotless and without blemish. They were to illustrate the perfect purity of Jesus Christ. Those called to the wedding banquet of the Lamb will seek the cleansing that comes from intimate relationship with the spotless Lamb of God.

A beautiful college in eastern Indonesia called UnKlab is situated in the mountains just outside the world-famous diving destination of Manado, in northern Sulawesi. It is known as the "green campus" because of the wonderful expanses of grass that greet the eye at every turn. Every day the students are up before dawn to rake the leaves before the sun rises over the horizon.

The campus contains several substantial buildings, and it seems that in this part of the world white is the favorite color to adorn any edifice. But while white looks beautiful against the jungle-green environment, it does have drawbacks when it rains. For not only are the buildings white, but the floors have white tiles as well. During the torrential rainy season some of the earthen walkways turn to mud, and it is not long before the white tiles get smeared with chocolate-brown dirt.

In North America the favorite color of flooring is brown, because it "hides the dirt" well. So one might be mystified as to why anyone would want to place white tiles where they would get dirty so quickly. But if you were to ask the cleaning people at UnKlab why they used this color for the flooring, they would answer, as if it ought to be self-evident, "So we can see the dirt." And sure enough, one day after a muddy rain they restore the tiles to a spotless state, with all dirt removed from the surface.

Let's face it—most of us don't want to see the dirt on our floors. We don't enjoy noticing it in our lives, either. As a result we do everything we possibly can to conceal the dirt by sweeping it under the carpet or comparing our polluted thoughts and actions with the world around us. But the Lamb of God is 100 percent pure and spotless. Jesus is pure so that when we come to Him, we can see the dirt in ourselves. And He will not only help us recognize our true condition, but has promised to cleanse us from all unrighteousness (1 John 1:9). So instead of trying to hide our dirt, we can go to Jesus and become clean through the Word of forgiveness.[158]

Lord, draw me near to Jesus so that I can clearly see the defects in my own character. I don't want to hide the dirt anymore—I want to be truly clean.

November 15

T he presence of a living prophet marked the early decades of the Seventh-day Adventist Church. Early Adventists believed that the visions and testimonies of Ellen G. White resulted from a direct connection with God. From 1844 to 1915 her books, articles, sermons, and private letters provided a constant stream of insight into how God viewed the developing movement. They dealt with living, everyday questions. The denomination located and built institutions on the basis of her recommendations. Also she both confirmed and at times denied the various results of Adventist Bible study.

The presence of a living prophet was challenging, but it also provided great security. Through interaction with the prophet, Adventist leaders could have a strong sense of God's direct guidance in the many difficulties the fledgling movement faced. They could solve theological and political issues with her prophetic guidance. Those fully committed to Ellen White's authority had a sense of certainty that few obtain in this life.

But in 1915 Ellen White died, stilling the living voice. No longer could the church address the problems of the moment with direct and specific guidance from God. While members could consult her voluminous writings, people could easily dispute their applicability to specific issues. A church accustomed to the living voice of God now had to struggle with the writings of a dead prophet—but it is the reality that most Christians have to cope with.

By 1919 the issue of what to do with a dead prophet was a serious issue for the young movement. So its leaders convened a Bible and history teachers' council. From July 30 through August 1, 1919,[159] all seemed to agree that it required much care and common sense to interpret her writings correctly. But in the aftermath of the council, a couple of those present began to spread the word that key Adventist leaders had abandoned true faith in the prophet. The death of a prophet can leave believers with more questions than answers.

How do you draw living lessons from the writings of a dead prophet? To rightly handle those of a dead prophet such as the apostle John, you have to take seriously the time, place, and the circumstances that led to the document in the first place. The writings of even dead prophets are always worthy of our time and of our careful attention.

Lord, thank You for giving me a desire to know Your will and Your ways. I choose to invest serious time in Your Word this week.

And I saw heaven standing open, and I observed a white horse, and **THE ONE SITTING ON IT IS CALLED FAITHFUL AND TRUE,** *and in righteousness He judges and makes war. His eyes are like a flame of fire, and upon His head are many crowns, having a name written which no one knows except Him. He was dressed in a garment that had been dipped in blood, and* **HIS NAME WAS CALLED "THE WORD OF GOD."** *And* **THE ARMIES OF HEAVEN WERE FOLLOWING HIM** *on white horses, dressed in fine linen, brilliant and pure.* REV. 19:11-14.

Kobe Bryant was born to greatness. His father had played in the National Basketball Association, the world's most respected professional league. From childhood on Kobe had been groomed to follow in his father's footsteps. The ability to dunk, shoot, and dribble was in his genes.

After a spectacular high school career (named national Player of the Year in his senior year) he entered the NBA at the age of 18, the youngest player ever to get into a game. At the age of 20 he was a starter on one of the best teams in the world, the Los Angeles Lakers, and made the All-Star team. By the age of 22, when most players are just entering the league as rookies, Kobe Bryant was unquestionably one of the best players in the world.

A handsome man, rich and famous, he could have lived the swinging life of an alpha male in a world that idolizes talent, wealth, and fame. Instead, in his early 20s he married the beautiful Vanessa Laine and became a family man, much to the disappointment of thousands of young women, to whom he was a hero. He also became a hero to many young men in the ghetto, who dreamed of a day when they could be like him.

Then tragedy struck. In early July 2003 he was staying at a resort hotel in Eagle, Colorado. He met a 19-year-old concierge in the lobby of the hotel, and she visited his room. No one but the two of them knows what happened next. She accuses him of rape, while he says what occurred took place with her consent. As I write, the painful round of charge and countercharge has been making its way through the courts. His wife and teammates have so far stood behind his story.

Whether or not Bryant was guilty of a crime, the anguish on his face, and that of his wife, as he admitted infidelity on national television was painful to watch. It was a reminder to all that life has only one Hero that we can honor without conditions—Jesus Christ. The minute we place others on a pedestal, or even try to climb on one ourselves, we invite failure. The one called The Word of God, who is always faithful and true, is the only hero truly worth following.

Lord, I need human mentors and guides, but I pray that I will place my ultimate trust only in You. I pray also that my daily actions might be an encouragement and not a disappointment to any who choose to look up to me.

November 17

And I saw heaven standing open, and I observed a white horse, and the one sitting on it is called FAITHFUL AND TRUE, *and in righteousness he judges and makes war.* REV. 19:11.

Why is it that the day after Thanksgiving is the biggest shopping day of the year? Isn't it fascinating that people in American society spend a whole day giving thanks for everything they have, then turn around and dash out the door to get hold of a lot more things that they don't have? It is almost as if the day of Thanksgiving alerts everyone to the fact that they don't have enough (which in most American homes, at least, is a silly idea).

But in my opinion, the strangeness of the day after Thanksgiving is exceeded by the day after Christmas. On Christmas Day (or Christmas Eve) Americans get more gifts than at any other time of the year. Then on the following day they rush out to obtain even more things (at special sale prices)! Something is seriously out of proportion here.

The morning after reveals more about our lives and character than the day before. While we might profess some noble sentiments on Thanksgiving or Christmas, the way we behave the morning after shows if sincere action actually supports our thoughts.[160] Let's face it. Human beings are natural consumers. Naturally self-centered, we want more and more. Unable to ever have enough, we are as fickle as fleas.

Jeremiah understood this all too well. He knew that even the best of us have a hard time following through the morning after. That is why he pointed to God's faithfulness as the only solid place on which we can base our lives: "Because of the Lord's great love we are not consumed, for his compassions never fail. They are new every morning; great is your faithfulness" (Lam. 3:22, 23, NIV).

You and I have a choice today. We can head out to seek our own way and gratify our own desires, living today as if it were the day after Thanksgiving or Christmas. Or this can be God's kind of new morning, in which we see things through His eyes. A morning in which, seeing the hunger and heartache all around us, we choose to serve rather than be served.

To live for Him today is to follow in His footsteps. He is faithful and true. His promises are so sure that they are like prophecies of His future behavior. His sentiments become His actions. I want to be more and more like Him.

Lord, I thank You for Your continuing faithfulness. If You were not faithful, I and everyone that I love would be lost. Today, help me to live according to Your ways and think according to Your thoughts.

And I saw heaven standing open, and I observed a white horse, and the one sitting on it is called "Faithful and True." . . . And **THE ARMIES OF HEAVEN WERE FOLLOWING HIM** *on white horses . . .* Rev. 19:11-14.

The last half of Revelation 19 contains some arresting images. Nevertheless, it was a small point of grammar in verse 14 that caught my eye one day. You see, the Greek language has four different ways to express the past tense. The Greek word behind the translation "were following" (in verse 14) is an imperfect indicative. This word form expresses continuous action in the past.

In other words, the action of riding together was continuous. The armies of heaven "were following" the rider on the white horse. Such following is not a one-time act, but an ongoing habit. They are accustomed to riding after their leader. Apparently success in heaven as well as on earth often depends on the team staying together.

A friend of mine saw an interview on public television between Charlie Rose and the well-known American cyclist Lance Armstrong.[161] Armstrong had just won the Tour de France for the fourth consecutive time (he now has seven consecutive victories). What makes Armstrong's story particularly compelling is not just the fact that he is the first American to be so successful in this unique event, but also that he has won the series of races in spite of a battle with cancer. His recovery from cancer and ongoing triumphs have inspired many around the world to keep fighting when the disease strikes.

Near the end of the interview Charlie asked Lance for the secret of his success in winning the three-week Tour de France. Armstrong could have given many answers, and all of them would have made a lot of sense. He could have talked about conditioning, determination, and strategic skill. But that is not how he responded.

He told Charlie that the secret to his success at the Tour de France was "never ride alone." You see, Lance is part of a team, the U.S. Postal team, which consists of nine riders. The team has one goal in mind: to support the one rider who has the best chance to win the race. So the rest of the team sacrifices itself for the sake of that one rider. They carry food for him and sometimes ride in front of him to break the wind. In general they manage the race in such a way that their leader is never stranded or struggling alone. Surrounded by his teammates, Lance never rode alone and was not vulnerable to the attacks of others. He remained strong throughout the race until the final victory.

"Never ride alone" is a heavenly principle that works for bike races *and* the race of life.

Lord, I need You to "ride" with me today. I can't make it through this day alone.

November 19

Out of [the rider's] mouth comes a sharp, two-edged sword, in order that he might strike down the nations with it. He will rule them with a rod of iron, and he will trample the winepress of **THE FURIOUS ANGER OF GOD ALMIGHTY.** *He has upon his garment and upon his thigh a name written: "King of Kings and Lord of Lords."* Rev. 19:15, 16.

The phrase "furious anger" is almost untranslatable. A literal reading would be "trample the winepress of the fury of the wrath of God Almighty." I'm not sure what the "fury of the wrath of God" attempts to say except that He is "really, really, *really* angry."

The book of Revelation takes us on a tour of the vocabulary of anger. The original Greek has expressions for such words as "anger," "angry," "wrath," and "fury." We are not surprised that the dragon is angry (Rev. 12:12, 17) or that prostitute Babylon is full of wrath (Rev. 14:8; 18:3). The bad guys in most stories tend to be types who can't control their feelings.

What *does* surprise us is how often the book portrays *God* as angry, furious, or wrathful (Rev. 11:18 and 14:10, for example). When we encountered the seven last plagues, the book told us that they are the full and final outpouring of God's wrath (Rev. 15:1). Naturally we had hoped that by the time we had gotten to Revelation 19 we would have been done with this troubling side to the divine personality.

One way to deal with this is to note that the Old Testament often depicts God as angry or wrathful. It is as if Jesus and the Old Testament God portray two dueling sides to the divine character. But Revelation does not allow us this illusion. It makes very clear that the Lamb also gets angry (Rev. 6:16, 17) and that He is approvingly present at the torment of those who accepted the mark of the beast (Rev. 14:10). Evidently anger can be a healthy thing or an unhealthy thing, depending on the circumstances and the motivation behind it.

The key, I think, is that the wrath of God is not an emotional thing—it is a judicial one. God isn't throwing a hissy fit. His wrath is a settled disapproval of anything that disturbs the happiness and tranquillity of the universe. He is the defender of victims and the rescuer of the oppressed. We shouldn't judge this language on the basis of our own dysfunctional emotions.

It reminds me of a speeding ticket I got in New Jersey a few decades ago. Written on it were the words: "The people of the state of New Jersey against Jon Paulien." Boy did I feel rejected! That really hurt—I mean, 8.6 million people upset at me! Then I realized no one was *really* angry with me, not even the police officer. I had just broken a small piece of the social contract that holds New Jersey together. The "wrath" of New Jersey has been a good motivator ever since.

Lord, I am thankful to know that You are there wherever injustice occurs. Help me to trust that You will set everything right in Your time.

*And I saw an angel standing constantly in the sun, and he cried out with a loud voice to all the birds that fly in midair, "Come, gather yourselves to **THE GREAT FEAST OF GOD** in order that you might eat the flesh of kings, and the flesh of generals, mighty men, horses and those that sit on them, and the flesh of everyone, whether free or slave, small or great." REV. 19:17, 18.*

We notice a lot of feasting going on in this chapter of Revelation. First of all, the Lamb is planning to marry His bride and wants to celebrate with a major feast (Rev. 19:7-9). In this passage we find another feast—a gruesome one—parallel to the first. The two feasts represent two destinies that follow from two possible decisions. People can choose either a relationship with Jesus or they can go their own way.

Great moments in relationship are often related to food. One of my favorite things in all the world it to have a date with my wife. Whatever else is involved, we like to eat at a restaurant. And two things are critical in the choice of restaurant: (1) the food must be tasty to us, and (2) it helps if it is a quiet and special place. Fast food is not always the best selection for a date.

Likewise, we build a relationship with Jesus by spending quality time in His Word. But people often give up daily reading of God's Word because they don't find it very "tasty." My dating experiences suggest some ways to enhance the devotional experience.

1. Make a Reservation—It requires no reservations to eat at McDonald's or Burger King. In fact, you don't even have to get out of your car! In many parts of the world, mealtime is more like a pit stop at Daytona than Thanksgiving dinner at grandma's house. Fast food won't do for a serious date. Just as you must make a reservation to eat at a fine restaurant, it helps to block out a daily time to feast at the table of the Lord (Ps. 23:5).

Now, just where are you going to find the time to make this reservation? How do I find time to date my wife? Making it a priority, we decide that the quality of our relationship requires the best of our time. If we say, "Let's see if we can fit it in," it won't happen. If necessary, we decide a week ahead. And we make sure that our date is at a time when we are wide awake and at our best.

2. Choose a Table—Next we ask for the best seat in the restaurant. We aren't content with a seat by the swinging door the waiters use or an open table surrounded by others, because we don't want to be interrupted. And we especially like quiet booths by the window with the sun shining in. With all this preparation and anticipation, we can hardly wait to see the menu.[162]

Lord, I remember many special moments with You. I want to make a fresh start with You today.

November 21

And I saw an angel standing constantly in the sun, and he cried out with a loud voice to all the birds that fly in midair, "Come, gather yourselves to the great feast of God in order that you might **EAT THE FLESH OF KINGS,** *and the flesh of generals, mighty men, horses and those that sit on them,* **AND THE FLESH OF EVERYONE,** *whether free or slave, small or great." Rev. 19:17, 18.*

The last half of Revelation 19 (verses 11-21) contains some gruesome images. The rider on the white horse wears a robe dipped in blood and strikes down whole nations with a sharp sword that comes out of his mouth like a cruise missile! The resulting carnage is so great that all the vultures in the world have difficulty cleaning up after the battle. Like many other parts of Revelation, this would not seem a promising place to find spiritual guidance for everyday living!

The plagues directed against Egypt in the book of Exodus are representative of the plagues yet to come. In the Exodus story Pharaoh kept backing off whenever God sent a new plague. Out of fear he would promise to let the Israelites go free, but as soon as the Lord let up on the pressure, he would go back on his promises. Pharaoh considered God's kindness a sign of weakness, a chance to take back what he thought he owned.

Islamic extremists believe that they are right in what they do. Convinced that they are fighting "The Great Satan," many have no difficulty hiding in orphanages and hospitals, using innocent women and children as shields, and even slaughtering their own people if they think it will advance the cause. They don't see such behaviors as wrong, but as necessary sacrifices in service of a greater cause. The fact that their enemies try to avoid killing civilians is not perceived as kindness or mercy but rather as weakness. They assume that if those who oppose them *truly* believed in their cause, they would slaughter everyone that got in the way, women and children included.

On the cross Jesus had the capacity to destroy His torturers and anyone who took their side. On that fateful Friday 2,000 years ago in Jerusalem His tormenters laughed at a Man who had willingly allowed Himself to be humiliated, beaten, and ultimately killed. They thought His refusal to even argue with His captors was a great sign of weakness.[163]

God had Revelation written to assure us that it will not always be so. His kindness toward Satan and those who take his side will not continue forever. Satan's days are numbered. The Lord's kindness is not weakness—it allows us time to repent of our own lack of kindness. In the end God will prove powerful enough to end injustice and deliver His people from evildoers.

Lord, teach me how to display Your kindness in spite of insult and injustice. Keep my eyes fixed on the final outcome.

And I saw the beast and the kings of the earth and their armies gathered to make war with the one sitting on the [white] horse and with his army. And the beast was captured, also the false prophet who performed miraculous signs before him (with these signs he deceived those who received the mark of the beast and worshipped his image). These two were thrown alive into the lake of fire that burns with sulfur. And the rest were killed by the sword that came out of the mouth of the one sitting on the [white] horse. And all the birds gorged themselves on their flesh. REV. 19:19-21.

When I was a teenage boy, these images fascinated me. I guess I had the youthful ability to disconnect an image from its gruesome reality. As I have gotten older, I have become less comfortable with parts of this passage. The thought of human beings burning in a fire or being impaled with a sword is not pleasant. (I even get wimpy when faced with the dentist's needle!)

We know from literature of New Testament times, however, that the apocalyptic images of Revelation 19 resonated with that generation. Again, God meets people where they are. The message of this violence is that the Lord will one day eliminate sin and evil from the earth. Abuse and torture will end when the beast and the false prophet meet their fate. It is like medicine for a sick world.

For most of human history bacterial infections were like a death sentence. Pneumonia, scarlet fever, syphilis, and festering wounds meant that few people lived beyond middle age. But on September 3, 1928, in London, a Scottish researcher named Alexander Fleming glanced at some petri dishes in his laboratory. They were about to be sterilized for reuse.

"That's funny," Fleming commented to himself. He noticed that the bacterial cultures in the petri dishes were dying off. The culprit seemed to be a liquid he called "mold juice," the product of spores that must have wafted in from a lab downstairs. Fleming determined that the spores were *Penicillium notatum* and renamed the fluid penicillin.

Having seen the horrors of infection during World War I, he was searching for a safe and powerful antibiotic. Up until that day he had found only an extremely weak one, called lysozyme, which he extracted from body fluids. Amazingly, even after the discovery of penicillin, it was still a decade before other scientists took notice of Fleming's work, purified penicillin for mass production, and turned it into a miracle drug.[164] Antibiotics are God's tokens within the natural world that He will one day purify the universe from sin and evil.

Lord, thank You for the promise that suffering, sin, and evil will not last forever. I open myself to Your cleansing spiritual antibiotics today, because I want to be more like You.

November 23

And I saw the beast and the kings of the earth and their armies gathered to make war with the one sitting on the [white] horse and with his army. . . . And the rest were killed by the sword that came out of the mouth of the one sitting on the [white] horse. And all the birds gorged themselves on their flesh. REV. 19:19-21.

I wrote the previous devotional early on the morning of Mother's Day. In the afternoon my family and I drove off to a friend's place where a number of families were getting together to celebrate the occasion. After a nice meal the group began to break up into smaller groups and found quiet places to talk in the house or around the wooded yard outside.

I joined a small group near the pool, which was slowly being filled from a hose. When one member of the group asked if I was anticipating any new publications, I mentioned that I had just published several, but a devotional book would keep me occupied for a while. Someone asked me what a devotional book on the book of Revelation would be like, and I shared the penicillin story on the previous page. And I said something to the effect that "the book of Revelation describes God's antibiotic for the universe."

A member of our group, who teaches business at the university, pondered the concept for a while and then inquired, "If God has an antibiotic for the universe, what do you see as the resistance to that antibiotic?"

Not having thought in those terms, I answered flippantly, "You can't make an illustration stand on four legs!" But the more I thought about his question, the more I felt that it might have some relevance to the issue of God's cleansing the universe of sin and sinners at the end of history.

You see, resistance to antibiotics occurs when people don't finish the bottle. They take just enough of the medicine to feel better, and then they stop. The problem is that the partial dose of antibiotic kills off the weaker bacteria in their system, but the remainder are strong enough to resist the next batch of antibiotic to some degree. If enough people take partial doses, new strains of bacteria that the antibiotic can no longer control may arise.

By way of analogy, resistance to God's saving work arises from free will. God allows us to frustrate His work in our lives if we so choose. When we apply the gospel just enough to feel better, but don't take the full dose of its cleansing power, our resistance to the gospel gradually grows. Over time we respond less and less to God's call. The day may come when the only way to overcome our resistance is through the destruction illustrated in the passage above.

Lord, give me the full dose of Your transforming power. May I never be satisfied with halfway measures. I accept Your complete Lordship of my life.

I saw an angel coming down out of heaven, having the key of the abyss and a great chain in his hand. And he seized the dragon, the ancient serpent, who is the devil and Satan, and bound him for **A THOUSAND YEARS.** *He threw him into the abyss, locked it, and sealed it over him in order that he might not deceive the nations any more until* **THE THOUSAND YEARS** *were finished. After these things he must be released for a short time.* REV. 20:1-3.

D o the 1,000 years take place before or after the second coming of Jesus? Three major views have sought to answer this question. In the *postmillennial* approach, Jesus comes after 1,000 years of human progress. While popular in the nineteenth century when education and scientific progress made many believe that the world was getting better, it doesn't, however, match the Bible's prediction that things will be very difficult before the end (2 Thess. 2:8-12; 1 Tim. 4:1-5; Rev. 13-19). Also, it also doesn't match the realities of today's world.

The *premillennial* view regards the millennium as a literal 1,000 years after the second coming of Jesus. In the *amillennial* view the millennium is not a literal period of 1,000 years but a symbol for the whole Christian Era from the cross to the Second Coming. The choice between these two may not make a huge difference from a devotional point of view.

Our family pediatrician recently approached me with a fourth view of the millennium. He said, "I get a little tired of all these arguments about whether the millennium is 'pre' or 'post' or 'a.' I've decided to develop a different approach."

"What's that?" I asked.

"I call it *panmillennialism!* That means everything will pan out in the end!"

Our pediatrician's position may make a lot of sense. I believe, however, that John clearly intended the 1,000 years of our text to occur after the Second Coming. By the time the millennium begins, characters such as Babylon and the beast have already passed off the scene (Rev. 19). The beginning of the millennium also comes after the mark of the beast and the forced worship of the beast's image (Rev. 13:15-17; cf. Rev. 20:4).

So if the millennium begins with the cross (the amillennial position), the events of Revelation 13-17 would have to have occurred before the cross. But I am aware of no serious scholar of Revelation who interprets the book in this way. While I want to respect the kinds of theological arguments that godly people make for the amillennial concept, that position does not seem to flow from the narrative of Revelation itself.

Lord, the arguments people have over the meaning of the Bible sometimes leave me confused and discouraged. Help me to trust that You will work it all out in the end.

November 25

And I saw thrones, and they sat on them, and **JUDGMENT WAS GIVEN TO THEM.** *And I saw the souls of those who had been beheaded because of the testimony of Jesus and the word of God. These did not worship the beast or his image, neither did they receive the mark upon their forehead or upon their hand. And they came to life and* **REIGNED WITH CHRIST FOR A THOUSAND YEARS.** *The rest of the dead did not come to life until the thousand years were finished. This is the first resurrection. Blessed and holy is the one having a part in the first resurrection. Upon these the second death has no power. But* **THEY WILL BE PRIESTS OF GOD AND OF CHRIST, AND THEY WILL REIGN WITH HIM A THOUSAND YEARS.** Rev. 20:4-6.

A returning missionary was rear-ended at a traffic light, causing minor damage to the car he had borrowed from a friend. When the officer arrived at the scene, he could not find the proof of insurance for the car, so he ended up receiving a ticket for $341. That news did not go well with his missionary salary. Even worse, it meant an appearance before a judge at the local courthouse. What was doubly frustrating was that the proof of insurance had been in the car all along! He had just not recognized it.

So here he was sitting in the court with a host of other felons and fiends, planning to throw himself on the mercy of the court. But before the bailiff called his name, another person appeared with a ticket exactly like his. The person merely produced the proof of insurance, and the judge pronounced the blessed words of mercy, "Dismissed!"

Now the missionary had reason for a little hope. When the judge called him to the bar, he produced the proof of insurance, and the judge again said, "Dismissed." The missionary walked out of that courthouse, into the morning sun, with a glad and grateful heart.[165]

The book of Revelation has a strong focus on judgment. But God's judgment is not something that His people need to fear. And it is more than just deciding who will be saved and who will be lost. The judgment in this text allows the saints to review the events of history and see that God has consistently done the right thing. That conviction is important for the health of the universe and everyone in it.

The amazing thing is that God is willing to submit Himself to judgment for our sakes. Caring about our feelings—even throughout eternity—He gives the redeemed a 1,000-year period to examine His actions. After careful review they will be satisfied both with His justice and with their position in His kingdom.

Lord, I am so grateful to know that You care about our feelings and our understandings. I trust that You will one day have the answer to all that troubles me now.

And when the thousand years have come to an end, Satan will be freed from his prison, and he will go out to **DECEIVE THE NATIONS** *which are in the four corners of the earth, Gog and Magog, whose number is like the sand of the sea, to gather them together for battle. And they marched across the breadth of the earth and surrounded the camp of the saints, the beloved city, and fire came down from heaven and consumed them.* REV. 20:7-9.

Ragged ruins jut like broken teeth from the fractured earth. Splintered remnants of uprooted trees, long since petrified, protrude from between blackened boulders. Sterile and still, the whole earth is a vast, cratered graveyard. Not a green thing trembles in the hot wind. Not a breathing thing stirs. Until, incredibly, living bodies begin to materialize out of the craters and the ruins. Bodies almost without number, varied beyond description. They range from strapping giants, seemingly in the prime of life, to hollow-eyed beings ravaged by age and disease.

Is this the opening scene of the latest sci-fi thriller? No, it is the scene implied by the sweeping story of Revelation 20. The 1,000 years have finally finished. It is time for the second resurrection—the resurrection of the damned at the end of the millennium. Why has God summoned these lost souls from sleep? Why not just let them remain in oblivion, since they refused to change? God does this to bring closure to the conflict between good and evil. He does it for the sake of the universe.

The wicked from the nations rise from the grave just the way they died, with the same kinds of thoughts, feelings, and passions. One last time they face the temptations of Satan. Again they fall for his deceptions. Doing what comes naturally, they attack the saints, who have returned to earth in the beloved city, the New Jerusalem (Rev. 21:2).[166]

Many find themselves wondering about a divine justice that saves some while allowing others to be lost. To human eyes, many of the saved will seem defective, and many of the lost will come across as righteous. Some wonder how God could judge between humans that appear so much alike.

But the events at the end of the millennium demonstrate that little acts of "harmless" selfishness have transformed the characters of the lost. Their minds and hearts have become quietly twisted to the point that nothing will turn them away from sin. Faced with a clear and public choice between repentance and destructive action, they once more choose the latter. In the process they verify God's judgment. The lines have been rightly drawn, and no doubts remain. History can now come to its sudden and final end. Sin, suffering, and death will disappear forever.

Lord, I see that little things have big consequences. Help me be faithful in the little things today.

November 27

And the devil, who deceived them, was cast into the lake of fire and burning sulfur, where also the beast and the false prophet are, and they will be **TORMENTED DAY AND NIGHT** *for ever and ever.* REV. 20:10.

A 10-year-old boy named Robert needed serious confrontation and ended up better for it. He was wild and uncontrollable. When a dentist ordered the boy into the dental chair, he refused repeatedly, finally threatening to take his clothes off if the man made him get into the chair.

"Take 'em off," the dentist replied. The boy took off everything but his pants. "OK, son, get into the chair."

"You don't understand—if you make me, I'll take *all* my clothes off!" Robert insisted.

"Son, take 'em off," the dentist ordered. The boy complied and got into the chair, naked as the day he was born. When the dentist finished the procedures, Robert asked for his clothes back.

"I'm sorry, but we'll be keeping them for the night. Your mother can pick them up tomorrow."

You can imagine the shock in the waiting room and the parking lot as the boy left with his mother. The next day the mother returned for the clothes and reported, "Robert has been blackmailing me about his clothes for years. But you're the first person to call his bluff. You have no idea what an impact this has had on him." [167]

Our text for today contains strong and disturbing language. Some sincere Christian thinkers take it to mean that the lost will literally undergo torment for an eternity of time, never dying, never having a break, never released from their suffering. But this is a misunderstanding of the Hebraic concept of "for ever."

The language of fire and sulfur recalls the destruction of Sodom and Gomorrah, which thoroughly destroyed the cities and their inhabitants but did not leave them endlessly twisting in the fire like a chicken in a rotisserie (Gen. 19:24). Jude 7 tells us that "forever" fire (same Greek word as Rev. 20:10) destroyed Sodom. The language also recalls the destruction of Edom, which was to be burned "forever" (Isa. 34:8-10), yet one finds no inferno there today. "Forever" in Hebrew is not so much an indication of time as it is an indication of thoroughness. When God confronts evil the last time, He will make a full end—it will never return.

Many people today would prefer that language like this didn't appear in the Bible. But evil will not go away quietly—it must be confronted. The universe will be a better place for its destruction.

Lord, I realize afresh that I can make no compromise with evil. Send the fire of Your Spirit to cleanse me today.

And I saw a great white throne and the one sitting upon it, from whose presence earth and heaven fled away, and no place was found for them. And **I SAW THE DEAD, BOTH GREAT AND SMALL, STANDING BEFORE THE THRONE.** *Books were opened, and another book was opened, the book of life.* **THE DEAD WERE JUDGED ON THE BASIS OF THE THINGS WRITTEN IN THE BOOKS, ACCORDING TO THEIR WORKS.** REV. 20:11, 12.

This scene is quite scary on the face of it. Everyone on earth—great and small, rich and poor—will one day be called to account. Nothing ultimately occurs in secret—all things will one day come out into the open. It is a powerful incentive to right living.

What we are talking about here is accountability. Accountability involves allowing others to help you keep watch over yourself. It means never having to face your problems alone. Someone else is there to encourage you and to help keep you straight. God is constantly available for this purpose. But for many people, accountability to God isn't incentive enough. They need a real flesh-and-blood person watching over them.[168]

Such accountability can take many forms. One type is a sharing group, such as Alcoholics Anonymous, which requires everybody to tell the truth and accepts them in their telling of it. A fascinating thing happens in such a group. As you learn to share your faults and struggles openly, you begin to find strength to deal with issues you were unwilling to face before. Knowing that you must give account to the group provides a check against your natural laziness or immoral behavior. As a result, accountability is a great motivator to right living.

Here is a suggestion for the few and the brave. Do you have a hard-nosed friend? Someone you trust, who loves you and cares deeply about you? An individual who would never want to see you hurt? Go to this friend and share with him or her your desire to make changes in your life. Tell the person that you will be completely honest and that you expect honesty in return.

That is scary, isn't it? Well, I couldn't live without it. I have three close friends in addition to my wife (one is a White American, one is an African-American, and the third is Hispanic). I know that these three men love me. Trusting in their love, I have given them the right to confront me about my faults anytime they see something negative. Whenever we get together, we have accountability sessions. We go out to eat or take a long walk and open up the deepest recesses of our hearts to each other.

The Bible suggests that nothing can be so precious as the wounds of a friend (see Prov. 27:6). And no friend is so true as the one who loves enough to tell the truth.

Lord, I want to be accountable to You in all things. Use my friends to keep me focused on Your purpose for my life.

November 29

And the sea gave up the dead which were in it, and **DEATH AND HADES GAVE UP THE DEAD WHICH WERE IN THEM,** *and everyone was judged according to their works.* REV. 20:13.

Buster was a fairly ordinary cat. Of no breed in particular, he was a delightful combination of the two characteristics that make cats so much fun. On the one hand, he was all cat. The mice, chipmunks, squirrels, moles, and birds in the area were all intensely aware of his presence whenever he ventured outside. The "mighty hunter" strode through his domain with an air of conscious superiority. On the other hand, when he was with children he was as gentle and affectionate as if there were not a violent chromosome in his whole genetic makeup. He was greatly loved. And he was never gone from the house for more than 12 hours.

One day he disappeared. We found no trace of him for 72 hours. Our worries and fears increased by the hour after the first day or so. After three days the family gathered for a special prayer session. I can still hear my wife praying, "Lord, even if he is dying somewhere, please bring him back so we can know what happened. Send your angel to carry him back if You have to. We need to know what has happened to him."

The next morning my wife was having devotions by the front window. Suddenly she screamed, "It's Buster! It's Buster! He's back! He's in the yard!" We all piled out of the house in various stages of dress and undress to greet the beloved wanderer. Our cat had a large hole in his side, filled with flies and maggots. With both tears and joy we realized that God had answered my wife's prayers. Buster had come home to say goodbye!

With broken hearts we gently carried him back into the house and called the vet. When treatment failed, the family went to the animal hospital to say a final goodbye. Seeing us enter, Buster struggled to his feet to greet us, then collapsed back to the floor of his cage, barely able to breathe or open his eyes. We knew that it was over. With loud wailing and two buckets of tears, the five of us expressed our love to him one last time. Although we walked out of the hospital into sunshine, the day seemed so dark.

It is comforting to know that death's days are numbered. One day we will be reunited with our loved ones, and separation will forever be a choice instead of something imposed on us. Will Buster be there too? I don't know. I know that nothing is impossible with God, but I don't know if He will preserve little pet personalities for eternity. Yet this I do know. If Buster isn't there, it is because God has something even better in store for us.

Lord, I long for the day when death "gives up." Until then, let me cherish every moment of this precious life You have given me.

DEATH *and Hades were* **THROWN INTO THE LAKE OF FIRE.**
This, the lake of fire, is the second death. REV. 20:14.

Death is an extremely ugly business. It would be bad enough if death simply lurked somewhere far in the future. But it constantly finds ways to insert itself into the lives of the living.

A chaplain arrived at the hospital one morning and found a note to call the psych ward. One of the doctors had left some information for him there, of all places. Was this some sort of joke?

The chaplain called the psych ward and a cheerful voice chirped, "One East." After identifying himself to the woman, he heard, "Oh, are you the chaplain who got bitten last week?"

"Yes, I'm the one." (It was a long story, not worth explaining to a stranger.)

"OK, the doctor said to tell you that the guy who bit you last week was HIV . . . [he heard the shuffling of papers as she searched for the document] . . . ummm . . . HIV. . . [the chaplain listened in frozen silence] negative!" she finally blurted out.

With pounding heart the chaplain gently reprimanded her "bedside manner" and hung up the phone.[169]

A woman in her late 40s refused to let her 88-year old mother die. Her mom came into the hospital for a new heart valve, but ended up on a respirator and wanted to be taken off the apparatus. The daughter thought she didn't really want to die. But doctors were required to honor the mother's wishes. The daughter, however, said plaintively, "I'm not ready for my mom to die."

My mom is 91 years old as I write. She is strong and still well able to take care of herself most of the time. But every so often she gets frustrated by her limitations of sight, hearing, and physical mobility.

"I want to make it to January 15—some checks are coming in then. After that, I just want to die and get it over with."

"You've probably got 10 years left in you, Mom," I say hopefully.

"Why would I want to live that long?" she asks (she did die on September 1).

Death and everything that leads up to it is a genuinely ugly business. The book of Revelation certainly doesn't sugarcoat the problem. But it confronts it with good news. Death is not a permanent fixture of reality—it's not natural to the universe. One day death itself will die! That's why Jesus died, so that one day He might destroy death itself. I'm looking forward to that day, aren't you?

Lord, thank You for the promise of a life that transcends death. May the reality of eternal life transform the way I look at death.

December 1

AND ANYONE WHO WAS NOT FOUND WRITTEN IN THE BOOK OF LIFE WAS THROWN INTO THE LAKE OF FIRE. REV. 20:15.

How does God feel about the destruction of the wicked? Is it "good riddance" along with a sigh of relief? Or is this the most difficult moment in the history of the universe? The following story gives me a sense of the answer.

Shirley was a high school guidance counselor when the phone rang one day. A student was on the line. "Jen says to tell you that maybe you should check on Todd. He may need you pretty badly. She broke up with him at noon."

Todd was Shirley's son. She hurried home to find an empty medicine bottle on the kitchen counter and a message on her son's computer: "It's hard to know what to say when you face death, but I thought I must say something. . . . Suicide is not the answer, but maybe it is a better way than life. . . . I want everyone concerned to know I love them—especially Jen. I love you so much that love has taken over my intelligence." Todd was all of 16 years old at the time.

Life had always mattered to the young man before this. As a student he was at the top of his class. At a convalescent center he had always been a responsible worker. Shirley slammed her fist down on the taunting computer. That morning a happy 16-year-old had left the home with a rose and a poem he had written for his girlfriend. He had never threatened suicide or been unduly depressed. Fitting in with his peers, he didn't drink or take drugs, had none of the classic symptoms of a suicide. Although Shirley had counseled others, she had no chance to counsel her own son.

Her husband had rushed Todd to the emergency room. The staff there pumped his stomach and put him on an IV drip. Thanks to rapid intervention Todd received another chance at life. Some time later he and his mother finally had a quiet chance to talk. The words gushed out in gulping sobs: "Mom, I didn't mean to hurt you! I didn't mean to hurt Jen! Why can't she love me? I begged her not to leave . . ."

"Cry, honey, just cry," his mother said.

"Mom, have you ever knelt and begged someone to stay, and they just turned and walked out?"

"No, son, I haven't."

Todd whispered softly, "God has—every time one of us walks away from Him."[170]

Lord, I sense a bit of the aching pain You feel every time I walk away from You, even if just for a moment. I know that an even greater pain is coming on that day when sin and sinners are eradicated from the universe. You have always been there when I needed You. I want to be there for You on that day.

And I saw **A NEW HEAVEN AND A NEW EARTH.** *For* **THE FIRST HEAVEN AND THE FIRST EARTH HAD GONE AWAY,** *and there was no more sea.* REV. 21:1.

According to this text, the new earth will be quite different from the world we know. But how can we be sure the earth will survive the end in a meaningful form? The studies of science are certainly not encouraging. They suggest that the universe is headed either for collapse and fiery meltdown or expansion and a big freeze. Neither option sounds attractive to me. But why worry about that? Long before the universe could come to an end, scientists anticipate a solar explosion that would leave no trace of earth.

So what hope is there that a new heaven and a new earth might replace the old ones? Scientist-theologian John Polkinghorne believes that we have only one source for such hope—the God of Abraham, Isaac, and Jacob.[171] He points out that we are not the first generation in which people questioned the promises of God. Jesus faced skeptics too.

Like many in our time, the Sadducees did not believe in an afterlife. They tried to trap Jesus with an ingenious story about a woman who became the wife of seven brothers, one after the other (Matt. 22:23-26). Each had died without children, leaving to the next the duty of marrying his widow. So, said the Sadduccees, "Whose wife will she be at the resurrection, considering she was married to all seven?" (see Matt. 22:28). In other words, if any kind of life exists after death, how could God untangle a relational mess like this?

The challenge did not catch Jesus off guard. Cutting right through their smoke screen, He reminded them of what God said to Moses at the burning bush: "Have you not read what God said to you, 'I am the God of Abraham, the God of Isaac, and the God of Jacob'? He is not the God of the dead but of the living" (verses 31, 32, NIV). Jesus' argument may be puzzling at first, but it is a powerful one. The patriarchs mattered to God when they were alive. Would they not still concern Him after their deaths? Would God simply discard them after they had ceased to exist? Wouldn't He rather retain their identities in His heart until he could make them alive again?

Our best hope for the future, therefore, is not in science or human ingenuity—it is in divine faithfulness. God put together this world and the life in it. If He did it once, He can do it again. To know Him is to trust Him. If He has promised a resurrection, He will be faithful to carry out what He vowed. The resurrection of Jesus reinforces the Old Testament promise (Isa. 26:19). Because God raised Jesus from the dead, we know that He will do the same for the followers of Jesus as well (1 Cor. 15:20-23). His faithfulness is our best hope.

Lord, You are the faithful God of Abraham, Isaac, and Jacob. You have proved faithful in the little things of my life. I will trust You to be faithful when the end comes.

December 3

I saw the Holy City, the New Jerusalem, coming down out of heaven from God, prepared as a bride adorned for her husband. And I heard a loud voice from the throne saying, "Behold, **THE TABERNACLE OF GOD IS WITH MEN, AND HE WILL TENT WITH THEM. THEY WILL BE HIS PEOPLE, AND GOD HIMSELF WILL BE WITH THEM AND BE THEIR GOD."** Rev. 21:2, 3.

A young woman diagnosed with a terminal illness learned that she had three months to live. So as she was getting her things in order she contacted her pastor to discuss certain aspects of her final wishes. She told him which songs she wanted sung at the service, what scriptures she would like read, and what outfit she wanted to be buried in.

Everything was in order and the pastor was preparing to leave when the parishioner suddenly remembered something very important to her. "There's one more thing," she said excitedly.

"What's that?" the pastor replied.

"This is very important," she continued. "I want to be buried with a fork in my right hand."

The pastor stared at the young woman, not knowing quite what to say.

"That surprises you, doesn't it?" she said.

"Well, to be honest, I'm puzzled by the request."

The young woman explained. "In all my years of attending socials and dinners, I always remember that when the dishes of the main course were being cleared, someone would inevitably lean over and say, 'Keep your fork.' It was my favorite part, because I knew that something better was coming . . . like velvety chocolate cake or deep-dish apple pie. Something wonderful—and with substance! So I just want people to see me there in that casket with a fork in my hand, and I want them to wonder 'What's with the fork?' Then you can tell them: 'Keep your fork . . . the best is yet to come.'"

Our text's description of the future is written with the past in mind. God's eternal reward for His people includes the restoration of both Jerusalem and the Garden of Eden. His people will live in a "garden city" that offers the best of both worlds: the peace and tranquillity of a garden combined with the bustling excitement of a beautiful city. And best of all, God Himself will be there with us.

Keep your fork.

Lord, from the beginning of my life I have sensed that there has to be something better ahead. Thank You for the precious promise of the New Jerusalem.

[GOD] WILL WIPE AWAY EVERY TEAR FROM THEIR EYES, *and there will be no more death, neither will there be any more sorrow or crying or any more pain,* **BECAUSE THE FORMER THINGS HAVE GONE AWAY.** REV. 21:4.

I love you, Dad."

It was the last thing that Howard had heard his daughter say. What had prompted her to make the phone call that ended with those words? Did she know that the bus she was about to board would explode? Wasn't he supposed to die before his child did? Howard felt alone in his grief. The apostle Paul had promised that God wouldn't lay on us burdens greater than we could bear (1 Cor. 10:13), but Howard wasn't so sure anymore. The heaviness in his chest left him breathless at times.

He sought comfort in the words of Jesus: "Blessed are those who mourn, for they will be comforted" (Matt. 5:4, NIV). But the promise did not seem to be fulfilled in Howard's experience. Although he read the text, he didn't feel comforted. A sense of loss continued to wrench him apart.

I wonder what Mary thought when she saw her Son on the cross, he pondered. *It's interesting that the Bible does not record any emotional outburst from her. She never cried out, "What are you doing to my Son?" Did she know that He was supposed to die? Did she understand it as part of some cosmic plan? Why didn't she run over and offer to take His place?*

When spring came, Howard felt a little better. As the roses began to bloom he remembered happy times with his daughter planting and enjoying the bushes. But then the rains came, and he felt gloomy again. "I still relive that tragedy-laden phone call as if it were yesterday," he said. "Lord, I still don't understand Your plan!"

One day he came across Revelation 21:4: "He will wipe away every tear from their eyes. There will be no more death or mourning or crying or pain, for the old order of things has passed away" (NIV). They were words from the future—words he was longing to hear. Howard came to realize that they explained Matthew 5:4 as well. Those who mourn do not always receive comfort in this life. The future tense is a promise that doesn't always apply to the here and now.

But both texts are clear in this. Howard will see his daughter again. Because he believes in eternal life, he has gradually found comfort in Revelation's vision of hope. Even though his daughter lies in a grave, he knows that Jesus will return again. And when He does, God will wipe every tear away and the mourners will be comforted forever.[172]

Lord, I have often felt frustrated by prayers that went unanswered, tragedies not prevented, loved ones I have lost. Help me trust Your future promise.

December 5

[GOD] WILL WIPE AWAY EVERY TEAR FROM THEIR EYES, *and there will be no more death, neither will there be any more sorrow or crying or any more pain,* **BECAUSE THE FORMER THINGS HAVE GONE AWAY.** Rev. 21:4.

Will God wipe away tears by causing us to forget all the hardships and suffering of this life? Or will we remember the hurts clearly, yet they won't devastate us anymore? How far will the "former things" have gone away? I suspect we will still remember, but the pain will be gone. The memories of our personal history are worth retaining—they are part of who we are and what we have become. When memory has lost its power to wound, it still retains its capacity to develop depth of character.

Those severely wounded by life can find it hard to imagine that time could strip painful events of their power to cause tears. But with God's help it can happen. And sometimes the process doesn't take long.

My youngest daughter and I staggered out of our beds at 1:30 in the morning. Recently baptized in the Red Sea, she had committed to a night climb of Mount Sinai. We set out with several others at 2:00 a.m., trailed by camel drivers certain we wouldn't make it to the top without help. "Camel, good camel, very nice," they mumbled to each of us every five minutes.

The darkness was deep, broken only by flashlights. As we dug the toes of our athletic shoes into the scrabbly red soil of the mountain, occasional shooting stars flashed by behind us. The 7,400-foot mountain became steeper and steeper as the path approached the great wall that signaled the last third of the climb. The camel drivers continued to follow, certain that some of us would soon succumb to muscular gridlock. And some did. But my daughter forged determinedly on.

The steepest part of the climb is the legendary staircase to the top—750 steps carved almost vertically out of the red rock. Rest stops became more and more frequent as bodies cried out for mercy. But we made it! No camels! No donkeys! Just sore muscles.

By midmorning my daughter and I returned to our hotel. She flopped facedown on her bed and lay absolutely still for a moment. Then her head popped up, and she said, "Remind me to never, ever, *ever* do anything like that again!" Her head dropped facedown into her pillow, and I didn't hear from her for several hours.

A few days later in Germany a bright-eyed girl looked up eagerly at me, without warning, and said, "Dad, when can we climb Mount Sinai again?" It took me by surprise, but it shouldn't have. The memory was fresh, but the pain had vanished. You could say that the "former things" had gone away, yet in another sense they had not.

Lord, give me patience to make it through this day, knowing I am one step closer to the new earth that You have in mind for us.

And the One sitting on the throne said, "Behold, **I AM MAKING EVERYTHING NEW!"** *And He said, "Write, because these words are faithful and true."* Rev. 21:5.

D
o you really want God to make *everything* new? Aren't there some things you like better when they are old? Isn't that warm coat, with the familiar colors and the fraying threads in the collar, better than the latest fashions, with the colors that don't quite suit you and the lack of features that you just can't live without? Doesn't that bald husband with the annoying leg twitch have features that you just wouldn't trade for a new model? any new model? Have you ever bought a new (or newer) car that just didn't feel as right as the old one? Sometimes old is better. Old things can be reliable and practical. The known is often better than the unknown.

Not long ago my university made the building I work in new. It had the old building gutted to the core and constructed a major addition incorporating many offices and classrooms. But I miss my old office greatly. In it I had bookshelves everywhere, even in the coat closet. Come to think of it, I *had* a closet in the old office—a place to hang a coat or a spare jacket, to store my graduation gown, to keep an extra pair of shoes and an umbrella, just in case.

The new office has an extra-large work space that I have industriously filled with clutter. But my new desk doesn't have as many drawers as my old, tiny one, and I have lost track of many papers as a result. The new office has space for far fewer books, and I have had to take many of them home, causing confusion and inefficiency as a result. I have less space for files, so I have also had to divide them between home and office.

But there is no going back. The powerful air handling system in the new building means no more students sleeping in class because the air is hot, stuffy, and stale (they have to come up with other excuses now). The technology of the new building allows us to explore teaching options that have improved learning a great deal. The configuration of the building has done wonders for the seminary community, enhancing the quality of relationships among students and teachers. And the suite of offices in which I work, in spite of their inefficiencies, is like a little piece of home away from home.

And I take comfort in the knowledge that in the new earth "I shall know fully, even as I am fully known" (1 Cor. 13:12, NIV). When God makes all things new, we will still recognize the ones we love. Our surroundings will be perfectly suited to our needs. In heaven the new will be constantly renewed, yet the familiar will be preserved. Only the flaws will be gone. Our joy will be complete. And I won't miss the fraying threads.

Lord, I can't wait to see that new world in which we will have no regrets.

December 7

And He said to me, "It is done. **I AM THE ALPHA AND THE OMEGA,** *the beginning and the end. To the one who is thirsty* **I WILL GIVE FREELY** *(without cost) from the spring of the water of life.* Rev. 21:6.

Our God is the greatest of all givers. In Jesus Christ He sent the greatest gift ever presented to the human race. Because of the cross, the water of life is freely available to all who recognize their thirst (John 7:37-39). Sin, however, makes many of us deeply unwilling to accept the gifts of God. To receive a gift is to, in some degree, lose control of our lives. As a result, many vulnerable people feel reluctant to take gifts, even those from God.

An e-mail I received some time ago well illustrates this human tendency. A friend, recounting evangelistic experiences in the Philippines, reported the following story.

"During the first night of the series I noticed a young preteen girl that seemed grumpy. She was constantly out of sorts with the people around her. When I bent down and simply asked what her name was, she seemed a little shocked but managed to blurt out, 'Sherry.'

"From that moment on I made it a special mission always to greet her and smile at her whenever I met her. Sherry would react ambiguously by both smiling and running away. At times she would run behind where I was sitting and lightly touch me on the shoulder and then disappear into the crowd.

"Sherry always wore a pin that kept her hair in a neat bun. Wanting to express my affection for her, I purchased another hairpin and gave it to her. She put the pin on once, but a few minutes later she reappeared with nothing in her hair. From that point on, Sherry wore nothing in her hair when she came to the meetings. The message was quite clear. Nobody gets close to her, and she was going to show me just who was in control of the situation.

"The last day of the meetings were coming up, and I decided to take a risk and buy the girl another present for her hair. This time it was a bright-pink heart with a rubber band attached. I had the hair clip in a plastic bag and dropped it in her lap while she was sitting. Sherry acted a little startled, and I walked away, because I knew I had disturbed her comfort zone.

"I didn't see the child much the rest of the day. I thought perhaps I shouldn't have risked giving her another gift. But as I was leaving, a hand reached out to faintly touch my elbow. Running away as usual, a smile on her face, in her hair Sherry had the bright-pink tie I had given her that morning! A deep sense of peace and satisfaction filled my soul. She had finally accepted the gift."[173]

Lord, give me the courage to accept Your greatest Gift and allow Him to mold my life in whatever way You will.

The one who overcomes will inherit these things, and I will be his God and he will be My son. To everyone who is a coward, unfaithful, corrupt, a murderer, a fornicator, a sorcerer, or an **IDOLATER,** *and to every liar, comes their portion in the lake burning with fire and sulfur, which is the second death.* Rev. 21:7, 8.

Idolatry was a major issue in New Testament times. At the top of the idolatrous food chain was the emperor of Rome himself. First-century Christians would have seen in Revelation a powerful declaration that the emperor "has no clothes." Caesar did not create this world (Rev. 4:11), he was not eternal (verse 8), and he did not redeem the people of the empire with his blood (Rev. 5:12). While the splendor of Rome was alluring and impressive, its claim for worship was foolish.

Just as first-century Christians resisted the attractions of empire to follow Jesus, so Christians today need to repudiate the idols of our generation. We often find ourselves drawn to worship the idols of science, technology, wealth, and commercialism. In the process we easily ignore the implications of Creation and the cross. But such contemporary idolatry may soon prove to be as foolish as the claims made by the empire once were.

In recent years the realization of the complex and sensitive conditions required for intelligent life to exist on earth has stunned the scientific community. The universe appears, in fact, to have been incredibly fine-tuned for the benefit of humanity on earth at this point in cosmic history. And scientists are discovering this insight across the board: in physics and astrophysics, classical cosmology, quantum mechanics, and biochemistry. The existence of intelligent carbon-based life on earth depends upon a delicate balance of natural conditions. If any part of this balance would become even slightly altered, life as we know it would not exist. Today we have space for only one brief example.

Water is one of the strangest substances known to science. Its specific heat, surface tension, and physical properties are different from the norm. For example, the fact that its solid phase is less dense than its liquid phase, so that ice floats, is virtually unique in nature. But this property of water is essential to life. If ice were more dense than water, it would sink to the bottom of bodies of water, where it would remain in the deepest parts until eventually all lakes and oceans would freeze solid. Instead, ice forms a protective skin on the surface of reservoirs of water, keeping them from freezing down to the bottom. This is one of many unique characteristics of water that are absolutely essential for heating and cooling, the formation of cell walls and membranes, and so many other aspects essential for human life.[174]

Lord, help me to discern clearly between the alluring claims of today's idolatry and the clear evidence of a loving Designer. Help me to build my life around the things that truly last.

December 9

The landscape along Interstate 57 in central Illinois is extremely flat, mostly farm fields and pasture, with an occasional stand of trees. One overcast day in mid–March I was a bit startled to see what appeared to be a gigantic gray cross barely visible against the gray sky in the distance. My first impression was that it must be some sort of industrial contraption that just happened to have the shape of a cross. But as we drew nearer, it became clear that it was truly a representation of the cross of Jesus Christ, the beams set in diamond-shaped metal, perhaps 80 feet high. There was no sign or other explanation as to why it was there by the road—it just was.

I wondered if that monument was someone's response to a special intervention by God. Perhaps he or she had been drowning in a lake and said, "Lord, if You'll save my life right now, I'll build You the biggest monument in the state!" Or perhaps it was supposed to be the bell tower to a church, but the congregation ran out of money before it could construct the church itself. Be that as it may, that cross is certainly the centerpiece of that portion of the Illinois landscape.

It is like that with the book of Revelation, also. If we are not careful, we might get the impression that the beasts, the vultures, the darkness, the earthquakes, and the hailstones are what the book of Revelation is all about. But they are more like the general landscape of the Illinois prairie. The true centerpiece of the book of Revelation is not war or catastrophe, not oil or the Middle East, but Jesus Christ and Him crucified.

One would expect that the arrival of the New Jerusalem would be an event in its own right. The enormous size, the radiance, the unusual shape, could easily be the centerpiece of the story. But this book is the revelation of Jesus Christ. So the New Jerusalem is no ordinary city. It is the bride, the wife of the Lamb. And John does not allow even the New Jerusalem itself to distract from the overwhelming focus on Jesus. To read this book without gaining a clearer picture of Jesus is to miss the key point.

Lord, in my excitement over the glories of the future world, never let me lose sight of the fact that You are the real reason anyone would want to live forever. I want to know You better every day for an eternity.

[The city] has a great and high wall, having twelve gates. And at the gates are twelve angels. And the names of the 12 tribes of the sons of Israel are written on the gates. Three gates are on the east, three on the north, three on the south, and three on the west. The wall of the city has twelve foundations, and upon them are twelve names of the twelve apostles of the Lamb. REV. 21:12-14.

D oes God have an exact and detailed plan for every person's life? Is there a "best decision" out there, part of God's perfect will for my life? Or does God have many possible roads to get me to the same goal?

For some of us, finding the very best route between two points can become an obsession. I once planned a road trip from Michigan, where I live, to Florida. I noticed that all the best routes seemed to pass through Chattanooga, Tennessee, so the big issue was how to go from Michigan to Chattanooga.

I noticed that we could go down through Indianapolis to Nashville, and then across to Chattanooga. Or we could head east from Louisville through Lexington and then south through Knoxville to Chattanooga. Or we could head east from Michigan or Indianapolis into Ohio and come down through Cincinnati to Knoxville and beyond.

I counted the miles and concluded that the shortest distance between my part of Michigan and Chattanooga is through Nashville. On the other hand, the stretch from South Bend to Indianapolis is painfully slow, with lots of traffic lights, and Nashville can be tough during rush hour. So if we headed east on I-80 into Ohio we could make the whole trip on superhighways. On the other hand, that route seemed to be almost 100 miles longer. On the other hand, the way through Lexington avoids Nashville, but is 40 miles longer. On the other hand . . .

Does God have the perfect route for all situations, or is the goal of our life what really counts? The goal of our lives is to develop character and be among the group that will live in the New Jerusalem. The shortest route, the easiest route, or the "best" route does not always develop character. Sometimes we achieve character only by taking a back road that leads to a detour that puts us onto some potholed, gravel road.

God knows what we need better than we do. He can make the most of every route we take. The thing that really counts is where we end up. The contrast between the golden city and the lake of fire couldn't be more plain. The slain Lamb has gone before us, so what counts is to follow Him no matter where the road of life takes us.[175]

Lord, I want to be with You in the Holy City. More than anything else I want my family and friends to be there too. Today I want You to be in charge of the map.

December 11

The one who spoke with me had a measuring rod made of gold, in order that he might measure the city, its gates and its wall. THE CITY IS LAID OUT SQUARE; *its length is equal to its width. He measured the city with the rod; it was 12,000 stadia,* THE LENGTH, WIDTH AND HEIGHT EQUAL. *He measured its wall, 144 cubits according to the measure of a man, which the angel was using. The material of the wall is jasper, and the city is pure gold as transparent as glass.* REV. 21:15-18.

The Bible is like a gigantic cycle: it begins with a beautiful place of safety and security (Gen. 1; 2); sin, doubt, and disobedience come in (Gen. 3); then we follow the story of sin and disobedience from the beginning (Gen. 3) to the end (Rev. 20). The New Jerusalem narrative attempts to describe the peace, security, and safety that will be in place after the destruction of sin (Rev. 21). Scripture would not present a complete picture without the book of Revelation, nor would Revelation be complete without these last two important chapters.

Is the New Jerusalem a literal city like those today? Or is it a symbol of an indescribable reality? If it is like ancient Jewish pictures of the glorious future, it is more symbolic than literal. God did not intend it to satisfy the reader's curiosity about the architecture of the future, but to teach spiritual lessons that will change lives today.

Tobit (in the Apocrypha), for example, describes an end-time Jerusalem whose gates consist of sapphire and emerald, and whose walls and streets are embedded with precious stones (Tobit 13:21, 22, Douay; 13:17, LXX). But this description is just one of many things for which Tobit praises God (Tobit 13:1, Douay). Isaiah predicts foundations of sapphire, jeweled gates, and walls of precious stones (Isa. 54:11, 12), but they too are there for praise (Isa. 60:10-18, especially verse 18). Zechariah, on the other hand, predicts that Jerusalem will be without walls, because the Lord will be a wall of fire around it (Zech. 2:4, 5). So to assume that all of this description is meant as literal is questionable.

What relevance does the vision have for us in a skeptical age? The images are those of the author's time and place, but the central theme is clear. Everything that human beings have hoped and dreamed for is attained, not by human effort, but in relationship with the Lamb. And that relationship begins now. The vision of the future New Jerusalem keeps our minds and hearts focused on the one thing that really matters.

Lord, help me to remember every day that paradise is not a Caribbean island, that the ideal city is not Hollywood, but that I will find the ultimate hopes and dreams of my life in relationship with You.

The foundations of the wall of the city were decorated with every kind of precious stone. The first foundation was jasper, the second sapphire, the third agate, the fourth emerald, the fifth sardonyx, the sixth carnelian, the seventh chrysolite, the eighth beryl, the ninth topaz, the tenth green quartz, the eleventh jacinth, and the twelfth amethyst. The twelve gates were twelve pearls; each gate was made of a single pearl. The main street of the city was made of pure gold, as transparent as glass. REV. 21:19-21.

For me the most unforgettable moment of 1984 occurred during a presidential debate. The race for the nomination of the Democratic Party was chiefly between Walter Mondale and Gary Hart. Gary Hart would later become infamous for his dalliances with women other than his wife. But at the time of this debate he was actually the leading candidate for the nomination. No one could have anticipated that the entire nomination would turn on a single phrase.

In the course of the debate, Gary Hart talked about his vision for improving the country. Walter Mondale responded that his opponent had a lot of things to say, but the really decisive issue was "Where's the beef?" Was the phrase a ploy to acquire the agriculture vote? No, his comment was not really about food, although it did recall a hamburger ad on TV.

In the ad a "little old lady" sat at the table of a rival hamburger chain. Someone placed a hamburger in front of her. The bun was generous in its proportions, but inside it held only a tiny piece of meat, about the size of a quarter. In stunned surprise she said with the quavering voice of the aged, "Where's the beef?" The campaign was a smash success. All over the country people began quoting the line. The little old woman became a star overnight at the age of 85.

The message of the advertisement was that claims don't matter when it comes to hamburgers. What counts is the meal that one actually receives. By invoking the phrase from the burger commercial, Mondale called his opponent's credibility into question. With a simple phrase he succeeded in turning his opponent into a national laughingstock even before his marital indiscretions became public knowledge and forever ruined his political career. Such is the power of allusion to the past.

Our text is largely a recitation of various stones in the foundation of the New Jerusalem. But they point to something deeper. The stones of the city's foundation are the same as those on the breastplate of Israel's high priest. Here, as so often in this book, the vision ties together the whole of God's revelation. In the Apocalypse of John all the books of the Bible meet and end. It is like the finale of the biblical symphony.

Lord, I want to go deeper and deeper into Your Word every day.

December 13

And I did not see a temple in her, for the Lord God Almighty is her temple, and also **THE LAMB.** *And the city has no need of sun or moon in order that they might give it light, for the glory of God has illuminated it and* **ITS LAMP IS THE LAMB.** REV. 21:22, 23.

What will it be like when we meet Jesus (the Lamb) in the Holy City? What thoughts will run through our minds? What will we feel? I suspect, if we have a true picture of what He went through for us, that a deep well of gratitude will burst forth in our heart and will swell more and more throughout eternity. We can only begin to sense it now, but we can at least make a start.

Imagine that on a hot July day you have to work in the fields all day long, 14 hours of hard labor.[176] I know that you cannot withstand a day like that, so at the last minute I step forward and take your place. You stay home and think all day about my experience: the hot sun, the flies, the backbreaking work, the sore muscles, the aches and pains, and the desire just to sit and rest in the shade. When I return, I tell you how the day went, and you say, "I see. Thank you, friend, for what you did." But do you really see? Do you really know what it was like—how every moment was agonizingly slow, how every step was torture to my feet?

Now just suppose that, instead of staying behind, you had come along with me that day. Actually watching me labor those 14 hours, you had seen me stooped, barely able to walk, my hands blistered by the hoe, my face burned by the hot sun. You would watch me stumble and sweat and look for relief, watching the hands on my watch move ever so imperceptibly. Had you done that, you would truly have begun to understand. You would not have felt the physical pain, but you would have better grasped just what I endured for you, and the gift that I gave of myself that day would stay with you forever.

So it is with the Crucifixion. When we think about it, we *maybe* picture Christ being whipped. How many times? Once? Twice? With what? Do you picture His flesh torn? Do you have any clue how that looks? Does that crown of thorns rest nicely on His head like a laurel wreath, or is it pressed deep into His flesh, causing rivulets of blood to stream down His face and body? What about the other beatings He endured? Scripture tells us that He was virtually unrecognizable (Isa. 52:14).

And all of this was after His only friends had betrayed and abandoned Him. The song goes, "His eyes were on the crowd that day, but He looked ahead in time. When He was on the cross, I was on His mind." When Jesus died that day He died for me. Once you and I truly understand this, it will be the basis for eternal gratitude.

Lord, I look forward to a face-to-face relationship with You. Until then, I will daily express and live my gratitude to You for what You have done for me.

And the city has no need of sun or moon in order that they might give it light, for
THE GLORY OF GOD *has illuminated it, and its lamp is the Lamb.*
REV. 21:23.

Where I live in Michigan, "lake effect" weather tends to produce gray skies as often as not. You see, Lake Michigan is about 300 miles long and more than 50 miles wide. It is large enough to create its own weather! On otherwise sunny days the prevailing wind picks up moisture over the lake and produces a seamless, gray cloud cover over the landscape to the east. I live in that "landscape." The first winter I spent in southwest Michigan we saw the sun only 12 days from September 1 to April 1. I didn't say that we had 12 sunny days, but that we "saw" the sun (sometimes only for a few minutes) on only 12 days out of more than 200!

While things have been a bit brighter in recent years (could global warming be a good thing in some places?), the sky is still a lot grayer in this part of the world than many other places. So when the sun breaks out and the sky is bright blue, Michiganders tend to rejoice more than most people would. Light, frankly, is a most glorious substance, especially when you don't get enough of it. It is no wonder that when the Bible speaks of light in the context of God, it uses the word "glory."

The very last reference in the Bible to the glory of God occurs in our text for today. The word "glory" has a number of meanings in the Bible. But when we narrow the focus to manifestations of God, glory designates something quite different than "beauty, ornament, pride, or boasting."

In the Lord's Prayer Jesus says, "Thine is the . . . glory" (Matt. 6:13, KJV). Glory is not an accidental feature of God's character, but an essential quality. But such glory is much more than just a radiant brightness. Exodus 34:6, 7, defines the glory of God as His character. God is "slow to anger, abounding in love and faithfulness, maintaining love to thousands, and forgiving wickedness, rebellion and sin. Yet he does not leave the guilty unpunished." (NIV). The glory of God expresses the fullness of His character, including both justice and mercy. That character clearly manifested itself in the words and the actions of Jesus (John 17:1-5).

In practical terms the place where we see the glory of God today is in His Word. It is the Bible that opens up the character of God to us in Jesus Christ. Other claims to glory may distract us, but we find the true glory in Jesus Christ through His Word. In the Word, God allows us to experience His glory, a foretaste of our experience in the New Jerusalem. There, what we have taken hold of here by faith will be visible to our sight.

Lord, I want to know You more and more. Fill my mind and heart with the glory of Your character today.

December 15

And **THE NATIONS WILL WALK BY ITS LIGHT,** *and the kings of the earth will bring their glory into it.* Rev. 21:24.

A popular joke tells about a heaven that perpetuates the old prejudices of earth. According to the joke, a Baptist heaven has lots of water and everyone dunks everyone else in it. In the Pentecostal heaven everyone raises their hands in the air, dances around, and falls over. There is Catholic heaven and Methodist heaven and so on. The joke is funny because in our heart of hearts we somehow know that God will abolish such distinctions in heaven. In the New Jerusalem people of every background will live together and will have learned the joyous acceptance that is in Jesus.

In the waning days of apartheid in South Africa, a White pastor drove home from church after an evening meeting. Halfway home on a four-lane highway he rode over hundreds of nails, experienced the consequences, and pulled to a stop. Seconds later two men came out of the darkness and attacked the car with crowbars, trying to force their way into the car. They managed to open one door and slashed the pastor's wife. The whole time, White members of his congregation rode past on their way home. An old Zulu man who arrived in a beat-up, rusted old truck finally saved the pastor and his wife.[177]

It is interesting how our definition of an outcast changes from generation to generation. The parable of the good Samaritan does not trouble us as long as we don't meet any Samaritans! But if Jesus were to retell the story today, how would He bring it home to us? Would the assaulted man be ignored by a televangelist and then the pastor of a megachurch? Would the Samaritan be replaced by a homosexual or an Islamic terrorist? The prejudice-free future of our text challenges us to take the principle and apply it to whatever circumstance we meet. We tend to be blinded, however, to our own version of the "outcast." The North Dakotan may be appalled by a White New Yorker's prejudice against Blacks, while holding similar prejudices against Native Americans. The New Yorker's attitude toward "yokels" from North Dakota may well be the reverse.

Even in the church we draw differences between people on the basis of how they interpret certain details of our doctrines, how they look when they come to church, where they live, or whether or not they clap their hands after a stirring musical performance. The gospel calls us to anticipate the glories of the New Jerusalem in the way that we treat people today. Jesus accepts us in spite of our own peculiarities and continues to work with us to recreate us in His likeness. The best way to return the love of Jesus is to treat others the way He has done us. That principle is at the heart of the life of heaven.

Lord, open my eyes to the hidden prejudices that govern the way I treat others.

December 16

And the city has no need of sun or moon in order that they might give it light, for the glory of God has illuminated it, and its lamp is the Lamb. And the nations will walk by its light, and the kings of the earth will bring their glory into it. And **HER GATES WILL NEVER EVER BE SHUT** *by day, for there will be* **NO NIGHT THERE.** Rev. 21:23-25.

Sometimes the positives in life are so overwhelming that you can describe them only in negatives. That's the way it is with the New Jerusalem. The reality of the New Jerusalem is indescribable. We learn that it will have no temple, no need of sun or moon, no night, and the gates will never shut. Its inhabitants will never have to deal with tears, death, mourning, crying, or pain (Rev. 21:4). The first taste of Paradise is an experience check: "Oops, no more death, no more night. Oops, no more locked doors. Oops, no more pain. This place is great!"

It reminds me of November 9, 1989. At 7:00 p.m. the East German Politburo, responding to weeks of peaceful demonstrations, announced that all citizens could leave East Germany at any crossing "immediately." After making this announcement they notified Harald Jäger, head of passport control at the Berlin Wall's Bornholmer Strasse checkpoint, that no one was to pass through unless they had the proper documentation.

Having faithfully watched over his border crossing for all of its 28 years of existence. Jäger determined to continue doing his duty this evening. But by 11:00 p.m. things began getting out of control. A crowd of 20,000 people pressed against the crossing, demanding to be allowed through, but most had not yet been able to secure the proper documents.

The crowd began to chant, "Open the gate! Open the gate! Open the gate!"

Jäger's men looked to him for instructions. But he had no orders for such a situation. He didn't know what to do. The border guards became insistent: "Tell us what to do!" Jäger held the fate of 20,000 people—yes, even a whole country—in his hands.

"What shall I do?" he implored his men, "Order you to shoot?" Jäger knew that the only way he could carry out his orders was through bloodshed.

Shortly after 11:00 p.m. he told his men at the gates, "Open them all!" By dawn an estimated 100,000 delirious East Germans had slipped past him on their way to a raucous celebration in West Berlin. Over the next few days revelers from both East and West hammered away at the symbol of Soviet communist oppression and toasted their freedom.[178] For them the symbol of hoped-for paradise was "Her gates will never ever be shut" again!

Lord, I thank You that none of the things that trouble or destroy today will long endure. Give me patience to wait for Your glorious liberation.

December 17

[The kings of the earth] will bring the glory and the honor of the nations into her. **ABSOLUTELY NOTHING THAT DEFILES WILL ENTER INTO HER, NEITHER ANYONE WHO PRACTICES SACRILEGE OR DECEIT.** *Only those [will enter] whose names are written in the Lamb's book of life.* Rev. 21:26, 27.

Three times (Rev. 21:8, 27; 22:15) the book of Revelation lists people who will not attain eternal life. But will those who receive eternal life really be the fortunate ones? Would you really want to do exactly what you are doing right now forever? Is it possible that eternal life could get a bit boring after a while? A former teacher used to tell the following story.

A fisherman dreamed that he was in heaven. An angel came up to him and said, "I understand that fishing is your favorite sport. I have just the place for you." He then took the fisherman to the best trout stream in all the universe. Delighted, the fisherman began pulling in some real big ones.

After a year the angel reappeared to find the man happily fishing away, a 10-foot-high pile of large fish on the ground behind him. The fisherman said, "This has been great. I love heaven. How about we go find another stream?"

"This is the best trout stream in the entire universe. I'm sure you will be disappointed with anything else."

"You're right," the fisher said. "This is the best!"

He continued fishing for 10 years and by now had a pile of fish 50 feet high behind him. When the angel returned, the fisherman repeated, "This has been great, but let's see what else there is."

Again the angel replied, "This is the best there is. You have the best stream and your favorite hobby. What else could you want?" So the man fished for another 90 years, and the fish pile behind him was now more than 300 feet high. When he finally saw the angel once more, the fisherman pulled his rod out of the water, slammed it to the ground, and said, "I'm sick and tired of this! It's the same thing again and again. This isn't heaven—it's hell!"

Smirking wickedly, the angel said, "It took you 100 years to figure it out?"

To live forever is not enough. An excess of pleasure and wealth will not guarantee that eternal life will retain its flavor. The joy of eternity will be found in the depth of relationship with God and others and in the work we will do to carry out God's ultimate purpose for us and for the universe. The good news is that we can begin living the life of heaven now. To know and obey God will be our science and song throughout eternity.

Lord, thank You for this glorious vision of a New Jerusalem. May this vision keep me focused on the things that truly matter.

December 18

And [the angel] showed me a river of **THE WATER OF LIFE,** *clear as crystal, flowing from the throne of God and of the Lamb.* Rev. 22:1.

The Kaufmann family got to experience a little bit of heaven on earth. They wanted a simple summer weekend cottage by their favorite stream called Bear Run, some 70 miles southeast of Pittsburgh, Pennsylvania. Edgar J. Kaufmann owned a department store in Pittsburgh during the Great Depression of the 1930s. For many years Bear Run had provided a rustic place for the Kaufmann family and their employees to get away from the city and spend time embraced in quiet nature. The family in particular enjoyed picnicking beside a 20-foot waterfall that sang its tireless song throughout the beautiful wooded area.

To build a unique weekend home beside this waterfall, Edgar Kaufmann engaged the noted, but mostly unemployed, 67-year-old architect Frank Lloyd Wright from Wisconsin. What he got instead was a masterpiece, aptly named "Fallingwater."

It seems that Wright was always long on vision but short on money and execution. After several months of delay Kauffman informed Wright that he would be driving from Milwaukee to the architect's studio in order to see plans for the house. Wright's apprentices afterward noted that the client's imminent arrival did not seem to bother their noted teacher at all. With topological map in hand, he made some preliminary sketches and warmly greeted Kauffmann.

After Wright explained how the house would be cantilevered over the waterfall, the very pragmatic Kaufmann remarked, "I thought that you would place the house near the waterfall, not over it." To this Mr. Wright replied, "E.J., I want you to live with the waterfall, not just look at it. I want it to become an integral part of your lives."

An integral part indeed. The house, with its strong horizontal lines, juts out from the rock outcroppings and comes to rest directly over the falling water. Whereas the visual effect of a house stretched over a descending stream is most dramatic, the sound of the water naturally and continually reverberating through the home is a wonder to hear.[179]

Fallingwater is considered great architecture because it is not just a cabin by a stream. The sound and sight of the living stream transform the entire structure. Likewise, the Master Architect wants to transform our lives with the living water of His Word. Like Fallingwater we can choose to structure our lives so that the Word is our constant companion, filling our existence with its sights and sounds. Move next to the Water. Let it become an integral part of your life. It will be a foretaste of heaven.

Lord, let me be attentive to the living Water You have prepared for me today. I want my life to be a living reflection of Your ways to all who meet me.

December 19

In the middle of [the city's] main street, and on each side of the river, was a tree of life bearing twelve fruits, which were produced month by month, and the leaves of the tree were for **THE HEALING OF THE NATIONS.** REV. 22:2.

The phrase at the end of this text has always fascinated me. If the New Jerusalem is part of a perfect world, what need is there of healing? Sickness and death are a thing of the past by this time (Rev. 21:4). So physical healing must not be what is in view here. The text says that the healing is not for individuals, but for "the nations." Often based on the Hebrew term goyim, the word refers to both foreign nations and Gentiles.

It has been suggested that the "healing" of Revelation 22:2 deals with national and linguistic barriers. People of all nations, tribes, and languages inhabit the New Jerusalem. The leaves of the tree of life represent overcoming the hurts and the barriers that keep people apart. The goal is the elimination of all mental and emotional barriers between Jew and Gentile, slave and free, male and female, and the bringing together of the saved into one united family in Christ Jesus (Gal. 3:28; Rev. 21:24-26).[180]

In recent years the world has seen a foretaste of this in South Africa. Eugene de Kock is a White South African who served for many years as the commander of state-sanctioned apartheid death squads. He is serving a 212-year sentence in a Pretoria prison for crimes against humanity. A Black female psychologist, Pumla Gobodo-Madikizela, interviewed De Kock for a total of 46 hours. For her safety, guards kept him chained to a chair bolted to the floor, and her chair was on wheels so she could roll to safety if he lunged at her.

De Kock, however, did not behave like the monster she expected. Instead, he asked permission to meet with the widows of several Black policemen, men whose executions he had arranged. He wanted to apologize to them privately. To the surprise of both De Kock and Gobodo-Madikizela, one of the widows confessed, "I was profoundly touched by him." To their even greater surprise, all the widows "instinctively" forgave him.

Did such a man deserve forgiveness? There is more to it than that. Forgiveness is something that seems able to transcend cruel reality and racial and cultural hatred to reach down to the heart and make things right even though it may seem impossible. And the amazing thing is that, more than absolving the one forgiven, forgiveness seems to heal the one who forgives. The White man's pain so moved the Black psychologist that at one point, oblivious to her own safety, she reached out and touched his shaking hand. The gesture startled them both. The healing of the nations had begun.[181]

Lord, I pray that the healing of the nations might begin in my heart today. Strengthen me to extend Your forgiveness to all within my reach.

In the middle of [the city's] main street, and on each side of the river, was a tree of life bearing twelve fruits, which were produced month by month, and the leaves of the tree were for **THE HEALING OF THE NATIONS.** REV. 22:2.

I am told that the following story is true, but even if it is only a parable, it touches my heart with a glimpse of what the healing of the nations is all about.

On the eastern shore of Maryland the gentle waters run in and out of the land like fingers. The Canadian geese know this place, as do the white swans and the ducks that ride the waves of Chesapeake Bay as they skim their way into harbor. In the autumn they come home by the thousands for the winter. The swans move toward the shores in a stately glide, their tall heads proud and unafraid. An indifference, almost a disdain, exists between the swans and the geese.

Once or twice each year snow and sleet move into the area. When this happens and a river is narrow or shallow enough, a freeze turns the water to ice. It was on such a morning that a woman looked out of her window as the snow laced the rim of the river's shore in white. For a moment she stood quietly, looking at the picture that the night's storm had painted. Suddenly she spotted a goose in the river, very still, its wings folded tight to its sides, its feet frozen to the ice.

Then she saw a line of swans in the dark skies. As the woman watched, the lead bird swung to the right, then the white string of birds became a white circle. It floated from the top of the sky downward. At last, as easy as feathers coming to earth, the circle landed on the ice. As the swans surrounded the frozen goose, she feared that those large swan bills might peck out what life the goose still had left. Instead, those bills began to work on the ice. After some time a narrow margin of ice instead of the entire creek now rimmed the bird. The goose's head lifted. Its body pulled. Then the goose was free and standing on the ice.

Then, as if he had cried "I cannot fly," four of the swans approached again. Their powerful beaks scraped the goose's wings from top to bottom and nibbled up its body, chipping off and melting the ice held in the feathers. Slowly, as if testing them, the goose spread its wings as far as they would go, brought them together, accordion-like, and spread them again. With the goose out of danger, the swans resumed their eastward journey—in perfect formation. Behind them, rising with incredible speed and joy, the goose swept into the sky. He followed them, flapping double time, until he caught up and joined the end of the line. The woman watched until they were out of sight, tears running down her cheeks.[182]

Lord, help me reach out in healing love today to those who are different from me.

December 21

And there will be no curse there anymore, and the throne of God and of the Lamb will be in it, **AND HIS SERVANTS WILL SERVE HIM.** REV. 22:3.

Why will God's people willingly serve Him for an eternity? Because, so to speak, He first served them. Their service will arise out of the delight and joy they have found in the marvelous sacrifice of the Lamb.

Socially isolated individuals often complain that they have received "the short end of the stick." They feel that the people in their lives have done bad things to them. We tend to remember most either the very good things that happen to us (the long end of the stick) or the very bad things (the short end of the stick). The beauty of service is that it extends to other people "the long end of the stick." Service, therefore, has a powerful impact on the lives of others.

Jim Park was reminded of the great power of service when he showed up at the Manila International Airport to take a flight to Guam. He had checked his baggage in and decided to visit the bathroom (they call it the "CR" or "comfort room" in the Philippines). As he entered, one of the attendants (there to assist people as if it were the bathroom of a high-class hotel) greeted him.

When they glanced at each other, each felt as if they had seen the other before. All of a sudden the attendant blurted out that he had met Jim two months earlier on a return trip from Bangkok. He had remembered that Jim was a missionary who had given him a nice tip as a reward for assistance.

Now, attendants see literally thousands of people every month. To remember one particular person in detail after a period of two months is an amazing thing. Quite astounded for a moment, Jim then remembered that after getting off the previous flight he had also visited the CR. The attendant had been kind enough to help Jim with some carry-on bags even though Jim had told him that he did not have any money to give him. Jim thanked him as he left and said he would be back to give him something after he got his checked luggage.

Several minutes later he returned and handed the attendant the 100 pesos (about $2) he had in his possession at the time. Apparently Jim's faithfulness to his word and the generous tip were so memorable that he still remembered the missionary a couple months later. Needless to say, on this return visit the attendant once again gave enthusiastic service. But this time he passed the tip on to a friend working with him. That meant three people were very happy.[183]

Lord, today I will meet many people. Help me to prepare for the service of eternity by giving each one the "long end of the stick."

THEY WILL SEE HIS FACE, AND HIS NAME IS UPON THEIR FOREHEADS. *And there will be no more night. They have no more need for the light of a lamp or the light of the sun, because the Lord God will shine over them and they will reign for ever and ever. [The angel] said to me, "These words are faithful and true. The Lord, the* **GOD** *of the spirits of the prophets,* **HAS SENT HIS ANGEL TO SHOW TO HIS SERVANTS WHAT MUST SOON TAKE PLACE."** REV. 22:4-6.

A Christian apologist once spoke to a group of atheists. After finishing his speech, one of the atheists complained to him, "Christians have their special holidays, such as Christmas and Easter; the Jews celebrate their national holidays, such as Passover and Yom Kippur. But we atheists," he said, "have no recognized national holidays. It's unfair."

As a humorous response the apologist replied, "Why not celebrate April 1?"

Those familiar with North American customs know that April 1 often goes by the name of April Fools' Day. Some believe that the holiday had its origins in France. It may be related to the vernal equinox of March 21 (the first day of spring). The vernal equinox was the beginning of the new year, according to the Julian calendar. Because of small inaccuracies in its calculations, the Julian calendar was 11 days off by the sixteenth century. So the vernal equinox was on April 1 until Charles IX implemented the Gregorian calendar in 1582. Then the vernal equinox reverted to March 21.

Before the calendar change people gave gifts to each other on April 1 in honor of the new year. After the date changed pranksters sent mock gifts to people they had selected, thus making them "April fools." The custom made its way around the world to many other nations.

Regarding atheists, Psalm 14:1 reports, "The fool says in his heart, 'There is no God'" (NIV). The fool is someone who is proud of his or her earthly knowledge and ignores the evidence of a higher power. In the words of media mogul Ted Turner, a fool believes that "Christianity is a religion for losers."[184]

Our text promises that in the new earth we will see the face of God. When looking at a person's face. you can often learn a lot about them, because they express character through their expressions. After years of experience I can often tell at a glance that a person has been heavily traumatized in the past. Our characters and life experiences have an impact on the features. So when the redeemed get to see God's face, it means that they will come to know His character and will be in intimate relationship with Him. Heaven will have no atheists.

Lord, I am awed by Your willingness to enter into intimate relationship with me. With You in my life I will be preserved from foolish thoughts and actions.

December 23

Behold, I am coming soon. Blessed is the one who keeps **THE WORDS OF THE PROPHECY** *of this book. I, John, am the one who heard and saw these things. And when I had heard and seen them I fell down to worship at the feet of the angel who showed me these things. But he said to me, "See that you don't! I am a fellow servant of you and of* **YOUR BROTHERS THE PROPHETS** *and of those who keep the words of this book. Worship God!" And he said to me, "Do not seal up* **THE WORDS OF THE PROPHECY** *of this book, for the time is near."* REV. 22:7-10.

Prophets are making a comeback in today's world. The tabloids are full of them. Perhaps you've heard of Nostradamus, the sixteenth-century French physician and chef of Jewish heritage. Born to a father forced to convert to Catholicism around 1501, Nostradamus became renowned because of predictions that seemed to come true a short time after he made them. He laid out his predictions in 1,000 four-line poems divided into "centuries" of 100 each. The most famous of Nostradamus' dated predictions was the one for the year 1999:

> "The year 1999, seven months,
> From the sky will come a great King of terror,
> To resuscitate the great king of Angoulmois;
> Before, after, Mars will reign by good luck." [185]

This language is clearly ambiguous. Many looked for its fulfillment in terms of a meteor shower or some other heavenly event. Most of them also anticipated that some significant conflict would break out during the year, if not in the month of July itself. But the date came and went, and no one observed anything of the sort.

In the mid-1960s another alleged prophet named Jeane Dixon caught the public imagination. I made note of two verifiable predictions on her part. One of them was that the unpopular views of Barry Goldwater, who lost the presidential race in 1964, would be vindicated within the next decade. The other was that the scrapping of a miniature missile project would prove to be a huge mistake by the end of the 1970s. Neither prediction ever came true as far as I know. The concept of prophets is something we're used to. But the concept of successful prophets is another matter.

The book of Revelation claims to be a written prophecy (Rev. 1:3 and 22:10). Unlike the works of Nostradamus and Jeane Dixon, this book bears the clear evidence of God's hand. As we study those prophecies already fulfilled, we learn how to interpret those that haven't yet come to pass.

Lord, open my eyes to see more clearly the purpose You had in giving these visions to John. May I direct my true worship to You alone.

Let the one who is unrighteous remain unrighteous, let the one who is filthy remain filthy, let the one who is righteous continue to do righteousness, and let the one who is holy remain holy. **BEHOLD, I AM COMING SOON!** *And my reward is with me, to pay back everyone according to his work.* REV. 22:11, 12.

When I was 9 years old, someone convinced my mother that Jesus would return in the year 1964. He noted the text "As it was in the days of Noah, so shall it be when the Son of Man comes" (Matt. 24:37) and reckoned that the days of Noah had lasted 120 years (the time it took Noah to build the ark). He added that period to the year 1844, which was significant to him for other reasons, and concluded that Jesus would come back in the year 1964. The idea impressed me enough to decide that I would have fun until around 1962 and would then get ready to meet Jesus!

In the year 1975 a pair of brothers held some studies in which they argued that Jesus would return in 1981. I was studying at the seminary then, and the men urged several of us to quit school and get down to the business of warning the world. Had I taken them seriously I might have done so, but I had already been through this once before. I had learned that one has to balance one's belief in the soon return of Jesus with an awareness that God wants us to prepare thoroughly for future service.

First-century Christians tended to read texts like the above in a similar fashion. As time went on it tempted them to think that the Lord was becoming slack in the fulfillment of His promises (2 Peter 3:9). But the apostle Peter pointed out that the seeming delay of the Advent was because of God's desire that all would come to repentance. The time between Christ's first and second comings is an extension of His grace. God's desire to save is so great that even those who scoff against the reality of His second advent receive more opportunity to repent.[186]

Those who have genuine faith, however, will find that it gets stronger and stronger as the delay gets longer and longer. The key to this text is not the timing of Jesus' return but the identity of the One who is coming. Those who are waiting for the arrival of a great friend find their anticipation growing as the time of separation increases. When I am traveling away from my wife, she gets more beautiful by the day, and my desire to be with her increases with time.

It is out of a living relationship with Jesus that we maintain our confidence in His soon return. While we should live each day as if it were our last one on earth, delay will not destroy that relationship. For each day of our lives the word is "He is coming soon!"

Lord, I thank You that the constant barrage of date-setting that we once experienced has faded. Help me to keep my focus on knowing You, which will make me ready for Your return.

December 25

Behold, I am coming soon! And my reward is with me, to **PAY BACK EVERYONE ACCORDING TO HIS WORK.** Rev. 22:12.

Today's text has two parts. We tend to seize on the former and ignore the latter. The crucial message is not the nearness of the end, but the fact that our behavior today affects our reward then. God gave prophecies such as those in the book of Revelation not to satisfy our curiosity about the future, but to teach us how to live today.

Some Christians invest a great deal of energy in determining the timing and nature of end-time events. Not only does this miss the point of Bible prophecy, it can have unfortunate consequences, as illustrated in the following story.

Michael tells the story of a religious camp meeting. After an open-air worship service and a potluck lunch, the young marrieds went on walks, the older marrieds went for their traditional "rest," and the teenagers either wandered toward the river or hung out by the lunch tables.

Will and Bobby were in the group by the tables. An 8-year-old girl with red hair and freckles sauntered up to their table and asked, "What's up?" Will said, "Nothing much," but Bobby quickly added, "Except a tornado is headed this way. Hail the size of golf balls are close behind, and we are directly in its path! It should be hitting us in about 30 to 45 minutes!"

The redhead's eyes opened wide, and she dashed off to warn everyone else of the impending danger. Within minutes most of those present were tuning in to all the local radio stations. Many began packing up and getting out of there. Of the hundreds of families camping there, about a third had evacuated within the space of 20 minutes, even though the sky did not have a single cloud and the tents were stifling hot because of the lack of a breeze.

Michael's first thought on hearing the report was *I should have brought a radio.* His second thought was *I wonder what Will and Bobby have to do with this?* So he went looking for the teenagers. Sure enough, Will and Bobby laughingly admitted to having told a redheaded girl of the impending disaster.

Searching for the child, Michael found her running to another part of the campgrounds. He stopped her, much to her agitation, and told her it was all a joke. She became really upset and argued that he was lying to her, that a tornado was really headed their way, and that he had better get out while he had the chance! And off she went on her mission to warn everyone. The weather that weekend was perfect. If a tornado ever does hit that campground, who will believe the warning?[187]

Lord, keep my study of prophecy focused on You more than on the events around me.

"I am the Alpha and the Omega, the first and the last, the beginning and the end. Blessed are those who wash their robes, in order that they might have rights to the tree of life and might enter into the gates of the city. OUTSIDE [THE CITY] *are dogs, sorcerers,* THE SEXUALLY IMMORAL, *murderers, idolaters and everyone who loves and practices lying."* REV. 22:13-15.

Even among Christians some take sin lightly. "I'm not so bad." "God isn't that particular." They do not seem to realize that forsaking sin is a crucial need in the Christian life. While our performance does not save us, a pattern of sin can have such a deep impact on our lives that we lose our way in the end.

We cling to cherished behaviors because they are exciting, attractive, or meet certain internal needs. Sexual attraction, for example, is particularly dangerous. A pastor named Randy Alcorn, therefore, offers a powerful solution for sexual temptation: "Whenever I feel particularly vulnerable to sexual temptations, I find it helpful to write out what effects, what consequences, my actions could have. Here's what I write:

"'If I go farther down this road, I will probably grieve the One who redeemed me. I will probably drag His sacred name into the mud. . . . One day I will have to look Jesus, the righteous Savior, in the face and give an account of my actions.

"'If I go farther, I will probably inflict untold hurt on my wife, who is my best friend and who has been faithful to me. I will lose my wife's respect and trust; I will hurt my beloved daughters. I will destroy my example and credibility with my children. I might lose my wife and my children forever. I could cause shame to my family.

"'I could lose self-respect. I could create a form of guilt awfully hard to shake. Even though God would forgive me, would I ever be able to forgive myself? I could form memories and flashbacks that could plague future intimacy with my spouse. I could heap judgment and endless difficulty on the person with whom I committed adultery. I could possibly reap the consequences of diseases like gonorrhea, syphilis, herpes, or AIDS. Maybe I could cause a pregnancy, and that would be a lifelong reminder of my sin. Maybe I would invoke shame and lifelong embarrassment on myself.'"[188]

What an incentive to end a train of thought or an affair in the making! And I would add to his list the danger of a place outside the Holy City, as our text warns. Over the short run, sinful actions may seem harmless, but in the long run the consequences are too heavy to consider.

Lord, I thank You for the challenge of this text. Help me to remove everything in my life that divides, separates, hinders, or fails to honor You.

December 27

I, Jesus, have sent my angel to testify to you **CONCERNING THE CHURCHES.** *I am both the root and the descendant of David, the bright and morning star.* REV. 22:16.

The church deacon had thoughtfully prepared a place for the guest speaker to look over her notes before the worship service. The speaker was seated at the church secretary's large desk just outside the pastor's study. A short while later three women came into the office and asked, "Have you seen our purses? We left them on the desk a half hour ago."

"I'm just a visitor here, not the receptionist," the speaker replied, "but no, I have not seen any purses, and I've been here for 15 minutes."

The women panicked, looking underneath the desk, beside it, and in the drawers, but still found no pocketbooks.

Just then the helpful deacon reappeared, and the frantic women asked him the same question.

"Yes, I have seen your purses," he said. "You left all three of them on top of the secretary's desk. So to make sure they were not stolen, I took all of them and locked them in the closet."

The women were understandably relieved.

But the deacon was not finished. He offered a gentle reprimand. "You should know better than to leave pocketbooks lying around anywhere. After all, although this is a church, it is not heaven!"[189]

The deacon was balancing the ideal and the real. While the church can offer a foretaste of heaven, it is not heaven in the fullest sense. It is very much a part of the great battle at the center of focus in the book of Revelation. The church family consists of human beings with a great number of imperfections.

In Revelation Jesus offers a clear testimony concerning the churches. This is true not only of the first three chapters of Revelation but of the entire book, according to this text. Every vision, every beast, every blessing, every war, every song of praise, has as its purpose to instruct the churches.

One thing is clear. The churches are not whitewashed in the book. Jesus applies a searching scrutiny to them and portrays their characters and experiences with rigorous honesty. While the churches contain many faithful ones, the people of God are still far from perfect. They deeply need the cleansing that comes from the blood of the Lamb (Rev. 1:5, 6; 7:14; 12:11). And they look forward to the transformation of all things that Jesus will effect when He returns.

Lord, help me to keep my balance between the ideal and the real in the church. When things go wrong, keep my eyes fixed on Jesus.

The Spirit and the Bride say, "Come." And let everyone who hears say, "Come." And let everyone who is thirsty come. **LET EVERYONE WHO WISHES TAKE THE WATER OF LIFE WITHOUT COST.** Rev. 22:17.

I sn't it amazing how many people wait until their deathbed to apologize to either a family member or a friend? It seems that when people are bedridden, or in a weakened state, or near death, they start to contemplate their life and the impact that they might have had on people. Hospital chaplains witness such deathbed confessions many times.

Why do people wait until the end? Why do they procrastinate until it is too late to undo the injured feelings that have partially destroyed someone else's life? Why didn't they make their amends when it would have done some good instead of waiting until they knew others would have pity on them? Is this not cowardice? fear? human pride?

People do not like to risk being made a fool. The fear of appearing to be foolish, or wrong, is so strong in most of us that we spend our lives pretending that everything is OK. We are afraid to admit that we were wrong, afraid to appear foolish to others—especially our own families!

But who was the biggest fool that ever lived, according to human standards? Who endured total humiliation in order to reestablish a relationship with you and me? Christ, of course. He never once feared making a fool of Himself. Even when others jeered, "He saved others, . . . but he can't save himself!" (Mark 15:31, NIV).

Jesus became the biggest fool that ever lived so that the real fools might come to love Him as He loved us. He put relationship before His own pride. Tempted to come down from the foolish cross, He still reached out to us, not caring if people called Him foolish.[190]

The book of Revelation, as we have seen, is full of unusual stories and even stranger creatures. It would be easy to get the impression that war, famine, pestilence, and judgment are its primary themes. But our text for today reminds us that the fundamental topic of the entire book is the "revelation of Jesus Christ."

Revelation reminds us that salvation in Christ came at infinite cost (Rev. 5:6; 12:11; 13:8), yet it is absolutely free to us. But the foolishness of the human heart rebels against receiving anything that it hasn't earned. We humans fear the foolishness of admitting that we are wrong, that we need what Christ offers (Rev. 3:17). But in His sacrifice we see that it is foolish pride that causes us to postpone the day of our salvation.

Lord, I accept the water of life that You offer so freely. My pride suggests that I do something special today to earn the gift. Help me to trust in Your loving and graceful provision.

December 29

I bear witness to everyone who hears the words of the prophecy of this book: **IF ANYONE SHOULD ADD [WORDS] TO IT, GOD WILL ADD TO HIM THE PLAGUES THAT ARE WRITTEN IN THIS BOOK, AND IF ANYONE SHOULD TAKE AWAY FROM THE WORDS OF THE BOOK OF THIS PROPHECY, GOD WILL TAKE AWAY HIS PART IN THE TREE OF LIFE** *and in the holy city, things that are written in this book.* REV. 22:18, 19.

At first glance it seems a rather threatening way for God to end the Bible! *"Don't mess with this book! If you touch even a word of it, you will be in such trouble that you will wish your life were over!"* While such ominous words undergird the authority of the book of Revelation in particular, they seem appropriate also for the Bible as a whole.

The Bible as it is does not contain all truth. "Two plus two equals four" is a truth, for example. But it doesn't appear in the Bible. "It is warmer at the equator than at the poles" is a truth. But it also isn't in the Bible. So the Bible is not a collection of everything that is true—it is like a yardstick, by which we measure claims to truth.

That's why it is important to leave the Bible as it is. God fitted it for its own purpose. To tamper with it, to ignore one part or another, would be to interfere with its divine purpose. And to add something or to leave something out would be to distort God's intent. It seems to me that has implications for us as well. Every one of us is unique. We too are fitted for a purpose. Sometimes we might want to add or subtract from the work God has done with us, but we would be wiser to accept His purpose and use our unique characteristics for His glory.

Kathleen Donovan, former missionary to Papua New Guinea, describes this humorously. "I have fat legs," she says, "multicolored because of varicose veins. . . . They're not things of beauty, . . . but they reach perfectly from the ground to my hips. . . . They never tempt other people to envy." She goes on to point out that because of her legs, she has learned methods of varicose vein management that are helpful to others. A friend even uses her legs as an illustration of the results of sacrificial missionary service. It turns out that the ailment was inherited rather than the result of standing for hours at operating tables. Nevertheless, the sight of Kathleen's legs inspired a mission presentation that convinced others to consider similar service. Some listeners might never have done so if Kathleen's legs "had been slim and beautiful." [191]

Donovan concludes, "Our job is to accept gratefully what we've been given, and find ways of using it to the glory of God." That would be true of the Bible as well. We should take it as God has given it, rather than try to manipulate its message to our own satisfaction.

Lord, help me to accept the way You designed me. Use even my less-desirable features as an illustration of Your benevolent purpose!

372

I bear witness to everyone who hears the words of the prophecy of this book: **IF ANYONE SHOULD ADD [WORDS] TO IT, GOD WILL ADD TO HIM THE PLAGUES THAT ARE WRITTEN IN THIS BOOK, AND IF ANYONE SHOULD TAKE AWAY FROM THE WORDS OF THE BOOK OF THIS PROPHECY, GOD WILL TAKE AWAY HIS PART IN THE TREE OF LIFE** *and in the holy city, things which are written in this book.* REV. 22:18, 19.

W e noticed in the previous day's reading that the Bible, as it reads, has been fitted by God for its purpose. To tamper with it, to ignore one part or another, would be to interfere with its divine mission. Having said that, I doubt that very many people have ever done this intentionally. Most of us sense that it would be wrong to cut large portions out of the Bible or add things that we or someone else had written. That kind of tampering is not really a major threat.

What concerns me more is the way we often add to or subtract from the Bible without even realizing that we are doing so. For example, take a passage such as Matthew 6:25-34. It tells us not to worry about our lives—what we will eat, drink, or wear. It even suggests that to spend a lot of time in anxiety about such things indicates weak faith (verse 30). Taken by itself, such texts can lead well-meaning Christians to conclude that whenever they are depressed, anxious about the future, or feel stressed, it indicates something wrong with them spiritually.

The bigger picture of the Bible, however, tells us that even the most faithful of God's servants have had episodes of depression, anxiety, and stress. Fueled by pain and depression, Job says some nasty things about God (Job 9:16-24; 10:3-17; 27:1-6)! Was there something wrong with him spiritually? His friends thought so (Job 8; 15:5, 6; 22:1-11). But God recognized differently. He said there was no one like Job in all the earth (Job 2:3; 42:7)!

Elijah became deeply fearful and depressed after his victory on Mount Carmel (1 Kings 19:3, 4). Did the Lord abandon Him? Absolutely not (verses 5-18). Paul came under such pressure that he was convinced his life was over (2 Cor. 1:8, 9). Was there something wrong with him spiritually? No, God continued to work with him (verses 9-11). Even Jesus felt deeply troubled emotionally on more than one occasion (Mark 14:32-34; John 11:33, 38; 12:27). Was there something wrong with Him spiritually?

Revelation 22:18, 19 implies that before we assert, "The Bible says," it would be wise to read *everything* Scripture has to say on the subject. Whenever we take isolated texts and use them to support our ideas, we run the danger of adding to or subtracting from the Word of God.

Lord, I don't want to add or subtract from the Bible's picture of You. I want to be attentive to Your whole counsel and not give distorted pictures of You to others.

December 31

*The One who testifies to these things says, "Yes, I am coming soon." Amen.
Come, Lord Jesus. May* **THE GRACE** *of our Lord Jesus Christ be with
everyone.* REV. 22:20, 21.

A woman once wrote to the famous columnist Ann Landers about the "best experience of my life." It happened on a bus in New York City. "It was a cold, rainy night—and also my birthday. . . . Having just moved from Phoenix to New York, I was feeling miserable, homesick, and alone in the big city. I boarded a crowded bus at Columbus Circle. The only seat left was at the back, behind the other bored and cold commuters, next to an elderly man."

She sat down feeling quite dejected. To her surprise, the elderly man turned to her and said, "You look so sad. What's wrong?"

Touched by the concern of this stranger, she poured out her heart and ended up sobbing. She finished saying, "I'm homesick and cold. It's my birthday, and nobody cares!"

As her tears continued to flow, the entire bus became quiet. Then the man began to sing: "Happy birthday to you . . ." Several people joined him, until soon everyone one on the bus was singing, "Happy birthday, dear . . . Happy birthday to you!"

Applause and laughter erupted.

The woman concluded her account to Ann Landers, "I was showered with good wishes and warm smiles all the way to my stop at 72nd and Broadway. It was the best birthday present I've ever received."

Compassion has a healing quality. This story of a lonely woman demonstrates that an act of compassion will soothe pain, heal hurt, ease fear, soften a blow, and relieve anxiety. Our world always needs compassionate people—those who have an awareness of the suffering of others and who also have the willingness to relieve it.[192]

Our journey through the book of Revelation has been a roller-coaster ride filled with war, famine, pestilence, wild beasts, earthquakes, and scorching fire. Through it all we have tried to maintain a focus on the book's primary theme, the revelation of Jesus Christ. The plagues of the book are a demonstration of His power to save. So it is not totally out of character for an action/adventure book such as Revelation to end with grace. Grace is a special manifestation of the divine presence and power, an expression of kindness, mercy, and good will. An excellent translation would be "healing compassion," the very thing the woman on the bus received.

As the book of Revelation draws to a close, I invite you to drink in the healing compassion of Jesus Christ. Let Him heal your wounds, soothe your hurts, and affirm your value as a person. There is no better friend when in need.

Lord, thank You for Your overwhelming grace. I accept it with my whole heart.

January

[1] Based on Stefanie Johnson, "Seeing Clearly," *Adventist Review,* Oct. 30, 2003, p. 37.

[2] Based on an e-mail from Paul Wangai, Oct. 29, 2004. See also Harvey Mackay, *We Got Fired! . . . And It's the Best Thing That Ever Happened to Us* (New York: Random House, 2004).

[3] John Bowman, "Book of Revelation," *The Interpreter's Dictionary of the Bible.*

[4] Based on an e-mail from Dan Millen, Oct. 18, 2002.

[5] See Craig S. Keener, *Revelation, The NIV Application Commentary* (Grand Rapids: Zondervan, 2000), p. 85, notes 22, 23.

[6] *Ibid.,* p. 89.

[7] Quoted in e-mail from Dan Millen, Oct. 27, 2004.

[8] For more information about Hekate, see David E. Aune, *Revelation 1-5, Word Biblical Commentary* (Dallas: Word Books, 1997), vol. 52a, pp. 104, 105.

[9] Keener, p. 100.

[10] *Ibid.,* pp. 104, 105.

February

[11] *Ibid.,* pp. 105, 106.

[12] Ellen G. White, *Testimonies for the Church* (Mountain View, Calif.: Pacific Press Pub. Assn., 1948), vol. 3, p. 21.

[13] Based in part on Jack Harris, "Wall of Glass," *Adventist Review,* Nov. 27, 2003, pp. 28-30.

[14] See Keener, p. 77.

[15] Ronald E. Dorsey, Jr., "The Tarnished Spoon," *Adventist Review,* Nov. 20, 2003, pp. 8-11.

[16] Ted Roberts, *Pure Desire* (Regal Books, 1999), pp. 162-164.

[17] Keener, pp. 114-117.

[18] Based on a personal interview (April 25, 2004) with Michael Lorentz, former defensive end for the University of Colorado and the University of Montana.

[19] Based on "The Martyrdom of Polycarp," in *Documents of the Christian Church,* ed. Henry Bethenson, 2nd ed. (London: Oxford University Press, 1963), pp. 9-12.

[20] Based on Renee Coffee, "Showers of Blessings," *Lake Union Herald,* February 2004, p. 15.

[21] The quotation is from Pliny *Epistulae* 96. Translated by Roland H. Bainton and quoted in Bainton, *Christendom: A Short History of Christianity and Its Impact on Western Civilization* (New York: Harper and Row, 1966), vol. 1, p. 57. Page 58 of the same book summarizes Trajan's response.

[22] Based on an e-mail from Samuel Thomas, Jr., Feb. 19, 2004.

[23] Thanks to Jim Park for the main idea behind this devotional. E-mail, Nov. 18, 2002.

[24] Jim Park, June 10, 2002, e-mail.

March

[25] Aune, p. 206.

[26] Eberhard Bethge, ed., *Dietrich Bonhoeffer: Letters and Papers From Prison,* trans. Reginald Fuller (New York: MacMillan, 1967), pp. xvii, xxiii; Keener, p. 146.

[27] William F. Ramsay, *The Letters to the Seven Churches of Asia and Their Place in the Plan of the Apocalypse* (London: Hodder and Stoughton, 1906), pp. 359-362.

[28] Aune, p. 225.

[29] Keener, p. 148.

[30] Based on an e-mail from Jim Park, Dec. 5, 2004.

[31] Based on an e-mail from Dan Millen, Feb. 17, 2003.

[32] Richard Corliss, "Breaking the Color Line," *Time,* Mar. 31, 2003.

[33] Keener, pp. 159, 160.

[34] Gwynne Dalrymple, "The Church of Laodicea," *Signs of the Times,* Nov. 14, 1933, p. 7.

[35] Ed Dickerson, "Dead Languages," *Adventist Review,* March, 2004, p. 28; based on Bruce Olson, *Bruchko* (Orlando: Creation House, 1973), p. 146.

[36] Ellen G. White, *Mind, Character, and Personality* (Nashville: Southern Pub. Assn., 1977), vol. 2, p. 579.

[37] E-mail from Dan Millen, Nov. 16, 2002.

[38] Based on actual events as described by Ed Dickerson in an unpublished manuscript entitled "The ABCs of Nurture," pp. 94-96.

April

[39] Inspired by an e-mail from Dan Millen, Nov. 25, 2003.

[40] E-mails on Dec. 1, 2003.

[41] Ranko Stefanovic, *The Backgrounds and Meaning of the Sealed Book of Revelation 5,* Andrews University Seminary Doctoral Dissertation Series 22 (Berrien Springs, Mich.: Andrews University Press, 1996).

[42] Keener, pp. 190, 191; Ellen G. White, *Testimonies,* vol. 4, pp. 9-11.

[43] Inspired in part by an e-mail from Jim Park, Dec. 26, 2004.

[44] Based on an e-mail from Dan Millen, Jan. 22, 2003.

[45] Based in part on Keener, pp. 246, 250.

[46] Based on Philip Yancey, "The Holy Inefficiency of Henri Nouwen," *Christianity Today,* Dec. 9, 1996, p. 80.

[47] Revelation 1:12-18 acclaims Jesus in language drawn from texts referring to Yahweh in the Old Testament. See the readings for January 22 and 23.

[48] John McRay, *Archaeology and the New Testament* (Grand Rapids: Baker Book House, 1991), pp. 355, 359-361.

May

[49] Kimberly Luste Maran, "Mending Broken Hearts," *Adventist Review,* Nov. 20, 2003.

[50] Based on Keener, pp. 208-211.

[51] *Ibid.,* pp. 204, 205.

[52] E-mail from Jim Park, May 19, 2003.

[53] Based on Keener, pp. 226, 227.

[54] Based on Rachel Whitaker, "Blessed Are the Weak?" *Adventist Review,* Oct. 30, 2003.

[55] Based on a biography posted at http://www.law.umkc.edu.

[56] Based on Keener, pp. 220, 224, 225.

[57] E-mail from Jim Park, Dec. 14, 2003.

[58] Richard Bauckham, *The Climax of Prophecy* (Edinburgh: T. & T. Clark, 1993), pp. 217-219.

[59] Dan Millen, e-mail, Apr. 28, 2002.

[60] Last two paragraphs indebted to Keener, p. 181.

[61] Based on Keener, pp. 248, 249.

[62] E-mail from Ali Kingston, Dec. 3, 2002.

[63] Kathleen Donovan, *Growing Through Stress* (Berrien Springs, Mich.: Institute of World Mission, Andrews University, 2002), pp. 28-32.

[64] E-mail from Jim Park, Aug. 17, 2003.

June

[65] Herbert Danby, ed. and trans., *The Mishnah,* first ed. (London: Oxford University Press, 1933), pp. 582-589. These pages reflect rabbinic traditions relating to the daily Tamid service in the Temple.

[66] E-mail from Jim Park, Dec. 13, 2004.

[67] Based on an e-mail from Christa Zarka, June 10, 2003.

[68] Based on Michael Nickless, "The Night America Panicked," *Michigan Memo 16,* no. 9 (October/November, 2004): 2.

[69] Based on John Hollenhorst, "Underground Shelters Abound in Paradise Valley," transcript of a television report posted at www.rickross.com on Mar. 2, 2004.

[70] Based on a British Broadcasting Corporation news report, Dec. 14, 2003, posted at www.bbc.co.uk.

[71] Inspired in part by Dickerson, "Dead Languages," pp. 27-29.

[72] Based on Keener, p. 274.

[73] Statistics based on the Trade and Environmental Database sponsored by American University: http://gurukul.ucc.american.edu/ted/ice/tigris.htm.

[74] Gordon Retzer, "Forgive—'No Matter What . . . ?'" *Lake Union Herald,* July 2002, p. 2.

[75] Story based on Martin Selak, "Grace in Hell," *Adventist Review,* May 13, 2004, pp. 12-14.

[76] E-mail from Dan Millen, Nov. 21, 2002.

[77] E-mail from Jim Park on Oct. 28, 2002.

July

[78] Stories based on Amanda Sauder, "Putting Headlines and Heroes Into Perspective," *Adventist Review,* May 20, 2004, p. 21.

[79] Based on Keener, p. 284.

[80] Based on an e-mail from Jim Park, July 6, 2004.

[81] Hiram Edson, manuscript fragment of his "Life and Experience" (Berrien Springs, Mich.: Ellen G. White Research Center, James White Library, n.d.), pp. 4, 5.

[82] John Polkinghorne, *The God of Hope and the End of the World* (New Haven, Conn.: Yale University Press, 2002), p. 20.

[83] Nathan Brown, "It's the Thought That Counts," *Adventist Review,* July 8, 2004, p. 20.

[84] Based on Keener, pp. 300, 301.

[85] *Ibid.,* pp. 301, 302.

[86] Robert McNamara, "Averting the Apocalypse," *Time,* Mar. 31, 2003.

[87] Story based on Cathy Booth Thomas, "Flying Faster Than Sound," *Time,* Mar. 31, 2003.

[88] See Austin G. Archer, "Living With Fear," *Adventist Review,* Jan. 8, 2004, pp. 14-16.

[89] Based on an e-mail from Dan Millen, Nov. 26, 2003.

[90] Based on Anita Hamilton, "A Bus Rider's Defiance," *Time,* Mar. 31, 2003.

[91] Based on an e-mail from Dan Millen, Apr. 7, 2004.

[92] Based on Douglas Brinkley, " 'One Giant Leap for Mankind,' " *Time,* Mar. 31, 2003.

[93] Based in part on Mart de Groot, "From Science to Faith," *Adventist Review,* Mar. 25, 2004, pp. 14-16.

[94] E-mail from Dan Millen, Mar. 1, 2003.

[95] For more detail about the experience of Christians in the first-century Roman world, see Jon Paulien, *The Deep Things of God: An Insider's Guide to the Book of Revelation* (Hagerstown, Md.: Review and Herald Pub. Assn., 2004), pp. 17-32.

[96] For those who wish a deeper understanding of the meaning of the cross, I have written a book called *Meet God Again for the First Time* (Hagerstown, Md.: Review and Herald Pub. Assn., 2003).

August

[97] E-mail from Jim Park, Feb. 24, 2003.

[98] James Poniewozik, "AA Takes Its First Steps," *Time,* Mar. 31, 2003.

[99] Amanda Ripley, "A Homegrown Nightmare," *Time,* Mar. 31, 2003.

[100] Howard Lutnik, "The Foreshadowing of 9/11," *Time,* Mar. 31, 2003.

[101] Story from "Family News With Dr. James Dobson," *Focus on the Family Newsletter,* March 2001, pp. 3, 4.

[102] Keener, pp. 346, 347.

[103] Based on Cheryl Doss, "I'll Be Back Someday," *Lake Union Herald,* February 2004, p. 14.

[104] In an e-mail from Jim Park, Oct. 26, 2003.

[105] Ted Roberts, *Pure Desire* (Ventura, Calif.: Regal Books, 1999), pp. 192-195.

[106] Adam Zagorin, "Finding the King's Fortune," *Time,* Mar. 31, 2003.

[107] E-mail from Dan Millen, May 7, 2003.

[108] Quoted in Clifford Goldstein, "Between the Strokes, Again," *Adventist Review,* Feb. 26, 2004, p. 29.

[109] Jackie Ordelheide Smith, "Balancing Cell Phones and Eternity," *Adventist Review,* October 2004, p. 6.

[110] Based on Lisa Takeuchi Cullen, "Unleashing an Era of Dread," *Time,* Mar. 31, 2003.

[111] With thanks to Miriam Taylor, "Look-alikes," *Adventist Review,* Feb. 27, 2003, p. 31.

[112] Based on Keener, pp. 364-366.

[113] Based on Lauren Schwarz, "The Consuming Fire," *Adventist Review,* Oct. 30, 2003, pp. 26-29.

[114] Based on Keener, pp. 358-360.

[115] Damien Johnson, "A New Song," *Adventist Review,* Dec. 18, 2003, p. 15.

[116] *Ibid.,* pp. 16, 17.

[117] *Ibid.,* pp. 14, 15.

[118] As told by Dwight K. Nelson in "Requiem and Resurrection for a Fallen Brother," *Ministry,* May 2004, pp. 5-8.

September

[119] Clifford Goldstein, "The Book of the Cosmos," *Adventist Review*, Mar. 28, 2002, p. 29.

[120] With appreciation to Dan Millen, e-mail, Nov. 9, 2002.

[121] E-mail from Samuel Thomas, Jr., Aug. 15, 2003.

[122] Inspired by an e-mail from Jim Park, Nov. 7, 2004.

[123] Roberts, pp. 188-192.

[124] John Stark, "Footnotes of a Walker," *My Generation*, November-December 2002, pp. 78-81.

[125] Based on Dana and Colleen Clark, "Dja-Dja," *Adventist Frontiers*, March 2004, pp. 10-13.

[126] Keener, p. 380.

[127] The story is told by Norman H. Young, "Arm-wrestling the Devil," *Signs of the Times* (Australian), August 2003, pp. 45-48.

[128] Based on an e-mail from Dan Millen, Mar. 29, 2003.

[129] Based on an e-mail from Samuel Thomas, Jr., Oct. 10, 2003.

[130] Story based on Josh Tyrangiel, "The King Finds His Voice," *Time*, Mar. 31, 2003.

[131] Based on an e-mail from Dan Millen, Aug. 11, 2003.

[132] Based on an e-mail from Jim Park, Feb. 1, 2004.

[133] For a more thorough coverage of the sanctuary in the book of Revelation, see Paulien, *The Deep Things of God*, pp. 124-133.

[134] Last half of devotional based on Keener, p. 400.

[135] Charles C. Mann, "The Bluewater Revolution," *Wired*, May 2004.

[136] Based on E. Lonnie Melashenko, "Revelation: The Book of the End," *Adventist Review*, Oct. 16, 2003, pp. 14-17.

[137] Based on an e-mail from Jim Park, Jan. 11, 2004.

[138] The last part of this devotional is based on Keener, p. 400.

October

[139] As told in Ansel Oliver, "Me? Meek? A Look at Jewish Humor and Meekness," *Adventist Review*, Oct. 30, 2003, pp. 22, 23.

[140] E-mail from Dan Millen, Mar. 31, 2003.

[141] For more information on the background of the term *Armageddon*, see Jon Paulien, "Armageddon," *Anchor Bible Dictionary* (New York: Doubleday, 1992), vol. 1, pp. 394, 395.

[142] Romesh Ratnesar, "The Dawn of Israel," *Time*, Mar. 31, 2003.

[143] Based on Madelyn Pugh Davis and Bob Carroll, "Falling in Love With Lucy," *Time*, Mar. 31, 2003.

[144] Reported from his own experience as a chaplain at Sequoia Hospital in California: Dan Millen, e-mail on Nov. 6, 2002.

[145] Based on Keener, pp. 438, 439.

[146] *Ibid.*, pp. 416, 417.

[147] Brett Anderson, "Give, and We Shall Receive," *Worth*, February 2004, pp. 64-70.

[148] Based on Keener, pp. 426, 427.

[149] Polkinghorne, pp. 104, 105.

[150] Anderson.

[151] Daniel Gross, "The Good We Do," *Worth*, February 2004.

November

[152] Based on Keener, pp. 441-444.

[153] *Ibid.*, pp. 440-447.

[154] Based on Melashenko, pp. 14, 15.

[155] Jim Park, e-mail, Oct. 16, 2002.

[156] John Kelley, "Outrunning the Aryan Myth," *Time*, Mar. 31, 2003.

[157] Based on Lauren Schwarz, "The Consuming Fire," *Adventist Review*, Oct. 31, 2003, pp. 26-29.

[158] Based on an e-mail from Jim Park, Mar. 28, 2004.

[159] In my summary of the council discussions I am particularly indebted to the transcripts and introduction found in *Spectrum* 10, no. 1 (1979): 23-57.

[160] Jim Park, e-mail on Dec. 2, 2002.

[161] *Ibid.,* Aug. 5, 2002.

[162] *Ibid.,* Mar. 31, 2003.

[163] Inspired by an e-mail from Dan Millen, Mar. 26, 2003.

[164] Michael Lemonick, "The Overlooked Miracle," *Time,* Mar. 31, 2003.

[165] Based on an e-mail from Jim Park, July 25, 2004.

[166] The first part of the devotional is based on Leslie Kay, "Judgment Day," *Adventist Review,* Oct. 23, 2003, pp. 24, 25.

[167] Adapted from "Family News With Dr. James Dobson," pp. 2, 3.

[168] See Ellen G. White, *The Desire of Ages* (Mountain View, Calif.: Pacific Press Pub. Assn., 1898), p. 297.

[169] E-mail from Dan Millen, Oct. 24, 2002.

December

[170] Based on Shirley Kromann, "Not the Answer," *Adventist Review,* May 20, 2004, pp. 22-24.

[171] Polkinghorne, pp. 82, 83, 94, 95.

[172] Based on Tamara Michalenko Terry, "Grief Observed," *Adventist Review,* Feb. 19, 2004, pp. 28, 29.

[173] E-mail from Jim Park, Nov. 2, 2003.

[174] Based on William Lane Craig, "The Teleological Argument and the Anthropic Principal," posted at www.lederu.com on Sept. 27, 2003.

[175] Inspired by Heidi Boggs, "Finding the Perfect Route," *Adventist Review,* July 15, 2004, pp. 14-16.

[176] The following is based on Rhonda Whetstone Neibauer's reaction to the movie *The Passion of the Christ,* which I received by e-mail from Dan Millen on Mar. 19, 2004.

[177] E-mail from Michael Pearson, Dec. 6, 2002.

[178] Based on Daniel Eisenberg, "Taking Down the Wall," *Time,* Mar. 31, 2003.

[179] Based on an e-mail from Jim Park, Mar. 10, 2003.

[180] Ranko Stefanovic, *Revelation of Jesus Christ* (Berrien Springs, Mich.: Andrews University Press, 2002), p. 593.

[181] Lance Morrow, "The Quality of Mercy," *Time,* Jan. 27, 2003.

[182] E-mail from Dan Millen on Mar. 25, 2004.

[183] Based on e-mail from Jim Park, Feb. 22, 2004.

[184] Leslie N. Pollard, "Fooled!" *Adventist Review,* October 2004, p. 24.

[185] Translation and discussion in Hillel Schwartz, *Century's End: A Cultural History of the Fin de Siècle From the 990s Through the 1990s* (New York: Doubleday, 1990).

[186] Paragraph based in part on Leslie N. Pollard, "The Lord Is Not Slack," *Adventist Review,* January 2004, p. 45.

[187] E-mail from Michael Pearson, Dec. 6, 2002.

[188] Quoted in Bill Hybels, *Christians in a Sex-crazed Culture* (Wheaton, Ill.: Victor Books, 1989), pp. 17, 18.

[189] Based on Wilma McClarty, "This *Is* a Church, but This *Is Not* Heaven!" *Adventist Review,* Mar. 18, 2004, p. 24.

[190] Based on an e-mail from Dan Millen, Sept. 22, 2004.

[191] Donovan, p. 36.

[192] Victor Parachin, "Healing Compassion," *Signs of the Times* (Australian), August 2003, pp. 17, 18.

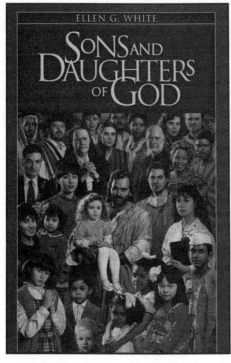